Charles Jelavich
History Department
Indiana University
Bloomington, Indiana

Man, State, and Society in East European History

MAN, STATE, AND SOCIETY

Other books in the series include:

Man, State, and Society in East European History

EDITED BY

Stephen Fischer-Galati

PRAEGER PUBLISHERS

New York · Washington · London

PRAEGER PUBLISHERS
111 Fourth Avenue, New York, N.Y. 10003, U.S.A.
5, Cromwell Place, London S.W.7, England

Published in the United States of America in 1970
by Praeger Publishers, Inc.

© 1970 by Praeger Publishers, Inc.

Library of Congress Catalog Card Number: 69–10516

Printed in the United States of America

INTRODUCTION

A variety of explanations has been offered for the historical retardation of Eastern Europe vis-à-vis Western Europe. Almost all have focused on the adverse effects of prolonged Habsburg, Ottoman, and Romanov domination. Thinkers and historians from the Enlightenment to the present have looked upon the "golden days" of early East European civilization as the model for restructuring an unnatural order that had been imposed upon their ancestors by the alien empires of the Habsburgs, Turks, and Russians. Like the men of the Renaissance of the West a few centuries earlier, the intellectuals of Eastern Europe (and, occasionally, their political leaders also) embellished upon the past and blackened the present, while giving little thought to the future.

In reality, with few exceptions, the "golden days of yore" were less bright in Eastern Europe than in the West. The values of ancient Greek and Roman civilization, which the humanists of the Renaissance sought to restore in the fifteenth and sixteenth centuries, had only a marginal influence on the evolution of Eastern Europe. The civilizing mission of the Greeks and Romans was trampled upon by the nomads from Asia long before the invaders reached the West. Many of these peoples settled voluntarily in Eastern Europe. Others, like the Magyars, accepted settlement in the East because their westward movement was arrested by militarily superior adversaries. By the tenth century, the separation of East and West was a *fait accompli*. It is true that the common bond of Catholicism assured closer ties between the Western Catholic world and the Western Slavs and Magyars than with Greeks, Southern Slavs, Rumanians, and other settlers who had gravitated toward Byzantium and Eastern Christianity. It is also true that because of the differing religious orientations—which were reflections of political realities—the nature of state and society in the various parts of the East differed from that of the West. But these differences were not nearly as significant as occasionally assumed by historians of Eastern Europe, because they ultimately mirrored the "objective historic conditions" of Europe as a whole.

With the exception of the few communities that were engaged in commercial activities connected with the Eastern sea or land trade, and in such oases of commercialism as Bohemia and Transylvania, feudalism prevailed throughout Eastern Europe before the emergence of the Habsburg, Ottoman, and Russian empires. The medieval empires of the Bulgarians, the Serbs, the Bosnians, and the great kingdoms of the Magyars and the Poles were in fact not the progressive entities deemed worthy of emulation, if not reconstitution, by the thinkers of the eighteenth century. Not even the Byzantine Empire, despite its relative modernity, could serve as a prototype for a new Eastern Europe. Rather, the strength of the medieval East European states rested on the development of advanced forms of feudalism: Eastern Europe was as much the bastion of conservative resistance to the commercial imperialism of the West as to the military imperialism of the Ottoman Turks. It is fair to say that by the fifteenth century Eastern Europe had become the repository of forms and values later identified with "Autocracy, Orthodoxy, and Nationality," and that these values and forms were the province of the dominant landed aristocracy, religious or secular. It is also fair to say that the *raisons d'être* and *d'état* of the Habsburg and the Ottoman rulers were essentially the same: to strengthen the medieval Catholic or Muslim theocratic orders.

The fifteenth and sixteenth centuries deepened the division between Eastern and Western Europe. The shift in the trade routes, and the resultant political and socio-economic changes in the West, bypassed the theocratic and authoritarian East, which was beset with political problems by that time obsolete in Western Europe. The Habsburgs in Eastern Europe sought to consolidate political power at the expense of the narrow class interests of the Bohemian and Magyar feudal aristocracies. The Ottoman Turks established a large terrestrial empire over the dead bodies of the feudal aristocracies of the subject nations. The reorganization of the socio-economic order in the conquered areas was geared toward the manning and supplying of armies of conquest, not to economic pursuits (other than agriculture). Such commercial activities as the Turks were prepared to condone were limited to the Eastern sea trade. But the Turks conducted their economic affairs for purposes other than those of the capitalist West. To the Turks, trade was for the enrichment of the sultan and the pursuit of war, not for economic development per se. In that respect, their views were similar to those of the Russian feudal autocrats. In Moscow, the tsars were struggling with the unruly feudatories and asserted, as well as derived, their power from the utilization of the land for military and political purposes and from their steadfast opposition to all Western "heresies." To Ivan III and his successors, Rome was their own "Third Rome"—the defender of "Orthodoxy and Autocracy," the ultimate conservative values of Eastern Europe.

By the seventeenth century, the overriding concern of the rulers of Eastern Europe was to resist challenges to their power from landed interests; the concern of the landed interests was to protect themselves against encroachment on their powers by the monarchs. Except during the relatively short period of continuing commercial activity in the Ottoman Empire and Transylvania (which ended de facto in the seventeenth century), the political drama involved feudal ruler, feudal lord, feudal

Church, and peasant. The fortunes of the contest varied for all but the peasant. By the end of the seventeenth century, the peasant was unfree even in those parts of the Ottoman Empire where he had enjoyed a relatively privileged position after the Turkish conquest. The feudal aristocracies fared better. In Poland, for instance, the power of the aristocrats was unlimited; the *szlachta*, the very model of feudalism triumphant and unchecked, were equated with the "nation."

By the eighteenth century, Eastern Europe was essentially a feudal domain caught up in the problems of feudal societies. The only notable exceptions were the enclaves controlled by Greek political and economic entrepreneurs, who were salvaging what they could from the disintegrating Ottoman Empire. But even the commercialism of the Greeks was insignificant in comparison with that of their Western counterparts; they were unable to form a middle class that would precipitate the modernization of the Ottoman Empire. The task of modernization rested with the autocrats themselves. But the motivations and aims of such men as Peter the Great and Joseph II were hardly the same as those of the modernizers of the West. The Eastern enlightened despots sought modernization for military purposes, for the strengthening of autocratic rule. Westernization was to be limited and achieved through the loyal bureaucracy and such allies as could be rallied against the conservative feudal oligarchies. Their ultimate purpose was not the creation of a bourgeoisie but the establishment of a centralized and secularized military-bureaucratic-autocratic state, manned by a compliant aristocracy.

Except for modernization of the military establishment and the limited introduction of Western mores and ideas, the efforts of the enlightened despots failed before the obdurate opposition of the vested landed interests. Only a handful of men—generally aristocrats, but also merchants, priests, and teachers—who read, studied, and traveled understood the meaning of the political ideas of the West. But their interpretation of the bourgeois ideology of the eighteenth century was based on the narrow concerns of their own class in Eastern Europe. They sought reform, not revolution; their demands ranged from equality with more privileged feudal groups to restoration of usurped rights and clearer definition of political, fiscal, and legal obligations. Ultimately, their argument was historical; their demands were focused on regaining the "national" rights enjoyed in the pre-Ottoman, pre-Habsburg, or, in the case of Poland, pre-Romanov past. Occasionally, when it suited the interests of the militarily modernized Habsburg and Russian empires, malcontents obtained the support of Austrian or Russian despots in their quest for restoration of abused national (class) interests. But that support was more often than not contingent on vassalage and was given for the attainment of imperial aims opposed to those of the solicitants. And at no time was this contradiction more evident than during the French Revolution and Napoleonic Wars. "Liberty, Equality, Fraternity," the slogan so dear to the reformists of Eastern Europe (although in fact so incompatible with their true class interests), was anathema to their imperial patrons.

To the reformists, the French Revolution stood for restoration of historic rights and states, in short, for narrow class nationalism. They were not seeking social and legal equality for all members of the nation but merely recognition by the supranational emperor of the rights of the elites. But the champions of theocratic legitimacy—the Habsburgs, the sultans, and above all, Tsar Alexander I—were determined to protect theocracy against all heresies ascribable to French revolutionary doctrine. The defeat of Napoleon provided the rationale for the containment of all demands for change, and the maintenance of the *status quo ante bellum.* By branding all reformers as "revolutionaries," by invoking the doctrine of imperial legitimacy and supremacy, and by placing divine authority above secular rights the rulers of the Eastern empires, as fearful of social reform as of national assertion, drove the moderate class-conscious reformers into more extremist positions than they had wanted to adopt. The intensification of "nationalist" demands, the creation of the nationality problems of nineteenth-century Eastern Europe, were indeed the product of imperial reaction and obstinacy more than of acceptance of the French revolutionary message by an essentially moderate, reformist elite. And the same was true with respect to the nationalist class confrontations of 1848. Only *in extremis* did the most radical of the revolutionaries, Louis Kossuth, extend the narrow class concept of the nation to encompass the Magyar masses; but he would not accede to the socio-economic and political demands of those of different nationality. To Kossuth, as to leaders elsewhere in Eastern Europe, the revolution of 1848 was to propel his own class or group into a position of power at the expense of the ruling establishment. It was not designed to alter the status of man, state, and society along the lines implicit in the revolutionary slogan "Liberty, Equality, Fraternity."

It is noteworthy that after 1848, just as in earlier times, any political and social change came from above. The gradual emancipation of the peasantry—the most radical social action of the nineteenth century—was decreed by the legitimate rulers. In the process, they secured the allegiance of the peasantry, thereby either precluding or controlling political change. And even when the ruling elites encouraged industrialization, for political reasons rather than because of any genuine commitment to modernization or the modification of the social order, they were able to retain control over that order. Whether in imperial or national state form, Eastern Europe remained basically agrarian and feudal, and resistant to modernization.

It was precisely because of the security provided by the paternalistic and, by Western standards, archaic socio-economic and political order that Western capitalism found expansion into Eastern Europe advantageous in the late nineteenth century. Agricultural products were cheap and plentiful; so were raw materials and industrial labor. The financial requirements of the elites could easily be met by the affluent West, and political bridges were built in the process. Encouragement of the primitive national goals of rulers of sovereign states and leaders of would-be national entities to be carved out of the body of the decaying Ottoman Empire, such as territorial aggrandizement and nationalist propaganda directed against the multinational empires, secured bases in the Balkans for Western powers seeking markets and political gains as well as for the Habsburgs and Romanovs concerned with the maintenance of their own East European interests.

The interaction of the forces of nationalism and imperialism in an area dominated by societies in the process of slow transition from the feudal to the industrial age was a primary cause of World War I. The war resulted in the destruction of the Eastern empires and, often by default, the triumph of the cause of national states. But the national states of Eastern Europe, representing in one form or another the restored states of the pre-imperial order, were as a rule no more advanced than the empires they replaced. Ostensibly, after World War I, the East European was free of foreign domination. He owned his land, although not always as a free man. The political order was democratic and constitutional, at least on paper. But these paper constitutions had no meaning, for in fact the state was regulated and directed by nonrepresentative elites. The state was national, and its governmental structure differed from that of the past. But it remained authoritarian and elitist, the domain of landlords and occasionally, as in Czechoslovakia, of the bourgeoisie. The leaders of the new states—with the notable exception of Czechoslovakia—had not learned the lessons of World War I. Chauvinism, irredentism, and nepotism were the dominant characteristics of Eastern Europe between the wars; social change, industrial growth, education of the masses—in short, modernization to meet the requirements of the twentieth century and to bring Eastern Europe to the level of the West—were regressive ones.

It has been said that the modernization of Eastern Europe was precluded by its lack of capital and by its location between Germany and Russia. This is true. But the actions of the establishments in the interwar years were determined by their desire to enjoy the fruits of victory or, conversely, to avenge defeat. It is true that historic values had to be preserved. But in their traditional forms landlordism, nationalism, and authoritarianism were obsolete in the postwar period. Their demise occurred in World War II, which also recorded the victory in Eastern Europe of the new totalitarianism of the Soviet Union.

A new order was to be built on the ruins of the historical tradition. Modernization was to be achieved through social revolution and industrialization. But the message that was to come from the East was not to be "Liberty, Equality, Fraternity," but "Autocracy, Orthodoxy, Nationality," according to the dogma of the new Russian emperors. That this was indeed more compatible with the historical traditions of Eastern Europe may be seen from the following selection of documents and articles relevant to the history of Eastern Europe.

STEPHEN FISCHER-GALATI

Boulder, Colo.
May, 1970

CONTENTS

Man, State,
and Society
in East European
History

ONE

The Historical Legacy: Eastern Europe Before the Fall of Constantinople

On May 29, 1453, Constantinople was conquered by the Ottoman Turks. The fall of the city signaled the collapse of the Eastern Roman Empire. On August 30, 1526, Louis II, King of Hungary and Bohemia, was killed in the Battle of Mohacs, also by the Ottoman Turks. Mohacs (together with the Turkish siege of Vienna of 1529) was representative of the Ottoman threat to the Holy Roman Empire in the struggle for domination of East-Central Europe. The conflict was soon to be joined by another claimant to the Roman legacy: the "Third Rome" of the Romanovs.

But the search for legitimacy, and the corollary extension of power and influence by Habsburgs and Romanovs in their struggle against the "Infidel Turk," merely obscured the political and socio-economic realities of East-Central Europe. In the fifteenth century, the states and societies of East-Central Europe bore only the most superficial resemblance to Rome. On the eve of the Turkish conquest of Constantinople, social and political life had reached a state of disarray that reflected the disintegration of the medieval order in the West and the impact of that process on the static socio-economic and political structure of the East-Central European state system.

That state system—if such it may be called—showed enormous diversity. In the Balkan Peninsula, over which the Byzantine emperors had lost control before the Ottoman Turks appeared in Europe, several loosely organized political organizations maintained a precarious existence. The once formidable Bulgarian Empires had disappeared, the Second destroyed by the Ottomans in 1396. The great Serbian Empire of Stephen Dushan had virtually disintegrated under Turkish blows and internal dissension. Albanian tribesmen and *condotieri*, led by the famous Skanderbeg, were readying themselves for a last ditch stand against the advancing Turks. The Greeks, who had been losing their imperial possessions since the mid-fourteenth century, were staging the final defense of their capital city. The Rumanian province of Wallachia had accepted Turkish suzerainty in 1418, while that of Moldavia was desperately trying to maintain its precarious autonomy against Polish and Turkish encroachments.

On the eve of the subjugation of the Peninsula, the state order was rudimentary in all the Balkan areas. Imperial and princely authority had become ephemeral. Such power as existed was wielded by the feudal nobility. The Orthodox Church, which had traditionally supported the secular leaders, reflected the waning power and prestige of the state. The Church also remained the principal link between rulers and ruled, the unifying force in a disintegrating society. The Church preached resistance to the Turks and blessed Christian crusades against the Infidel. It remained implacably opposed to the Church of Rome, and, on occasion, to the Patriarch in Constantinople as well. In this sense, the Orthodox Church may be said to have encouraged nationalistic feelings among the Christian inhabitants of the various parts of the Balkan Peninsula.

In the western areas of East-Central Europe, the disintegration of the state order was less evident but nonetheless real. Bohemia was caught up in a major civil-religious war. Hungary, the bastion of Catholic resistance to Turkish imperialism and of political resistance to Habsburg imperialism, was weakened by internecine struggles and foreign wars. Only the Polish-Lithuanian state in the north enjoyed a modicum of stability. Unlike the Balkan states, however, Bohemia, Hungary, and Poland had meaningful state organizations in which the dominant secular and spiritual aristocracies exercised well-defined political functions. Their social order was also more complex than in the southeast, reflecting a higher level of economic activity and corresponding social stratification.

The overwhelming majority of the population of East-Central Europe in the mid-fifteenth century consisted of peasants at various levels of servitude. Serfdom was most prevalent in Hungary, least so in Serbia and the mountainous areas of the Balkans. With the consolidation of feudalism, the peasants' rights to property and liberty diminished, and communal organizations such as the *zadruga*—the extended patriarchal family once so prevalent among the Southern Slavs—gradually disintegrated. A middle class existed only in such economically developed areas as Bohemia and Transylvania. This class was generally of different nationality from the peasantry and even the aristocracy: Frequently, it was German, Levantine, or Jewish. But national differences—in a sense, primitive "nationality problems"—were not confined to merchants alone. In Hungary, for instance, the majority of the population was Slav and Rumanian; there was also a heterogeneous population in the Polish-Lithuanian state. The ruling aristocracies and monarchs were nationally homogeneous, but the nationality they represented was not always that of their subjects.

In this checkered and unstable social and political order, the majority of men enjoyed neither peace nor prosperity. Constantly harassed by war and encroachment on his patrimonial rights, the peasant sought relief through monarch and Church while organizing himself for passive or active resistance against foreign invaders and domestic landlords. Frequently, he joined roving guerrilla bands—such as the legendary *hajduks* of the Balkan mountains—or staged *jacqueries* in defense of his rights. The more privileged members of society, however—at least in Bohemia, Hungary, and Poland—enjoyed material well-being and shared in both the cultural legacy and the Renaissance of the West. The Byzantine aristocracy, intellectuals, and churchmen continued to preserve and even to export the civilization of the Eastern Empire. But as the Turks extended the area of their conquest and control, the cultural and socio-economic differences in the Balkans were leveled. By the end of the fifteenth century, a new order with new values had replaced the Byzantine-Balkan social and political systems.

In Hungary, the turmoil and ferment of the Matthias Corvinus era (1458–90), exciting and challenging as it was, led to the exacerbation of internal problems and external conflict. In pursuit of his imperial ambitions, Matthias Corvinus alienated the Hungarian aristocracy and ravaged Bohemia, thereby paving the way for the expansion of Turkish and Habsburg power in East-Central Europe. By 1526, the Habsburgs had asserted their rights of inheritance over a prostrate Bohemia and fought the Turks for the control of a ravaged Hungary. With the exception of Poland, which remained independent after Mohacs, all of East-Central Europe was consolidated into the new imperial orders of the Habsburgs and the Osmanlis. The years 1453 and 1526 were indeed watersheds, marking the beginning of a fateful new era for the men, states, and societies of Eastern Europe.

1

EASTERN EUROPE IN WORLD HISTORY

E. C. HELMREICH

[In the diverse historical experience of the peoples of Eastern Europe prior to the establishment of the Ottoman and Habsburg Empires are to be found most of the problems that plagued the empires until their dissolution in the twentieth century. The basic and recurrent problems of Eastern Europe—geopolitical, religious, demographic, and national —are succinctly summarized by Professor E. C. Helmreich.]

THE SETTLEMENT OF CENTRAL-EASTERN EUROPE

Early Migrations. Although most of the peoples of this region have remained fairly stationary since approximately the tenth century, certain groups seem to be more indigenous than others to the areas where they center today. Starting in the Balkans, we have the Greeks, the scattered Kutzo-Wallachs in Macedonia, who are best identified today with the modern Rumanians, and the Albanians. Although the matter is a subject of much dispute among anthropologists and historians, some of them also place the Rumanians of the Carpathian area in the same category. We are on surer ground when we come to the Baltic littoral. Here the related Finns, Estonians, and Livonians have resided since very early times, along with another group, the Latvians and Lithuanians. The Germans and Slavs have a more varied history. They are indigenous to certain areas, but were more inclined to wander, and at different times in history they occupied and dominated vastly different territories.

At about the beginning of the Christian era, the various German tribes occupied not only the territory beyond the Rhine-Danube frontier of the Roman Empire but were also in control fairly well down the valley of the Vistula toward the Black Sea. Driven by an increase in population,

Reprinted, by permission, from Joseph S. Roucek and Associates, *Central Eastern Europe: Crucible of World Wars* (New York: Prentice-Hall, 1946), pp. 6–18.

the need for better grazing and hunting preserves, and urged on by the inroads of enemies and the desire for plunder, these tribes began to move about. This migration of nations (*Völkerwanderung*) was primarily concentrated in the fourth and fifth centuries, although the process continued well beyond that period. It had catastrophic effects on the old Roman Empire and eventually led to the establishment of new Germanic kingdoms in Western Europe. The direction of the migration was south and, as the Germanic tribes moved out, their places were taken by Slavs and newcomers from the Asiatic reservoir of humanity. The gap between the Urals and the Caspian, leading to the flat plains to the north of the Black Sea and the beckoning Danube valley, formed a broad highway into the heart of Europe, and along this highway, in the fifth century, came Attila and his Hunnish bands, soon to be followed by the Avars. These were to be absorbed by later arrivals, and today, as a synonym for complete oblivion, there is the proverb "to perish like the Avars without leaving a trace."

The expansion of the Slavs was less spectacular but more enduring than the advent of the Huns and Avars. The best that ethnographers can do to locate the early Slavs is to place them in the region northeast of the Carpathians in the upper basins of the Vistula, Pripet, Dniester, and Dnieper rivers—a region about halfway between the Baltic and Black seas in what is sometimes referred to as the Isthmus of Europe. From here the Slavs radiated like spokes in a wheel. To the east went what were later to be known as the White Russians and the Great Russians, to the south and west went the Little Russians (Ruthenians), the principal inhabitants of modern Galicia and the Ukraine. The main direction of Slav migration in this early period was westward, and the Slavs soon overran Central Europe, reaching even beyond the Elbe and to the classic frontiers of Italy and Greece.

The claims of the Slavs to Central and Eastern Europe were not, however, to go unchallenged. The Germans reversed their westward migratory trend and began to erect a series of barriers (marches) against them. Charlemagne (800–814) was the first ruler to do this on a grand scale. His biographer enumerates no less than four wars against the Slavs.

The Danubian Basin. The Slav expansion to the west and south was challenged not only by the Germans but by a new series of Asiatic invaders. Toward the end of the seventh century the Bulgars, an Asiatic Turanian tribe akin to the Huns and Avars and to the modern Finns, Estonians, and Magyars, crossed the Danube delta and spread into the Balkans. Although they conquered the Slavs, who by that time had taken possession of these lands, they were absorbed in turn, so that today they are Slavs with little but their name to remind them of their ancient origin. By the eighth century, the Khazars had established a strong kingdom north and east of the Black Sea. The conversion of their Khan to Judaism, even though the majority of the Khazars later accepted Muhammadanism, indicates the extent of Jewish influence in this area. More important than the Bulgars and Khazars were the Magyars, who settled in the great Danubian plain (Alföld) in the ninth century and extended their conquests up to the southeastern German marches.

The great body of Slavs was thus permanently divided into two sections, for to the east of the Magyars the breach was continued by the Rumanians, with their basic Latin culture. The Slavic group to the north and west consisted of the Wends, the Sorbs, the Czechs, the Slovaks, and the Poles. The southern group consisted of the Slovenes, the Croatians, the Slavonians, and the Serbs. Of these groups, the Wends (near Berlin) and the Sorbs (in Silesia) have been entirely absorbed by the Germans. The Slavonians are really Serbs who reside in a region known as Slavonia and have a history quite distinct from that of the other Serbians. In this they resemble the Montenegrins, who are racially among the purest Serbs, but who receive special mention because they inhabit the territory of the Cernagora (Black Mountain) and have a distinct regional history.

Later Invasions. Following the Magyars, additional invaders swept westward across the vast steppes of southern Russia. As conquerors they influenced the history of this region, although in most cases they founded no modern national groups of significance. More important than the Petchenegs in the tenth century and the Cumans in the eleventh century were the Mongols. Having created a vast empire under Genghis Khan in Central Asia and China, they raided Europe, reaching Bohemia in 1241. Destruction and disorganization were left in the wake of their armies. Under Batu they established an "Empire of the Golden Horde," with its capital at Sarai on the Volga, from which they ruled a large part of Eastern Europe.

Not all invaders followed the easy route north of the Black Sea. The Seljuk Turks struck south into Anatolia, revitalized the Muhammadan Saracenic Empire, and soon challenged the power of the Byzantine Empire at Constantinople. This threat furnished the pretext for the Crusades (1095–1270), with their great influence not only on Western Europe but on the East as well. More important than the Seljuks were the Ottoman Turks, who replaced them and who were to become the founders and organizers of the great Turkish Empire. Although the Ottoman Turks extended their power up to the gates of Vienna, and thus had a tremendous effect on the peoples of Southeastern Europe, they ruled as conquerors. They established no large Turkish national groups, but only small minorities here and there to add to the babel of tongues.

Colonization. A consideration of early indigenous groups and groups which became indigenous as a result of somewhat later mass migrations does not suffice to account historically for the mosaic of peoples which is the most fundamental characteristic of Central and Eastern Europe. This must be traced also to an important colonization movement into the region throughout the course of history.

Under the Roman Empire the province of Dacia was colonized, and the modern Rumanians claim they are the descendants of these colonists and of the tribes originally occupying this area. Traders in the Middle Ages established small national colonies in remote regions. This type of colonization is well illustrated by the settlements of the German merchants of the Hanseatic League in the Baltic States. Colonists also followed the Cross: Witness the activity of the Teutonic Knights in the Baltic regions of East Prussia, Estonia, and Latvia, and the German settlers who followed the German missionaries into Bohemia. In later years many groups of settlers migrated to escape religious persecution, either Muhammadan, Roman Catholic, Greek Orthodox, or Protestant. Conquest of new territories also brought new colonists, as illustrated by Swedish expansion along the shores of the Baltic, German expansion into the eastern marches, and Russian expansion into the Baltic and Black Sea regions.

Colonization by groups of nationals was, however, largely the result of direct invitation by ruling princes who wanted settlers to work the lands, businessmen to conduct the trade of the cities, and soldiers to protect the frontiers. This process has gone on continually. Such settlers obtained not only special land grants but, equally important, special governing privileges. The large immigration of Saxons into Transylvania in the twelfth century is a perfect example of this type of colonization. These famous Siebenbürgen Saxons were recognized as a separate nation by their overlords and were granted autonomy. They have jealously guarded these rights and in part maintained them to this day.

After the devastation of the series of wars in the seventeenth and eighteenth centuries, when the Turks were gradually driven back beyond the Danube, the Habsburg rulers regularly invited peoples to settle in this area. Many of the settlers who responded were Germans, but there were also many Slovaks and Serbs. The Swabians along the lower Danube, for the most part, migrated to this region in the eighteenth and nineteenth centuries. The Cossacks, with their historic special privileges in the Ukraine, originated as a group of frontier guards. The Habsburgs down to 1867 maintained against the Turks a special Military Frontier staffed largely by Croats and Serbs who had special privileges and were subject directly to the Ministry of War in Vienna.

The reason for these grants of special privilege to colonists is not hard to find. They arose primarily out of the need to entice immigrants to increase the prosperity and wealth of the ruler's domains. Colonists would not come unless they were accorded special rights because they were often accustomed to a more highly developed state of law in their mother country than existed in the regions to which they were migrating. This was especially true with regard to towns, which accounts for the fact that many German communities in Eastern Europe (notably in Poland) were governed by German municipal codes. In fact, *Magdeburger Recht* did not disappear from Russian Poland until 1831. This recognition of special legal systems had the same purpose as the capitulations in Turkey and extraterritorial rights in China and Japan. In addition, there was the concept of personality of law so prevalent in medieval Europe, especially among the Germans, according to which a man took his law (the law of his tribe or nation) with him wherever he went and expected to be tried and judged by it.

By granting such legal and other privileges, the ruling prince sought also to win the support of the immigrants against his obstreperous nobility or the majority nationality. But while special minority privileges satisfied and pacified their recipients, they also often antagonized the more numerous native population. The greater centralization of the state in recent years and the passing of power to majority groups through the democratization of government have resulted in the curtailment of special minority privileges, a fact that accounts in part for the acuteness of minority problems today.

Among the racial and religious minorities who were often granted special privileges were the Jews. These grants did not have to be extensive to attract the Jews, who were generally under severe persecution in Western Europe. A number of rulers in fourteenth-century Poland and Lithuania were especially well disposed toward them, however, and many Jews came to live in these territories. Later, these Jews were restricted to certain areas, which became known as the "Pale." But there were also many Jews scattered beyond the Pale, particularly in the rest of Galicia, Hungary, and Rumania. Eastern Europe thus became the world center of Jewish population.

Religious Development

The great variety of peoples is naturally a divisive force in Central and Eastern Europe The same is true of religion which has often been closely associated with nationality in this region. In the Middle Ages there were two main missionary centers: Rome and Constantinople. Roman Catholicism spread from the first; Eastern Orthodoxy from the second. The former brought with it a Western orientation, Western culture, and the use of the Latin alphabet. Eastern Orthodoxy brought about contacts with the civilization of the Byzantine Empire and, except in the case of the Rumanians, the use of the Cyrillic alphabet. After the Muhammadan conquest of Constantinople (1453) and the Balkans, the isolation of the Eastern churches from the rest of Christendom was increased.

On the eastern (i.e., Greek Orthodox) side of the religious demarcation line which extends vertically across Europe are the Greeks, the Bulgars, about one-third of the Albanians, the Serbs, a greater part of the Rumanians, and the Russians. To the west, and predominantly Roman Catholic, are the Poles, Czechs, Slovaks, Magyars, Austrians, Slovenes, and Croats. Constituting a sort of border line in Galicia and sections of Rumania are the Uniates: Catholics in full communion with Rome but following Eastern rites of worship.

This religious division of Central-Eastern Europe was disturbed but not materially changed by the Protestant Reformation. Although the Protestant movement originally swept large sections of Bohemia, Slovakia, Austria, Hungary, and Poland, the reaction of the Counter Reformation regained much of this territory for Roman Catholicism. In the north, where Protestant Sweden controlled Finland, Estonia, and Courland,

Lutheranism was introduced and remains the dominant religion. The secularization of the Teutonic Order left Protestantism in control in East Prussia and in portions of the Baltic littoral. In Hungary, Protestantism was able to preserve itself in some places against the Catholic power of the Habsburgs, particularly in the eastern sections which remained longer under Turkish rule, and in Transylvania, which enjoyed a peculiar autonomous status. In this region, as early as 1571, Roman Catholicism, Lutheranism, Calvinism, and Unitarianism received official recognition and toleration. The Orthodox faith, however, remained outside the fold. The Turkish conquest of Southeastern Europe brought with it Islam and added a new divisive element. This was important in its day but has no marked present significance. . . .

POLITICAL DEVELOPMENT TO 1450

General Pattern. It is difficult to work out a coherent political pattern for Central-Eastern Europe. At the time when the Balkan Peninsula was the home of Greek civilization, the territory from the Danube to the Baltic was inhabited by unknown wandering tribes. The Roman Empire extended its control somewhat beyond the Danube, but essentially it remained a Mediterranean power. Nevertheless the influence of the Roman Empire, with its heritage from Greece, eventually spread throughout Central-Eastern Europe. Insofar as that influence derived from Rome, it was similar to the heritage of Western Europe where the Church asserted supremacy over the State.

To a great extent, however, Central-Eastern Europe derives from Constantinople, where Roman and Greek traditions merged into the civilization of the Byzantine Empire. It was from Constantinople that the first missionaries were sent to the Slavs and with them went the concept that the State was not only closely related to the Church, but was dominant over it. Often the ruling prince took the lead in bringing his people into the Christian fold and, having done so, retained a directing hand over the Church. *Cuius regio eius religio* was a doctrine enforced in Central-Eastern Europe long before the Reformation wrote into the public law of the Germanies that a prince should determine the religion of his subjects.

From Rome the imperial tradition was passed on to the Germans, from Constantinople to the Russians. Some of the people who separated the two—Poles, Hungarians, Serbs, Bulgarians—were also inspired by the imperial concept and at various times attempted to establish empires of their own. Yet on the whole these peoples, as will be pointed out below, became the parts out of which rival imperial states were built. The persistence of the imperial idea in Central-Eastern Europe was in part due to the relatively late rise of nationalism and democracy there. Although these forces did in time disrupt the established imperial states, they did not end the imperial tradition—a fact amply demonstrated by contemporary world politics.

By about 1350 a turning point in the history of Central-Eastern Europe can be discerned. To the east the Mongols, the last invaders to sweep across the steppes of Russia, were still firmly established on the Volga. To the southeast, the Byzantine Empire was in the throes of revolution. In 1354, the Ottoman Turks established their first foothold in Europe. Already beset by the Black Death, which ravaged Europe about 1350, the people were soon to add to their litanies a prayer for protection against this new scourge. Between these powers on the east and the states of Western Europe, Central-Eastern Europe consisted of a number of independent or semi-independent states which owed their freedom largely to the weakness of their neighbors. To the west lay an enormous and grasping but weakly organized empire.

The Holy Roman Empire. The Holy Roman Empire was a loose confederation of feudal states, mostly Germanic. The Emperor, who laid claim to universal rule as heir of the Roman emperors, always had difficulty in controlling both his Italian and his German subjects. The emperorship was an elective office, a fact which frequently led to bitter rivalries. In the famous Golden Bull of 1356, the election procedure was formally organized by assigning the task to seven electors. Three of them were ecclesiastics: the Archbishops of Mainz, Trier, and Cologne. The other four were lay rulers: the Count Palatine of the Rhine, the Duke of Saxony, the Margrave of Brandenburg, and the King of Bohemia. Bohemia had become a recognized part of the Holy Roman Empire after Boleslav I had been forced to accept German suzerainty in 950. When the line of succession failed in Bohemia in 1526, the crown passed to the Habsburgs.

The fact that the Catholic Habsburgs could thus always unite with the three ecclesiastical electors to assure the election of a Habsburg emperor was of fateful significance to the history of all Europe. Vague and shadowy as the power of the emperors came to be, the Habsburgs would have cut a relatively minor figure in Eastern European history had they not been backed by the influence, prestige, and power that they obtained as emperors of the Holy Roman Empire. Equally fateful was the fact that at times the welfare of Central-Eastern Europe was sacrificed to support Habsburg policies in Germany, Spain, and Italy. Via the Habsburgs and the Empire, the wars and troubles of Western, Central, and Southeastern Europe were to be inextricably intermingled. Thus the states of Central-Eastern Europe led a precarious existence between their imperialistic neighbors.

The Baltic Region. In the far north, the Swedes had conquered the Finns in the twelfth century, but the Finns nevertheless maintained a high degree of autonomy. The loose organization of the Swedish kingdom and its complex relationship to the other Scandinavian kingdoms in this period made Swedish suzerainty little more than nominal. Along the Baltic littoral and in the islands of the Baltic, the Hanseatic League maintained important trading centers which actually served as German outposts. The Peace of Stralsund (1370) between the League and Sweden marked the high point of the power of the Hansa in this area. Strong though it was, however, the Hansa was forced to share its control of the Baltic with the Teutonic Knights. In 1200 the Pope had proclaimed a Crusade against the Baltic heathen, and the German Knights of the Sword (joined later by the Teutonic Knights) had responded eagerly to this summons to "Christian warfare." The Knights had colonized and Christianized East Prussia and then, expanding their rule northward from their base at Riga, had finally won Estonia from its Danish overlords in 1346.

The Order of Teutonic Knights also sent its colonists deep into Poland and into Lithuania, but they were never able to subjugate these territories. At this time Lithuania was the most powerful state in Eastern Europe, and in 1386 the Duke of Lithuania brought about a federation with Poland by a marriage alliance. The allies were able to defeat the Teutonic Order in the famous Battle of Tannenberg in 1410. This defeat marked the beginning of the end for the Teutonic Order and the corresponding rise of the Polish-Lithuanian state, which in the sixteenth century was to control the vast territory from the Baltic to the Black Sea and from east of the Oder River and the Carpathians to the headwaters of the Volga.

Bohemia-Moravia. Before and after the Polish-Lithuanian federation, Poland at various times entered into relations with Bohemia and Hungary, which lay beyond its southern mountain frontier. In Bohemia the Czechs had established a state as early as the seventh century, only to be absorbed by the kindred state of Moravia in the tenth century. As mentioned above, Bohemia in 950 became a recognized part of the Holy Roman Empire. This tie with the government of Germany, often very tenuous, was nevertheless to last in one fashion or another down to the rupture of the Germanic Confederation in 1866 and, through the continuing connection of Bohemia with Austria, even longer.

The middle of the fourteenth century is often regarded as the Golden Age of Bohemia. Under its King Charles I (1347–78), the famous Charles IV of the Empire, Bohemia took the lead in imperial affairs. The University of Prague was founded in 1348 and soon it nourished a national-religious leader in the person of John Hus (1369–1415). He was to pay with his life for his denunciations of abuses within the Catholic Church and of German dominance in Bohemia. His death at the stake by order of the Council of Constance (1415) unleashed the civil conflicts known as the Hussite Wars (1420–33) and laid the basis for the bitter religious national struggles against the Habsburgs in the seventeenth century. Failure of a direct line of succession united Bohemia through dynastic ties with Hungary and, as we have seen, in 1526 with the Austrian Habsburgs.

Hungary. The Magyars, who had reached the Danubian plain in 896, organized and obtained Western recognition of their state of Hungary in the year 1001, when King Stephen was crowned with a special crown blessed by the Pope. Certainly by the end of the tenth century the Magyars were in control of modern Slovakia, which remained from that time until 1918, except for a very brief episode or two, an integral part of the Hungarian state. In this period Hungary also held modern Transylvania, but here a varying degree of autonomy was always the rule until 1867. Croatia-Slavonia, which Hungary conquered in the eleventh century, likewise enjoyed a measure of autonomy under the crown of St. Stephen.

Under Louis the Great (1342–82), medieval Hungary reached the peak of its power. Louis forced the princes of Serbia, Wallachia, and Moldavia to recognize his suzerainty, established control over Ragusa and most of Dalmatia, and even was elected King of Poland. But this great Hungarian-dominated federation, extending from close to the Baltic to the Mediterranean and Black seas, was only a flash in the pan, for it centered too much in the person of the king. Poland, after its union with Lithuania (1386), became a dangerous rival. Moreover, the princes to the southeast took their oaths of allegiance lightly, and the inroads of the Turks soon placed the Hungarian kings on the defensive.

The Slovenes. While the Croats came under Magyar rule, the Slovenes were conquered by the Germans in the ninth century and, like the Czechs, were to be associated thenceforth with the history of the Holy Roman Empire. Their territories (mainly Carinthia, Carniola, and Styria) were ruled by different princes subject to varied allegiances, but in the course of the thirteenth and fourteenth centuries all of them came into the hands of the Habsburgs, who had won possession of the neighboring territory of Austria under Rudolf I (1273–91). This long association of the Slovenes with Vienna and with the Habsburg champions of Catholic Christianity has profoundly affected their cultural and economic development.

The Balkans. The hundred years from 1350 to 1450 brought tremendous changes south of the lower Danube. The Bulgarian Empire had collapsed under the attack of the Byzantine emperor in 1018, and for the following century and a half Bulgaria had been an integral part of the Eastern Empire. In 1186 a second Bulgarian Empire had arisen and had maintained a precarious existence for two centuries. In the middle of the fourteenth century, the Bulgarian Tsar married the daughter of Stephen Dushan (1331–55), the greatest of Serb rulers. Under Dushan, the Serbs dominated the Balkan Peninsula for a few brief years. In 1389, however, the Ottoman Turks defeated a coalition of Balkan armies in the famous Battle of Kossovo. This victory marked the first great Turkish success in Europe. After conquering most of the Balkan Peninsula, the Turks turned to besiege Constantinople, which they had originally by-passed. With the capture of this city in 1453, the Byzantine Empire came to an end. Within the next few years the Turks completed their conquest of the Balkans, mopping up the few remaining Greek outposts in Morea and extending their control to Wallachia (1462), Bosnia (1463), and Albania (1479).

The fall of the Byzantine Empire marks an epoch in world history. Now the Roman Empire had truly come to an end, the control of the holy places had definitely passed into Moslem hands, and the Cathedral of St. Sophia, the symbol of the leadership of Eastern Orthodoxy, was converted into a mosque. At the same time Christian Europe, itself beset with ever increasing religious controversy, was confronted by a powerful new ideological foe. In the east a rising new power, the Principality of Moscow, laid ominous claim to the imperial heritage of the Byzantine emperors.

Russia. By the middle of the ninth century, a number of important city-states were located along the so-called eastern water route from the Baltic to the Black Sea—Novgorod in the north, Smolensk in the middle, and Kiev in the south. These cities controlled the important trade with Constantinople. Kiev, thanks to the aid of certain Viking invaders (known as *Varangians* in Russian history), established its supremacy in the period 882–1132. During this time of Kiev's dominance, the Russians received Christianity as taught by the Church at Constantinople. Subsequent invasions, particularly the Mongolian incursions, caused the Kiev state to disintegrate into many principalities. The rulers of the Golden Horde exercised only weak control over the more westerly sections of their empire. By the middle of the fourteenth century, the Dukes of Lithuania extended their dominance to the plains of the Black Sea. Many of these peoples were only too glad to come under the protection of Christian Polish or Lithuanian princes in order to escape the harsher levies of the Tartar Khans.

To the east of the Lithuanian state, the Principality of Moscow began to achieve prominence. Its first ruler of significance was Ivan I (1325–41), who received the surname Kalita (Moneybag) because of his parsimony. He purchased special privileges from his Tartar overlords and in turn was commissioned by them to collect tribute from other princes. "To him who hath shall be given," and the princes of Moscow prospered, gradually adding one bit of territory after another to their domain. The creation of modern Russia is an expansion of the Principality of Moscow, much as the creation of modern France is a result of additions of territory to the Capetian possession of Île-de-France.

In 1462 Ivan III, to be known in history as "Ivan the Great" and as the first sovereign of the modern Russian state, became Prince of Moscow. The Khans of the Golden Horde had already been weakened by new attacks from Asia under Timur the Great (1369–1405), and Ivan now broke their domination in Russia. In 1472 he married the niece of the last Byzantine emperor and announced himself heir of the Roman emperors and Protector of the Orthodox Church. The double eagle of the Byzantine Empire was adopted as the Russian coat of arms. Genealogists went so far as to trace Ivan's descent, by a stretch of imagination, back to Caesar Augustus.

2

THE BACKGROUND OF THE HUSSITE REVOLUTION

FREDERICK G. HEYMANN

[The history of medieval Bohemia, like that of modern Czechoslovakia, reveals characteristics unique in Eastern Europe. In the late fourteenth and early fifteenth centuries, Bohemia was socially, economically, and culturally advanced by West European as well as East European standards. The interaction of class conflict, incipient nationalism (the rivalry between Bohemians and Germans), and religious conflict (between Czech intellectuals and theologians and the Church of Rome) led to the Hussite Revolution of the fifteenth century, the "first Protestant revolution." These phenomena are described and analyzed in the context of Bohemian and European history in the following selection from Frederick G. Heymann's masterly study of the Hussite Revolution.]

The years of [John] Žižka's * youth—the sixties and seventies of the fourteenth century—coincided with that period in which Bohemia's "Golden Age" reached its fullest flowering. It is the second half of the reign of Charles IV. A combination of favorable economic, political, and social trends had been fully used and reinforced by this great ruler, a man as shrewd and calculating in his ways and means as he was conscientiously devoted to his high tasks. The first in the long line of Bohemian kings to bear the imperial crown of the Holy Roman Empire, he did much for the vast regions under his sovereignty, and the judgment that he was the Empire's "archstepfather" has long been discarded. Yet it is true to say that his special love belonged to the country of his birth, that he was proud of being, through his mother, a descendant of the old Slavic royal house of

* John Žižka was supreme military leader of the Hussites from 1420 until his death in 1424.—ED.

Reprinted, by permission, from Frederick G. Heymann, *John Žižka and the Hussite Revolution* (Princeton, N.J.: Princeton University Press, 1955), pp. 36–60.

Přemysl, and that under him the country, and especially its capital, rose
to be the political and cultural center of Europe north of the Alps. None
of the great cities of the Old World shows to this day the stamp of a
fourteenth-century ruler as impressively as Prague shows the stamp of
Charles. From the great St. Vitus Cathedral on Hradčany Hill across the
beautiful stone bridge which bears his name to the New Town, his building and planning can be traced, and long before his death the University,
founded by him in 1348, had begun to equal in fame such older places
of learning as Bologna, Paris, and Oxford. With Brandenburg added to
its dependencies, the Crown of Bohemia ranked, at this time, as one of
the strongest of Europe's powers. Though technically it still formed
part of the Holy Roman Empire its role in the ancient superstate was
practically limited to the identity of the ruler. It was not as Emperor
that Charles ruled over Bohemia, rather was he the King of Bohemia
who had been elected to rule the Empire as well.[1] And in comparison
with the widely unsettled conditions in most of Germany, the Bohemian
state presented a picture of order, prosperity, and cohesive strength.

This situation changed considerably when, at the age of only seventeen, Wenceslas IV followed his father in 1378. The inexperience, personal incompetence, and inconsistency of this ruler contributed much
to the weakening of the royal power and with it to the resumption of
those domestic struggles which Charles's stronger hand had been able to
suppress almost completely. In the Empire the ineffectiveness of Wenceslas's rule led to his deposition by the electors in 1400, in Bohemia to
the rise of the League of Lords, to the repeated imprisonment of the
King, and to the unwelcome interference in the affairs of the Kingdom
by other Luxembourg princes, especially Sigismund of Hungary and Jost
of Brandenburg.

It would, however, be wrong to hold Wenceslas's deficiencies as a ruler
responsible for all the troubles or conflicts which began to beset Bohemia
during his reign. To a considerable extent their roots go deeper into past
history. They can well be described as the growing pains of a young and
vigorously developing society, a society which was exposed to unusual
problems and challenges and eventually reacted in equally unusual ways.
A mere record of events during the rule of Wenceslas would contribute
but little to an understanding of them. It seems more helpful to attempt
to analyze, as clearly as it is possible in the space of a short chapter, the
structure of Bohemian society and the basic tendencies of its development
in the last decades before the outbreak of the great storm of 1419.

We are accustomed to thinking of the whole part of late medieval

[1] While Bohemia had been made a hereditary kingdom in 1156, its character as fief
of the Empire had all but disappeared when the Golden Bull, granted in 1212 by
Frederick II to Přemysl Otakar I, renounced the right of the Emperor to confirm the
election of the King and freed the Kingdom from all financial obligations toward the
Reich. Only the fact that Bohemia's kings kept insisting on their role as the ranking
temporal electors of the Empire (with the hope of acquiring for themselves the imperial
dignity) prevented the complete separation between Bohemia and the Empire.

Europe belonging to the Church of Rome as something like a unit, and usually describe its social structure as feudal. Regional differences, however, were considerable and highly significant. Thus the degree of stratification which society had reached in Western Europe even before the fourteenth century was nowhere attained in the East, and the main reason for this lesser rigidity of the social texture can probably be found in the fact that all through the thirteenth century the eastern countries of the Roman-Christian world, especially Poland, Bohemia, and Hungary, were still in the process of lively colonizing activities. There were still empty spaces to be filled, forests to be cleared, new settlements to be founded. By far the most active (though not, as it is sometimes assumed, the only) national group engaged in these activities were, of course, the Germans. In Bohemia especially, German colonization, favored both by the royal power and the Church, had proceeded unchecked during the rule of the late Přemyslide kings. Early in the fourteenth century, however, this process came to a halt, having lost its original drive as well as the possibilities for new settlement. The end of the colonizing period led to stronger competition and friction, not only between the two nationalities but also between the main strata of society regardless of ethnological origin.

There were other elements in this process making for more differentiation as well as for increasing tendencies toward stratification. Population as a whole was growing again, soon after the years of the Black Death (1348–50) had temporarily—and rather mildly in the case of Bohemia and Moravia—checked this development. And the balance of social forces existing in the twelfth and thirteenth centuries had been shaken, with gains for some and losses for other groups, by the impact of a budding merchant capitalism and a money economy which, though still primitive in its methods, at least in comparison to Italy, had already spread through the whole of society.

All these changes, however, and the dynamic forces responsible for them, have to be seen against the background of an overwhelmingly agricultural society. The distribution of the soil was and remained the predominant factor in determining the relative strength of each social group. And here again we are faced by a significant difference between the situation in Bohemia and that in most other European countries.

The Church was a very great landowner everywhere in Europe, but it seems unlikely that in any other country the proportion of Church-held land was quite as huge as in Bohemia. The clerical estate, the Archbishop of Prague and the bishops, the chapters and especially the monasteries, owned together no less than one-half of all the land. (In other countries this proportion was probably nearer one-third.) Against this tremendous collective wealth we find, as the greatest single owner, the King with about one-sixth of the total soil, a good deal of it forest land. All other social groups—high nobility, lower nobility, towns, and free peasants— had to share the remaining third.

Among these last-named groups the greatest landowners were still the lords, not only individually but also collectively. Yet compared with earlier times they had lost much, while the Church had gained. Split inheritance, combined with the need for cash caused by an ever increasing personal standard of living, had been among the main causes for this development. Consequently, the number of vast baronial holdings, such as had still been frequent in the twelfth and early thirteenth century, had shrunk considerably. Hardly more than half a dozen of the great clans were still rulers of extended domains, each holding large numbers of villages, several castles, and a few dependent towns. Most or all of these we shall encounter in the course of the revolutionary years: the Rosenbergs and the Wartenbergs, the Lords of Dubá, Kolovrat and Sternberg, the Kunštats and the Lichtenburgs. (The predominantly German names, taken from their main castles, are only the reflection of the fashion of an earlier time to give German names to those castles. The men themselves were very conscious of belonging to the Czech nation, the "lingua bohemica.") Apart from those leading families, few lords owned more than one or two castles and ten villages, and one castle with five to eight villages can be considered the average baronial holding of the late fourteenth century.

The reduction in the property status of the high nobility strengthened the tendency of that group toward exclusion and rigid stratification. In earlier times the borderline between higher and lower nobility had been distinct but not impassable. In the late fourteenth and early fifteenth century, on the other hand, few if any members of the lower nobility succeeded in rising to the higher class even if—for instance, due to the favor of the king—they had been able to amass a considerable landed property or to occupy an office of high standing. Nor did the barons permit any political influence to be wielded by the gentry as a class. Though they were represented in the great diets of the kingdom, their role there was strictly secondary, as was generally that of the towns as well. How much any decision of the diet was considered as a decision by the barons emerges very clearly from reports written during the Hussite wars. Even though in reality the two other estates were then no longer politically weak, some chroniclers still talked of "the barons" when they wanted to refer to the diet as a whole.

If, inside the baronial caste, a degree of differentiation had developed between the few very rich and powerful houses and the main body of the class, the same was true to a much stronger degree of the lower nobility. Indeed, we can almost say that this term (the gentlemen or *vladyky*) includes not one but two social classes or groups: the knights (*rytíři*), and the squires (*zemané*). Generally the status of knight, as social rank, implied the ownership of a "castle," which, however, might be a fairly modest building. (The Czech language contains a special word, *tvrz*, for the small, not necessarily stone-built castle.) In addition knightly families would hold one or two villages, some very well-to-do ones even a slightly larger number. The ordinary squire would, on the other hand, just own one village or hamlet and not infrequently would even have to be content with sharing this small property with another member of his class. This increasing differentiation was, to some extent, due to the same reasons which had led to the relative impoverishment of part of the high nobility: split inheritance and needs for cash money, which could not be fully satisfied by the sale of agricultural produce.

The poor squire would thus hardly differ in his economic position from any well-to-do freeholder. But whereas there is no clear or rigid dividing line between the knights and the squires, the line between the poorest squire and the richest peasant of "ignoble" origin is drawn with the greatest strictness. The squire has his coat of arms which also appears on his seal—an important instrument of personal identification at a time when even noblemen could not all be counted upon to know how to write. No social contact, especially no intermarriage, was possible between noblemen and those below them. The line was thus much stricter than that between the lords and the gentry, where it was still possible, though unusual, for a baron to marry the daughter of a squire without loss of rank.

It was, as we have seen, from the rank of the squires that Žižka emerged. And in his case we can well observe the fate of the economically weakest members of this estate, men who had lost or were about to lose their old basis of existence and station, their land, under the pressure of the economic changes of the time. He was only one of many who had to look for a different living, lawful if possible, in the service of one of the lords or perhaps of the King or, if there was an opportunity, of a foreign ruler who needed experienced soldiers; unlawful, that is as brigands, if no other employment seemed available. This widespread impoverishment was bound to create dissatisfaction and resentment among the lower gentry, and in the case of Žižka—where we find a very poor squire living in the shadow of the richest baron of the country—it seemed tempting to see something like a class struggle in the historically documented early fight between the former squire of Trocnov and the Lord of Rosenberg. We have earlier expressed our doubts concerning such an interpretation, and even if an element of such feelings should have been present in Žižka's actions in the early years of the fifteenth century it would still have been more a personal than a class reaction. In general the economic troubles of the gentry were different in degree rather than in substance from those of the higher nobility, and what antagonism there was between the two classes had a political rather than a strictly socio-economic character, though a rise in the legal and political stature of the gentry would, of course, be looked upon as a chance for safeguarding or improving its economic position. In the course of the Hussite Revolution the gentry had ample opportunity to strengthen itself. It emerged from the struggle with very solid gains, both economic and political, and with its special status recognized by its representation in the diet as a separate *curia*, or house. In a way, thus, the miraculous career of the squire of Trocnov can be said to have symbolized (and to some extent to have directly influenced) the fate of his class. But to understand how this was possible we shall have to watch the whole gigantic struggle itself.

The masses of people living in rural areas were, of course, peasants. Without the rich manpower derived from the villages of Bohemia, Žižka could never have built up his revolutionary armies which were to prove superior to the great international crusades sent against them from west and east. The peasants, streaming to the banners of Tabor in the early years of the Hussite wars, were, at this stage, a revolutionary class, even though none of their better-known leaders derived from peasant origin. Should we conclude from this knowledge that Bohemia's peasants, in the period before the outbreak of the Hussite Revolution, were especially badly off, that they had been oppressed or exploited beyond endurance? This somewhat primitive notion about the causes of revolutions has been discarded quite generally, and it would be just as mistaken in reference to the Bohemian Revolution of the early fifteenth century as it is in reference to the French Revolution of the late eighteenth century.

It can probably be said that at no time before, and at no time again until the early nineteenth century, Bohemia's peasants were as relatively well off as in the period preceding the Hussite wars. Slavery—a common institution in Eastern Europe during the early Middle Ages—had disappeared in Bohemia in the course of the twelfth century. The Bohemian peasants of the fourteenth century were personally free and were not bound to the land as were the serfs of Western Europe under the manorial system. They could move and, in the period concerned, made ample use of this right.

The proportion of freeholders, on the other hand, was very small. Quite generally duty-free ownership of the land by peasants was the exception rather than the rule. More frequent was an institution called *lhota* in which land was given to peasants for clearing and free use on a temporary basis. After a fixed (but locally different) number of years this status could be terminated by either side or could be made permanent with the land either to be paid for by the tenant over a certain period or to be rented by him for a fixed annual rent.[2] In the second case the relationship between peasant and landlord approached the status which was prevailing in Bohemia in the fourteenth century: that of a hereditary tenant farmer with limited duties both in payment of rent and in services, and with the right to the full and free use of the soil. This advantageous position of the peasants of Bohemia had at least partly been due to the introduction, in the twelfth and early thirteenth centuries, of the "German Law," that is, those legal advantages by which it had been possible to induce German settlers to come to Bohemia.[3] The need to keep the peasant on his farm against the competition of other landlords—first among

[2] The frequency of the institution can be gauged from the large number of villages which, to this day, are named Lhota or Lhotka.
[3] The "German Law" was by no means the prevailing legal status of the peasantry in Germany. Conditions were different in different regions and in some of them manorial serfdom was no longer unknown.

them the Church—made it necessary to meet the general demand of the peasants for equally good conditions, especially with the help of written contracts. The duties, under these circumstances, were not overly heavy. True, the barons could try to exert pressure as, in most cases, they had the right of jurisdiction over the peasants on their estates. But Charles IV limited the punishment they could inflict, and, more important, the peasants could appeal against baronial decisions to the royal courts.

All this, of course, does not mean that the peasants had no complaints. It rather meant that they were far enough advanced to voice their complaints with determination. And it is characteristic of the general mood prevalent in the late fourteenth century that those complaints found considerable support among those men who had begun to think first and foremost in terms of religious reforms. Thus one of Hus's "forerunners," Thomas of Štítný, accused some of the lords of putting heavier taxes on the peasants than they themselves had to deliver to the King, and Hus himself described as atrociously unfair the fact that the compensation (apart from punishment) to be paid for the killing of a lord was as much as ninety-five threescores of groše whereas for a peasant it only amounted to five threescores. There was special resistance to the "*odúmrt*," that is, the claim of the lord to have the land whose tenant died without leaving a direct heir in his house revert to him. (It had its parallel in the French *mortmain*.) The demand for its abolition was also taken up by the religious reformers. There was, thus, an early tradition of social conscience which would make the reform movement attractive to the peasants long before any thought of revolution could have entered the heads of either the reformers or the peasants. Indeed neither Hus nor his friends ever considered any radical change in the structure of society, at least not in regard to the temporal estates.

The way, however, in which the peasants could try to help themselves most effectively in cases of real hardship was to make use of their freedom of movement. The way of collective departure and resettlement was hardly open any longer, but for the individual there was always the chance to go into one of the royal cities. His fate there might be doubtful, and it was not too easy for the recent immigrant from the rural areas of the country to acquire the rights and advantages of citizenship. Yet considerable numbers of peasants flocked to the cities, some driven by pressure, others lured by the expected advantages of town life. There, eventually, they contributed to the growth of the *chudina*, the masses of the people with little or no property, dependent on whatever wage labor was available at the time. In Prague especially, this group of people was large and was to have some influence on the development of the Hussite movement, especially during the earlier years of the revolution.

The overwhelming importance of the towns in changing the social structure of European society in the late Middle Ages has long been recognized, but the main examples which come to mind when this fact is stressed are the cities of Italy, France, the Netherlands, and the Hanseatic towns of Germany. The degree to which Bohemia and Moravia had become an important town region is less well known. Here again it is the reign of Charles IV, the years from 1346 to 1378, which saw the full flowering of a development which had started long before. Toward the end of his life Bohemia (without Moravia or any of her other dependencies) counted about a hundred walled towns, thirty-five of them royal cities. Under Wenceslas IV this number increased still further, though not very considerably. But more important than the increase in the number of towns was the increase of their economic and political strength.

Some of these towns were, of course, very small communities of a couple of thousand or even less, and dependent, in the main, on agricultural pursuits. But in the majority of the royal towns the trades, and with them the guilds, were very fully developed in the fourteenth century, and in the greatest of them agriculture had already ceased to be of paramount importance for the main body of the citizenry, except those people living in the suburbs outside the town walls. Cities like Hradec Králové, Pilsen, Žatec, and many others had not only become markets and trading centers by the end of the fourteenth century but also seats of a highly diversified manufacture. In a class by itself was Kutná Hora (as well as the Moravian town of Jihlava) because of its highly productive silver mines. The role which Bohemia's silver production played for the rapid economic development of the country has probably not yet been quite fully evaluated. It did then, and in a lesser way, for Bohemia what the bullion of the New World did in the sixteenth century for Western Europe. It accelerated the replacing of older forms of trading and of payment for services by money transactions. It made possible the importation of goods beyond the capacity of the country to export, even though Bohemia's export was growing and included such items as linen and woolen cloth, ceramics, leather, knives, beer, wine, and various agricultural products. Bohemian silver, which paid for the balance, was used all over the neighboring countries, especially in Germany. The income from the silver mines made the King less dependent on the readiness of the estates to grant him additional taxation and thus, by strengthening royal power, helped in the pacification and unification of the country under Charles IV. It was on the basis of silver that Kutná Hora became the second city of the kingdom, but once this position had been achieved it flourished in many ways, its guilds were highly diversified, building proceeded in an impressive way, and the Hussite wars confirmed the city's importance by the many actions fought for its possession.

But even Kutná Hora's prosperity paled when compared to that of Prague, Bohemia's old, immemorial capital. Castle, market, and seat of the early Bohemian dukes in the ninth century, seat of a bishop in the tenth, it was, before the end of the first millennium, a busy trading center with many churches and with some houses of stone. From early times the settlement included two boroughs, the Small Town (Small Side) lying on the left bank of the Vltava under the protection of the royal castle on Hradčany Hill, and the Great Town, later Old Town, across the

Vltava in the bend formed by the river. By the middle of the twelfth century the two towns were connected by a stone bridge which lasted for almost two hundred years. The succeeding structure was built early under Charles IV. Its grave and solid beauty has survived six centuries and does not show any signs of decrepitude.

The time of Charles was the great era for Prague. The city's growth was spectacular. The building of the New Town, in which the King-Emperor took a very personal part, constituted one of the most impressive feats of the late medieval town planning. It just about doubled the area of the city, which from now on consisted of three autonomous boroughs. Before Charles's death the New Town contained a population roughly equal to that of the two other boroughs. The capital as a whole had, by that time, approximately 40,000 inhabitants which made her one of the largest cities of Europe, roughly on a par with London and the leading Flemish cities and outranked only by Paris. But the intensive side of its growth was even more amazing. Prague was now, beyond dispute, the cultural hub of Central and Eastern Europe. The development of learning, powerfully supported by the King and the University, was equaled by a magnificent flowering of the arts, with architecture in the lead and painting not far behind. And while, under Wenceslas, Prague too began to feel the beginnings of the social and political crisis, the arts continued to prosper. We have a report from a Milanese ambassador who visited the city just at the turn of the century. This man who knew the wonders of Italy's early Renaissance was deeply impressed by the magnificence of the northern capital which, so he said, approached the beauty of Rome. And all this splendor reflected not only, and perhaps not even in the first place, the copious patronage of a great ruler but also the pride of the citizens who, in their own churches, city halls, and many of their private houses, exhibited their individual and collective wealth.

But the wealth was, of course, not truly collective or general. On the contrary the social and economic differentiation which characterized Bohemia's development in the fourteenth century was nowhere as distinct and even extreme as it was in the cities, more especially in the capital. Three classes are fairly clearly discernible there, and the differences in their social status are almost as great, in their economic status even greater than those between the classes in rural areas. The predominant position, economic as well as social and political, was held by the old patrician families of the great merchants. Their wealth can be gauged from the fact that many of them acquired considerable landed property and had little difficulty in gaining acceptance (and intermarriage) at least with the lower nobility. In their hands had long been the government of the cities, and only relatively late in the fourteenth century could the urban middle class, the craftsmen and artisans, gain a foothold in the city councils. The separate government of the New Town was more accessible to them as it was this social group which constituted the majority of the full citizens of that borough. They were, or course, backed by their great professional organizations, the guilds.

The fight of the guilds for more influence in the town governments is a feature of the contemporary town history all over Europe. In Bohemia and Moravia it was conducted with considerable vigor. Charles IV still supported the patricians against the claims of the guilds, going at times so far as to order some of the latter to be dissolved. But in the seventies and eighties of the fourteenth century they were gaining strength again. In 1378 we find them, in Brno, openly rebelling against the patrician rule, and in the following decades various similar moves followed. Wenceslas IV, unlike his father, tolerated this strengthening of the guilds if he did not favor it outright.

This large class of craftsmen and artisans was to become the leading group during the subsequent struggle, and the German chronicler Andrew of Ratisbon was hardly wrong when he accused the guilds of Prague of having given strong support to the Hussite Revolution. Yet we should not think of this class, either before or during the Hussite movement, as a fully homogeneous and politically united social body. They acted in unison only as long as they shared their antagonism against the great patrician families, an antagonism, as we shall soon have to discuss, in national and religious as well as in social terms. But once their common adversary was removed their unity disintegrated. The richest, most firmly established layer of this middle class actually took the place of its former social superior and, having acquired a strong vested interest in forms similar to those of the older town aristocracy, turned conservative and anti-revolutionary. Cooperating closely with the more conservative leaders of the academic clergy and also with the high nobility, it obtained, after the first years of revolution, the upper hand in the Old Town and eventually in the whole city. The rest of the middle class—numerically weaker—was much less inhibited in its revolutionary tendencies. It was more open to influences from radical sectarianism and provided, in the early years of the Revolution, the decisive backing for the greatest and perhaps the most interesting among the radical clerics of the Hussite movement, Priest John Želivský, formerly a monk at the Premonstratensian monastery of Zeliv.

It is hardly surprising that, in following the leadership of this gifted and fascinating orator and politician, the lower middle class found itself accompanied and reinforced by the third and lowest social stratum, the masses of the "proletarians" of the city, the people without any possessions and without any guild standing, especially the day laborers. In the contemporary sources they appear as "the poor people," the *chudina*. Many of them had been recent immigrants from the rural areas, people who still had their roots in the country and could perhaps go back to their villages if opportunities for employment became scarce (for instance if the building activity slackened) or if the wage level fell. For others this possibility no longer existed. It is obvious that, in an increasingly revolutionary situation, these people could follow the line that seemed to promise them an approach to better living conditions under a more egalitarian society. Thus they did, at times, provide something like an increased dynamism to the revolutionary movement. At no time, however, did they play an independent role or assume any leadership of their own. All the men who under the guidance of John Želivský later appeared as spokesmen of the revolutionary masses belonged, as far as their names are known, to the craftsmen who were organized in the guilds and who probably had acquired in those organizations the experience necessary for political leadership. In this way the role of the city "proletariat" in the Hussite movement was quite similar to that of the peasants, who had equally to rely on their social superiors—the squires—for leadership in the common struggle.

We have tried so far—in what was necessarily a very cursory presentation—to show that, in the course of the later fourteenth century, Bohemia had developed in its social and economic structure into one of the most progressive, most differentiated, and most dynamic societies of late medieval Europe. Yet many of the features discussed can be found elsewhere, and even the looseness and weakness of the government of Wenceslas IV, which failed to discourage internal strife and thus let social frictions develop rather freely, was paralleled in other countries, for example, in the France of Charles VI, without leading to open revolution. In England, it is true, the great peasant revolt of 1381, supported as it was by part of the citizenry of London, testified to the increasing force of the social tensions of the time, and it can well be argued that even earlier movements like the peasant revolt which started in Flanders in 1324 or the great French *jacquerie* of 1358 were, as phenomena of social history, basically of the same nature as the revolution which followed, just a century after the Flemish outbreak, in the land of John Hus. But all those movements were limited in scope and were quickly and completely defeated. The very different course and outcome of the Hussite movement would remain inexplicable if it were to be understood as a purely socio-economic development. Its scope and success was largely due to the fact that the social forces and tensions were reinforced and largely directed by the two other great elements which are manifested all through its course: the Czech nationalism which had begun to be a strong and effective force rather early in the fourteenth century, and the movement for religious reform which, though acquiring its elementary strength only at the beginning of the fifteenth century, was to overshadow all other issues once the struggle had become an open clash. The question how those three elements—the social, the national, and the religious—influenced and reacted upon one another is intricate, largely debatable, and beyond the scope of this study. In this context we may say that the social and the national tendencies which led up to the revolution were very intimately interwoven at an early stage, whereas the trend for religious reform seemed originally to have different sources, partly even foreign, and to be fairly independent from the other two trends.

Czech national feelings are expressed quite unmistakably as early as at the beginning of the twelfth century in the first great and coherent attempt at writing the history of Bohemia: in the Latin Chronicle of

Cosmas of Prague. Even then it finds its basis in a defensive attitude against the Germans. Cosmas writes of "the innate arrogance of the Germans, who in their puffed-up pride always hold in contempt the Slavs and their language." It is a sentence which might well have been used by Czechs eight centuries after Cosmas wrote—so constant has been the resentment against German encroachments throughout Bohemian history. But German influence in Bohemia, exerted with varying intensity all through the high and late Middle Ages, was far from having only negative results for Bohemia. We have mentioned before the improvement in the life of the peasants due to the introduction of the "German Law." The German settlers in the cities whose immigration had been favored especially by the later Přemyslide kings in the thirteenth century con- tributed greatly to the development of commerce and of the trades and crafts in the country. Even in the "Golden Age," the time of Charles IV, much of the great cultural progress was due to German participation, though French and Italian influence was far from negligible. The active role of the German element in the country thus proved a constant challenge to the Czech population. The need to compete with the older and more varied experience of the immigrants resulted in strong and highly successful efforts on the side of the Czechs to meet the challenge, to match the achievements of the foreigners. It was in this hard school of national competition that Czech craftsmen, Czech artisans, but also Czch artists and Czech scholars developed their abilities and became as competent in all these endeavors as any of the townsmen in the great civilizations of late medieval Europe. But with the increased ability of the Czechs to cope with all the technical, economic, and cultural tasks of a steadily progressing society there arose, understandably, the desire for a role of social and political equality. And here they came up against the strongly entrenched groups of Germans who, on their side, tried to keep the most important as well as the most profitable positions to themselves. This was true in the Church where many of the leading prelates were Germans, among them the holders of some of the richest abbacies. It was just as true in the cities where the ruling patrician families were almost exclusively German. It is characteristic that up to the early four- teenth century few Czechs succeeded in entering the closed rank of the city councilors. Then, however, things began to change. By the middle of the century small numbers of Czech councilors were to be found in several cities, for example in Pilsen and Žatec, and before 1400 Czechs were already in the majority in a number of important city governments, such as Hradec Králové, Louny, and Beroun.

Most grimly contested, however, were the governing positions in the capital. True, the New Town which, from the beginning, was settled almost exclusively by Czechs, had a majority of Czech councilors as early as 1356. The Small Side followed somewhat later. But in the Old Town, still economically as well as politically the most important of the three boroughs, there were seldom more than two or three Czechs among the councilors until the early years of the fifteenth century, although the

Germans constituted rather less than one-third of the population. Only in 1413, when Czech nationalism in close connection with the religious reform movement had already assumed a highly militant character, was the proportion of Czechs in the council, by order of King Wenceslas, determined to be at least one-half. The measure was not accepted without considerable resistance which even led to some bloodshed.

It is understandable that this slow and only grudgingly accepted progress did not really satisfy the Czechs. And the struggle for full recognition of the nation in its own national affairs became more and more allied to and interwoven with the social struggle of the urban middle class against the rich patricians. To identify completely the relationship between patricians and urban middle class with that between Germans and Czechs would be an oversimplification. There were some Czechs among the richest of the citizens of Prague, and there were many Germans among the craftsmen and artisans, at least in the Old Town. Yet for the Czechs in the lower social groups the German patrician, lording it over the city, was clearly and increasingly the object of social as well as of national antagonism. And this resentment was fanned into even stronger hostility when the twofold adversary eventually proved also to be the enemy of the great religious reform movement.

Here again the identification of Germans with enemies of the reform movement was hardly anything basic or innate. Indeed the very first of the many clergymen who preached the need for moral reform and religious revival in Bohemia was a German: Conrad Waldhauser, the Augustinian whom Charles IV had called from Vienna to Prague in 1358, hoping thus to counteract the clerical corruption which the King-Emperor, for all his benevolence to the clergy, could not fail to perceive. Waldhauser's immediate successor, Milič of Kroměříž, was a Czech from Moravia, but his sermons (he preached in both Czech and German) found an equally enthusiastic audience among members of both nations. The Czech character of the reform movement in Bohemia is more clearly expressed in the following generation by the great reform preachers of the last quarter of the fourteenth century, foremost among them Thomas Štítný and Matthew of Janov. But their emphasis upon writing and preaching in Czech, though a conscious deviation from custom, was directed against the monopoly of Latin rather than German and expressed the idea that religious life had to be more than a ritual performed in a language which the common people could not understand. In this sense, trying to open up the sources of full religious experience to the masses of the people, the growing reform movement had truly democratic implications which were also inherent in Matthew of Janov's insistence upon the frequent, if possible daily, partaking of the Holy Communion by all the people. It was in this spirit of creating free access to religious experience for everybody that two wealthy Czech citizens of Prague founded in 1391 the Chapel of Bethlehem, to be used exclusively for Czech preaching. And this church became the center of the reform movement when its pulpit was occupied by a man whose mental stature, moral fiber, and reformatory zeal surpassed in creative strength that of all his predecessors and contemporaries: John Hus.

Hus was so great a man, and his role in the history of his country and the Western church was of such vast dimensions, that any attempt at an adequate description or evaluation within the framework of this chapter would seem hopeless. Fortunately both his personality and his work have been covered by rather extensive studies and writings in English. There is no special need to go into the difficult and intricate questions of Hus's contributions to the development of Christian theology and dogma. The claim, once made by an influential scholar, that Hus was not much more than a popularizer of the teachings of [John] Wyclif, has been quite definitely refuted. But theological speculation was not in the center of Hus's thinking. "He never stresses doctrinal reconstruction for its own sake, but always in connection with some effort at moral reform or religious awakening. Wyclif's writings provided him with much help and inspiration, and he thought highly of the great Oxonian. Yet there was also much in Wyclif's doctrines that he felt he had to reject, and he gave his life not for the truths of Wyclif but for the truth of Christ and the Scriptures as he understood them.

Perhaps it was partly this stronger emphasis upon the religious practice which enabled Hussitism even in its early stages to achieve, within Bohemia, the universality which none of the earlier reform movements, including Lollardy in England, had been able to reach: The struggle for religious reform in Bohemia became a great general upsurge which received and absorbed many of the social and national strivings which we tried to describe earlier in this chapter. And though the later Hussite Revolution, especially in its more radical developments, surely went beyond what Hus personally ever had advocated or would have welcomed, nevertheless Hus himself must quite largely be credited with, or made responsible for, the wide scope of the reform movement. True he never consciously advocated any basic change in the stratified structure of society. But his passionate defense of the common people, the little ones and poor ones, and his whole insistence upon the active role of the lay population within the Church as an all-inclusive community, gave his activities the democratic tinge which was just as strongly felt by his friends and adherents as it was understood and decried by his enemies. Like Luther after him, he vitalized the religious services of his country, drawing in all his congregation by developing the religious song.

Hus's social credo was based still more on the general demand for moral decency and the humane ethics commanded by Christ and the Scriptures than on any program for a better society. It was revolutionary only to the extent that the actual practices of the rulers of his society, and of the Church in particular, were incompatible with those principles of Christian ethics. Yet some of Hus's bitterest conflicts with the great power structure of the Roman Church arose over issues which had economic significance, such as the question of simony on which Hus wrote one of his most impressive and militant books, and the sale of indulgences in

1412 by a papal emissary (incidentally a German prelate by the name of Thiem) to which Hus reacted with a determination not surpassed by Luther in his much more famous quarrel with Tetzel a century later. In the fight against indulgences Hus went so far as to declare that believing Christians did not have to obey the Pope if his commands went against the Law of Christ. To the adherents of papal supremacy this was clearly an act of brazen rebellion.

That anyone who still considered himself a faithful son of the Church could take so audacious a stand against the Pope can only be fully understood against the background of the Great Schism which had, by then, lasted for thirty-four years and had discredited the institution of the Papacy in the eyes of many otherwise fully orthodox people. The purpose for which John XXIII* had ordered the sale of indulgences actually grew out of the Schism. With them he wanted to finance a crusade against King Ladislas of Naples who supported the older Roman rival-Pope, Gregory XII (in addition to whom there was still a third Pope, Benedict XIII, residing at Avignon).

The Great Schism had, even earlier, provided causes for national friction inside Bohemia and had thus, indirectly, caused Hus to become something like the spiritual leader of his nation. In 1408 a struggle had broken out between the conciliar party, which hoped to heal the great breach by calling a church council to Pisa, and the party which fully recognized the Roman Pope Gregory XII against his Avignonese rival. The latter group was supported by Archbishop Zbyněk of Prague, whereas King Wenceslas supported the calling of the council. When the matter was brought before the University as the highest authority in ecclesiastical law the majority of that institution decided against the King. The vote had to be taken in "nations" of which there were (as at Paris) four: the Bohemian, Bavarian, Saxon, and Polish. The majority was formed by the three last-named, most of them actually Germans. Only the Bohemian "nation" voted, in agreement with the King, for the conciliar solution.

The Czech members of the University had long complained about the fact that they could be outvoted by foreigners, and under the impact of the decision on the issue just described, King Wenceslas decided to heed their demand for a change. By the Decree of Kutná Hora, issued on January 18, 1409, the King granted three votes to the Bohemian nation against one to be held by the three foreign nations.

The Decree of Kutná Hora, enforced by the King against the fierce protest of the Germans (with the Rector von Baltenhagen at their head), had highly important consequences. It led to the exodus of large numbers of German masters and students (who, in their majority, subsequently founded the University of Leipzig). It changed the character of the University from an international into a national institution. And while it harmed the prestige which the school had had all over Europe, it established all the more firmly its position as the spiritual center of the Czech nation.

* Baldassarre Cossa, who was the antipope, John XXIII, from 1410 to 1415.—ED.

The rectorship (presidency) of the University which Herr von Baltenhagen had to lay down was now taken over by Hus. Though not all
of the masters followed his leadership it can be said that, from now on,
the University became both the spiritual testing ground and the increasingly firm platform on which the reform movement could develop. And just as the University had become a national institution so
the reform movement became ever more clearly a national movement.
The social implications inherent in it, at least as far as they tended to
divide the Czechs internally, were temporarily forgotten or at least
overshadowed by the common enthusiasm for a cause in which, religiously and nationally, Czechs of all stations could unite. The King
himself seemed to approve of it, at least to the extent of backing Hus
against the increasing hostility of the papal party and of Archbishop
Zbyněk. Queen Sophia quite openly sided with Hus, often visited the
Chapel of Bethlehem to listen to him (where, as we have heard before,
she was sometimes accompanied by Žižka) and even made the great
reformer her confessor. Among the members of the Royal Court, among
the high nobility and the gentry, Hus found an ever growing number
of friends and adherents, and the masses of the Czech city population of
Prague began to look to him as their God-sent leader and almost a saint.

During the years 1410 and 1411 the struggle centered around the issue
of Wyclif's writings, seventeen of which had been declared heretical by
the Curia, whereas the University, under Hus's leadership, contested this
ban. Archbishop Zbynek demanded that all of Wyclif's writings then in
the personal possession of members of the University be handed in to
him for inspection. When this demand had generally been complied
with, he had them summarily burned. Energetic protests on the side
of Hus and his adherents were answered by Zbynek with temporary
excommunication of Hus and his friends, but Hus kept preaching.

The conflict became still more bitter in 1412 through Hus's intervention, mentioned earlier, against the sale of indulgences which drove him
to challenge openly the Pope's right to demand general obedience. This
time Pope John XXIII not only confirmed Hus's excommunication but demanded the demolition of the Church of Bethlehem as a "nest of heretics," and laid the interdict upon Prague. To alleviate the situation, following an appeal from the King, Hus went in the summer of 1412 into
a sort of voluntary exile which lasted for two years. He spent them in the
south, dwelling part of the time in the castle of Kozí near Bechyněl where
he produced some of his most important writings. But at least as conse-
quential was his continued preaching activity. His listeners, now, were
mostly peasants who came from all over the country to hear his sermons,
delivered often under the open skies. The seed of this activity was to grow
until eventually the rural masses, especially in south-central Bohemia,
became the active and enthusiastic supporters of the great sectarian movement of Tabor. And the wide adherence of the peasantry to the reform
movement completed, as it were, the truly national support which Hus
could count upon when early in November, 1414, equipped with a safe
conduct from the Roman King Sigismund, he arrived at Constance to

justify himself before the greatest and most significant church council to have assembled for centuries.

Hus's trial for heresy before the Council of Constance is one of the famous court procedures in history, and its course and outcome represents one of those truly moving tragedies by which reality has sometimes challenged the art of the dramatist. There seems little doubt that, for all the personal enmity which Hus encountered, especially among some of his Bohemian accusers, the majority of the assembly would have been glad to see him revoke and thereby save his life. It is equally clear that Hus was not, as it has sometimes been asserted, the stubborn dogmatist who, for his own major glory, consciously sought the crown of the martyr. He often declared that he would be glad to revoke any error that should be proved to him out of the Scriptures. But this insistence on the Bible as the supreme authority challenged the basic claim of the Church to be the sole judge of divine truth and therefore had to be rejected if the Church was to retain its indisputable mastery over the religious life of the Christian world. To this extent, then, compromise seemed from the first well-nigh hopeless. But in addition to those differences touching upon the very basis of the struggle, it can hardly be denied that Hus was never given the opportunity for a proper and unfettered self-defense, however little this might have helped him. The demands of the Council to revoke such theses of Wyclif's as Hus himself had never held [4] were, in the eyes of the Czech reformer, so many demands for him to deviate from the truth by self-accusations which would have been lies before God. The letters which he wrote home from Constance, especially those written in prison at a time when he knew himself to be doomed, movingly express the greatness and purity of this noble soul, the sublime idealism which motivated him, and the deep love for his people to whom he had given a new, strong, and dynamic understanding of Christianity.

Many attempts have been made to justify not only the sentence of the Council but even the breach of the safe conduct by which Sigismund, as protector of the Council, had assured Hus of free and unmolested return to Bohemia. But there surely is no excuse for this breach short of the fantastic claim that no Christian need keep faith with a heretic, and Sigismund himself acknowledged the flagrant wrong he felt compelled to do, not only by violently blushing when the sentence was pronounced and Hus looked at him, but also by his earlier attempts at stalling when Hus was first arrested. The accusation that he was guilty for the death of Hus followed Sigismund through most of his life and seems to have burdened his conscience, as he made considerable efforts, throughout the following years, to prove his innocence.

Hus died at the stake on July 6, 1415. When the news arrived in Bohemia it caused an outcry of fierce indignation all through the country. A diet of the estates of Bohemia and Moravia was called to Prague which, on September 2, addressed a note of protest to the Council of Constance couched in the strongest language. The diet protested the innocence

---

[4] Especially the theory of remanence.

and excellence of Master John Hus and declared that anyone claiming that there was heresy in Bohemia "speaketh lies as a treacherous enemy of our kingdom and our nation, being himself a malicious heretic, and even a son of the Devil, who is the father of lies." Immediately afterwards the majority of the lords present at the diet, under the leadership of Čeněk of Wartenberg, Lacek of Kravaŕy, and Boček of Poděbrady, concluded a covenant to last for six years by which they obliged themselves to defend the freedom of preaching on all their estates, to obey the bishops only as long as those acted according to the Scriptures, and to acknowledge the University of Prague as the highest authority in disputed matters of faith. The document received the signatures of 452 lords and knights, the overwhelming majority of Bohemia's nobility. A Catholic counter-league, based on the promise of obedience to the King, the Church of Rome, and the Council of Constance, achieved the adherence of only fourteen lords.

The violent reaction of the majority of the Czech people did not serve as a warning to the Council. Sigismund had some difficulty in preventing the Council from indicting his brother King Wenceslas and Queen Sophia. The 452 signatories of the national covenant, together with some of the prominent followers of Hus among the masters of the University, were summoned to Constance to undergo a trial for heresy. They never considered following the summons, of course, but one of Hus's foremost clerical friends, Jerome of Prague, who had gone to Constance to testify on Hus's behalf, was now subjected to a procedure similar to that accorded to Hus. At one stage, cowed by the fear of death, he revoked completely, but while still in prison repented his weakness and strongly protested Hus's innocence and his own agreement with him. Therefore, as one relapsing into heresy, he was burned on May 30, 1416.

The thunder from Constance made no impression upon the majority of the people of Bohemia, except perhaps in stiffening their attitude. Their defiance of the Council's commands was more clearly expressed in the rapid spread of the custom, first practiced by the eminent master of the University, Jacobellus of Stříbro, to dispense the Holy Communion in both kinds to laymen of both sexes, though the Council had only in June 1415 solemnly condemned this practice, maintaining that only priests were allowed to partake of the wine. The new custom (in reality a return to the oldest form of the Eucharist) had been approved by Hus in one of his last letters from Constance. It now became so crucial to all adherents of the reform that in many places all over the country those priests who were not prepared to adhere to it were driven from their churches. On March 10, 1417, the University of Prague approved of the custom, declaring the Communion in both kinds as indispensable for salvation. From now on the chalice was the official symbol of the reformed Church of Bohemia, and its adherents became known as Calixtines or (from the Latin form for "in both kinds," *sub utraque parte*) Utraquists.

But even in this early stage of its development the Hussite movement showed the tendency almost necessarily inherent in any such movement once it starts deviating from the firm basis of an established dogmatic structure: the tendency toward further splitting into differing groups. There was, for instance, some disagreement among the masters of the University on whether Jacobellus of Stříbro did not go too far in demanding the Communion, always in both kinds, also for children right from the time of their baptism. Deeper, however, went the difference between the views of the Utraquists as represented by the University of Prague, and large sectarian groups which had arisen in some of the rural areas, especially in the south of Bohemia not far from the centers where Hus had done his preaching in the years from 1412 to 1414. The most important of these sectarian groups was, at an early stage of the Hussite Revolution, to become known as Taborites from the Biblical name of Mount Tabor, and though we cannot be sure when this name was first used by them we can, for the purpose of identification, apply this denotation even now in talking of those religious radicals. They were chiliasts and expected the coming of Christ at an early date. And whereas the Utraquists were determined to discard all those parts of the ritual which seemed to be incompatible with the Scriptures, the Taborites went a great step further, discarding everything that could not directly and unmistakably be inferred from the Bible.

The Taborite radicalism soon worried the University, and a declaration issued by the masters in February, 1418, warned against them. In September of the same year a synod called to Prague tried, for the first time, to lay down the religious principles of the Utraquists in twenty-three precise points, among them the prescription that all those beliefs and rituals of the Roman Church which did not directly contradict either the Scriptures or the moral principles were to be upheld.

For all the deep changes that had occurred in the religious life of the nation, the political situation within Bohemia during the first three years after the death of Hus did not yet show any clear signs of the impending storm. The Council of Constance had, to the last moment, clamored for radical measures against the Hussite movement. But in April, 1418, the great assembly dissolved after having achieved at least one of its main tasks: the liquidation of the Great Schism. After the resignation of Gregory XII and the deposition of John XXIII and Benedict XIII the Council elected Cardinal Colonna who, under the name of Martin V, inherited the difficult task of dealing with the greatest heretical movement that had ever arisen within the framework of the Western Church. The opportunities to eradicate the heresy largely depended on the attitude of King Wenceslas, and for the time being the King seemed determined not to yield. As late as June, 1418, he issued an order forbidding his subjects to follow any summons before an ecclesiastical court outside the Kingdom. But the tensions inside as well as the pressure from outside were still growing, and some months later his constancy waned. And with it waned the precarious peace which so far had been maintained in Bohemia.

TWO

The New Imperial Order: Continuity and Change (1453–1789)

The establishment of the Ottoman imperial order after the fall of Constantinople, and the de facto subjugation of all the Balkan states by the beginning of the sixteenth century, virtually destroyed the historical socio-economic, cultural, and political order of Southeastern Europe. The Ottoman Turks may be regarded as the continuators of the Eastern Roman Empire only to the extent to which they revitalized the military and economic activities of that empire and retained key personnel to execute their own mission. In theory, that mission was the spread of Islam; in practice, it was the enrichment of the Sultan and the leaders of Islam. The national identities of the subject peoples— Bulgarians, Serbs, Greeks, Albanians, Bosnians—were eradicated, as were the boundaries of the states they inhabited at the time of the Muslim conquest. However, they were allowed to retain their religion, and they enjoyed the protection of the Sultan as long as they remained loyal to him.

The Ottoman Empire was a theocracy: Rights, privileges, and relations with Constantinople were ultimately a function of religion. As the frontiers of the Ottoman Empire were extended beyond the Danube into Hungary, the pattern of economic and political relations between conquered Christian and Muslim conqueror varied with local conditions. But in the Balkans, at least, the basic nature of state and society remained constant until the end of the sixteenth century. In the same period, the vassal states of the Turks—Wallachia, Moldavia, Montenegro, even Transylvania—showed remarkable political and enonomic stability.

The primary reasons for the stability of areas under direct or indirect Turkish control were the prosperity and the military strength of the Ottoman Empire. The wealth and power of the Turks in the golden period that began with the feats of Muhammad the Conqueror (1451– 81) and ended with the defeats of Selim II (1566–74) permitted the maintenance of the hybrid state organization and stable social order associated with the Pax Ottomanica. The inhabitants of areas under direct Turkish control were jealous of their socio-economic rights and freedoms, even when they resented the rapid centralization of religious and secular power by the Greek Orthodox Patriarchate in Constantinople. They remained aloof from entreaties to rebellion against the Infidel by such would-be crusaders and "liberators" of the Peninsula from the Turk as the Spanish and Austrian Habsburgs, the Papacy, and the Venetians. They engaged in economic pursuits without hindrance; the peasantry, especially, welcomed the restoration of usurped property rights.

The prosperity of the Ottoman Empire was derived primarily from successful exploitation of the Eastern trade route and from looting by victorious armies of weak or preoccupied enemies. This prosperity began to wane as the sixteenth century drew to a close, and by the mid-seventeenth century it proved insufficient to maintain socio-economic and political stability. The shift in the European balance of power that followed the shift in trade routes, the commercial revolution, and the consolidation of the European state system forced the Turks to reassess the economic and military potential of their empire. The Turks were by then faced with determined Western opposition, led by their traditional enemies, the Habsburgs, seeking implementation of their own imperial motto: "*Austriae est imperare omni universo.*"

Until the mid-sixteenth century, the struggle for hegemony in Eastern Europe that began with Mohacs had favored the Turks. The Turks had humiliated the Holy Roman Emperor and the King of the Romans repeatedly between the siege of Vienna of 1529 and the Habsburgs' acceptance of the role of vassals of their holdings in Hungary in 1547. While Charles V watched the spread of Turkish influence in the Mediterranean, his brother Ferdinand saw the conquest and parceling of his Hungarian inheritance. Turkish Hungary was larger and more prosperous than the meager area dominated by the Habsburgs. Transylvania —the most advanced region of the old Hungarian Kingdom—became a locus of anti-Habsburg activities under the protection of the Turkish suzerain. The spread of Protestantism into Turkish Hungary, particularly Transylvania, provided an added incentive, or rationale, for the "liberation" of those lands from the "enemies of the true faith." The long drawn-out struggle over the Hungarian inheritance ended de facto by the end of the seventeenth century with the recovery of all of Hungary and Transylvania by the Habsburgs. The Treaty of Karlowitz of 1699 recorded the humiliation of the Ottoman Empire and its retrenchment to frontiers commensurate with its actual power. The Habsburg Empire, however, which stretched from Austria to Wallachia, was overextended.

The economic and political problems that faced the Habsburgs and the Turks at the end of the seventeenth century defied easy solution. The Turks had to cope with a peasantry gradually alienated by the abuse of their property rights and liberties by restless Turkish armies and insubordinate feudatories and government officials. They had to counter the attempts by the Habsburgs to subvert the Christian peasant and foment revolution against the Sultan. They had to cope with the deterioration of imperial authority, the disintegration of their political structure, the weakening of the state order, and the loss of revenue from foreign trade. Their attempted solutions, however, were crude and short-sighted: the brutal repression of "revolutionaries" and the forced mass conversion of Christian subjects, accompanied by strengthening of the fiscal, religious, and political authority of the Constantinople Greeks over the Christian masses (the *rayahs*). These ad hoc measures for containing unrest, controlling subversion, and maintaining the integrity of the empire and the prosperity of its rulers proved less and less effective as the fortunes of the Porte declined further in the eighteenth century.

If the Turks were able to avoid the collapse of their far-flung empire, it was partly because the Habsburgs were unable to cope with their own complex problems. The temporary stabilization of the European political order at the end of the Thirty Years War allowed the successful military "liberation" of Hungary and Transylvania. But the Habsburgs' commitment to the protection of their interests and possessions in both Western and Eastern Europe precluded consolidation of their gains. The resistance of the Bohemian nobility to the consolidation of Habsburg power had indeed been crushed at the Battle of the White Mountain (1620), but that of the Hungarian aristocracy had not. Despite a temporary decline in its fortunes during the period of Turkish occupation, the Hungarian nobility retained sufficient strength to defend its historic rights against the Habsburg "liberators." The Rakoczi rebellion **and** the ensuing Peace of Szatmar (1711) guaranteed the maintenance **and**

confirmation of these rights by an overcommitted Austrian dynasty. The
Magyar aristocracy in Transylvania also secured Habsburg acceptance of
its traditional rights. The power of the Magyar aristocracy in the Hungarian lands was never to be broken by the Habsburgs.

It is not that the Habsburgs did not try to consolidate and expand their
power in Eastern Europe, even after Szatmar. They did so militarily in
two major wars against the Turks (1716–18 and 1736–39). During the
first, they made their deepest penetration into the Balkans, "liberating"
parts of Serbia, Bosnia, and Wallachia. In the process, however, they
complicated the already complex nationality pattern of their empire by
increasing the size and number of national groups within it. This was
not necessarily adverse to the Habsburgs' plans for consolidation of imperial authority, for in their view the "have-not" nations of Southeast
Europe could be used as leverage against the Magyar "haves." The "have-
nots" could have been won over to the imperial cause through the
civilizing influence of the "enlightened emperors" and through the recognition of their national identity and their socio-economic, religious,
and political rights. In the view of the enlighted despots of the eighteenth
century, the Habsburg Empire could have become a melting pot of all the
religions, nationalities, and socio-economic groups in Eastern Europe: a
supranational empire ruled by Maria Theresa or by the most enlightened
of the East European rulers of that century, Joseph II. Unfortunately
for the Habsburgs—and perhaps for the inhabitants of Eastern Europe
in general—their "mission" was a political one. It was therefore resisted
by all those who opposed the centralization of imperial authority and
the expansion of Austrian power; it was also resisted by opponents of
social reform. Maria Theresa and Joseph II were hampered by the restrictions imposed by the Hungarian aristocracy on Emperor Charles VI
as the price of acceptance of the Pragmatic Sanction. Even without those
restrictions, however, they would have been unable to overcome the
resistance of the Catholic Church and the feudal aristocracy, short of
supporting a social revolution by the masses. In the absence of such a
commitment—which was incompatible with their interests and their
power—the Habsburgs merely inflamed the aspirations of the underprivileged and strengthened the opposition of the privileged. The opening
of the Pandora's box brought demands for political, socio-economic, and
religious rights from such "non-nations" as the Rumanians of Transylvania. It also encouraged the spread of reformist ideas—of a far more
radical nature than envisaged by the enlightened despots—among intellectuals and aristocrats.

The modernization and ensuing turmoil in the Habsburg lands did
not affect the Ottoman Empire. The turmoil there, and in the autonomous Rumanian provinces, was partly ascribable to Habsburg military
actions against the Porte. But it was chiefly due to Russian imperialism
and the corollary deterioration of the Ottoman state order. The Ottomans' unsuccessful defense against Austrian and Russian military aggression in the eighteenth century brought devastation to the Balkan Pen-

insula and steady deterioration of the rights of both Christian and Muslim masses. The relocation of displaced Ottoman feudatories, the decline in imperial authority, the strengthening of local governmental powers (and abuse thereof), the growing financial difficulties of the Porte, and the unrest of the defeated armed forces all contributed to the development of the revolutionary spirit—and occasional revolutionary manifestations—among the dispossessed and destitute peasantry. This unrest was further aggravated and exploited by Russia's inflamatory call to arms against the Infidel.

Moscow's assumption of the role of liberator of Balkan Christendom was formally enunciated and forcibly implemented by Peter the Great and his successors. The common bond of Orthodox Christianity may not in itself have been strong enough to justify the Balkan Christians' joining the Russian "armies of liberation," but added to this was their disaffection with the Turks and with the Turks' political and economic representatives in the Peninsula, the Phanariote Greeks. This disaffection was particularly strong among the Rumanian aristocracy and clergy, whose residual power and influence had been sapped by the Greek clerical and secular aristocracy. But throughout the Peninsula, oppressed priests and peasants entertained anti-Greek and anti-Turkish sentiments, with the resultant development of a national consciousness in the Balkans. Thus, gravitation toward the "Third Rome," rather than toward Constantinople, assumed national as well as religious connotations.

The expectations of the underprivileged, and of the privileged as well, were not realized, however, since the Russians were neither social reformers nor political liberators. Awareness of Russia's imperialistic motives grew slowly, especially in the Balkans. But it was inescapable for the politically conscious in those parts of East-Central Europe where Russian imperialism showed its true cynicism; the partitioning of Poland most clearly exposed the correlation between the "protection of coreligionaries" and territorial aggrandizement. The participation of the Habsburgs and the Prussians in the desecration of the Polish state contributed to the political education of the people of East-Central Europe (and of the West European powers as well).

As the eighteenth century drew to a close, socio-economic and political unrest in Eastern Europe began to assume new dimensions and to take on new characteristics. The forces threatening destruction or alteration of the internal and external balance of power in Eastern Europe, inflamed by those seeking political advantage or socio-economic change, turned East-Central Europe into an arena for war and revolution. The French Revolution and the Napoleonic Wars clashed with the forces of conservatism and theocratic imperialism, with lasting consequences for the region.

3

TURKISH LETTERS

OGIER GHISELIN DE BUSBECQ

[In Western eyes, the Ottoman Turks have been associated with various tyrannical practices directed against the Christian tradition in general and the Christian population of Eastern Europe in particular. This image is placed in perspective by the observant Habsburg ambassador to Constantinople, Ogier Ghiselin de Busbecq. The following is an excerpt from the first of Busbecq's "Turkish Letters," written in September, 1555. Busbecq provides a colorful and poignant description of life in the Ottoman Empire in the sixteenth century.]

I undertook, when we parted, to give you a full account of my journey to Constantinople, and this promise I now hope to discharge with interest; for I will give you also an account of an expedition to Amasia, which is by far the rarer treat of the two.

To an old friend like yourself* I shall write very freely, and I am

* The letters were written to one Nicolas Michault.—ED.

Reprinted from Charles Thorton Forster and F. H. Blackburne Daniell, *The Life and Letters of Ogier Ghiselin de Busbecq* (London: C. Kegan Paul & Co., 1881), I, 76–111.

sure you will enjoy some pleasant passages which befell me on my way; and as to the disagreeables, which are inseparable from a journey so long and so difficult, do not give them a thought, for I assure you that, though they annoyed me at the time, that very annoyance, now they are past and gone, only adds to my pleasure in recalling them.

You will remember that, after my return home from England, where I attended the marriage of King Philip and Queen Mary, in the train of Don Pedro Lasso, whom my most gracious master, Ferdinand, King of the Romans, had deputed to represent him at the wedding, I received from the last-mentioned Sovereign a summons to undertake this journey.

The message reached me at Lille on November 3, and without any delay, except such as was entailed by a detour to Bousbecque for the purpose of bidding adieu to my father and my friends, I hurried through Tournai, and thence to Brussels.

Here I met Don Pedro himself; and he, to use an old proverb, gave the spur to a right willing horse, by showing me a letter he had received from the King, in which he charged him to make me set out as soon as possible. Accordingly, I took post-horses, and came with all speed to Vienna. Even at this early stage my journey brought troubles of its own, for I was quite unaccustomed to riding, and the time of year was by no means favorable to such an expedition, involving as it did bad weather, muddy roads, and short days. I had, therefore, to pursue my journey long after nightfall, and to gallop over a track, which hardly deserved the name of a road, in complete darkness, to the great danger of my neck.

On my arrival at Vienna I was presented to King Ferdinand by John Van der Aa, a member of his privy council. He received me with the kindness which invariably marks his intercourse with those of whose loyalty and honesty he has formed a favorable opinion. He told me at great length his hopes with regard to me, and how important it was to his interests that I should accept the office of ambassador, and start forthwith. He informed me he had promised the Pasha of Buda that his ambassador should be there without fail by the beginning of December, and he was anxious there should be no want of punctuality on the part of his representative, lest it should furnish the Turks with a pretext for not fulfilling the engagements which they had undertaken in consideration of this promise.

We were within twelve days of the date. There was barely time to make preparations for a short journey, and I had a long one before me.

Even from this short space I had to deduct some days for a hurried visit to John Maria Malvezzi at Komorn, whither I went by the commands of the King, who considered it of great importance that I should have an interview with Malvezzi, and receive from his own lips such information and advice as he might be able to give me with regard to the character and disposition of the Turks, inasmuch as I myself had no knowledge or experience of them.

He had been for some years Ferdinand's ambassador at the court of Suleiman, to which post he was first appointed when the Emperor

Charles, for diverse weighty reasons, negotiated a truce with the Turks
through Gerard Veltwick; for on that occasion he had also made a truce
with them for eight years on behalf of King Ferdinand.

Now, Malvezzi had been one of Veltwick's companions, and on his
return he was sent back to Constantinople by Ferdinand to act as his
ambassador, in the hope that his presence at the Sultan's court would
be of service in checking the raids of the Turks in the kingdom of Hungary, as there would be someone on the spot to remonstrate with Suleiman with regard to the outrages committed by his officers, and demand
satisfaction.

But it happened, not long after, that an opportunity, which Ferdinand
felt he could not afford to lose, occurred for reuniting Transylvania with
Hungary. In this he was warmly supported by the Hungarians, who
looked on Transylvania as an appanage of the kingdom. Accordingly, he
came to an understanding with the widow and son of John the Voivode,
who had formerly usurped the title of King of Hungary, and recovered
Transylvania in exchange for other provinces.

When the Turks got wind of these transactions—and, indeed, they
could not have been kept secret—Roostem, the son-in-law of Suleiman
and chief of the councillors who are called Vizierial Pashas, summoned
Malvezzi to his presence and asked him whether the news was true. He,
without the slightest hesitation, contradicted the report and offered,
moreover, to stake his life on the result and to submit to their worst tor-
tures if his statement proved incorrect. But when, on Ferdinand's taking
possession of the whole of Transylvania, the truth became clear, and
further concealment was impossible, the Sultan was furious with Roostem
for having placed so much confidence in Malvezzi's assurances, and
Roostem was still more enraged with Malvezzi, and often declared that
he had cheated him. Not to make too long a story, Malvezzi was thrown
into prison, his goods confiscated, and his servants sold as slaves. In this
prison he was kept in close custody for nearly two years. Sickness attacked
him, and as he was not allowed to receive any medicines, he contracted
a disease which, some time after, terminated his life. The Turks, in such
matters, have no idea of moderation; they are excessively complaisant
when they wish to show their friendship, and excessively bitter when
their anger is roused. But when their troubles at home made them
desirous of peace, and their attempt to recover Transylvania by force
of arms was unsuccessful, they were easily induced to leave off fighting
and to arrange the dispute by negotiation. The Turkish demand was that
the whole of Transylvania should be restored; but inasmuch as his treaty
with the Voivode was the result of neither force nor fraud, Ferdinand maintained that it ought not to be set aside and declined to evacuate Transylvania. With a view to satisfying the Turks on these matters, he dispatched
to the Sultan's Court two ambassadors, in whose loyalty and zeal he
had the greatest confidence—Antony Wranczy (or Verantius), Bishop
of Erlau, and Francis Zay, the commander of the ships the Hungarians
call Nassades. On their arrival Malvezzi was released from his dungeon

and sent back to Ferdinand with dispatches from Suleiman. Shortly after this, the King desired him to return to Constantinople to act as his ambassador in ordinary when peace should have been concluded. Accordingly he set out, but a fresh attack of the disease he had contracted during his confinement compelled him to stop at Komorn, a fortress which lies at the point where the River Waag joins the Danube and is our farthest outpost against the Turk.

He felt that his end was drawing near and wrote to Ferdinand, asking him to appoint someone to take his place as ambassador. The King did not altogether believe what Malvezzi said, nor, on the other hand, was he disposed to think it quite without foundation. However, he was rather inclined to suspect that his reason for avoiding the office of ambassador was not so much the severity of his attack as the recollection of what he had suffered before and the dread of what might be in store for him in the future; at the same time, he felt that he could not in decency compel a man who had done good service to King and country to proceed on an errand for which he declared himself unfit. The death of Malvezzi a few months afterwards gave ample proof that his illness was neither an excuse nor a sham. The result of all this was that I became Malvezzi's successor; but inasmuch as I had no experience in the tactics and character of the Turk, the King, as I told you before, thought that a visit to Malvezzi would be useful, since he could give me directions and suggestions as to the best method of dealing with Turkish chicanery. Accordingly, I spent two days with Malvezzi and learned as much as I could in so short a time of the policy to be followed and the things to be avoided in one's daily transactions with the Turk. Thence I returned to Vienna and set to work, as hard as I could, to get together what I wanted for my journey. But there was so much business to be done, and the time was so short, that when the day came on which I had arranged to leave I was not ready. The King kept pressing me to go, and I had been busy arranging and packing since three o'clock that morning; but it was with great difficulty that I managed to complete my preparations shortly after dusk. The gates of Vienna, which at that hour are locked, were unbolted, and I set out.

The King had gone hunting that day; and when he left he told me he felt quite sure that before he returned in the evening I should be on my road. And so I was; but there was very little difference between the time of his return and of my departure.

At 11:00 P.M., we reached Fiscagmund, a borough town of Hungary, four miles * from Vienna, where we stopped for supper, for in our haste we had left Vienna supperless and then pursued our way toward Komorn. One of the king's instructions was that I should get hold of one Paul Palyna at Komorn, who had great knowledge of the raids and robberies of the Turks, and take him with me to Buda; since, if he were at hand to prompt me, I should find it a great advantage when remonstrating

* Busbecq's miles are German Stunden, each equal to approximately 2.5 American miles.—ED.

with the Pasha concerning the outrages and demanding satisfaction for
the same. But that I should start punctually appeared to Palyna the
most unlikely thing in the world, and accordingly, when I arrived at
Komorn, he had not yet left his home, and not a soul could give me any
information as to when he was likely to arrive. I was intensely annoyed.
I dispatched a report of the matter to Ferdinand, and devoted the
next day to waiting for this precious companion of mine at Komorn.
All in vain; so on the third day I crossed the River Waag and pursued
my way towards Gran, the first fortress within the Turkish boundary line.

The officer in command at Komorn, John Pax, had given me an
escort of sixteen hussars, as the Hungarians call these horsemen, with
orders not to leave me until we came in sight of the Turkish outposts.
The Turkish officer in command at Gran had given me to understand
that his men would meet me midway between that town and Komorn. For
three hours, more or less, we had advanced through a flat and open
country, when four Turkish horsemen appeared in the distance; my
Hungarians, however, continued to ride with me, until at last I advised
them to retire, fearing that, if they came nearer, some troublesome
breach of the peace might ensue. When the Turks saw me coming, they
rode up and, halting by my carriage, saluted me. In this manner we advanced a short distance, conversing with each other, for I had a lad who
acted as interpreter.

I was not expecting any addition to my escort, when suddenly, as we
came to a spot a little below the level of the rest of the country, I found
myself surrounded by a troop of 150 horsemen, or thereabouts. I had
never seen such a sight before, and I was delighted with the gay colors of
their shields and spears, their jeweled scimitars, their many-colored
plumes, their turbans of the purest white, their robes of purple and dark
green, their gallant steeds and superb accoutrements.

The officers ride up, give me a courteous welcome, congratulate me on
my arrival, and ask whether I have had a pleasant journey. I reply in
terms befitting the occasion, and so they escort me to Gran, which consists of a fort situated on a hill, at the foot of which flows the Danube,
and a town hard by on the plain, where I take up my quarters. The
archbishop of this place stands first among the nobles of Hungary, both
in rank and in wealth. My lodging had more of the camp than the city.
Instead of beds there were planks covered with coarse woollen rugs; there
were no mattresses, no linen. And so my attendants had their first
taste of Turkish luxury! As for myself, I had brought my bed with me.

Next day the Sanjaq-bey in command of the place repeatedly urged
me to visit him. This is the title which the Turks give to an officer in
command; and the name comes from the sanjaq, or standard, which is
carried in front of his squadron of cavalry; it consists of a lance, on the
top of which is a brass ball plated over with gold. I had no dispatches
or commission for this officer, but he was so persistent that I had to go.
It turned out that all he wanted was to see me, to go through some
civilities, ask my errand, urge me to promote a peace, and wish me a

prosperous journey. On my way to his quarters I was surprised to hear the frogs croaking, although it was December and the weather was cold. The phenomenon was explained by the existence of some pools formed by hot sulphur springs.

I left Gran after a breakfast, which had to serve for a dinner as well, as there was no resting place between it and Buda.

In spite of my entreaties that he would spare himself the trouble of paying me so great an attention, the Sanjaq-bey must needs escort me with all his household and the cavalry under his command. As the horsemen poured out of the gates, they engaged in mimic warfare and also performed several feats, one of which was to throw a ball on the ground and to carry if off on the lance's point when at full gallop. Among the troopers was a Tartar with long, thick hair, and I was told that he never wore any other covering on his head than that which nature afforded, either to protect him against weather in a storm, or arrows in a battle. When the Sanjaq-bey considered that he had gone far enough, we exchanged greetings, and he returned home, leaving an escort to conduct me to Buda.

As I drew near to the city I was met by a few Turks, who were by profession cavasses. These cavasses act as officials and execute the orders of the Sultan and Pashas. The position of cavasse is considered by the Turks to be one of high honor.

I was conducted to the house of a Hungarian gentleman, where, I declare, my luggage, carriage, and horses were better treated than their owner. The first thing the Turks attend to is to get carriage, horses, and luggage into safe quarters; as for human beings, they think they have done quite enough for them if they are placed beyond the reach of wind and weather.

The Pasha, whose name was Touighoun (which, by the way, signifies a stork in Turkish), sent a person to wait on me and pay me his respects; and asked me to excuse him from giving me audience for several days, on account of a severe illness from which he was suffering, and assured me that he would attend to me as soon as his health permitted.

This circumstance prevented my business from suffering at all by Palyna's delay and enabled him also to escape the charge of willful negligence. For he used all diligence to reach me in time and shortly after wards made his appearance.

The illness of the Pasha detained me at Buda for a considerable time. The popular belief was that he had fallen sick from chagrin on receiving the news that a large hoard of his, which he had buried in some corner, had been stolen. He was generally supposed to be an arrant miser. Well, when he heard that I had with me William Quacquelben, a man of great learning and a most skilful physician, he earnestly desired me to send him to prescribe for his case. I made no objection to this proposal, but my consent was like to have cost me dear; for when the Pasha gradually got worse, and a fatal termination to his illness seemed probable, I was in great alarm lest, if he joined his Muhammad in Paradise, the Turks should accuse my physician of murdering him, to the danger of my excellent friend and my own great disgrace as an accomplice. But, by God's mercy, the Pasha recovered, and my anxiety was set at rest.

At Buda I made my first acquaintance with the Janissaries; this is the name by which the Turks call the infantry of the royal guard. The Turkish state has 12,000 of these troops when the corps is at its full strength. They are scattered through every part of the empire, either to garrison the forts against the enemy or to protect the Christians and Jews from the violence of the mob. There is no district with any considerable amount of population, no borough or city, has not a detachment of Janissaries to protect the Christians, Jews, and other helpless people from outrage and wrong.

A garrison of Janissaries is always stationed in the citadel of Buda. The dress of these men consists of a robe reaching down to the ankles, while, to cover their heads, they employ a cowl, which, by their account, was originally a cloak sleeve, part of which contains the head, while the remainder hangs down and flaps against the neck. On their forehead is placed a silver-gilt cone of considerable height, studded with stones of no great value.

These Janissaries generally came to me in pairs. When they were admitted to my dining room, they first made a bow and then came quickly up to me, all but running, and touched my dress or hand as if they intended to kiss it. After this they would thrust into my hand a nosegay of the hyacinth or narcissus; then they would run back to the door almost as quickly as they came, taking care not to turn their backs, for this, according to their code, would be a serious breach of etiquette After reaching the door, they would stand respectfully with their arms crossed and their eyes bent on the ground, looking more like monks than warriors. On receiving a few small coins (which was what they wanted) they bowed again, thanked me in loud tones, and went off blessing me for my kindness. To tell you the truth, if I had not been told beforehand that they were Janissaries, I should, without hesitation, have taken them for members of some order of Turkish monks, or brethren of some Muslim college. Yet these are the famous Janissaries, whose approach inspires terror everywhere.

During my stay at Buda a good many Turks were drawn to my table by the attractions of my wine, a luxury in which they have not many opportunities of indulging. The effect of this enforced abstinence is to make them so eager for drink that they swill themselves with it whenever they get the chance. I asked them to make a night of it, but at last I got tired of the game, left the table, and retired to my bedroom. On this my Turkish guests made a move to go, and great was their grief as they reflected that they were not yet dead drunk and could still use their legs. Presently they sent a servant to request that I allow them access to my stock of wine and lend them some silver cups. With my permission, they said, they would like to continue their drinking bout through the night; they were not particular where they sat; any odd corner would do for them. Well, I ordered them to be furnished with as much wine as they could drink, and also with the cups they asked for. Being thus supplied, the fellows never left off drinking until they were one and all stretched on the floor in the last stage of intoxication.

To drink wine is considered a great sin among the Turks, especially in the case of persons advanced in life: When younger people indulge in it the offense is considered more venial. Inasmuch, however, as they think that they will have to pay the same penalty after death whether they drink much or little, if they taste one drop of wine they must needs indulge in a regular debauch; their notion being that inasmuch as they have already incurred the penalty appointed for such sin in another world, it will be an advantage to them to have their sin out, and get dead drunk, since it will cost them as much in either case. These are their ideas about drinking, and they have some other notions which are still more ridiculous. I saw an old gentleman at Constantinople who, before taking up his cup, shouted as loud as he could. I asked my friends the reason, and they told me he was shouting to warn his soul to stow itself away in some odd corner of his body, or to leave it altogether, lest it should be defiled by the wine he was about to drink, and have hereafter to answer for the offense which the worthy man meant to indulge in.

I shall not have time to give you a full description of the good town of Buda, but that I may not pass it over altogether, I will give you a sketch of such sort as is suitable for a letter, though it would not be sufficient for a book. The town is built on the side of a hill, in a most delightful situation, the country around being rich and fertile. On the one side it is bordered by vine-clad hills, and on the other it commands a view of the Danube, as it flows past its walls, with Pest beyond, and the broad fields on the other side of the river. Well might this town be selected as the royal capital of Hungary. In past times it was adorned with the magnificent palaces of the Hungarian nobility, some of which have fallen down, while others are only kept from falling by a liberal use of props and stays. The inmates of these mansions are generally Turkish soldiers, who, as their daily pay is all they have to live on, can spare nothing for the purpose of mending the walls or patching the roofs of these vast buildings. Accordingly, they do not take it to heart if the roof lets in rain or the wall cracks, provided they can find a dry spot to stable their horses and make their own bed. As to the chambers above, they think it is no concern of theirs; so they leave the rats and mice in full enjoyment of them. Another reason for this negligence is that it is part of the Turkish creed to avoid display in the matter of buildings; they consider that a man proves himself a conceited fellow who utterly misunderstands his position if he aims at having a pretentious house, for he shows thereby, according to their notion, that he expects himself and his house to last for ever. They profess to use houses as travelers use inns, and if their habitations protect them from robbers, give them warmth and shade, and keep off rain, they want nothing more. Through the whole of Turkey it would be hard to find a house, however exalted or rich its owner may be, built with the slightest regard to elegance. Everyone lives in a hut or cottage.

The great people are fond of fine gardens and sumptuous baths and take care to have roomy houses to accommodate their retinues; but in these you never see a bright verandah or a hall worth looking at, nor does any sign of grandeur attract one's attention. The Hungarians also follow the same practice, for with the exception of Buda, and perhaps Presburg, you will scarcely find a city in the whole of Hungary containing buildings of any pretension whatever. For my own part, I believe that this is a very old habit of theirs and arises from the circumstance that the Hungarians are a warlike nation, accustomed to camp life and expeditions far from home, and so, when they lived in a city, they did so as men who must shortly leave it.

While at Buda, I was much struck with a spring which I saw outside the gate on the road to Constantinople. The surface of the water was boiling hot, but at the bottom you could see fish swimming about, so that, if they were caught, you might expect them to come out ready boiled!

At length, on December 7, the Pasha was ready to receive me. I gave him a present with a view to securing his favor and then proceeded to complain of the arrogance and misdeeds of the Turkish soldiers. I demanded the restitution of the places which had been taken from us in violation of the truce, and which he had undertaken in his letters to restore to my master on his sending an ambassador. The Pasha replied with complaints as heavy as mine about the losses and injuries he had sustained at the hands of our people. As to restoring the places, he took refuge in the following dilemma: "I," said he, "either did not promise to restore these places or I did promise to restore them. In the former case, I am not bound to restore them; while in the latter case, a man of your intelligence must comprehend that I made a promise which I have neither the right nor the power to keep; for my master has assigned me the duty of enlarging his dominion, not of diminishing it; and I have no right to impair his estate. Remember it is *his* interest that is in question, not *mine*. When you see him, you can ask him for whatever you like." He concluded by remarking that it was "very wrong of me to bother a man still weak from illness with a long discourse about nothing."

When he had delivered this decision, with the air of a judge, I had leave to go. All I gained by my interview was the conclusion of a truce until an answer should be brought back from Suleiman.

I observed, when we were presented to the Pasha, that they kept up the custom of the ancient Romans, who put in the word "feliciter" at the end of their speech and used words of good omen. I noticed also that in most cases the left-hand side was considered the more honorable. The reason they assign for this is that the sword confers honor on that side, for if a man stands on the right, he has in a certain sense his sword under the hand of the man who flanks him on the left, while the latter, of course, would have his sword free and disencumbered.

Our business at Buda being thus concluded, in so far as we were able to accomplish it, my companion returned to the King, while I, with my horses, carriages, and people, embarked on some vessels which were waiting for us and sailed down the Danube towards Belgrade. This route was not only safer than that by land but also occupied less time, for encumbered as I was with baggage, I should have been twelve days at the very least on the road, and there would also have been danger of an attack from Heydons—for so the Hungarians call the *banditti* who have left their flocks and herds to become half soldiers, half brigands. By the river route there was no fear of Heydons, and the passage occupied five days.

The vessel on board which I sailed was towed by a tug manned by twenty-four oarsmen; the other boats were pulled along by a pair of sweeps. With the exception of a few hours during which the wretched galley-slaves and the crew took food and rest, we traveled incessantly. I was much impressed on this occasion with the rashness of the Turks, for they had no hesitation in continuing their voyage during the night, though there was no moon and it was quite dark, amid a gale of wind. We often, to our very great danger, encountered mills and trunks and branches of trees projecting from the banks, so that it frequently happened that the boat was caught by the gale and came crashing onto the stumps and branches which lined the riverside. On such occasions it seemed to me that we were on the point of going to pieces. Once, indeed, there was a great crash, and part of the deck was carried away. I jumped out of bed and begged the crew to be more careful. Their only answer was "Alaure," that is, "God will help us;" and so I was left to get back to my bed and my nap—if I could! I will venture to make one prophecy, and that is, that this mode of sailing will one day bring about a disaster.

On our voyage I saw Tolna, a Hungarian borough of some importance, which deserves special mention for its excellent white wine and the civility of the people. I saw also Fort Valpovar, which stands on high ground, as well as other castles and towns; nor did I fail to notice the points at which the Drave, on the one side, and the Theiss, on the other, flow into the Danube. Belgrade itself lies at the confluence of the Save and the Danube, and at the apex of the angle where these streams join, the old city is still standing; it is built in an antiquated style and fortified with numerous towers and a double wall. On two sides it is washed by the rivers I mentioned, while on the third side, which unites it to the land, it has a citadel of considerable strength, placed on an eminence, consisting of several lofty towers built of squared stone.

In front of the city are very large suburbs, built without any regard to order. These are inhabited by people of different nations—Turks, Greeks, Jews, Hungarians, Dalmatians, and many more.

Indeed, throughout the Turkish Empire the suburbs, as a rule, are larger than the towns, and suburbs and town together give the idea of a very considerable place. This was the first point at which I met with ancient coins, of which, as you know, I am very fond, and I find William Quacquelben, whom I mentioned before, a most admirable and devoted fellow student in this hobby of mine.

We found several coins, on one side of which was a Roman soldier standing between a bull and a horse, with the inscription "Taurunum."

It is a well-ascertained fact that the legions of Upper Moesia were quartered here.

Twice in the days of our grandfathers great efforts were made to take Belgrade, on the first occasion by Amurath, and on the second by Muhammad the captor of Constantinople. But the efforts of the barbarians were on both occasions baffled by the gallant defense of the Hungarians and the champions of the Cross.

It was not till the year 1520 that Belgrade was taken. Suleiman, who had just ascended the throne, advanced against the city with powerful forces. He found it in a weak state, the garrison not having been kept at its proper strength, owing to the neglect of the young King Louis and the feuds of the Hungarian nobles; consequently, he made himself master of the city without much loss. We can now see clearly that Belgrade was the door of Hungary and that it was not till this gate was forced that the tide of Turkish barbarism burst into this unhappy country. The loss of Belgrade entailed the death of Louis* on the battlefield, the capture of Buda, the enthrallment of Transylvania, and the utter prostration of a flourishing realm, amid the alarm of neighboring kingdoms lest their turn should come next. The loss of Belgrade ought to be a warning to the Princes of Christendom that they, as they love their safety, should take the utmost possible care of their forts and strongholds. For the Turks resemble in this point great rivers swollen by the rains; if they can burst their banks in any single place, they pour through the breach and carry destruction far and wide. In yet more fearful fashion do the Turkish hordes, when once they have burst the barriers in their path, carry far and wide their unparalleled devastations.

But we must now return to Belgrade, with full purpose to make our way straight to Constantinople. Having procured in the city what we thought needful for our journey by road, leaving Semendria, formerly a stronghold of the Despots † of Serbia, on our left, we commenced our journey toward Nissa. When we came to high ground, the Turks showed us the snow-capped mountains of Transylvania in the distance, and they also pointed out by means of signs the place near which some of the piles of Trajan's bridge may still be seen. ‡

After crossing a river, called Morava by the natives, we took up our lodgings in a village named Jagodin, where we had an opportunity of seeing the funeral ceremonies of the country, which are very different from ours. The body was laid in a chapel, with its face uncovered, and by it was placed food in the shape of bread and meat and a cup of wine; the wife stood by the side, and also the daughter, dressed in their best clothes; the latter wore a headdress of peacock's feathers. The last present

---

* At the Battle of Mohacs.—Ed.

† The Princes of Serbia were called "Despots" in Greek and "Cral" in their native language.—Ed.

‡ The bridge erected by Emperor Trajan's architect Appolodorus in the second century A.D. is located in present-day Rumania, in the town of Severin on the Danube.—Ed.

which the wife made to her husband, after he had been waked, was a purple cap of the kind that young ladies wear in that country.

Then we heard wailing and crying and complaining, as they asked the dead man, What they had done that he should desert them? Had they in any way failed in showing submission to him or in ministering to his comfort? Why did he leave them to loneliness and misery? etc., etc. The religious ceremonies were conducted by priests of the Greek Church. I noticed in the burial ground a great many wooden figures of stags, fawns, etc., placed on the top of posts or poles. On inquiring the reason, I was informed that the husbands or fathers placed these monuments as memorials of the readiness and care with which the wives and daughters had discharged their domestic duties. On many of the tombs were hanging tresses of hair, which the women and girls had placed there to show their grief for the loss of relations. We heard also that it was the custom in these parts, when the elders had arranged a marriage between a young man and a young woman, for the bridegroom to seize his wife by force and carry her off. According to their ideas, it would be highly indelicate for the girl to be a consenting party to the arrangement.

Not far from Jagodin we came to a little stream, which the inhabitants call Nissus. This we kept on our right, skirting its bank until we came to Nissa (Niš). Some way on, we found on the bank (where the trace of an old Roman road still remained) a little marble pillar with a Latin inscription, but so mutilated as to be undecipherable. Nissa is a small town of some account to which the people of the country often resort.

I must now tell you something as to the inns we make use of, for that is a subject on which you have been for some time wanting information. At Nissa I lodged in the public inn, called by the Turks a caravanserai—the most common kind of inn in those parts. It consists of a huge building, the length of which somewhat exceeds the breadth. In the center is an open space where the camels and their baggage, as well as the mules and wagons, have to be quartered.

This open space is surrounded by a wall about three feet high, and this is bonded into the outer wall surrounding the whole building. The top of the former is level, and about four feet broad. This ledge serves the Turks for bedroom and dining room, and kitchen as well, for here and there fireplaces are built into the outer wall, which, I told you, encloses the whole building. So they sleep, eat, and cook on this ledge, three feet high and four feet broad; and this is the only distinction between their quarters and those of the camels, horses, and other beasts of burden.

Moreover, they have their horses haltered at the foot of the ledge, so that their heads and necks come right over it; and as their masters warm themselves or take their supper, the creatures stand by like so many lackeys and sometimes are given a crust or apple from their master's hand. On the ledge they also make their beds; first they spread out the rug which they carry for that purpose behind their saddles; on this they put a cloak, while the saddle supplies them with a pillow. A robe, lined with skins and reaching to the ankles, furnishes their dress by day and their blanket at

night. And so when they lie down they have no luxuries wherewith to provoke sleep to come to them.

In these inns there is no privacy whatever; everything is done in public,
and the only curtain to shield one from people's eyes is such as may be
afforded by the darkness of the night.

I was excessively disgusted with these inns, for all the Turks were
staring at us and wondering at our ways and customs, so I always did
my best to get a lodging with some poor Christian; but their huts are so
narrow that oftentimes there was not room enough for a bed, and so I
had to sleep sometimes in a tent and sometimes in my carriage. On certain
occasions I got lodged in a Turkish hostel. These hostels are fine, convenient buildings, with separate bedrooms, and no one is refused admittance, whether he be Christian or Jew, whether he be rich or a beggar.
The doors are open to all alike. They are made use of by the pashas and
sanjaq-beys when they travel. The hospitality which I met with in these
places appeared to me worthy of a royal palace. It is the custom to furnish
food to each individual who lodges there, and so, when supper time
came, an attendant made his appearance with a huge wooden platter as
big as a table, in the middle of which was a dish of barley porridge and a
bit of meat. Around the dish were loaves, and sometimes a little honey in
the comb.

At first I had some delicacy in accepting it, and told the man that my
own supper was being got ready, and that he had better give what he
had brought to people who were really in want. The attendant, however, would take no denial, expressed a hope that I "would not despise
their slender fare," told me that "even pashas received this dole, it was
the custom of the place, and there was plenty for supplying the wants
of the poor. If I did not care for it myself I might leave it for my servants."
He thus obliged me to accept it, lest I should seem ungracious. So I used
to thank whoever brought it, and sometimes took a mouthful or two. It
was not at all bad. I can assure you that barley porridge is a very palatable
food, and it is, moreover, recommended by Galen* as extremely wholesome.

Travelers are allowed to enjoy this hospitality for three full days; when
these have expired, they must change their hostel. In these places I found,
as I have already told you, most convenient lodgings, but they were not
to be met with everywhere.

Sometimes, if I could not get a house to lodge in, I spent the night in a
cattle shed. I used to look out for a large and roomy stable; in one part of
it there would be a regular fireplace, while the other part was assigned to
the sheep and oxen. It is the fashion, you must know, for the sheep and
the shepherd to live under the same roof.

My plan was to screen off the part where the fire was with my tent hang-
ings, put my table and bed by the fireside, and there I was as happy as a
king. In the other part of the stable my servants took their case in plenty

* The Greek physician of the second century A.D. Allusions to Galen were quite
common in Busbecq's day.—Ed.

of good clean straw, while some fell asleep by the bonfire which they were wont to make in an orchard or meadow hard by for the purpose of cooking our food. By means of the fire they were able to withstand the cold; and, as to keeping it burning, no vestal virgin at Rome was ever more careful than they. I dare say you will wonder how I managed to console my people for their bad lodgings. You will surmise that wine, the usual remedy for bad nights, is not easily found in the heart of Turkey. This is quite true. It is not in every district that you can get wine, and this is especially the case in places where Christians do not live. For ofttimes, getting wearied of Turkish insolence, they leave the neighborhood of the high road and take refuge in pathless wilds, where the land is poorer, and they themselves are safer, leaving their conquerors in possession of the more fertile spots. When we drew near to such places, the Turks warned us that we should find no wine there, and we then dispatched a caterer the day before under the escort of a Turk to obtain a supply from the neighboring Christian districts. So my people did not lack this solace of their hardships. To them wine supplied the place of feather beds and bolsters, and every other comfort that induces sleep. As for myself, I had in my carriage some flasks of excellent wine, which supplied my own private table.

I have now told you how I and my people provided ourselves with wine; but we had one hardship almost worse than want of wine, and this was the dreadful way in which our nights were broken. Sometimes, in order to reach a good halting place betimes, it was necessary to rise very early, while it was still dark. On these occasions it not unfrequently happened that our Turkish guides mistook the moonlight for the approach of dawn, and proceeded to wake us soon after midnight in a most noisy fashion. For the Turks, you must know, have neither hours to mark their time nor milestones to mark their roads.

They have professional people, called talismans, set apart for the service of their mosques, who use a water-glass; and when these talismans know that morning is at hand, they utter a cry from a lofty minaret built for that special purpose, in order to call and invite the people to the performance of their devotions. They utter the same cry when one quarter of the day has elapsed, at midday, again when three quarters of the day are over, and, last of all, at sunset; each time repeating the cry in shrill quavering tones, the effect of which is not unpleasing, and the sound can be heard at a distance that would astonish you.

Thus the Turks divide their day into four portions, which are longer or shorter according to the season. They have no method for marking time during the night.

But to return to my subject. Our guides, deceived by the brightness of the moon, were wont to give the signal for striking camp when the day was yet far distant. Up we jumped in haste, for fear of causing any delay or being blamed for any misadventure that might ensue. Our baggage was got together, the bed and tents thrown into the wagon, our horses harnessed, and we ourselves stood ready and equipped, waiting for the signal to start. Meanwhile, our Turks had found out their mistake and turned into bed for another sleep.

When we had waited some time for them in vain, I would send a message to tell them that we were quite ready and that the delay rested with them. My messengers brought back word that the Turks had "returned to their bedclothes, and vowed that they had been atrociously deceived by the moon when they gave the signal for starting; it was not yet time to set out, and we had much better all go to sleep again." The consequence was that we had either to unpack everything at the cost of considerable labor, or to spend a good part of the night shivering in the cold. To put a stop to this annoyance, I ordered the Turks not to trouble me again and promised to be responsible for our being up in good time, if they would tell me the day before when we ought to start, assuring them that I could manage it, as I had watches that could be trusted. "They might continue their slumbers," I added, "relying on me to have the camp roused at the proper time."

My Turks agreed but were not quite comfortable about it; so at first they would come early and wake up my servant, bidding him go to me and ask what the fingers of my timepieces said. On his return he would tell them, as best he could, what the time was, informing them that it was nearly morning, or that the sun would not rise for some time, as the case might be. When they had once or twice proved the truth of his report, they trusted the watches implicitly and expressed their admiration at their accuracy. Thenceforward we were allowed to enjoy our night's rest without having it cut short by their uproar.

On our way from Nissa to Sofia we had fair roads and good weather, considering the season of the year. Sofia is a good-sized town, with a considerable population of both residents and visitors. Formerly it was the royal city of the Bulgarians; afterwards (unless I am mistaken) it was the seat of the Despots of Serbia, whilst the dynasty still existed and had not yet succumbed to the power of the Turk. After quitting Sofia we traveled for several days through fruitful fields and pleasant valleys belonging to the Bulgarians.

The bread we used through this part of our expedition was, for the most part, baked under ashes. The people call these loaves "fugacias." They are sold by the girls and women, for there are no professional bakers in that district. When the women hear of the arrival of strangers, from whom they may expect to earn a trifle, they knead cakes of meal and water without any leaven and put them under the hot ashes. When baked they carry them round for sale at a small price, still hot from the hearth. Other eatables are also very cheap. A sheep costs thirty-five aspres,* a fowl costs one; and fifty aspres make a crown. I must not forget to tell you of the dress of the women. Usually, their sole garment consists of a shirt or chemise of linen, quite as coarse as the cloth sacks are made

---

* An *aspre* (or *asper*) was the lowest coin in the Ottoman Empire. At the rate of exchange prevalent before World War I, approximately 50 aspres were worth 1 cent; but in Busbecq's time, the Turkish coin had a considerably higher value.—Ed.

of in our country, covered with needlework designs of the most absurd and childish character, in different colors. However, they think themselves excessively fine; and when they saw our shirts—the texture of which was excellent—they expressed their surprise that we should be contented with plain linen instead of having worked and colored shirts. But nothing struck us more than their towering headdresses and singular bonnets—if bonnets they can be called. They are made of straw, woven with threads; the shape is exactly the reverse of that which is usually worn by our women in country districts; for their bonnets fall down on the shoulders and are broadest at the lowest part, from which they gradually slope up into a peak, whereas in Bulgaria the bonnet is narrowest at the lowest part; above the head it rises in a coil about three-quarters of a foot; it is open at the top, and presents a large cavity toward the sky, so that it seems expressly made for the purpose of catching the rain and the sun, just as ours are made for the purpose of keeping them off.

The whole of the bonnet, from the upper to the lower rim, is ornamented with coins and figures, bits of colored glass, and anything else that glitters, however rubbishy it may be.

This kind of bonnet makes the wearer look tall, and also obliges her to carry herself with dignity, as it is ready to tumble off at the slightest touch. When they enter a room you might imagine it was a Clytemnestra or Hecuba such as she was in the palmy days of Troy, that was marching onto the stage.

I had here an instance of the fickleness and instability of that which, in the world's opinion, constitutes nobility. For when, on noticing some young women whose persons had an air of better breeding than the rest, I inquired whether they belonged to some high family, I was told that they were descended from great Bulgarian princes and, in some cases, even from royal ancestors, but were now married to herdsmen and shepherds. So little value is attached to high birth in the Turkish realm. I saw also, in other places, descendants of the imperial families of the Cantacuzeni and Palaeologi, whose position among the Turks was lower than that of Dionysius at Corinth.* For the Turks do not measure even their own people by any other rule than that of personal merit. The only exception is the house of Othman; in this case, and in this case only, does birth confer distinction.

It is supposed that the Bulgarians, at a time when many tribes were migrating of their own accord or under compulsion, left the Scythian river Volga to settle here, and that they are called Bulgarians (an equivalent for Volgarians) from that river.

They established themselves on the Balkan range, between Sofia and Philippopolis, in a position of great natural strength, and here they long defied the power of the Greek emperors.

---

* John Cantacuzene became Byzantine Emperor John VI in 1341, and abdicated in 1354. The Palaeologi were Greeks who ruled the empire from 1261 to 1453. Dionysius, the deposed tyrant of Syracuse, became a schoolteacher in Corinth.—Ed.

When Baldwin * the elder, Count of Flanders, gained possession of the imperial throne, they took him prisoner in a skirmish and put him to death. They were not able to withstand the power of the Turks, who conquered them and subjected them to their heavy yoke. They use the language of the Illyrians, as do the Serbians and Rascians.

In order to descend to the level country in front of Philippopolis it is necessary to cross the mountain by a very rough pass. This pass the Turks call "Capi Dervent" †—that is to say, The Narrow Gate. On this plain the traveler soon meets with the Hebrus, which rises at no great distance in Mount Rhodope. Before we had crossed the pass I mentioned above, we had a good view of the summit of Rhodope, which stood out cold and clear with its snowy covering. The inhabitants, if I am not mistaken, call the mountain Rulla. From it, as Pliny tells us, flows the Hebrus, a fact generally known from the couplet of Ovid:

> Quâ patet umbrosum Rhodope glacialis ad Hamum,
> Et sacer amissas exigit Hebrus aquas.

In this passage the poet seems to refer to the river's want of depth and its scant supply of water; for though a great and famous stream, it is full of shallows. I remember, on my return, crossing the Hebrus by a ford close to Philippopolis, in order to reach an island, where we slept under canvas. But the river rose during the night, and we had great difficulty the next day in recrossing and regaining our road.

There are three hills that look as if they had been torn away from the rest of the range. On one of these Philippopolis is situated, crowning the summit with its towers. At Philippopolis we saw rice in the marshes growing like wheat.

The whole plain is covered with mounds of earth, which, according to the Turkish legends, are artificial, and mark the sites of the numerous battles that, they declare, took place in these fields. Underneath these barrows, they imagine, lie the victims of these struggles.

Continuing our route, we followed pretty closely the banks of the Hebrus, which was for some time on our right hand, and leaving the Balkans, which ran down to the Black Sea, on our left, we at last crossed the Hebrus by the noble bridge built by Mustapha and arrived at Adrianople, or, as it is called by the Turks, Endrene. The name of the city was Oresta until Hadrian enlarged it and gave it his own name. It is situated at the confluence of the Maritsa, or Hebrus, and two small streams, the Tundja and Arda, which at this point alter their course and flow toward the Aegean Sea. Even this city is of no very great extent, if only that portion is included which is within the circuit of the ancient walls; but the extensive buildings in the suburbs, which have been added by the Turks, make it a very considerable place.

---

* Baldwin, tenth Count of Flanders, was elected Emperor in 1204 and taken captive by the Bulgarians in 1205. After his death, he was succeeded by his son Baldwin, eleventh Count and second Emperor of that name.—Ed.

† The pass commonly known as "Trajan's Gate," or the "Pass of Ikhtiman."—Ed.

After stopping one day at Adrianople, we set out to finish the last stage of our journey to Constantinople, which is not far distant. As we passed through these districts we were presented with large nosegays of flowers, the narcissus, the hyacinth, and the *tulipan* (as the Turks call this last). We were very much surprised to see them blooming in mid-winter, a season that does not suit flowers at all. There is a great abundance of the narcissus and hyacinth in Greece; their fragrance is perfectly wonderful, so much so that, when in great profusion, they affect the heads of those who are unaccustomed to the scent. The tulip has little or no smell; its recommendation is the variety and beauty of the coloring.

The Turks are passionately fond of flowers, and though somewhat parsimonious in other matters, they do not hesitate to give several aspres for a choice blossom. I, too, had to pay pretty dearly for these nosegays, although they were nominally presents, for on each occasion I had to pull out a few aspres as my acknowledgment of the gift. A man who visits the Turks had better make up his mind to open his purse as soon as he crosses their frontier, and not to shut it till he quits the country; in the interval he must sow his money broadcast and may thank his stars if the seed proves fruitful. But even assuming that he gets nothing else by his expenditure, he will find that there is no other means of counter-acting the dislike and prejudice the Turks entertain toward the rest of the world. Money is the charm wherewith to lull these feelings in a Turk, and there is no other way of mollifying him. But for this method of dealing with them, these countries would be as inaccessible to foreigners as the lands that are condemned (according to the popular belief) to unbroken solitude on account of excessive heat or excessive cold.

Halfway between Constantinople and Adrianople lies a little town called Tchourlou, famous as the place where Selim was defeated by his father, Bajazet. Selim,* who was saved only by the speed of his horse Caraboulut (i.e., the dark cloud), fled to the Crimea, where his father-in-law exercised supreme power.

Just before we reached Selimbria, a small town lying on the coast, we saw some well-preserved traces of an ancient earthwork and a ditch, which they say were made in the days of the later Greek emperors and extended from the Sea of Marmora to the Danube.

These fortifications were intended to defend the land and property of the people of Constantinople, which lay within their defenses, against the inroads of barbarians. They tell of an old man in those days who declared that the existence of these works did not so much protect what was inside as mark the surrender of the rest to the barbarians, and so encourage them to attack, while it damped the spirit of the defenders.

At Selimbria we stopped awhile to enjoy the view over the calm sea and pick up shells, while the waves rolled merrily onto the shore. We were also attracted by the sight of dolphins sporting in the waters; and, in addition to all these sights, we enjoyed the heat of that delicious clime. I cannot tell you how warm and mild the air is in this charming spot.

* Selim was the father of the Sultan to whose court Busbecq was accredited.—ED.

As far as Tchourlou there was a certain amount of cold, and the wind had a touch of the North about it; but on leaving Tchourlou the air becomes extremely mild.

Close to Constantinople we crossed over the bridges, which spanned two lovely bays. If these places were cultivated, and nature were to receive the slightest assistance from art, I doubt whether in the whole world anything could be found to surpass them in loveliness. But the very ground seems to mourn its fate, and complain of the neglect of its barbarian master. Here we feasted on most delicious fish, caught before our eyes.

While lodging in the hostels, which the Turks call imaret, I happened to notice a number of bits of paper stuck in the walls. In a fit of curiosity I pulled them out, imagining that there must be some reason for their being placed there. I asked my Turks what was written on the paper, but I could not find that they contained anything which could account for their being thus preserved. This made me all the more eager to learn why on earth they were kept, for I had seen the same thing done in other places. My Turks made no reply, being unwilling to answer my question either because they were shy of telling me that which I should not credit, or because they did not wish to unfold so mighty a mystery to one outside the pale of their religion. Some time later I learned from my friends among the Turks that great respect is paid to a piece of paper, because there is a possibility that the name of God may be written on it. Therefore, they do not allow the smallest scrap to lie on the ground but pick it up and stick it quickly in some chink or crack, that it may not be trodden on. There is no particular fault, perhaps, to be found with all this, but let me tell you the rest.

On the day of the last judgment, when Muhammad will summon his followers from purgatory to heaven and eternal bliss, the only road open to them will be over a red-hot gridiron, which they must walk across with bare feet. A painful ordeal, methinks. Picture to yourself a cock skipping and hopping over hot coals! Now comes the marvel. All the paper they have preserved from being trodden on and insulted will appear unexpectedly, stick itself under their feet, and be of the greatest service in protecting them from the red-hot iron. This great boon awaits those who save paper from bad treatment. On some occasions our guides were most indignant with my servants for using paper for some very dirty work and reported it to me as an outrageous offense. I replied that they must not be surprised at such acts on the part of my servants. What could they expect, I added, from people who are accustomed to eat pork?

This is a specimen of Turkish superstition. With them it is a fearful offense for a man to sit, even unwittingly, on the Koran (which is their Bible); in the case of a Christian, the punishment is death. Moreover, they do not allow roseleaves to lie on the ground, because they think that the rose sprang from the sweat of Muhammad just as the ancients believed that it came from the blood of Venus. But I must leave off, or I shall tire you with these trifling matters.

I arrived at Constantinople on January 20, and there I found the colleagues I mentioned above, Antony Wranczy and Francis Zay. The Sultan was away in Asia with the Turkish army, and no one was left at Constantinople except the eunuch Ibrahim Pasha, governor of the city, and Roostem, who had been deprived of his office. Nevertheless, we visited the ex-chief Vizier, showed him every courtesy, and gave him presents to mark our esteem, for we did not forget the great influence he once had and his prospect of shortly regaining it.

4

THE OTTOMAN SYSTEM

WALTER LIVINGSTON WRIGHT, JR.

[The strength of the Ottoman Empire in the fifteenth and sixteenth centuries has traditionally been ascribed to the military prowess of the sultans and the modernity and efficiency of the state system. However, that system required strong leaders in order to function, because of the conflicts that arose from the distribution of powers between Christian and Muslim interests in the empire. The following selection offers a scholarly evaluation of the strengths and weaknesses of Ottoman rule in the sixteenth century.]

Fortunately, Western Europeans of the sixteenth century took a great interest in the Ottoman Empire of Suleiman the Magnificent. To them it seemed "a daily increasing flame, catching hold of whatsoever comes next, still to proceed further." Thus in the works of contemporary writers, diplomats, soldiers, travelers, and members of the organization itself, it is possible to find the materials for an accurate picture of the empire at its height. It is intended here to give no more than a brief summary of the main features of that government.

The Ottoman Government was organized on a most peculiar and unnatural basis. At its head was the sultan, regarded as absolute ruler, though in fact limited by two very definite conditions. One was the Islamic constitution of the state, a relatively complete set of laws both civil and religious, which were based upon the word of God—the Koran—and the sayings of Muhammad—the Hadith. This code had become finally fixed before the Osmanli [Ottoman] state was established and was not only venerated by the people in general but also guarded jealously against infraction by the great class of 'ulema, which included almost every educated person who had been born a Muslim. The other restriction to the sultan's

Reprinted, by permission, from Walter Livingston Wright, Jr., *Ottoman Statecraft* (Princeton, N.J.: Princeton University Press, 1935), pp. 21–28.

legislative power was the extremely conservative and backward-looking attitude of his subjects—an attitude which forbade inflexibly any sudden alteration in the recognized customs of the country or policies of the government. The ruler, therefore, was barred from practically all the usual fields of legislation, for these were covered by this Sacred Law, or *Sheri'a*. But the world refused to stand still, and modification became imperative, especially in the field of administration. The solution of this problem led to the development of two characteristic Ottoman practices. In the first place, for legislation covering the state as a whole there was revived an ancient pre-Islamic Turkish tradition which attributed complete lawmaking authority to the ruler, and under cover of this minor changes in the code were accomplished. These changes, however, were of small effect unless supported by the almost unanimous sympathy of the people at large and approved by decisions of the established heads of law and religion. The latter, in fact, more than once decreed the deposition of sultans who were accused of disregarding the Sacred Law.

In the second place, the code tended to restrict so narrowly the power of a ruler over his Muslim subjects that the discipline necessary for the administration of a vast empire could rarely be maintained. To control effectively the governors of distant provinces, men possessing very great power and prestige, the sultan had need of absolute rights over their life and liberty. Denied these rights over Muslim subjects save in the execution of the Sheri'a, he avoided the difficulty by building up an administration composed almost entirely of slaves. Over these the master had the power of life and death. Consequently a system was developed in which every administrative office was held by a slave of the sultan and every member of the standing army was his private property. Thousands of these slaves, ranging in rank from the grand vizier to the humblest private in the ranks of the janissaries, constituted the *Ruling Institution*. On the other hand the entire judicial organization was in the hands of freeborn Muslims.

As has already been noted, the restrictions upon the legislative power of the head of the state were so great that the government made few new laws. Its principal function was, therefore, administration pure and simple. The sultan was the chief executive, while under him were thousands of slaves whom he could command, punish, promote, disgrace, or kill in accordance with his slightest whim, without fear of complaint or revolt. Under the long line of able and energetic rulers who preceded Suleiman the system was perfected; each member of the immense slave family was carefully trained and ultimately appointed to that station for which he seemed best fitted; promotion was the result of ability and faithfulness. The sultans themselves were sent out as youths to be provincial governors and gained experience which helped to fit them for the colossal task of directing every detail of this vast machine, and for centuries the dynasty of Osman produced princes capable of holding firmly the reins of authority in times both of peace and war.

The heads of the various departments of government constituted the Divan, or council of state, over which the sultan at first presided in person, acting as his own prime minister. Later this function was delegated to the grand vizier, who was in every respect the sultan's deputy. The members of this council represented both of the great classes of officials, the Ruling Institution and the Muslim Institution. Each class requires a further brief explanation.

The Ruling Institution "included the sultan and his family, the officers of his household, the executive officers of the government, the standing army composed of cavalry and infantry, and a large body of young men who were being educated for service in the standing army, the court, and the government. . . . They conducted the whole of the government except the mere rendering of justice in matters that were controlled by the Sacred Law, and those limited functions that were left in the hands of subject and foreign groups that were non-Muslim. The most vital and characteristic features of this institution were, first, that its personnel consisted, with few exceptions, of men born of Christian parents or the sons of such; and second, that almost every member of the Institution came into it as the sultan's slave, and remained the sultan's slave throughout life, no matter to what height of wealth, power, and greatness he might attain."[1] Many of these were obtained through the *devshirme* or tax in boys levied upon the Christian inhabitants of European Turkey; others had formed part of the sultan's share of prisoners captured in war; still others were bought in the slave market of the capital or received as gifts from wealthy officials or foreign rulers. Every year some three or four thousand youths between the ages of ten and fifteen entered the Institution. Highly trained officials examined and classified them, choosing approximately one-tenth to enter the schools of pages which were maintained in the imperial palaces, while the rest were sent to Anatolia to spend several years in the service of feudal landholders. There the latter were expected to learn Turkish, to harden their bodies with physical labor, and to become converted to Islam. Later they would be recalled to the capital to become janissaries or common soldiers in one or the other of the various smaller military corps.

Meanwhile, the relatively small number who had been chosen because of their apparent ability and handsome appearance were being carefully trained to become the great men of the empire. Living under strict discipline, watched over by white eunuchs, instructed by learned Muslims in Turkish, Arabic, and Persian, together with such other subjects as were considered essential to the ruler of the day, they received also a thorough schooling in military matters and the ceremonies of the imperial court. After rising through several ranks they might attain membership in the small group of pages who waited upon the ruler's person. At the age of twenty-five, each was sent out from the palace to some minor position in the provinces to gain experience in administration and war. A capable man might then rise through all the various ranks of the hierarchy of officials and eventually attain the position of grand vizier. As slaves of the ruler,

[1] A. H. Lybyer, *Government of the Ottoman Empire in the Time of Suleiman the Magnificent* (Cambridge, 1913), p. 36.

all were subject only to his will and to no other. They were neither taxed
by the state nor subject to the ordinary laws of the land; they were
in servitude and at the same time were rulers and members of a highly
privileged class, which, however, could not transmit its rights to descendants, who became ordinary members of the Muslim population.

From the great community of Muslim-born Turks were drawn the
three members of the Muslim Institution who had places in the Divan,
the *mufti*, and the two *qadi'askers*. These had pursued a long and difficult
course of training in the *medresehs*, or religious colleges, where they
studied especially Arabic and through it the religion and law of Islam.
Graduating thence, they entered the service of the government in the
judicial branch and eventually became judges. Passing through various
ranks with ever widening jurisdictions, each parallel to a similar administrative division, there were open to them these two positions at the
summit of the legal hierarchy; one that of chief judge of Rumelia, or
Europe, the other Anatolia, or Asia. Another group who received a similar
training might choose the career of juriconsult or *mufti*, an official who
was regarded as a sort of court of appeal or reference by the regular judges.
Each province and city had its mufti, and at the head of all was the
Shaykh ul-Islam, who was mufti of the capital and the highest religious
and legal authority in the empire, and indeed in Islam as a whole, after
the sultans proclaimed themselves caliphs.

In addition to these numerous members of the religio-legal hierarchy
who administered or interpreted the Sacred Law, there were many other
members of the Muslim Institution in every town and village in the
empire. Some were professors in the *medresehs* or teachers in lower
schools; others were connected with monasteries as dervishes, or with
mosques as preachers and scribes. All had received some education and
were trained in the hard logic of Arab scholasticism, accepting the utter
finality and complete inflexibility of the Sacred Law and the institutions
both social and political which were based upon it. Closely connected by
family ties with the whole body of the Muslim population, this 'ulema,
or learned class, was an almost immovable obstacle to innovation or
arbitrary change of any sort whatever. It embodied the conservatism both
of Islam in particular and of the Orient in general. By reason of its origin
and training, this class was of necessity in some sense a rival of the
Ruling Institution and was continually receiving new recruits of inherited strength and ability. As the guardians and executors of the law,
members of the Muslim Institution were also privileged.

Mention has already been made of the representatives of the Muslim
Institution who were entitled to attend the Divan. A brief description
of the other high officials usually present will serve to make clear the
various departments of administration. The most important was, of
course, the grand vizier. At first the mere "burden bearer" of the sultan,
this officer came to occupy an increasingly powerful position as the ruler
began to pay less attention to the duties of government than to the plea-
sures of palace life. Eventually he became the virtual head of the state,

acting both as chief executive officer and chief justice. Under him were two *beylerbeys;* the *qapudan pasha;* the *agha* of the janissaries, representing the military classes of the empire; the *nishanji,* or chancellor; the *defterdar,* or treasurer; and the *chaush bashi,* or head of the palace functionaries. In addition there were the *re'is efendi,* or chief scribe, and his assistants. Each of these officials was head of a department with many subordinates at the capital, while in each administrative division of the empire there was a corresponding council held under the presidency of the local governor.

The beylerbeys were originally two in number, corresponding to the qadi-'askers, one with authority over Europe, the other over Asia; but later there were appointed others who were merely governors-general of large divisions of the empire. The beylerbey was head of both civil and military employees of the sultan in the territory under his jurisdiction. Himself responsible directly to the grand vizier, he had under him *sanjaq beys,* or provincial governors; *alay beys,* or rulers of counties; and *subashis,* or commanders of towns. From the highest to the lowest rank, these officials had authority similar to that of their chief. Each commanded not only a force of the standing army stationed in his district, but also the levy of feudal warriors and landholders. The latter deserve a word of explanation. All were Muslim fighting men to whom the income from certain taxes in a greater or smaller area was given in return for military service. Their position was handed on from father to son under ordinary circumstances, but the commanders of this cavalry army were invariably slaves of the sultan. In every territorial division of the empire there was, therefore, a governor who was at the same time civil administrator and head of a considerable body of both infantry and cavalry, all ready to take the field at a moment's notice.

The qapudan headed a naval organization similar in form. Under his command were both the "standing" navy, with its headquarters at Istanbul, and the feudal navy, consisting of galleys provided by certain beys in return for lands situated in the area surrounding the Aegean Sea—a region over which this pasha possessed an authority similar to that of the beylerbeys.

The agha, or general, of the janissaries, who had no civil functions, completed the list of the members of the Divan who were called "people of the sword." His sole function was that of commanding the turbulent footsoldiers of the slave family, of making them dangerous to the enemy in time of war and harmless to their master in time of peace.

Turning now to the "people of the pen," or *ehl-i qalem,* the *nishanji,* or *nishanji bashi,* first demands attention. As head of the imperial chancery it was his business to prepare all official documents, to keep records or copies of them, and whenever required, to affix the *tughra,* or decorative signature, of the sultan to any paper on which it was required. Under his orders were numerous minor functionaries who had charge of making and preserving a record of every act of the government.

The defterdar was head of the treasury department, with control of all the incoming and outgoing funds of the state. His department was divided into twenty-five bureaus, in which were kept complete records of the financial transactions of the government, including the sale of tax farms and custom-house concessions.

Just as the beylerbey was represented in each province, no matter how small it might be, by a lieutenant, so also each of the other members of the Divan was represented by an official of lower rank but similar function in the subordinate Divan, which sat under the presidency of each governor of a district in the empire. Everywhere, the central government was duplicated by organizations under its control and restricted to narrower boundaries. Always there was a member of the Muslim Institution side by side with each representative of the beylerbey.

In time of war, this administrative system became the army. The members of the Divan accompanied the sultan and grand vizier to war and were followed in turn by all the provincial governors, with the troops, both feudal and regular, of their districts.

Such, in brief, was the Ottoman government in the days of its prime. Inconsistent details—and they were many—have not been mentioned. . . . It must suffice for us to know that it was of some such complete and powerful structure as this that Mehmed Pasha was thinking when he raised his voice in criticism of what he saw about him. And well might he lament the passing of that mighty machine of government which had been built by his predecessors to enable an autocrat to rule a vast empire which lacked racial, geographical, or religious coherence and could be held together only by the overpowering force of a political system which was ruled by a single will and an administration which was also the army.

5

THE CAPITULATIONS OF 1675

[The Eastern trade routes provided the Turkish sultans with substantial income to pursue their military activities and maintain a stable economic and political order. The elaborate trade agreements concluded between the Ottoman Empire and other trading nations—the so-called Capitulations—indicated the Turkish interest in keeping the trade routes open, even at the cost of granting extraterritorial rights to the subjects of those nations.

The Capitulations of 1675 differed but little in form from the earliest capitulations of the second quarter of the sixteenth century. By 1675, however, the income derived from foreign trade had declined considerably, a change reflected in the rapid deterioration of the Ottoman state system during the seventeenth century.]

SULTAN MEHMED, MAY HE LIVE FOREVER!

"Let every thing be observed in conformity to these Capitulations, and contrary thereto let nothing be done."

EXTENSION TO BRITISH SUBJECTS OF PRIVILEGES GRANTED TO FRENCH, VENETIANS, POLES, ETC.

THE command, under the Sublime and lofty Signet, which imparts sublimity to every place, and under the imperial and noble Cypher, whose glory is renowned throughout all the world, by the Emperor and Conqueror of the Earth, achieved with the assistance of the Omnipotent, and by the especial grace of God, is this:

We, who by Divine grace, assistance, will, and benevolence, now are the King of Kings of the world, the Prince of Emperors of every age, the

Reprinted from Edward Herstlet (ed.), *Treaties and Tariffs Regulating the Trade Between Great Britain and Foreign Nations: Turkey* (London: Butterworths, 1875), pp. 8–13.

Dispenser of Crowns to Monarchs, and the Champion, Sultan Mehmed, Son of Sultan Ibrahim Chan, Son of Sultan Muhammad Chan, Son of Sultan Murad Chan, Son of Sultan Selim Chan, Son of Sultan Suleiman Chan, Son of Sultan Selim Chan.

The most glorious amongst the great Princes protesting the faith of Jesus, and the most conspicuous amongst the Potentates of the nation of the Messiah, and the Umpire of public differences that exist between Christian nations, clothed with the mantle of magnificence and majesty, Charles the Second, King of England, Scotland, France, and Ireland (whose end terminate in bliss!), having sent an Ambassador to the Sublime Porte in the time of our grandfather Sultan Murad (whose tomb be ever resplendent!) of glorious memory and full of divine mercy and pity, with professions of friendship, sincerity, devotion, partiality, and benevolence, and demanding that his subjects might be at liberty to come and go into these parts, which permission was granted to them in the reign of the Monarch aforesaid, in addition to various other special commands, to the end that on coming and going, either by land or sea, in their way, passage, and lodging, they might not experience any molestation or hindrance from anyone.

He represented, in the reign of our grandfather Sultan Mehmed Chan (whose tomb be ever resplendent!) to our just and overshadowing Porte, his cordial esteem, alliance, sincere friendship, and partiality thereto. As such privilege, therefore, had been granted to the Kings and Sovereigns of France, Venice, and Poland, who profess the most profound devotion for our most eminent throne, and to others between whom and the Sublime Porte there exist a sincere amity and good understanding, so was the same through friendship, in like manner granted to the said King; and it was granted him that his subjects and their interpreters might safely and securely come and trade in these our sacred dominions.

The Capitulations of sublime dignity and our noble commands having been, through friendship, thus granted to the Kings aforesaid, and the Queen of the above-mentioned kingdom* having heretofore also sent a noble personage with presents to this victorious Porte, which is the refuge and retreat of the Kings of the world, the most exalted place, and the asylum of the Emperors of the Universe (which gifts were graciously accepted), and she having earnestly implored the privilege in question, her entreaties were acceded to, and these our high commands conceded to her.

ARTICLE I

LIBERTY OF COMMERCE; NAVIGATION

That the English nation and merchants, and all other merchants sailing under the English flag, with their ships and vessels, and merchandise of all descriptions, shall and may pass safely by sea, and go and come into our dominions, without any the least prejudice or molestation being given

* Kings James I and Charles I, and Queen Elizabeth I.—ED.

to their persons, property, or effects, by any person whatsoever, but that they shall be left in the undisturbed enjoyment of their privileges, and be at liberty to attend to their affairs.

ARTICLE II

LIBERTY OF BRITISH SUBJECTS

That if any of the English coming into our dominions by land be molested or detained, such persons shall be instantly released, without any further obstruction being given to them.

ARTICLE III

LIBERTY OF BRITISH VESSELS TO DEPART

That English ships and vessels entering the ports and harbors of our dominions shall and may at all times safely and securely abide and remain therein, and at their free will and pleasure depart therefrom, without any opposition or hindrance from anyone.

ARTICLE IV

VESSELS DRIVEN INTO PORT BY STRESS OF WEATHER

That if it shall happen that any of their ships suffer by stress of weather, and not be provided with necessary stores and requisites, they shall be assisted by all who happen to be present, whether the crews of our imperial ships, or others, both by sea and land.

ARTICLE V

SUPPLIES TO SHIPS

That being come into the ports and harbors of our dominions, they shall and may be at liberty to purchase at their pleasure, with their own money, provisions and all other necessary articles, and to provide themselves with water, without interruption or hindrance from anyone.

ARTICLE VI

WRECKS

That if any of their ships be wrecked upon any of the coasts of our dominions, all beys, cadis, governors, commandants, and others our servants, who may be near or present, shall give them all help, protection, and assistance, and restore to them whatsover goods and effects may be driven ashore; and in the event of any plunder being committed, they shall make diligent search and inquiry to find out the property, which, when recovered, shall be wholly restored by them.

ARTICLE VII

PROTECTION TO PERSONS AND PROPERTY

That the merchants, interpreters, brokers, and others, of the said nation, shall and may, both by sea and land, come into our dominions, and there trade with the most perfect security; and in coming and going, neither they nor their attendants shall receive any the least obstruction, molestation, or injury, either in their persons or property, from the beys, cadis, sea captains, soldiers, and others, our slaves.

ARTICLE VIII

DEBTORS; BANKRUPTS

That if an Englishman, either for his own debt, or as surety for another, shall abscond, or become bankrupt, the debt shall be demanded from the real debtor only; and unless the creditor be in possession of some security given by another, such person shall not be arrested, nor the payment of such debt be demanded of him.

ARTICLE IX

ADMINISTRATION OF JUSTICE; CIVIL SUITS

That in all transactions, matters, and business occurring between the English and merchants of the countries to them subject, their attendants, interpreters, and brokers, and any other persons in our dominions, with regard to sales and purchases, credits, traffic, or security, and all other legal matters, they shall be at liberty to repair to the judge, and there make a *hoget*, or public authentic act, with witness, and register the suit, to the end that if in future any difference or dispute shall arise, they may both observe the said register and *hoget*; and when the suit shall be found conformable thereto, it shall be observed accordingly.

Should no such *hoget*, however, have been obtained from the judge, and false witnesses only are produced, their suit shall not be listened to, but justice be always administered according to the legal *hoget*.

ARTICLE X

INJURIES INFLICTED BY AN ENGLISHMAN; INTERFERENCE OF AMBASSADORS

That if any shall calumniate an Englishman, by asserting that he hath been injured by him, and producing false witnesses against him, our judges shall not give ear unto them, but the cause shall be referred to his Ambassador, in order to his deciding the same, and that he may always have recourse to his protection.

ARTICLE XI

FUGITIVE OFFENDERS

That if an Englishman, having committed an offense, shall make his escape, no other Englishman, not being security for him, shall, under such pretext, be taken or molested.

ARTICLE XII
RELEASE OF BRITISH SUBJECTS FOUND IN SLAVERY

That if an Englishman, or subject of England, be found to be a Slave in our states, and be demanded by the English Ambassador or Consul, due inquiry and examination shall be made into the causes thereof, and such person being found to be English, shall be immediately released, and delivered up to the Ambassador or Consul.

ARTICLE XIII
EXEMPTION OF BRITISH SUBJECTS FROM TRIBUTE

That all Englishmen, and subjects of England, who shall dwell or reside in our dominions, whether they be married or single, artisans or merchants, shall be exempt from all Tribute.

ARTICLE XIV
APPOINTMENT OF CONSULS

That the English Ambassadors shall and may, at their pleasure, establish Consuls in the ports of Aleppo, Alexandria, Tripoli of Barbary, Tunis, Tripoli of Syria, Scio, Smyrna, and Egypt, and in like manner remove them, and appoint others in their stead, without anyone opposing them.

ARTICLE XV
PRESENCE OF INTERPRETERS AT TRIALS

That in all litigations occurring between the English, or subjects of England, and by any other person, the judges shall not proceed to hear the cause without the presence of an interpreter, or one of his deputies.

ARTICLE XVI
DISPUTES BETWEEN ENGLISHMEN; DECISION OF AMBASSADOR OR CONSUL

That if there happen any suit, or other difference or dispute amongst the English themselves, the decision thereof shall be left to their own Ambassador or Consul, according to their custom, without the judge or other governors our slaves, intermeddling therein.

ARTICLE XVII
NON-RETENTION OR DETENTION OF BRITISH VESSELS AT SEA

That our ships and galleys, and all other vessels, which may fall in with any English ships in the seas of our dominions, shall not give them any molestation, nor detain them by demanding anything, but shall show good and mutual friendship the one to the other, without occasioning them any prejudice.

Article XVIII

Capitulations, &c., Granted to French, Venetians, and Others

That all the Capitulations, privileges, and articles granted to the French, Venetian, and other Princes who are in amity with the Sublime Porte, having been in like manner, through favor, granted to the English, by virtue of our special command, the same shall be always observed according to the form and tenor thereof, so that no one in future do presume to violate the same, or act in contravention thereof.

Article XIX

Restoration of Captured Vessels. Punishment of Offenders

That if the corsairs or galliots of the Levant shall be found to have taken any English vessels, or robbed or plundered them of their goods and effects, also if anyone shall have forcibly taken anything from the English, all possible diligence and exertion shall be used and employed for the discovery of the property, and inflicting condign punishment on those who may have committed such depredations; and their ships, goods, and effects shall be restored to them without delay or intrigue.

Article XX

Execution of Capitulations

That all our beylerbeys, imperial and private captains, governors, commandants, and other administrators, shall always strictly observe the tenor of these Imperial Capitulations, and respect the friendship and correspondence established on both sides, everyone in particular taking special care not to let anything be done contrary thereto; and as long as the said Monarch shall continue to evince true and sincere friendship, by a strict observance of the Articles and Conditions herein stipulated, these Articles and Conditions of peace and friendship shall, in like manner, be observed and kept on our own part. To the end, therefore, that no act might be committed in contravention thereof, certain clear and distinct Capitulations were conceded in the reign of our late grandfather, of happy memory (whose tomb be ever resplendent!).

6

THE RAYAHS AND THE LANDED ESTATES

SARI MEHMED PASHA

[The Pax Ottomanica, which provided social, political, and economic stability in Southeastern Europe in the sixteenth century, had all but disappeared by the eighteenth century. Among the principal causes of the deterioration of the balance between Muslim and Christian interests was the abuse by Muslim landholders and officeholders of the traditional rights of the Christian peasantry and of the legal provisions regulating land tenure in the Ottoman Empire. Sari Mehmed Pasha, a Turkish official in the eighteenth century, justly appraised the nature and consequences of these problems in the following account of the status of the peasantry and of the feudal order in the Ottoman Empire of his time.]

EXPLANATION REGARDING THE CONDITION OF THE RAYAHS AND THE HARMFULNESS OF TYRANNY AND OPPRESSION

One should abstain utterly from tyranny and guard oneself against being helper to the tyrant. One should seek to defend the oppressed, striving and persevering to gain the hearts of the poor and to draw down upon oneself their blessings. The Prophet of God (on whom be the salutation and commendation of God) has said: "Its answer accompanies the prayer of the poor." Verses:

Reprinted, by permission, from Walter Livingston Wright, Jr., *Ottoman Statecraft* (Princeton, N.J.: Princeton University Press, 1935), pp. 116–20 and pp. 142–48.

Take under thy care the heart of him who is poor;
His soul is ill; his heart is sad.
Because of prayer God has made
The petitions of the poor acceptable.

The Prophet (on whom be the commendation and salutation of God) has said: "Guard yourselves against the prayer of the poor man, even though he be an unbeliever." That is to say: "The prayer of him who is oppressed remains not on earth; even if he be an unbeliever it is accepted." "Oppression is darkness on the Day of Judgment." Verses:

Every man who has oppressed those under his power,
Tomorrow that oppression becomes darkness for him.
When the hour of death seizes his throat
Giving up his soul is sorrow.

Let them neither oppress the poor rayahs * nor cause them to be vexed by the demand for new impositions in addition to the well-known yearly taxes which they are accustomed to give. All the experienced sages have likened the taking for unessential expenditures of more money than they can endure from the poor rayahs to taking from the foundation of a building and transferring it to the roof. For weakness comes to the foundation because earth is taken from it, and the roof retains not strength to bear the weight of this load. So it causes complete destruction. Such being the case, the poor peasants should not be troubled by any sort of evil innovations. The people of the provinces and dwellers in the towns should be protected and preserved by the removal of injustices, and very great attention should be paid to making prosperous the condition of the subjects. Care should be taken in ordering their affairs, and it is above all else extremely essential that exact attention be paid to making their districts joyous and flourishing and to protecting and preserving the property and lives of travelers on the roads.

According to men of justice, it is correct to call the rayahs benefactors. His Imperial Majesty the late Sultan Suleiman Khan, whose dwelling is Paradise (God's grace and pardon be upon him), one day in his honored court made to his private and confidential companions this pearl-scattering speech, deigning to say, "Who are the benefactors of mankind?"[1] When everyone, united in opinion, said: "It is his imperial majesty the sultan, surpassing in merit, sovereign of horizons," this reply from his noble attendants was not accepted by the padishah, possessor of justice. He deigned to answer: "Verily, the benefactors are the rayahs, who, in their agriculture and husbandry, make repose and comfort unlawful to

* The term rayahs is used here to include the entire peasant population, both Christian and Muslim.—ED.

[1] It is not at all surprising that the courtiers answered as they did, for in Turkish the sultan and other persons of high rank or great power were always addressed in the plural. Thus the original question was susceptible of a double interpretation. The language of the author in describing this incident is typical of the florid style generally used by court historians and poets in speaking of the ruler.

themselves and feed us with the blessings which they have earned." May God give his holy soul a thousand blessings! In view of this consideration also, the essence and reality of the matter is that protection of the subjects is among the most extremely important affairs of the Exalted Government.

On the other hand the entering of the rayahs into the military class must be avoided carefully. Disorder is sure to come when those who are not sons or grandsons of sipahis [2] are all at once made into sipahis. For if it become necessary for rayahs to enter the military class, the rayah class becomes less, resulting in deficiency of the Treasury income; [3] and in this way the organization of the Exalted Government is ruined. For the Treasury exists through abundance of subject people. The rayahs are a trust from the Creator of men and the universe. The state exists through them and the treasure produced by them. If the subjects be always protected, they become not wretched, but increase. Kindness to them and protection of their affairs from the hand of tyrannical oppression is [a form of] worship.

Yet too much indulgence must not be shown to the rayahs. It is necessary not to permit their displaying adornment, like sipahis, on clothing or house furnishings or on their horses. On the other hand, if their wealth and livestock be abundant, they should be protected against the interference of anyone. If a rayah be employed in numerous public services which deserve a *timar* [4] from the abundant favor of the padishah, and if he become a sipahi, his relatives and his father should not be protected.[5] Or if he become a *danishmend,*[6] he escapes from the rayah class, but his household are still rayahs. They are not freed from the impositions.

It is necessary that the roll of rayahs be registered in the record office of the exalted Divan. Every thirty years a census must be taken, the dead and the ill must be separated off, and those not on the rolls must be newly recorded.

If the rayahs of a region, because of tyranny and oppression, go to another place, the ruler of the latter should send them back to their old

[2] Feudal cavalry, holders of *zi'amet* and *timar.*

[3] The purpose of the sultans in using government property to establish feudal estates was that of obtaining armed horsemen to keep subject populations under control and to fight against external enemies. The income of the lands conferred was carefully recorded, and the amount intended for the support of the sipahi and his helpers (*jebeli*) were stipulated in the *berat* of appointment. Since it was the return from certain taxes which provided the sipahi with a large part of his income, the state received proportionately less from the land put under such a lord. Mehmed Pasha tacitly admits that the arrangement had by his day so far broken down that the Treasury and army both suffered by the creation of new sipahis, for the latter rarely appeared for their military duties.

[4] The class of feudal holding with the smallest income, less than 20,000 aspers yearly.

[5] I.e., protected from the taxes imposed on rayahs through the aid of the relative who has entered a more privileged class.

[6] The word usually means "one learned in the law," but in the Ottoman Empire it referred technically to the highest of the three classes of students of the *medreseh,* or college of religion.

home and should cause them to settle down in accordance with the ancient law, in order that the country may not be ruined.

His excellency the grand vizier should not deem it permissible to turn aside from justice and moderation, nor from the execution of established usages, nor should he close his eyes to the [wisdom of] treating kindly those under his power, lest the subjects turn their faces from obeying their masters, and their affairs in the end be spoiled and ruined. For it has been said: "Without men of consequence there is no ruler, and without property there are no men of consequence, and without prosperity there is no wealth, and without justice and good administration there is no prosperity." That is to say: "The basis of the ruler's system is the man of consequence, and the raising of troops requires the paying of ready money by the Treasury, and the prosperity of the country comes through its healthy condition, and the flourishing of the country comes through the granting of justice and the punishment of oppressors."

EXPLANATION REGARDING THE ZI'AMET AND TIMAR

The condition of the *zi'amet* and *timar*[1] is also one of the matters to which careful thought should be given in the interests of good order in government. Very great care is necessary in their[2] appointment. It has been written: "Vacancies which occur should be given to deserving persons, and the grand viziers should not give great numbers of *zi'amet* to their own dependents, who should be satisfied with *timar*." When they are given out, they must not be conferred upon men known for their avarice and meanness. For very often it has been observed during campaigns that there are persons who, let us suppose, possess a *zi'amet* or *timar* that has a revenue amounting to at least three, four, or even five or six purses of aspers, or five or seven or eight hundred piastres.[3] Such men, though required to bring men-at-arms[4] in proportion to their income when a campaign becomes necessary, actually go entirely alone. They do not disburse and spend the income of the *zi'amet* or *timar* for the weal of the

---

[1] These are estates held by Muslim freemen who were obligated to perform military services in return for the grant of land by the state. The relationship was therefore semi-feudal in nature. The *timar* had a yearly income of less than 20,000 aspers, and the *zi'amet* of 20,000 to 100,000.

[2] I.e., the holders of these feudal grants.

[3] The author is disturbed because certain holders of *zi'amet* and *timar* have come into possession of lands yielding incomes vastly higher than the upper limits prescribed by law.

[4] *Jebeli*. In general, the rate was one *jebeli* for each 5,000 aspers of annual revenue above the *qilij*, or basic minimum, which differed from province to province.

campaign. They themselves put on an appearance of wretchedness and are good for nothing. The majority [of them] are "under protection."[5] They flee from the place of struggle and combat, from war and from blows. Men who possess *zi'amet* of four or five purses of aspers and should take the field with one man never fulfill their obligation. It seems most fitting that such men as these should be taught a lesson and perhaps punished or even not assembled during the campaign, and that useful and experienced *jebelis* to as great a number as they can bear be taken from them.

These *zi'amet* and *timar* are for Muslim veterans and useful men. The law regarding their appointment is explicit. The ancient law must be respected. But the *alay beys*,[6] saying, "Certain *qilij timar* are worthless," unite them together and give them to persons of unknown name, making a practice of embezzling their income.[7] If one who seeks [such a *timar*] appears, they say "It has been awarded," and refuse him. They also take money beyond all bounds under the name of "petition money" for the vacant *timar*, and give them to useless men. Stringent orders are needed that such vacant *timar* be given to brave men who can manage horses and to bold young warriors. Care and menaces [of punishment] are needed [to prevent] several fiefs from being united together. For as a result of the fact that they have been given to listless men who lack energy, on most campaigns feudal troops of use in labor or difficulty or service are very rare.

Most of them have gathered together two or three thousand aspers' worth of *timar*.[8] Perhaps they have made out *berats*[9] for their own unfreed slaves or for persons whose names no one knows. Among the *alay beys* and even among the timariots there are persons who are freed slaves.[10] With the help of the *alay beys* [the *timar*] have been made their subsistence. Their name is "basket *timar*." They call "basket *timar*" one whose holder is designated on campaigns, at fortresses, and in trenches as weaver of wicker hurdles and bringer of basketwork. As for these, they are not found performing this service. Their *berats* also are kept in the

[5] *Himaye.* Entering the service of more powerful men, either great landholders or government officials, they serve such individuals rather than the sultan, and in return receive protection from all enemies, including government officials attempting to enforce the laws. This arrangement is reminiscent of commendation in the later Roman Empire.

[6] These stood between the *sanjaq bey* and *za'im* in rank and income. Their fiefs, called *khass*, paid from 100,000 to 1,000,000 aspers yearly.

[7] I.e., a fictitious name is inscribed on the official rolls, and the *alay bey* himself collects the income.

[8] This sum is so small that one suspects the author of copying from an older work written when the asper had a much greater value than in his own time.

[9] A patent or warrant for the fief, giving in detail the extent and income of the property.

[10] The higher the rank of an official in the Ottoman system the greater the probability that he was a slave (*qul*) of the sultan—hence the form in which the author gives this statement.

basket.[11] There has come to be need of the greatest care in catching this sort of person. For at one time some of the recorded incomes were too great, and the holders of *zi'amet* and *timar*, saying "The recorded income of our *zi'amet* or *timar* is very large, and our [actual] revenue small," made it seem that they had separated off their worthless [holdings] and had subtracted these from their *berats*, and had diminished their recorded revenues. Later on, when an applicant for the part[12] which had been subtracted made his appearance and received appointment, they would themselves again actually occupy the subtracted parts. Their campaigns and services are naught. Moreover, they regretted that they had renounced [these estates] and diminished [their holdings], saying "[They belong] to our *qilij*, to the total of our *zi'amet* or *timar*; their union is long-standing," and they claimed them and have taken them [back]. In such matters as this has their artfulness been witnessed. Such persons are extremely numerous. If careful investigation be made, benefit both from [the discovery of unrecorded] soldiers and from substitute money is certain.[13] Yet there is need of the very greatest exertions.

The concealment and complete lack of care of the *alay beys* in the matter of commutation payments for *jebelis* and of interim revenues [14] is clear. The recent issuance of orders commissioning the *alay beys* themselves to collect the substitute money for *jebelis* has been an unmixed benefit.[15] With the aid of Him who is Exalted very great benefit to the Treasury is to be expected.

There is need for reform in the condition of *zi'amet* and *timar* which have been spoiled by the lack of care on the part of officials who formerly made appointments. The historians of [our] ancestors have written that the sultans of times past conquered castles and countries in great number by means of the holders of *zi'amet* and *timar* who, while they were in perfect order, gained well-deserved honor wheresoever they were face to face

[11] *Sepet* is the Turkish word for basket. The information given by the author regarding the origin of the term *sepet timari* is plausible, but confirmation has not been found in other writers. In general, the term *sepet timari* referred to any fief which was illegally under the direct or indirect control of a wealthy courtier or official and was therefore not serving its appointed purpose of providing the army with warriors.

[12] *Hissa*. Meaning originally "share," this word has in the present instance a technical significance: "a revenue-producing property which, though of the same character as any other feudal estate, is not in itself an independent holding, but may be added to an already existing fief."

[13] *Bedel*. This was a fine paid by those who failed to appear for active service when called to the colors. The word is used for any sort of substitution, but especially for a payment in commutation of military service.

[14] I.e., revenues from vacant holdings. These were naturally the property of the government while there was no regularly appointed holder of the fief to perform the required military services.

[15] This statement is not clear, since the author has just been condemning these same officers for their negligence. It is possible that he is suggesting the payment of the substitute money to the *alay beys*, who will be entitled to keep it and will consequently have a personal interest in seeing that payment is made. Other sources have not thrown light on this obscure passage.

with enemies of the Faith. But the great men and notables and persons possessing other positions have placed these *zi'amet* and *timar* for the most part under unfreed slaves or have made out *berats* to non-existent names. Hence among the people it is known and universally recognized that there are men who hold five or six *timar*. Of such persons the majority exist in name but not in body. Those who are actually men are dressed in *'abba* [16] and *kebbe* [17] instead of cuirass and mail, and who are given one or two thousand aspers as pocket money when imperial campaigns take place, are mounted on nags with pack saddles and are sent to war. Since the *zi'amet* and *timar* are in this way plundered and ruined, openings are presented for the spread both of the enemies of the Faith and of the brigands who appear in Anatolia and of the *hajduk* [18] unbelievers in Rumelia.

It is among the most necessary of necessities that endeavors be made to reform these, but with inspection alone the *timar* which are "in baskets" will not come into the open. In the year 1011 (A.H. = A.D. 1602–03) in the time of Yemishji Hasan Pasha, and later on, in the period of Nasuh Pasha, imperial orders were issued for getting the *timar* out of the "baskets" and for conferring them on deserving persons. Hasan Pasha was appointed [for this task] by the imperial court. The reform did not come to pass. Nasuh Pasha also caused the holders of *zi'amet* and *timar* situated in Rumelia to come to divinely protected Edirne.[19] The servants and slaves were present in person at the place of review and were inspected. Not a single *timar* appeared [out of the "basket"].

But if orders be given to the governor of every *eyalet* and the *beylerbey* of every *sanjaq*, and if the *beylerbeys* inspect with suitable investigation and inquiry on the basis that there must be no wrong or aggression against anyone in their jurisdictions, it will be self-evident and publicly known who are the old and brave members of the *ojaq* [20] who are settled in every *eyalet* and *sanjaq*. The *timar* and *zi'amet* which are under strangers [21] bearing the names of other persons, and under servants and slaves, and those which are held by aghas [22] will become known and clearer than day. When orders are issued for distributing the *timar* of such persons and conferring them upon those who deserve them, the son will not take the part of his father, nor the brother of his brother. Coming at a gallop, several men will seize upon some *timar* of this sort, saying, "This *timar* or *zi'amet*

16 A cloak or coat of coarse woolen cloth.

17 A large and heavy felted horse cloth.

18 The name given to Christian brigands who infested the mountainous parts of the Balkan Peninsula. The word originally meant "cattle-lifter" but acquired a more respectable standing as these brigands came to be regarded as the first heroes of the Balkan independence movements.

19 Adrianople.

20 This may refer both to members of the feudal class and to veterans from the janissary or other slave corps.

21 I.e., strangers to the class of timariots, *rather* than strangers to the district.

22 The context makes it clear that this refers to the *alay beys*. The title *agha* was given to any country squire.

is under a stranger," and they will claim it and apply for it. It will be impossible to conceal a single *timar*, and it will be understood that the *beylerbeys* cannot give a *timar* to an unfit person. Far-sighted men of wisdom among our ancestors saw this sort of wise opinion and judicious proposal and wrote what they had agreed upon. In short, it is in every way meet for both Faith and state that the greatest endeavor and perseverance be used in rectifying the conditions among these *zi'amet* and *timar*.

May the Lord Creator (glorious and majestic is He!) make possible the reform and may He in the manner most easy grant to the Exalted Government good order and regularity in every affair. Since we [23] are overwhelmed with the benefactions of this exalted state, we should practice the loyalty and uprightness with which we are charged, in order that in the Day of Judgment we may not be morally accountable and blameworthy. And we should in no way whatever avoid making communication and explanation to the full extent of our ability.[24] Every dawn the commencement of our scroll of praises should be prayers that we may be attentive to the command of the pearl-like sacred being,[25] that personage of royal attributes who is ornament of the throne, who until the rising up of the Resurrection is the embellishment of the honored seat which is the dwelling of the ruler of the Ottoman dynasty. May the Supreme Master accept him and may he purify and cleanse with the broom of good policy the garden of the blessedly prosperous one from the thorns and weeds of traitors' attacks. Amen.

[23] The writer and government officials in general.

[24] I.e., on each official rests the responsibility for reporting to his superior all abuses which he discovers, and for suggesting measures of reform.

[25] The Ottoman sultan.

7

ON SERBIAN KINGS

PAISI

[Disaffection with Ottoman rule, combined with Orthodox Russia's promise to "liberate" the Christian masses, inspired intellectuals and theologians in Southeast Europe to draft plans for a better future. In general, these plans involved restoring the "golden age" that existed before Turkish rule. In this respect, one of the most celebrated historical works of the eighteenth century was the *Slavonic-Bulgarian History*, written by the Bulgarian monk Father Paisi Hilendarsky. Paisi's fame rests less on the accuracy and quality of his writings—which may best be described as modest—than on their nationalistic fervor, which has caused him to be known as the father of Bulgaria's cultural awakening. The following excerpt, which treats the early history of the Serbian monarchy, is representative of the work as a whole.]

Here we beg the reader's attention, that we may speak briefly about Serbian kings.

Simeon Nemanya became known and honored in Serbia. From him originated the line of Serbian Kings, and the good fortune of the country. The Serbian Kings were of Latin, not Serbian, stock; they drew out their tribe from Likinia, while taking women from other kings and emperors. Consequently, they had no people of Serbian stock, male or female. Neman Zupan, the chief, became a monk, went to Mount Athos, built the Khilandar Monastery, and moved there. A healing chrism emanated from his remains. His son Stephen became the first Serbian King. Before his death, he also became a monk. To this day, his relics remain whole in Studenica [a monastery].

Stephen had three sons. The first, Radoslav, became King and banished his brother Vladislav. He stood his stead, then departed this life.

Translated by Diane Norman from Paisi, *Istoriia Slavnobolgarskaia* (Sofia: Bulgarska Akademia, 1914), pp. 45–50.

Vladislav became King. Before his death he, too, became a monk and was buried in the Milosevo Monastery. Their brother Uros then became King. After some time, his son Dragutin rose, banished his father from the kingdom, and became King. But after a time his conscience began to bother him, and he left the kingdom to his brother Milutin, ending his life in repentance. . . . For forty years, this most glorious and good King [Milutin] reigned. He extended the Serbian lands, taking territory from the Greeks and founding many monasteries and churches. There has never been a Serbian King like him in glory or honor, or in his gratitude to God for his possessions.

Milutin's son Stephen succeeded him. During his father's reign, he had wanted to become King and organized an army to do battle. But his father cleverly summoned him, seized and blinded him, and imprisoned him in Constantinople. After a time, his sight was returned by Saint Nicolas. He became King of the Serbs and lived in a holy manner, piously and justly. But his son Stephen rose up against him and strangled him with a rope. Thus in martyrdom did he end his life. His remains are whole and uncorrupted to this day in Decani and perform many miracles.

Stephen, the son of a King, murdered his father, a saintly man. Stephen left for Greece and seized from the Bulgarian King lands extending as far as Solun and Ohrid. In Solun, he concluded a peace treaty with the Greeks, returning to them several towns. He returned to Ohrid, taking the royal family, the Fathers Vukasin and Marko Kralevik. Vukasin and Marko Kralevik were wise, brave, and handsome men, and Stephen was amazed at their cleverness and courage. He brought them to Serbia with him and made Vukasin his right-hand man and Prince Lazar the second in rank. They were the highest ranking nobles in Stephen's court.

Stephen became Emperor by his own will in Skopje; no one, neither emperor nor king, gave him the imperial title. Thus he provided a patriarch for the Serbs without the permission of the other four patriarchs. Stephen was King and Archbishop of the Serbs, but, in his own mind and in his wisdom, he adopted the imperial and patriarchal titles. For this folly, the other kings and emperors ridiculed him, nicknaming him "Stephen the Mighty." He who first murdered his father and then proclaimed himself Emperor, thus improperly supplied a patriarch for the Serbs. The four patriarchs jointly condemned him and banished him from the law [of the Church]. Thus did Stephen bring down upon himself the curse of the patriarchs and the wrath of God for the murder of his father and his indiscretions. With him the [Nemanyich dynasty] ended. Thus he who had proclaimed himself "Emperor" lost the Serbian kingdom and died in damnation and exile.

But some Serbs, who resemble him in their indiscretions, hide his deeds. They still call him "Stephen the Mighty" and regard him as a saint, although he killed his father, died in damnation and ostracism, and ended the family and line of Simeon Nemanya. Those people have never looked closely at him, nor do they do so now, but praise him above the other holy kings. They elevate Stephen and the Serbian glory for which he was responsible over that of his grandfather Milutin. His supporters adapted the works of a certain Latin philosopher—who had written of kinships and national titles throughout Europe, the census, place names, and boundaries—to Serbian conditions. Those Serbs adapted the story they had found to "Stephen the Mighty"; they wrote a chronicle about him that indicated that those places and peoples had been subject to and under the control of Stephen. In this dubious way did they write about Stephen; they listened to old women without checking the register of Serbian Kings, where his name, his deeds, and the lands he held were recorded. Instead, they recounted how great was his power and how evil befell him.

They wrote in a similar manner about Tsar Constantine, in the Shishman chronicle, where they reproach him and his son Tsar Michael. They call Michael the "cruel" Shishman. Constantine and his son Michael had wives from the Serbian royal family whom they banished, which is the basis for the animosity between the Serbs and the Bulgars. Tsar Michael was killed by a Byzantine ruler in a battle the Serbs glorify, while ridiculing the House of Shishman and the Bulgarians. In all those years, the Serbs conquered and killed in battle only one King, but they pride themselves on it and write accounts. The Bulgars ruled for many years, killed many tsars, and made many tsars submit to tribute. But the Serbians had no words of praise for the Bulgars. Even now, they blaspheme the Shishman and Bulgarian domain while praising "Stephen the Mighty" and concealing his patricide. Therefore, a brief account of the Serbian and Shishman Kings is provided here. Nowhere in Bulgarian history is Constantine remembered, but because his name was "Shishman," he was written about by the Serbs.

Before his death, Stephen installed Vukasin in his house and kingdom. Vukasin did not want Stephen's imperial title. He described himself as Tsar of the Greeks and Bulgars, as a result of which there was discord. Vukasin wanted his own kingdom and a Bulgarian Empire, for he was of the lineage of Bulgarian Emperors and was a relative of Elena, the Empress of the Stephens. Elena was the daughter of Smilets, the Bulgarian Emperor. Vukasin murdered the son of the Stephen family, Uros, and became the Serbian and Ohrid King. He returned to Ohrid and Prilep, commanded the Serbs, and controlled much territory. Prince Lazar remained in the lands of the Danube in Shumadija and in Moravia, and opposed Vukasin. Consequently, the Serbian lands were divided in two for several years. When the army of Sultan Murad attacked Prince Lazar, Vukasin did not go to his aid. Murad killed Lazar on the Kosovo field and straightway seized his lands. With this, King Vukasin rose against the Turks, and his army drove them from Serbia to Adrianople; but the Turks again fortified themselves against Vukasin and forced him back. He was killed by his servant at the Maritsa River near Pazarcik. Marko transgressed against his father Vukasin and fled with the Turkish Tsar to Adrianople.

At Vukasin's death, Tsar Bajazid placed young Pasha Marko in Prilep and Ohrid. Bajazid, who was the son of Maria, a daughter of Bulgarian Tsar Alexander, in turn a son of the Shishman Constantine, loved Marko

Kralevik like a brother, though it was said that Vukasin and Marko were from the line of the Constantine. Many years later, there was another Maria, a descendant of the Serbian woman who had married the Turkish Tsar: she was named Kalamaria, daughter of the despot Bur. Later, the son of Prince Lazar, one of her descendants, paid tribute to the Turks and Magyars and possessed some land in Srem and Smederevo. They called themselves despots, and for nearly one hundred years these Serbian despots pursued the Turks, overrunning and seizing them. Marko, son of Vukasin, stayed in Prilep a long time, built many churches, and collected much tribute from the Albanians. Though the Ohrid lands were under the Turks, Marko controlled them and there were no Turks there. Later, the Turkish Emperor called Marko to join the struggle against Wallachia, and Marko went there. As soon as he saw Christian crosses and icons before the Wallachia army, he wept and refused to fight against Christians. So Marko was killed in Wallachia, and the Turks placed a Turkish pasha in his place, thenceforth and to this day.

Such was the end of the Vukasins and Markos for the Serbs. From Simeon Nemanya, the first Serbian King or chief, to Uros, the son of Stephen, the seventh generation with which ended the Nemanyich line, were 250 years. The Serbs had no cities, nor is it known who stayed where, who built monasteries and beautiful churches, who had compassion or honor, or who was glorified on earth and before God. Their kingdom was exceedingly small; under Stephen, some land was taken from the Greeks and Bulgars, but for only a short time did his kingdom exist and did he subjugate the Ohrid King and the local Bulgarians and call himself King of Bulgaria. Nevertheless, in a short time, these Kings destroyed and ended its royal house. Later they regained their Bulgarian lands, the Stephen government of the Bulgarians was resumed, and the Turks similarly seized it, from the Bulgarians, from Vukasin. He was the last Bulgarian and Serbian King in Ohrid.

This brief account was written for the reader because the Serbs reproach the Bulgarians and in their ignorance maintain that they are superior, that they, rather than the Bulgarians, were first blessed with a kingdom, an army, and a country. It was not so. Bulgarians know all the world's languages, and every history attests to and agrees with what is written about Serbia. There are no words in Latin or Greek history that testify to the contrary. Beginning with Simeon Nemanya, there are royal documents and royal legends on the holy Kings. But there is no agreement as to which of these documents pertain to which King. Each one has been written differently, and they are not in agreement. Some wrote as they wished and others based their accounts on what they heard from the common people. It is therefore impossible to learn the truth, for the facts are not in agreement. To this day, no one has uncovered anything new; the Serbs embroider history with empty phrases but do not have evidence to go on, as the Bulgarians do, from the Greek and Latin histories.

8

IS THE CAUSE OF THE BOHEMIAN ESTATES JUST OR NOT?

[The legitimacy of Habsburg rule in the Kingdom of Bohemia had been challenged by dissident members of the Bohemian nobility ever since the succession of Ferdinand I, in 1526. The protracted struggle between the Bohemian aristocracy, jealous of its usurped rights, and the Habsburg emperors, seeking absolute rule, erupted in open warfare in the early seventeenth century. The case for "civil disobedience" by the Bohemian nobility is clearly stated in this document of 1619. Little more than a year later, however, the Habsburgs triumphed over the Bohemian insurgents in the Battle of the White Mountain.]

THE QUESTIONS

Is the cause of the Bohemian estates just or not? Do the estates have the power to depose a King and elect another in his place? Upon what grounds have they refused to accept Ferdinand [II] as their King? Are their reasons good? Under what conditions have the Bohemians consented to the election of the King?

Translated by P. Sonnichsen from Rudolf Stanka, *Die böhemischen Conföderationsakte von 1619* (Berlin: Ebering, 1932), pp. 173–76.

THE ANSWERS

The justice of our cause is shown by the fact that this land [Bohemia] is an elected kingdom where free elections have been held for a span of six heads of state; that these elections were all constitutional; and that all the Kings, whether of the House of Luxembourg, of Poland, of the Lithuanians and other parts, and even of those selected from among their own barons, were all revered. And later on, Kings were even selected from Hungary and from the House of Austria.

Through free elections the Bohemians deposed an impertinent and prodigal King by the name of Vencilianos, elected another, refused to accept a King whose name was George, and put yet another in his place; finally, in the year 1608, they freely elected Rudolf, who was King of Bohemia for three years before he became Emperor.

If one wishes to argue that the House of Austria reached harmonious understanding and agreement with the estates to stabilize the succession of that King [Rudolf], we answer that those agreements were made under duress.

It may also be maintained that the estates are subject to the Empire and should not do anything contrary to the wishes of the Emperor. To this, the estates respond that in the Golden Bull there is no provision for de facto subjection to the Empire if the king has not been freely elected.

It is true that the King of Bohemia, as one of several electors, should invest the Emperor and the empire; but Emperor Matthias, upon being elected King of Bohemia, invested Emperor Rudolf. Ferdinand was not elected by the Bohemians and did not receive the investiture from Emperor Matthias; from which one can deduce that the House of Austria did not hold that investiture in much esteem.

One should also consider that we are not servants subject to imperial dictates. The reasons why the estates have refused to accept Ferdinand as their King, or, better said, the reasons why they reject him as King, are as follows:

He has acted contrary to his promises, contrary to the conditions under which he secured the election, which were that he should not enter into negotiations with the Bohemians so long as Emperor Matthias lived;

He has permitted investigations by the Jesuits, thereby disrupting the peace and tranquility of the kingdom;

He has brought foreigners into the government and has abused the privileges of the estates;

He has forced the people to go to mass.

He has humiliated the churches.

Against all right, he has subjected the churches, which properly belong to the governors of the kingdom, to the jurisdiction of the Archbishop of Prague. And, finally, he has subjected the privileges of the estates to a bishop.

For these and other reasons, the estates are compelled to renounce King Ferdinand and to urge their followers—in the name of the common good and fundamental law—to seek a sovereign acceptable to all.

9

THE RULING CLASS OF HUNGARY

HENRY MARCZALI

[The consolidation of the Habsburg imperial inheritance was frustrated in the sixteenth and seventeenth centuries, primarily by the Turks. It was finally achieved at the end of the seventeenth century, but even then in a manner unsatisfactory to the monarchy. By that time, the principal opposition to the centralization of imperial power came from the Magyar aristocracy. The reasons for the strength of the ruling class of Hungary (in contrast to that of the Bohemian aristocracy, for instance) are carefully delineated by Professor Henry Marczali in the following analysis of the rights, privileges, and bases for power of the Hungarian aristocracy in the eighteenth century.]

As the state of the country became more settled, it grew daily more evident that her constitution and internal organization were not menaced by any serious danger—and still less her nationality. The conditions and men of the age of Leopold* had given place to others. In consequence of the combined efforts of the prelates and nobility, the national form of government held its own against the foreign absolutist and Germanizing system, not only in the country itself but also in the territories newly recovered. It is true that such strong bulwarks of the liberty of the estates as the election of kings and the right of armed resistance had ceased to exist (1687). The system of permanent taxation, the standing army, the Pragmatic Sanction, the *locumtenentiale* council, and the vacancy of the office of Count Palantine all seemed to aim at making the power of the king unlimited. Yet all these measures had no tangible results. Not only did the Hungarian organism not yield an inch before the imperial system; it actually gained ground upon it. We must indeed, acknowledge that this fact was due in

---

* Leopold I, Holy Roman Emperor, 1658–1705.—ED.

Reprinted from Henry Marczali, *Hungary in the Eighteenth Century* (Cambridge, England: The University Press, 1910), pp. 3–12.

part to the religious loyalty with which King Charles III (as Emperor Charles VI) observed the terms of his coronation oath. There can be no doubt, too, that the course of events was influenced by his foreign policy, the exigencies of which rendered peace at home desirable. But this had been, more or less, the state of things in the seventeenth century too. That the country was now more settled was due in particular to the new element, the Hungarian "dynastic party." After the Peace of Szatmar, the Palffy, Eszterházy, Erdödy, Károlyi and Batthyány families began to assume increasing prominence. Most of the high temporal and spiritual offices were in their hands, and their estates were continually being increased. In the counties they took the lead either as hereditary high sheriffs or as bishops. At the Court they overshadowed everybody else by their pomp and wealth. They felt the breath of the spirit of foreign countries; they were influenced by the favor of the Court; but they remained Hungarians, as is proved by their correspondence, by their testaments, and by their whole lives.

The Hungarian nobility had reached a very important turning point in their evolution. The seventeenth century in Hungary was still pre-eminently an age of chivalry, in both a bad and a good sense. Its symptoms were: frequent changes of parties, the grossest sensuality, and a contempt for the law, since the magnates were above all privileged knights. In their fortified castles, surrounded by their henchmen, they ruled practically as independent princes. They were engaged in the affairs of their estates, or at most of their counties. However paradoxical the statement may seem, the country was never so badly off for great statesmen of distinguished birth: Only the eminent personality of Nicholas Zrinyi was capable of rising higher and acting from a national point of view. The transitional stage is then represented by the Eszterházys, whose resolute political and religious activity shows unmistakable signs of the influence of the great Peter Pazmany.

After the Peace of Szatmar, there was only one law and one army in the country. Neither was foreign to such an extent as to compel practically all classes of the country to entertain the idea of resistance, or sufficiently tainted with the spirit of the Hungarian oligarchy to allow of rebels' thinking they might resist with impunity. The magnates left their dark "eagles' nests," below which, in the valleys, rose stately manor houses, the homes of luxury and enjoyment, in the center of extensive gardens laid out in French or Dutch style. As early as 1683, the castle of the Count Palatine Eszterházy at Kismarton, which represents the transitional stage between the fortified residence and the manor house, was erected. Immediately after the Peace of Szatmar, in 1714, the superb manor of Cseklesz was begun; that of Edeleny was built between 1720 and 1727, those of the Palffys at Nagy-Gurab and Kiralyfalva in 1725, and that of the Károlyis at Erdod in 1730. Consequently the aristocracy renounced all attempts at resistance not only by law but in actual fact. The defense of the country was entrusted by them to the king and his army, and the most the aristocrats did was to endeavor to secure the predominance in the latter. The

great merits of John Palffy are familiar to everybody.* The greatness of
the Festetics family was established by an ancestor of theirs who was a
general at that time. The activity of the aristocracy, however, displayed itself more particularly in the field of politics. The great lords of those days
stand midway between the feudal lords of the Middle Ages—whose birth
was in itself a sufficient guarantee of their participating in the rule of the
country—and the modern aristocracy, whose power of acting a part in the
government is due more especially to their wealth and social privileges.
Their birth, indeed, was sufficient to entitle them to aspire to power, but
it was their education which fitted them for government. They may justly
be compared to the contemporary English aristocracy, which after a long
series of civil disturbances took some time to become reconciled to a
foreign ruler. The chief difference between the state of things in the two
countries is that, whereas in England the accession of the foreign dynasty
meant the triumph of Protestantism, in Hungary it involved the victory
of Catholicism; consequently, whereas in England it was the temporal
peers who secured the predominance, in Hungary the spiritual peers won
the ascendancy. The latter joined hands with the Court, but by so doing
succeeded in reconciling the dynasty to the interests of the Hungarian nation and its constitution.

Most conspicuous was the power of the magnates, those few many-
acred families; but the sphere of activity of the gentry had its significance.
The latter, too, laid down their arms or took service in the Emperor's
army. Besides looking after their estates, they also engaged in the administration of the counties, which, as the bulwark of the defense protecting
the interests of nobility and nationality, maintained their importance even
when those causes which rendered them institutions of such significance
during the Turkish wars had ceased to exist. This importance has been
recognized by historical and political tradition. In my opinion, however,
the county had other significant spheres of authority in the eighteenth
century. It prevented the individual members of the gentry from appearing as mere atoms in their connection with the Court or even the
wealthy and powerful magnates. In Poland, the nobility became gradually
divided into *slahcic*-es (peasant-nobles)—dependent upon the favor of
miniature kings—and into *pans* (barons), but although the fundamental
elements of such a development were also to hand, in Hungary this evolution was prevented by the county system. In Transylvania, where the
county institution was not so fully developed, the conditions were actually far more similar to those in vogue in Poland. As the institution representing the whole gentry, the county stood in the way not only of
foreign Turkish and German influences, but of the preponderance of the
magnates and peasant-nobles of Hungary. It thus supported the moderate
elements in their struggle to maintain the balance between extremes. At
its head stood a magnate or prelate acting as high sheriff, it also con-

* John Palffy, as Commander in Chief of the Austrian Forces, signed the Treaty of
Szatmar (April 30, 1711) for the Habsburgs. He was subsequently Palatine of the
Kingdom of Hungary, 1741–51.—ED.

tained numerous violent peasant-proprietors, but the chief influence was in the hands of the gentry, possessing estates of medium size and representing national and county interests alike, from whose ranks the county court assessors and sheriffs were recruited.

To the county life is due the fact that from this period the chief occupation of the gentry became legal science. It was in the law, stated in Verböczi's *"Tripartitum opus iuris consuetudinarii Inclyti regni Hungariae"* (1514),* and in the later Acts supplementing it, that they found the surest basis for their political position and for the security of their property. The exercise of judicial functions in most cases gave the gentry an opportunity of rising to high offices in the State. In general, the distinction between magnates and gentry was still very unsettled, new families were constantly rising into prominence beside the older ones, either by royal favor or as a reward for their particular merits.

In our days a great writer has compared the French nobility before the Revolution to an army degenerated by a long period of peace. Their fall was inevitable, for they were no longer capable of doing their duty and yet imposed burdens on others. Such a comparison shows the capability of the Hungarian nobility to govern and the necessity for their government, for if ever there was a nobility that deserved the name of army, such was indeed the Hungarian nobility. Ever since it was established, it had not ceased to extend and defend its country at the price of its own blood. Although in Hungary itself a long period of peace had now begun, the Hungarian nobility still continued to serve their monarch in every battlefield of Europe. Ten years after the Peace of Szatmar they actually complained that no member of the gentry was admitted to the army, and that the number of Hungarian regiments was being reduced. Civil administration, the estates, the church, and education—in a word, every weapon of power and influence was in their hands; they had their reward, for the country was theirs, but they did their duty well. The *perpetuus miles* was unable to replace the *posse comitatus*, and the *contributio* was supplemented by voluntary donations.† In France, the administration of the country was in the hands of an army of civil officers, in Hungary of the landed gentry. In France, literature was in the hands of laymen and *roturiers*; in Hungary it was controlled by the Church, which was itself a part of the nobility. In France, the king controlled everything; in Hungary, Parliament also had a voice in the decision of affairs of State. In a word, in France the privileged classes were a Gothic ornament that had become superfluous; in Hungary they were the column supporting the whole edifice. In France these classes were rendered unnecessary by the parallel development of

---

* The *Tripartitum* was the legal code adopted after the celebrated peasant revolt of 1514, led by George Dosza; it legalized the servitude of the peasant.—ED.

† The *posse comitatus* ("muster of the nobles") was the obligation of the nobles to go to war when summoned by the king; this obligation was the basis for the nobles' tax exemption. The *perpetuus miles* was the standing army established in 1715 to replace the *posse comitatus*. The *contributio* was the war tax paid by the peasants and burghers for the maintenance of the *perpetuus miles*.—ED.

the royal power and of the bourgeoisie; in Hungary they replaced both and ruled because they rendered service to the country.

At the conclusion of this short sketch, which has touched upon the various events only in so far as they served as the material for building up the future, as a necessary consequence of what has gone before, the question must naturally arise: What was the reason that the Hungarian nobility maintained this social, political, and intellectual superiority in an age when monarchical absolutism got the upper hand all over the continent?

This fundamental idea, which was general throughout Europe, made its influence felt in Hungary just as much as elsewhere. Whether consciously or unconsciously, Leopold I and his sons followed in the steps of their enemy Louis XIV, while Maria Theresa and her sons were just as powerfully influenced by the political organization of their great enemy the King of Prussia. Yet, whereas everywhere else on the Continent princes were enthroned on the ruins of aristocracies and revolutions were arising, in Hungary, despite every attempt to overcome them, the nobility stood unbroken, and did not resign their rights until 1848—and that too in a spirit of self-sacrifice unparalleled in the history of the world.

Ranke himself in one place declares that the medieval constitutions remained intact in Protestant countries as contrasted with Catholic states, where absolutism prevailed. This is true so far as England and France are respectively concerned, but is incorrect with regard to other countries. The kingdoms of Prussia, Denmark, and Sweden, which were pre-eminently Protestant countries, soon fell under the yoke of absolutism. In Hungary the Catholic majority did not prove at all dangerous to the Constitution. Nor has the degree of development anything to do with the matter. In Russia, a country on a far lower level of culture than Hungary, arose a species of unlimited monarchy similar to the others—though it admittedly owed much to the aid of foreigners.

Nor can we accept the somewhat chauvinistic view that the reason why the Hungarian nobility could not be overcome was that they were more energetic in their defense of their liberties than the others, and that the spirit of the nation itself stood in the way of oppression. History itself contradicts this supposition. The German historians of the twelfth century reproach the Hungarians with blind subservience to their sovereigns, just as later historians do with feudal license in the eighteenth and nineteenth centuries. According to Otto of Freising, the great medieval historian, who journeyed through Hungary in 1147, the Hungarians "are so subservient to their master that they consider it a crime, I will not say to anger him by open contradiction, but to affront him even by secret whisperings." Naturally this submissiveness to the king appeared in his eyes as an absurdity, and a proof of the barbarism of Hungary, for at that time the Germans were distinctly feudal in character. But at any rate the statement proves that we must find some other reason for the non-effacement of the Hungarian nobility.

The great historians of France are particularly fond of showing how the power of the kingship was increased by its appearing as the representative of the national unity. The bourgeoisie and the commons simply put the dictatorship into the hands of the king, to be used in the interests of the country. The Prussian kingship also went through a similar evolution. Peter the Great too was a dictator who used violence even toward the people, though he worked in the interest of great national ideals. Even in Hungary there is no lack of examples of the kind. King Matthias Corvinus ruled almost as an absolute monarch, in spite of all constitutional forms; the same may be said of Gabriel Bethlen,* however defiant his Parliaments might be: and the fact is that these rulers were not only powerful men, but men from whom the nation expected the realization of its ideals. Consequently, one of the principal causes contributing to the unlimited character of a monarchy is that, in the interests of its unity and position in foreign affairs, the nation should be ready to renounce its autonomous rights.

In its struggle for predominance, the kingship did not stand alone. Everywhere in Europe it found a sure and decisive support in the bourgeois elements, who, as a result of their wealth, intelligence, and tractability, were able to turn the scale. In France, the kings raised the *noblesse de robe*, the officials and judges, to a level with the *noblesse de' épée*, the feudal nobility. In Prussia, the kings were supported by a bourgeois bureaucracy. In Sweden and Denmark, it was simply the loyalty of the bourgeoisie and peasantry that raised the kings above the heads of the senators.

In Hungary too there was no lack of towns. Burgesses were invited to attend at the parliaments, and the inhabitants of the towns were for the most part well-to-do and thrifty. The number of towns—as estates of the realm—increased. The Parliament of 1715 incorporated a whole series of royal free boroughs, extending the rights of political representation to them also. In the constitutional struggles up to this time they had been for the most part royalist: Even Debreczen redeemed its liberty from Rakoczy † by a sum of money and offered excuses for its action to the royal government. The towns had, above all, to be circumspect. But, until the public feeling of the nation had raised Budapest to the position of a great city, the towns were almost inimical to the national spirit. They kept to themselves and, although composed of merchants and manufacturers, did not lead the way except in material respects. Albeit they were the seats of universities or university colleges, they had as little influence on the spirit of the students as if the monastic system of education had been still in vogue. Any member of the bourgeois class who rose above his fellows by his breeding and capabilities attained to a position of eminence either abroad or in holy orders. There could be no question of unity or of common interests.

The explanation of this phenomenon is to be found in the fact that the

---

* Gabriel Bethlen was Prince of Transylvania in 1613–29. The Golden Age of Transylvania is identified with his enlightened rule.—Ed.

† Ferenc Rakoczy II (1676–1735), Prince of Transylvania, was the leader of the war of insurgency against the Habsburgs in the early eighteenth century.—Ed.

towns were foreign in point of speech—and in spirit too, with the exception of those in the Szepesseg (Szepes Zips District in Upper Hungary). Apart from Debreczen and Szatmar-Nemeti they were nearly all German and Slav. As passive factors in the work of resistance they stood in the midst of the turbulent county and political life of Hungary. If they joined any cause, the fact was sufficient in itself to make that cause suspicious. In Hungary, no unlimited monarchy could develop, because there was no bourgeoisie.

We are struck by another consideration if we examine the development of absolutism all over Europe.

Wherever we see this peculiar form of government, characteristic of the early period of the modern age, starting to develop, we find a dynasty whose fate had for centuries been bound up with that of the nation. In France, the classic home of absolutism, the formation of a nation practially coincides with the rule of the Capet dynasty. The kings of Castile, whose power was developed by Philip II, were descended from Pelayo (750). The Grand Dukes of Russia, the ancestors of Peter, took their origin from Rurik; and the rule of the Hohenzollerns, the youngest dynasty, coincides with the cultural advance of Brandenburg. Could the nation have any political interest—particularly in its relations with other nations—which was not at the same time that of the king?

In England, on the other hand, we see that in 1603 a foreign dynasty [Stuart] ascended the throne; and, ever since that date, England has been governed by foreign rulers. In Poland, the national dynasty of the Jagellons became extinct in the sixteenth century, and, as no other national dynasty could be founded, the Poles were compelled to protect themselves against foreign influence by *pacta conventa*, wrung from their elected kings. It seems therefore that an essential preliminary condition for an unlimited monarchy is that it should be established by an old dynasty capable of securing unity and the triumph of the nation in the face of foreign foes. So absolutism is not purely the work of court cabals and oppression: It has sprung into existence wherever the kingship has been engaged in performing duties of an entirely national character.

The fundamental bases of human states and societies are hidden deep in obscurity: and, as the poet says, "If the word were revealed to our intellects, who would presume to utter it?"

10

THE PRAGMATIC SANCTION

[The consolidation of the forces resisting the absolutist tendencies of the Habsburg emperors was facilitated at the beginning of the eighteenth century by the absence of male heirs in the Habsburg line. To ensure succession for his only heir, Maria Theresa, Emperor Charles VI reaffirmed and confirmed the rights and privileges of the aristocracy. The Pragmatic Sanction, issued in 1713 and approved by the Hungarian Diet in 1723, records the imperial dilemma with reference to Hungary.]

The Estates and Orders of the Kingdom and of those parts annexed to the same render express their gratitude to His Imperial Royal Majesty for his paternal and most clement strengthening of the liberties and prerogatives of the same upon the advent of His Most Sacred Person into the midst of the Estates.

ARTICLE THE FIRST

Understanding humbly the paternal and most clement propensity of the Most Sacred Imperial and Royal Majesty toward the Estates and Orders of the Kingdom gathered together most felicitously in the present Diet and in such large number as has scarcely been seen at any other time, both for the perpetuation of the same and the increase of the public state of the Kingdom of Hungary and of the parts annexed to the same, and for the strengthening of the union with neighboring kingdoms and hereditary provinces against every misfortune, even against external force; and understanding his immediate care and solicitude for the preservation of domestic tranquility from the Royal letters of the same Most Sacred Imperial and Royal Majesty, which have been most mercifully promulgated to the Estates and Orders of the Kingdom and of those parts annexed to the same, and from proposals which have very recently been made (which we hold) with a devoted zeal of homage and fidelity to the same. For

Translated by David Engstrom from Gustav Turba, *Die Pragmatische Sanktion* (Vienna [n.p.], 1906), pp. 188–94.

93

this singular vow of fatherly affection and graces most humbly exhibited toward the same: namely, that notwithstanding whatever most serious cares and labors touching the Holy Roman Empire and European peace, he will betake himself into the midst of his faithful Estates and, like a father, console the same to the highest degree with his personage, which is revered by the same; and first and before all else, with no previous and most humble supplication omitted on the part of the faithful Estates and Orders; out of a genuine paternal affection toward the same entire Estates and Orders of his hereditary Kingdom of Hungary, and of the parts and kingdoms and provinces annexed to the same, in all, both diplomatic and whatever other rights, liberties, privileges, immunities, customs, prerogatives, and laws granted and established up to the present time, and to be established in the present Diet, and even in diets in the future, had deigned to offer to preserve both the same, and most clemently to confirm each one of the same; therefore, they return the humblest and greatest thanks they can to His Most Sacred Imperial and Royal Majesty: He has deigned not only to give his approval to the pious and salutary prayers of his faithful Estates and Orders, but piously and clemently and with gracious mind to accept also the feminine sex of his most August House of Austria to the descendancy of the same and from the same, which is lacking to the Royal Crown of Hungary, and the parts, kingdoms and provinces pertaining to the same sacred Crown, which by a free vote of the unanimous kingdoms of the universal Estates and Orders, and parts annexed to the same, has been proclaimed, and through an appointed deputation, called likewise an oblation, sent to the Highest Imperial and Royal Majesty, but likewise he would wish the succession in the sacred Crown of the Kingdom of Hungary and in those parts annexed to the same to be directed, preserved, and guarded by the same order of primogeniture, as of males, according to the norm in the rest of the kingdoms of His Most Sacred Majesty, and in the hereditary provinces and in the places outside Germany through her as ordained, established, made known to the public and inseparably accepted; and she is held in equality of degree, of the same lineage, by the reason of the prerogative of males. Thus, that she, be her heir male or female, issue forth an heir of the kingdoms and provinces of the August House of Austria, according to the mentioned norm of primogeniture which is accepted in the August House of Austria; by the same hereditary law of succession, for these and whatever future cases, and also for the infallible King of Hungary and of those parts annexed to the same, which are to be equally and individually understood, be held and crowned.

ARTICLE THE SECOND

Concerning the royal, hereditary, continuous succession of the Most Sacred Imperial and Royal Majesty of the feminine sex of the August House of Austria in the sacred crown of the Kingdom of Hungary, and the parts annexed from ancient times to the same.

Although the faithful Estates of the Royal Majesty and the Orders of the Kingdom of Hungary and of the parts annexed to it, seeing the lively and flourishing, greatly constituted age, strength, and health of the same, and having trusted as greatly as possible in the divine benediction that the same is to be blessed most bountifully with great and glorious successors of the masculine sex, for which the prayers also of his faithful states have been poured forth and must unceasingly be poured forth to the thrice most great God, were trusting as much as possible that the faithful Estates of the Kingdom must be consoled through an unceasing order of male heirs; but since they have especially in mind, too, that kings and princes are equally subject to the fate of mortality in common with other men; therefore weighing with forethought and deliberation the many and great acts and deeds, both those of the once divine predecessors of the Most Sacred and Imperial Royal Majesty, Leopold, his father, and his brother, Joseph, most glorious Kings of Hungary, and even especially the very deeds of His own Most Sacred Imperial and Royal Majesty, for the increase of his father's public good and for the perpetual safety of his faithful citizens, most glorious acts and deeds performed equally in war and peace.

While he not only preserved this his hereditary Kingdom of Hungary and the parts annexed to the same placed in a state by his aforementioned glorious predecessors; but even on the occasion of the very recent Ottoman War, guarded the same zealously against the most heated attacks of the same; with victorious and fortunate armies he extended into the kingdoms annexed to the same, and the provinces, with the immortal glory of his name and of the Estates and Orders, and with the perpetual security of the private citizens of the kingdom; with the result that it can be preserved in whatever succeeding times, from all external and even domestic turmoil and dangers, and indeed endure in a nourishing and continuous tranquility, and sincere union of minds against every force, even external; solicitously wishing to take precautions against even revolutions, and the evils of an interrgnum, known very well from former times, and which usually arise easily among the Estates and Orders of the Kingdom; prompted by the praiseworthy examples of their ancestors; and wishing most humbly to show themselves grateful and faithful to the Most Sacred Imperial and Royal Majesty, their lord, their most clement lord; in this lack of the masculine sex from the Most Sacred Imperial and Royal Majesty (which lack may God most mercifully deign to avert), the hereditary right of succession of the Kingdom of Hungary, and the Crown and the parts pertaining to the same, provinces and kingdoms, now retained and to be retained by divine aid; even to the feminine sex of the August House of Austria; indeed, in the first place from the high-fated and now ruling Most Sacred Imperial and Royal Majesty, then in defect of him, from the once divine Joseph, this also lacking, then from the lineage of the once divine Leopold, as a descendant of the Emperors and Kings of Hungary; and to their legitimate Roman Catholic successors: The archdukes of each sex of Austria, according to the order of primogeniture established by the Most Sacred Imperial and reigning Royal Majesty in his own kingdoms and others, and hereditary provinces in and outside Germany; with law and order being set forth, indivisibly and inseparably, one by one and at the same time, and together with the Kingdom of Hungary and the parts, kingdoms, and provinces annexed to the same to be possessed, and to be ruled and governed, do make transfer of and accept the mentioned succession; and likewise they establish, according to the above order, the same feminine succession in the August House of Austria, introduced and recognized in articles two and three of 1687, extended for the succession, now, instead of that time, equally articles two and three of the year 1715; the succession is to be accepted and ratified through the aforementioned feminine sex of the House of Austria, and the heirs and successors of the same declared in the previous manner, and together with the aforementioned state documents, most clemently confirmed by the Most Sacred Imperial and Royal Majesty, and other formerly declared liberties and prerogatives of the Estates and Orders of the Kingdom, and of the parts and of the kingdoms and provinces annexed to the same, determine that the succession is to be observed according to the tenor of the previously cited articles, always in the future, on the occasion of a coronation; and except after every kind of defect of the aforesaid sex, do they reserve the old and ancient, and accepted custom and prerogative of the Estates and Orders to be understood to have a place in the election and crowning of kings.

11

THE EDICT OF TOLERATION OF JOSEPH II

[The "civilizing mission" of the enlightened despots generally involved the consolidation or securing of political absolutism. Emperor Joseph II made use of the ideas of the Enlightenment for that very purpose. In the process, however, he raised the level of culture and of political awareness of the heterogeneous population of his empire. Among the most troublesome problems facing both the emperor and the masses was the equating of political prerogatives with Catholicism by the landed interests opposed to Joseph II's rule. To weaken their power, and to place imperial power above that of any religion, Joseph II issued the Edict of Toleration of October 13, 1781, which granted equality of opportunity and of rights of worship to the Lutheran, Calvinist, and Uniate (Greek Orthodox) subjects of the Habsburg Empire. The Edict of Toleration is representative of the sweeping reforms undertaken by Joseph II in his effort to divide and conquer and, in the process, modernize the Habsburg Empire.]

Beloved subjects: Convinced on the one hand of the perniciousness of all moral constraints and on the other hand of the great benefits that accrue to religion and the state from true Christian tolerance, we have been moved to grant the right of private worship to the Lutheran, Calvinist, and Uniate religious sects everywhere, without regard to whether the same have hitherto been practiced or introduced. The Catholic religion shall retain its pre-eminence in public religious services. The right of private worship shall be permitted to both Protestant religions [Lutheran and Calvinist] as well as to the Uniates in all areas where the bulk of the population is of these religious faiths, where this does not interfere with the Catholic faith, and where non-Catholics are not already in possession of the right of public worship. Especially we grant:

First: to non-Catholic subjects, where 100 families live in a rural area without benefit of a chapel or clergyman and are several hours distant

---

Translated by Max Riedlsperger from Berold Bretholz, *Lese und Quellenbuch zur böhmisch-mährischen Geschichte* (Augsburg: Johannes Stauda, 1927), pp. 320–322.

from the same, the right to build their own chapel adjacent to their school. Those even further removed may journey to the nearest existing chapel, so long as it is within the Crown lands, as often as they wish. They may also visit their clergymen and coreligionaires and owe to them, and to the sick, the necessary instruction and spiritual and physical comforts; however, they may not hinder, under the heaviest penalty, the calling of a Catholic clergyman if requested by one or another of the sick.

With regard to the chapel: chimes, bells, and towers, as well as public entrance from the street, are expressly prohibited, except where such already exist. Otherwise, said subjects are free to build as they choose, of whatever material they desire. All administration of their sacraments and practice of their religious services shall also be permitted, not only in the village but also to the sick in affiliated districts. Public funerals in which their clergy participate shall be completely permissible.

Second: Non-Catholic subjects remain at liberty to employ their own schoolmasters, who are to be maintained by the congregation, over which, however, our provincial school board has jurisdiction in matters of instruction and regulation. Likewise, we grant:

Third: to non-Catholic inhabitants of a village, if they endow and maintain their pastors, the choice of their own pastors. If, however, the village authorities want to assume the financial responsibilities themselves, they may enjoy the right to choose their pastors themselves. However, we reserve to ourselves in advance the right of confirmation, to such a degree that where there are Protestant consistories, confirmations may take place, and where there are none, the same should be conferred either by the already existing Czech or Hungarian Protestant consistories, until circumstances demand that they erect their own consistories in the provinces.

Sixth: From now on, the customary written declaration at marriage by non-Catholics with regard to the upbringing of their offspring in the Roman Catholic religion is to be totally dispensed with; all children of a Catholic father, be they of the male or the female sex, are to be raised in the Catholic religion, since this is regarded as a prerogative of the dominant religion. In the case of a Protestant father and a Catholic mother, the male offspring shall be raised in the Roman Catholic faith.

Seventh: Non-Catholics may in future be permitted to purchase houses and estates, to enjoy full urban and civil rights, to be admitted to the academic ranks and to the civil service, and are to be restrained by no form of oath other than that which is in accordance with their religious beliefs. Neither are they to be required to attend processions or services of the dominant religion, unless they so desire. All assignments and promotions shall be made without regard to religious belief, as is done daily in our military without hesitation and with the greatest fruitfulness. Such selections shall be based on integrity and ability rather than solely on considerations of the Christian and moral behavior of the competitors.

These our highest final decisions you will make known to the district officials, magistrates, and dominions through individual printed circulars published in greater number than usual. Permission shall also be granted to the publisher of each province to supply to everyone who demands them such printed circulars, which shall be disseminated in sufficient number in the other provinces.

12

A SHORT DESCRIPTION OF THE HERMANNSTADT MUNICIPAL EVANGELICAL GYMNASIUM (1778)

[The following description of the sources of revenue, obligations, and concerns of the faculty of a secondary school in the Transylvanian town of Hermannstadt reveals the discrepancy between the purposes of the education policies of the Austrian enlightened despots of the eighteenth century and the possibilities for their effectual implementation in the Habsburg Empire.]

In order to give a true picture of the condition of the schoolteachers at the Hermmanstadt Municipal Evangelical Gymnasium, one must examine the school personnel and the funds from which they are maintained. The funds shall be considered first, and then the salaries, duties, and obligations of each teacher shall be described.

The Gymnasium has the following sources of income for teachers' salaries:

I. From the city treasury:

1. The annual sum allotted for teachers' salaries is 478.20 florins. This is paid quarterly by the Tax Collector to the Rector, in exchange for a receipt. The Rector then distributes the money [to the teachers] in twelve installments.

2. Under the rubric wood money, the Tax Collector pays, in exchange for a receipt from the Rector, 46 florins annually in Otober. Eleven schoolteachers benefit from this.

3. From the granary, the city makes a single contribution annually, in April, of thirty-one bushels of wheat to students living at the Gymnasium, against a receipt from the Director of Students. This is used up during the six winter months, when the Rector gives to each fellow

Translated by Max Riedlsperger from Friedrich Teutsch, *Die siebenbürgischsächsischen Schulordnungen* (Berlin: Hofmann & Co., 1888), I, 338–46.

schoolteacher one loaf of bread, up to a yearly total of six loaves of bread per person. This rest is divided among the students.

II. From the Church treasury: Since 1757, monies received from a fund that originated in 1540 and has gradually increased over the years have been designated by the trustees and the donors for the payment of six school lecturers . . . in the annual amount of 691.36 florins.

III. From funerals: These include:

1. Funerals at which a sermon is delivered: a general or one-hour funeral, 2 florins; processional funerals, 1.52 florins. Four school colleagues divide the income from these, which amounts annually to about 103.20 florins.

2. Funerals at which no sermon is delivered (so-called special funerals): 50 florins.

All students who attend funerals divide the income thus derived into some seventy-odd parts. Two of the students who lecture publicly and are therefore considered school lecturers receive about 45 florins annually therefrom.

IV. From the Prebend (a collection that the Gymnasium arranges annually during Lent throughout the city): The entire income is about 1,360 florins, from which eight schoolteachers receive about 105 florins each. The surplus is divided among the students.

V. From the Calefactory monies (money provided by the schoolchildren): The older children contribute 0.17 florins, the younger ones 0.7 florins, for the whole winter, for a total of about 57 florins. Of this amount, the Rector pays yearly to four school colleagues 26.40 florins. From the surplus, he pays for the heating of the auditorium and five classrooms.

VI. From fines: about 40 florins yearly. One-third of the money derived from fines charged for negligence is deposited; one-half of the rest is paid to the Rector. The balance is used to maintain the school bakery and to make small repairs in the school.

In the two school bakeries, the above-specified twenty-five bushels of wheat are used in baking. The revenues from the bakeries revert to the bakeries. Each Sunday, the bread for the week is divided among the students; since, however, approximately eight loaves of bread are not enough to feed so many students, only those who are present at a sermon given by a student in the auditorium receive a piece of bread, larger or smaller in proportion to the number of students attending. (Since no revenue from the baking of bread accrues to the teachers, and only the poorest students need free bread, the provisions of this article have not been enforced.)

VII. From choral singing: On the three Church high feast days, the students sing in front of doors and throughout the city. The income from each performance is divided fairly among all the members of the school, but the students singing in the choir and the choir leaders receive a larger share. The two soloists receive annually about 27 florins.

VIII. The Senior collects from each schoolchild 0.15 florins quarterly, for a yearly total of 9 florins.

The revenues in money and in kind (i.e., thirty-one bushels of wheat) total 1,611 florins.

The school personnel and student body consist of:
I. Regular students, about 500 in all, including:
1. Students who have been promoted from the grammar school. These are further divided into those who wear the usual student dress, live at the Gymnasium, and enjoy a part of those benefits stipulated above (*studiosi togati*), and those who are not uniformed, live in quarters in the city, and enjoy no benefits (*studiosi non togati, seu chlamydati*). All together, they number more than 100.
2. Schoolchildren who have not yet been promoted from the grammar school. These include:
a. School attendants (about thirty). The majority of these (about twenty-three) live in the house of the Rector. He clothes them, gives them schoolbooks, paper, etc., cares for them when they are sick, and buries them if they die, all from a fund that he derives from a performance these poor children put on yearly during Advent throughout the city. A few exceptions enjoy no benefits.
b. The remaining schoolchildren, who are children of local citizens or of parents of means who live out of town.
Together, they number 400 or more.
II. Lecturers, who lecture publicly fourteen times a year. The duties and salary of each individual are, according to a two-and-one-half-century-old set of regulations, as follows:
1. The Rector is chosen by majority vote of the city magistrate and the citizenry, at the city hall. His duties are the following:
i. Instruction: He lectures three hours daily throughout the week, with the exception of Saturday afternoons, on religious dogma, ethics, philosophical argumentation, natural law(with particular reference to the Transylvanian state), and moral philosophy. Of these subjects, he regularly offers only religious dogma. Natural law and moral philosophy, as well as ethics and philosophical argumentation, are offered in rotation.
On Sundays and holidays, he delivers a sermon to all schoolchildren in the auditorium. After vespers, he presides over catechism classes, taught alternately by the head of the students and the Assistant Rector. On days of repentance, four times a year, he gives a lecture on repentance to adult students, and he preaches on the second day of all high holidays in the parish church. He supervises all the courses taught in the Gymnasium. According to the directions of the city pastors, he leads school inspectors into the teachers' classes and tries to place the teachers in positions for which they are qualified by training. To ensure proper instruction, in accordance with those directions, he also visits all lecture halls at least twice a week and more often if necessary. He arranges public examination of all classes twice a year, once in the spring and once in the fall, and personally supervises the graduates. Together with the Assistant Rector, he examines all those who have completed their studies and are going to German universities and issues an attestation

of their capabilities to His Excellency, the Provincial Governor. He oversees the moral advice given by his school colleagues to students living at the Gymnasium and in the city, and supervises the students' moral training. He also conducts a meeting every Saturday with all school-teachers, where all abuses and mistakes noticed by each one present are declared and precautionary measures are suggested. Every two weeks he conducts a public hearing, during which all offenses committed by resident students are considered and punishments are meted out.

ii. He assigns students who live at the Gymnasium to their rooms, ob-serves their behavior throughout the day, and gives them, insofar as possible, a moral education.

iii. He directs the school economy, supervises the bakery, and keeps accounts of all activities.

iv. He has supervision over the two free tables, at which twelve of the poorest students enjoy a meal once a day, and he assigns foster children to it with the consent of the donor family.

v. He takes care of the school library and keeps the accounts thereof.

vi. He clothes and cares for the school poor and sees that they are provided with books and all necessities.

vii. He has supervision over the choir and over all public processions.

The annual revenues received by the Rector total, from all sources, 438.20 florins. He also receives free living quarters at the Gymnasium.

2. The Assistant Rector lectures three hours daily six days of the week. He instructs one hour each in logic and metaphysics (alternating for six months each); in Greek and Hebrew; and in world and Transyl-vanian history. On Sundays, he alternates with the Rector in the audi-torium and in the catechism classes. He substitutes for the Rector whenever the latter is sick or absent from the school, and also, when required, on visits to other schools. The salary of the Assistant Rector, from all sources, totals 350 florins, plus a free room in the city.

3. The First Lecturer lectures three hours daily: two hours in rhetoric (one in the morning and one in the afternoon) and one hour in geog-raphy. The salary of the First Lecturer, from all sources, totals 125 florins, without a free room.

4. The Second Lecturer lectures a total of three hours daily, two hours on poetry and one hour on theology. His salary, like that of the First Lecturer, is 125 florins, also without a room.

5. The Third Lecturer lectures three hours daily: two hours on speech and mathematics, including applied mathematics, according to the de-cision of the faculty, and one hour on natural history. His salary is also 125 florins, without a room.

6. The Choir Director directs music in the auditorium three times a week, for one hour each, directs all Church music and funeral processions, and also sings in the choir. His salary, from all sources, totals 99 florins, without a room.

7. A Second Assistant lecturers three hours daily, two hours on chron-ology and one hour on beginning Hebrew and Greek. He attends all

funeral processions where a funeral sermon is delivered. For these duties, his salary, from all sources, is 66.5 florins, without a room.

8. A Third Assistant lecture on syntax four hours daily during the week, gives all Sunday catechism instruction, and accompanies all funeral processions. His salary is also 66.5 florins, without a room.

9. A Fourth Assistant lectures three hours daily to the beginners who come out of the village schools as adults and therefore cannot be included among the schoolchildren. This includes two hours on the essentials of the German and Latin languages, and one hour in elementary logic. His salary, from all sources, totals 37.20 florins and six bushels of corn, without a free room.

10. A First Extraordinarius on Grammar lectures four hours daily and on Sunday teaches the catechism. His salary, from all sources, is 29.30 florins, without a room.

11. A Second Extraordinarius lectures four hours daily to the so-called German class, in which children who do not study Latin are instructed in the Christian religion, reading, writing, and the basic knowledge necessary to citizenship. On Sundays, he teaches the catechism. His salary, like that of the First Extraordinarius, is 29.30 florins, without a free room.

12. The Praefectus lectures on basic theology four hours daily, teaches the catechism every Sunday, first in class and then to the poorest students, who are to be given basic information. He has some supervision over the students, calculates the revenues from special funerals and choral performances, and apportions the same. His salary, from all sources, totals 74.40 florins and also a free room at the Gymnasium.

13. The Senior Studiosorum Togatorum lectures on elementary literature for four hours daily to the smallest schoolchildren. He receives, from all sources, a total salary of 46.20 florins, and also shares a room with four other students at the Gymnasium.

The grand total of the above salaries is 1,611 florins and 50 crowns.

14. One student gives a drawing lesson daily; for this he receives 10 florins from the Rector. No other funds are designated for him, since the subject is a new one. The relationship between the work and the remuneration is noteworthy.

The first eleven of the above-cited teachers must have studied at well-endowed German universities, since at the Gymnasium (it can well be said) few scholarships are available. We have only the following scholarships: (a) the Doboss, in the amount of 100 florins, available only to a Transylvanian and a Swabian, for a duration of three years each; (b) the Klockner (12 florins annually); and (c) the Biegler (6 florins). These scholarships are shared by many. (The author of this report has received a total of 12 florins in scholarships in five years at the university.)

Moreover, they serve ten, twelve, and even more years at the school, and then four or more years in the capacity of priest, to which they are promoted from the school service, before they finally receive a parish that will support them. (The author has served almost four years at a salary of 29 florins.) Thus many die before they secure a parish, and as a result leave their bereaved families destitute. The income in the service itself does not permit even the slightest luxury; only a few are able to purchase the necessary books on such a meager income, which hardly suffices for quarters. The majority struggle to get by despite want and worries, but all completely lose the fortitude necessary for lecturing in their subjects.

We therefore invite our critics to look into the justness of our complaints and determine how worthy our faithful services are of redress of grievances. Through these little-known services, people in all walks of life are educated for the service of the state; all those who will be employed in the civil service (and, with few exceptions, those who go to the universities), all those in the military service, all country priests and schoolteachers and, finally, all citizens of the Saxon nation, without exception, come out of the hands of these schoolteachers who serve in the gymnasiums. Only their devotion to their profession maintained the fortitude of the colleagues of the Hermannstadt school in one of the severest tests they have undergone, a few years ago, when for three consecutive years they did not receive the major part of their salary, which comes from the Church treasury, because of lack of funds. This same devotion helps them to maintain their courage, and they will not tire; they will exhaust themselves in the service of the Fatherland of which they have the good fortune to be citizens and in the service of humanity. They only ask the support of every friend of humanity who has the power and opportunity to help them.

13

THE POLISH CRISIS OF THE EIGHTEENTH CENTURY

ROBERT H. LORD

[The vast power enjoyed by the Polish aristocratic ruling class (*szlachta*) was ultimately fatal to the Polish state in the eighteenth century. The following case study of a closed aristocratic society, reprinted from Robert H. Lord's classic analysis *The Second Partition of Poland*, reveals the strengths and weaknesses of a national feudal state in an age of imperial ascendancy in Austria and Russia, and of secularization in both Eastern and Western Europe.]

The Polish question owes its origin to the desperate and well-nigh irremediable decadence which overtook the Polish Republic about the middle of the seventeenth century and, continuing unchecked for a hundred years, brought the country to the verge of ruin. The causes of this decline and of the ensuing catastrophe have been discussed by numerous historians and publicists with intense interest, although generally with too little knowledge and too great national or party bias. A final explanation

Reprinted, by permission, from Robert H. Lord, *The Second Partition of Poland* (Cambridge, Mass.: Harvard University Press, 1915), pp. 6–25.

has not been given, nor can it be given in the present state of investigation.

It seems clear, however, that the decline of Poland is to be traced primarily to political causes, to the defects of a wretched system of government. Whatever other causes of weakness one may discover—for instance, the lack of a strong middle class, the oppression of the peasantry, religious intolerance, racial antipathies, intellectual or moral retrogression—these are all of but secondary importance. These evils, or equally grave ones, could be met with in other European states of the old regime, and yet no other great state atoned for them by the loss of its existence. For everywhere else there was a government strong enough to curb or diminish the destructive tendencies and to produce or assist invigorating ones. Poland alone had no such correcting or ameliorating force. Poland had no effective government whatever. The nation lived in an anarchy thinly concealed under the forms of an elaborate republican constitution. It is in the unfortunate historic evolution of that constitution that the explanation of the decline of Poland is to be sought.

The constitution of the Republic in its later years was so nearly unique in Europe that there was—and still is—a widespread tendency to regard it as something quite *sui generis*, as an entirely original creation of a misguided and fantastic people. In reality it was only an exaggerated and one-sided development of a type of political organization once almost universal on the Continent, of what the Germans call the *monarchisch-staendische Staat* or the *Staendestaat*. Nearly all the supposed peculiarities of the Polish constitution can be traced to principles and tendencies inherent in the *Staendestaat*; almost all of them find analogies in other countries in the same stage of development. Even the Liberum Veto,* which is often held up as the most unique and most monstrous institution of Old Poland, to be explained only from a national lack of political common sense, or else from a survival of primitive Slavic anarchism—even the Liberum Veto was merely a logical extension of the idea pervading medieval parliamentarism that the vote of a majority cannot bind a minority In the Aragonese Cortes, for example, a valid decision required the assent of all four *brazos* (orders) and of every member of every *brazo*. In Catalonia a single nobleman, by uttering the words "*Yo dissent,*" could stop the proceedings of the Cortes, much as the Polish deputies did with their famous "*Nie Pozwalam*" ["I forbid"]. But when all the parallels have been drawn—and they are very numerous—the fact remains that the *Staendestaat* produced in Poland very different results from those that it brought forth in most other countries.

The main difference is briefly this: that in Poland the struggles of the *Staendestaat* period resulted in the victory, not of the Crown over the Estates (as in most other lands), nor of the Estates collectively over the Crown, but of a single class over the Crown and the other classes alike; this triumphant class then failed to organize its power in such a manner as to give the country an effective government; and finally the ruling class— the *szlachta* [gentry]—maintained its monopoly of power far too long. A

* The Liberum Veto is discussed on page 115.—ED.

one-sided constitutional development, the failure to create a new political mechanism adapted to the new distribution of power in the state, and then prolonged anarchy and stagnation—these seem to be the essential causes of the decline of Poland.

The *szlachta*, the military land-owning class, began to play a political role only in the latter part of the fourteenth century, but thereafter its progress was surprisingly rapid, its triumph only too sudden and complete. Three circumstances especially contributed to its victory over the Crown: These were, the extinction of the ancient dynasty of the Piasts (1370), and the uncertainty as to the succession under the next few kings, which led (by 1434 at the latest) to the recognition of the principle that the Crown was elective; the weakness of character shown by most of the Polish monarchs after the time of Casimir the Great; and finally, the extraordinary military and financial needs of the Crown, resulting from the Hundred Years War with the Teutonic Order, the struggles against the efforts of the Polish kings to establish their dynasty on the thrones of Bohemia and Hungary. "The attempt to play the part of a great power of the modern type with only the resources of a medieval feudal state" inevitably brought to the front the class on which the maintenance of the new position and the success of the new policy of expansion primarily depended. The *szlachta* knew how to improve the opportunity to the utmost. The cornerstone of their power was laid by the Privilege of Kaschau (1374), by which King Louis of Anjou, in order to assure his daughter's succession to the throne, granted the *szlachta* exemption from all taxes (with one rather insignificant exception) and from all duties to the state except unpaid military service. After that, one privilege followed fast upon another. In 1454, Casimir IV was obliged to grant the Statutes of Nieszawa, the Magna Carta of the Polish nobility, by which he promised not to make new laws or to order the *pospolite rus-zenie* (the general rising of the nation in arms) without the consent of the *szlachta*. The gentry were thus for the first time legally admitted to a share in legislation, and as they were also free from any military or financial burdens, save those they might voluntarily lay upon themselves, their position in the state was commanding.

These far-reaching concessions required the creation of an organ through which the *szlachta* might regularly exercise their new functions. That need was met by the Diet, which, slowly taking form in the latter half of the fifteenth century, received its definitive organization and legal sanction through the Statute *Nihil Novi* in 1505.

Set over against this vigorous new institution, the Crown steadily lost both prerogatives and prestige, although it retained a considerable measure of independence as long as the Jagellonian dynasty survived. But with the extinction of that family in 1572, the foundations of Polish royalty crumbed. The nine-month interregnum that followed saw a change of really revolutionary character. The theory at once spread that, now that the old dynasty had disappeared, the *szlachta* no longer had any master over them and the supreme power had lapsed into their hands.

Hence they hastened to take possession of the state, acting by means of armed provincial associations, or "Confederations," which, replacing the royal courts and officials undertook to provide for the unity and security of the country and for the establishment of a new government. It was true that the *szlachta* did proceed to the election of another king; but the theory of election had now changed utterly. While the Jagellonian dynasty lasted, the practice of election meant hardly more than the designation of the natural successor by birth and an act of submission to him; the nation had little real freedom of choice, and the Jagellonian princes retained most of the prestige of hereditary monarchs. But from 1572–73 onward, it was understood that the *szlachta* were quite free to choose whom they would, and that the prince whom they chose was only their delegate, entrusted by them with a rigidly limited portion of authority, which might be revoked in case he overstepped his mandate. The *szlachta* had thus anointed themselves with the majesty that had once pertained to the Crown, and henceforth it became their chief concern to see that the sovereignty did not slip away from them. The state had become in fact, as well as in name, a republic.

After this revolution, save for rare instances, the King of Poland was merely the "painted monarch," the crowned figurehead, whose impotence could be compared only with that of the conventional *doge* of Venice. Surrounded by pomp and circumstance, he was yet without any of those effective powers which even in modern constitutional states remain to the monarch. The chief prerogative left to him was the right of appointing to innumerable offices, civil and ecclesiastical; but as appointments were made for life, and the king possessed no means of control over officials once appointed, this prerogative was of little avail. Indeed, it is probable that the jealousies, disappointments, and resentments provoked by the use of the royal patronage quite outweighed any profit that the Crown may have drawn from it. Certainly nothing contributed more to the suspicion that haunted the *szlachta* in the last centuries of Old Poland than the fear that the kings were corrupting the nation and endangering liberty by their insidious and unscrupulous use of the appointing power; nothing did more to keep alive that sleepless and ineradicable distrust of the Crown, which proved so formidable an obstacle to every attempt to restore some strength to the executive.

A long series of Polish historians, from Naruszewicz down to Bobrzyński, have deplored the abasement of the royal power as the primary cause of the decline of Poland. It has often been said that so vast, so exposed, and so heterogeneous a realm as this could survive only under a strong monarchy; that Poland needed to go through the wholesome discipline of enlightened despotism like the Western nations; that Poland fell because she tried to omit a stage in her evolution. But the more recent historiography tends toward a quite different view. It is urged that Poland might have attained the results that Western nations secured through absolutism by other methods, through the admission of all classes of society to a fair share in the government of the Republic. More serious, more decisive than the victory of the *szlachta* over the Crown, was the victory of the *szlachta* over the non-noble classes. These elements, unfortunately, showed themselves incapable of furnishing support to the falling kingship, or of forcing the *szlachta* to share with them the power wrested from the Crown, or even of defending their own political and economic existence against the attacks of the nobility. If the Polish state fell completely under the control of a single class, with the most disastrous results, it was not so much because in Poland the kings were weaker and the nobility more aggressive than elsewhere, as because the lower classes, and especially the bourgeoisie, exhibited a weakness unparalleled in any Western country.

In the fourteenth and early fifteenth centuries an admirable equilibrium existed between the various classes in Poland. Each class enjoyed a fair measure of rights and privileges, and no class was able to encroach seriously upon the others. This equilibrium was broken down, however, in the later fifteenth and sixteenth centuries, when the *szlachta* established their complete political and economic preponderance over townsmen and peasantry alike.

As against the peasantry, the *szlachta* were impelled by the same imperious economic needs that were about the same period converting the *Grundherr* into the *Gutsherr* and the free peasant into the serf in Eastern Germany, Bohemia, Hungary, and Russia. Into the causes and history of this vast transformation in the agrarian life of Eastern Europe it is impossible to enter here. This economic change coincided in time with the rise of the *szlachta* to political power and their conquest of the right of legislation through the Diet. The result was a series of "constitutions" (the most important of them between 1496 and 1573), which bound the peasant to the soil, increased his obligations in rent and labor, deprived him of the protection of the law, and even subjected his religion to the dictates of his master. Whether or not the lord was legally vested with the *jus vitae et necis*, it was assumed that he possessed it, and there are not lacking examples of its being exercised. The peasant thus sank into the most abject kind of bondage; the landowner was lord of his land, his property, his life, and his conscience.

The degradation of the Polish peasantry is not surprising in view of what was occurring elsewhere in Eastern Europe; but the abasement of the towns before the *szlachta* is less easy to understand, and in fact an entirely adequate explanation has not yet been offered. In the fifteenth and early sixteenth centuries the Polish cities were at the height of their prosperity. Politically, they were by no means negligible factors. Even earlier than the *szlachta*, they had learned to assert their rights by means of Confederations; their approval was frequently sought by the Crown for important political acts; and all through the fifteenth century their representatives often appeared at those loosely organized and little-known national assemblies out of which the Diet developed. But when that body was finally organized through the Statute *Nihil Novi*, the cities found themselves virtually excluded. Cracow alone, by special privilege, enjoyed a clear legal right to representation in the Diet; but the exercise of that right encountered such opposition from the *szlachta*, and the deputies of the capital were subjected to such humiliations when they ventured to show themselves, that by the end of the sixteenth century they had ceased to appear. It is true that the cities never quite lost their rank as one of the constitutional estates of the realm. Throughout the seventeenth and eighteenth centuries four or five towns continued to participate in elections to the throne, in extraordinary Diets, and in Confederations. The right of the towns to be represented at ordinary Diets was never formally abolished or renounced; but for practical purposes, from the beginning of the sixteenth century on, the cities had lost their place in the national assembly and in the political life of the nation.

This elimination of the bourgeois element from the Diet was a phenomenon not entirely peculiar to Poland. In Hungary, Bohemia, and Moravia—lands whose constitutional development closely resembled that of Poland and might, perhaps, have paralleled it completely, but for the fortunate advent of the House of Habsburg—the role of the city deputies at the Diets was gradually reduced to little more than the right to be present; in Bohemia that right was restricted to Prague alone, and in Hungary and Moravia in the later years of the old regime all the cities together had only a single vote. But nowhere else did the city estate fall so completely as in Poland, so suddenly, or, what is strangest, with so little apparent effort at self-defense.

The explanation most commonly advanced for this surrender by the cities is the fact that the Polish towns in the Middle Ages were peopled chiefly by Germans living according to German law, separated from the rest of the nation by language, customs, and interests, and neither willing nor able to take an effective and continuous part in the political life of the kingdom. It is true that in the sixteenth century the towns were rapidly being Polonized but this transformation came too late; the cities then found that their cooperation was not wanted, and that the doors of the Diet were closed against them. They were the less able to defend their political interests, because, despite the external appearance of prosperity, economic decline was setting in. The primary cause was the shifting of the world's trade centers at the close of the fifteenth century and the ruin of the Black Sea traffic at the hands of the Turks. The Polish towns thus lost that transit-trade on which their prosperity in the Middle Ages had chiefly rested, and henceforth they went steadily downhill. This decline was accelerated by the encroachments of the *szlachta*, who, as soon as they had come into power, rained blow after blow upon the sinking bourgeoisie. The latter were excluded from offices in the state and from the higher places in the Church; they were forbidden to own land outside their walls; their municipal liberties were virtually destroyed in the seigniorial towns, and in the royal cities greatly restricted. Above all, their trade was nearly ruined by the selfish and short-sighted legislation passed by assemblies of country squires, bent only on assuring their own fortunes and ignorant of the first principles of a sound national economy. As typical of this legislation, one may cite the law of 1565, which forbade native merchants to export or import any goods whatsoever, or the enactment of 1643 that native merchants were to sell at a profit of no more than 7 per cent; foreigners, of 5 per cent; Jews, of 3 per cent. The prosperity of the cities might possibly have survived the activity of the Polish Solons; but the terrible devastations suffered during the wars against Swedes, Turks, and Muscovites dealt it the final blow. By the eighteenth century the once brilliant and busy towns presented a perfect picture of desolation: the houses deserted or falling in ruins, the streets grown up to grass, and business confined to the wretched operations of Jewish money-lenders and petty traders. Poland was thus left destitute of the element most important for a sound political life—a strong, prosperous, and progressive middle class.

Though supported by great wealth and by the prestige naturally attaching to the Church among an ardently Catholic people, the Polish clergy also failed to oppose an effective barrier to the omnipotence of the *szlachta*. It is true that the bishops acquired and maintained a place in the Senate, and that in the fifteenth century the lower clergy were occasionally represented at the Diets. But in Poland, as in England, the clergy preferred to tax themselves and to regulate their relations with the Crown in their separate assemblies; as an estate they soon dropped out of the Diet; and then they too became the object of the attacks of the *szlachta*. Failing in their direct onslaughts, especially in their attempt to oust the bishops from the Senate, the gentry nevertheless succeeded in their essential aim. By securing a monopoly of the higher positions in the Church for members of their own class, they removed the main cause of antagonism and turned the hierarchy into an aristocratic body, one with themselves in birth, manners, ideas, and interests. With that the victory of the *szlachta* over all opposing elements was complete. They were the State. The struggles of the *Staendestaat* period had led in Poland to a result radically different from that attained in most other states, and one for which there is nowhere else an exact analogy. The result was the omnipotence of a single caste carried to a point unparalleled in any other European country.

Even this development need not have proved so disastrous, if the *szlachta*, after gaining the supreme power, had only properly organized it. An efficient aristocratic government, awake to national needs and able to concentrate the power and resources of the country for great national tasks, might have provided a tolerable substitute for absolute monarchy. But it was the supreme misfortune of Poland that the *szlachta*, after appropriating the sovereignty, seemed bent, not on using it for great national aims, but rather on dividing it equally among all the members of their class, taken as individuals. The authority lost by the Crown passed not to the Diet but to the local assemblies (Dietines) and, in the last analysis, to each country gentleman. The supreme power was atomized until it simply vanished, leaving anarchy.

The explanation of this unhappy phenomenon is chiefly to be sought in the geographic and historical conditions under which the *szlachta* had worked their way to power. The Republic embraced an enormous area;

it was larger than any of the other states which at that time experimented in popular government. In the German territories, Bohemia, Sweden, or Aragon, for example, all nobles might, without too much difficulty, attend the central parliament; but in Poland, as in Hungary, this proved impossible, and hence the need for the election of representatives, for local assemblies, for local self-government. The mere size of Poland rendered decentralization indispensable.

The particularist spirit had also been fostered by the historical evolution of Poland. After a short period of unity under the Piasts, in the twelfth century the realm had been divided into numerous principalities, which soon possessed no connecting links whatsoever. This period of disintegration, which lasted nearly two hundred years, left very deep and abiding traces. It was then that the various Polish "lands"—the principalities of that age, the palatinates of the next—took permanent shape and acquired their marked individuality, their separatist instincts, traditions and prejudices. The reunion of the country effected by Wladyslaw Lokietek at the beginning of the fourteenth century, was only a hasty and mechanical process, each "land" retaining its own assemblies of dignitaries and magnates, its own law, its own separate life and self-consciousness. Though some progress toward real unity was made under Lokietek and his successor, the speedy extinction of the dynasty and the subsequent weakening of the royal power, which had always been the chief bond of union in Poland, largely arrested this salutary process.

It was at this moment, when the integration of the country was still so incomplete, that the *szlachta* made their entry into political life. Naturally they acted through the agencies with which they were most familiar, namely, the local organizations, and in accordance with those ideas of local independence to which they were accustomed. So it happened that they entrenched themselves first of all not in a central parliament, but in the local assemblies—the Dietines. About the beginning of the fifteenth century the old provincial councils of dignitaries and magnates were transformed (except for judicial purposes) into assemblies of the whole community of the *szlachta* of each "land." The *Sejmiki* or Dietines originally concerned themselves only with modest local affairs; but as the *szlachta* extorted one privilege after another from the Crown, it was through the Dietines as their chief organs that they exercised their new functions. For purposes of taxation and, after the Statutes of Nieszawa, for calling the *pospolite ruszenie* and for legislation (at least legislation affecting the rights and privileges of the *szlachta*), the King was obliged to consult all the Dietines separately. That procedure was slow and awkward; what was needed was a concentration of the local machinery in a general parliament.

The nucleus of such a body existed in the *Wiec*, the assembly of the chief magnates and dignitaries of the entire kingdom which, as a royal council, under the first Jagellonians already exerted great influence over the decisions of the Crown in matters of general policy. Throughout the fifteenth century, *szlachta* and townsmen and, to some extent, the lower clergy not infrequently attended the meetings of the *Wiec*; but it is still uncertain what form their representation took and what part they had in the deliberations of the assembly. At any rate, an organic connection between the Dietines and the *Wiec* (or Diet, as it came to be called), was definitely established only at the close of the century. The Dietines slowly formed the habit of sending deputies to the central body; and in 1493, for the first time—as far as we know—deputies from all the Dietines in the kingdom assembled in the general Diet at Piotrkow. That was the Polish Model Parliament. The Diet took shape as a bicameral body: The deputies from the Dietines formed the Chamber of Nuncios, from which the city representatives soon disappeared; and the upper house was formed by the Senate (i.e., the old royal council or *Wiec*, made up of the archbishops, bishops, palatines, castellans, and the great officers of the Crown), which through the Statute *Nihil Novi* was placed on a footing of equality with the Chamber of Nuncios with respect to legislative rights.

The success of Polish parliamentarism now depended on the question of what the relation would be between the newly formed Diet and the older provincial assemblies. The predominance of the former would mean the continuation of the unification of the realm and perhaps the development of a strong central government; the predominance of the Dietines, on the other hand, would involve decentralization, disunion, impotence. At the outset, the decentralizing tendency prevailed. The deputies of the Dietines represented only their respective "lands"; they were bound by instructions, usually precise and imperative, from their electors; the Diet resembled a congress of ambassadors. Under Sigismund II a determined effort was made by the Protestant *szlachta* to end this state of things and to give the Diet the character of a real parliament by eliminating imperative mandates, establishing the majority rule in voting, and subordinating the Dietines to the Diet. But this effort failed, chiefly owing to the opposition, and later the weakness, of the King himself.

In the next generation, the tide set strongly in the opposite direction. The doctrinaire theories of the age about the "freedom" and "equality" of the *szlachta*, the heightened sense of their own importance produced by the events of 1572 in the minds of the gentry, their natural preference for deciding all matters directly in their local assemblies, rather than through deputies to the Diet, who might be insidiously influenced by the King or the magnates—all these things combined to assure to the Dietines a preponderance such as they had never before enjoyed. Restricted under the later Jagellonians to a very narrow sphere of activity, these assemblies now extended their encroachments so far and assumed such a plenitude of power and independence, that in the seventeenth century the Republic came to resemble a loose federation of fifty or sixty sovereign states. Not only did the various palatinates develop to the utmost their judicial and administrative autonomy, but decentralization was also carried to dangerous lengths in the financial and military system, on which the strength and security of the Republic primarily depended. The Dietines granted or refused taxes, either through their deputies to the Diet or directly, when the question was referred to them, as frequently happened; they themselves assessed and collected the taxes, turning over to the treasurers of the Crown only so much as they saw fit; and they raised and maintained military forces, which they tended to regard as their own provincial armies.

This excessive decentralization was, indeed, partially overcome during the eighteenth century. The unity of the army was restored; and the Diet of 1717, by establishing permanent taxes levied according to a fixed scale by officials of the central government, put an end to the financial powers of the Dietines, except for the raising of local rates. But by this time it was hard to undo the effects of one hundred years of disorganization and chaos, to curb the deeply rooted particularist spirit, to bring the state back to the path towards unity, on which it had started in the sixteenth century. And above all, even in the mid-eighteenth century nothing had been done to remedy the worst evil produced by the long preponderance of the Dietines, namely, the impotence of the Diet.

That impotence was due chiefly to the system of the imperative mandate. Since 1572 the instructions given by the Dietines to their deputies had grown more and more lengthy, detailed, and strict. The deputies might be ordered to put through a project at all costs, or not to allow one to pass under any consideration. Then the custom had grown up of holding so-called "Dietines of relation" (*Sejmiki relacyjne*) at the close of each Diet for the purpose of hearing the reports of the returned deputies. These Dietines of relation not only kept the nuncios in wholesome awe of disobeying their instructions, but also, while they could not de jure alter or nullify what the Diet had done, de facto they not infrequently did so.

The result of this system was to hamper the action of the Diet to the utmost. Whatever was to come up in the central parliament was discussed and virtually decided in advance by the Dietines, and the latter decided these matters—questions, it might be, of the most general nature, affecting the whole Republic—on the basis of local interests, local knowledge, local prejudices; decided them prematurely, categorically, in final instance, without regard for what the assembly of the whole nation, after a more comprehensive survey of the situation and more mature deliberation, might be inclined to favor. The fate of every question thus depended not so much upon the debates in the Diet as upon the referendum taken in fifty or sixty tumultuous gatherings of—for the most part—ignorant and narrow-minded country squires.

The logical development of the system of imperative mandates and the crowning anomaly of the Polish constitution was the famous Liberum Veto: the right of any member of the Diet to interpose a veto, which had the threefold effect of defeating the particular proposition that had aroused opposition, dissolving the Diet, and nullifying all the decisions previously taken by the assembly.

The Liberum Veto was a late constitutional development. In the sixteenth century Diets a determined minority was generally able to check the action of the majority, but if the dissenters were very few, little attention was paid to them. In the seventeenth century, however, with the strong tendency of that age to "liberty," and its antipathy to "tyranny" of any sort, the conception of the rights of the minority developed, until in 1652 for the first time a single deputy, Siciński, by his veto "exploded" the Diet. After that the use of the Liberum Veto, although it rested on no written law and was in itself a defiance of common sense, became an established constitutional practice—and a chronic evil. The Dietines often expressly ordered its application, taking pleasure in this means of showing their importance. The mass of the *szlachta* regarded it as a useful safeguard against injustice or tyranny—in fact as the "palladium of liberty," the "jewel of the constitution." Of the fifty-five Diets held between 1652 and 1764, forty-eight were "exploded," almost one-third of them by the veto of a single deputy. During the thirty-year reign of Augustus III* not a single Diet lived out its normal time. As the Diet met only once in two years, and then for six weeks only (provided it escaped being "exploded"), and as each Diet was generally brought to a violent and premature end with nothing accomplished, the result was that the national parliament had virtually ceased to function. And yet, after the collapse of the royal power, the Diet was the one institution that might have given the country a government!

One means of getting around the Liberum Veto existed, but, as has frequently been pointed out, it was a remedy worse than the disease. This was the "Confederation," i. e., a voluntary armed association of individuals formed for the purpose of putting through its specified projects in the face of any opposition whatsoever. Confederations—a characteristic medieval constitutional device—were much in vogue in Poland in the late fourteenth and fifteenth centuries; they then disappeared for a time, but recurred frequently in the period after 1572—one symptom more of the reversion in type that marked Polish constitutionalism in that age. Confederations were of three kinds: (1) those formed during interregna in order to prevent disorders and hold the realm together; (2) those formed during the lifetime of a king for the purpose of assisting him in some great emergency; and (3) those formed in opposition to the kings—of which there are only too many examples. Associations of the first two kinds were useful; indeed, a Confederation formed "at the King's side," might be merely a technical device for putting through a project in spite of the opposition of a minority, since in a Diet held "under the seal of a Confederation" the majority ruled. But a Confederation was under any circumstances a hazardous expedient, for it always brought with it the danger of civil war. Nothing reveals in a more glaring light the defects of Polish constitutionalism. Nothing could be more detrimental to stability, legality, and order than a system under which the ordinary authorities might at any moment be violently replaced by a set of ambitious private persons, who usurped control of the administration, the courts, the treasury, and the army, called a Diet, put through what legislation they pleased and dispersed only when their aims were attained. The right of confederation, as Moltke declared, was revolution legally organized. It

* King of Poland, 1734–63.—Ed.

gave rise to the epigram that the government of Poland was anarchy tempered by civil war.

Were there any truth in the old liberal maxim that those states were happiest that were governed least, the Polish Republic must have approached the acme of perfection. The activity of its government had been reduced to the vanishing-point. "No people," said Burke, "have ever taken greater precautions to secure the possession of a sober and well-regulated freedom, than the Poles have to preserve themselves in their present anarchy." In order that the King might not make himself a "tyrant," he had been stripped of well-nigh every prerogative. In order that the Diet might not endanger "liberty," it had been reduced to complete impotence. The Dietines, in which the Liberum Veto also prevailed, were, as organs of governments, scarcely more respectable. In Poland, Raynal declared, "everyone has the power to prevent action, and no one the power to act. There the will of any individual may thwart the general will; and there alone a foolish, a wicked, or an insane man is sure to prevail over a whole nation." Montesquieu rightly affirmed that "the object of the laws of Poland was the independence of every individual," that is, of every nobleman.

The *szlachta* had, in fact, attained the most complete freedom, not only from every kind of oppression but from any sort of obligation or constraint. From the latter part of the seventeenth century on, they ceased to render military service, since the development of warfare had made the old feudal levies an anachronism; nevertheless they continued to consider themselves the sword and buckler of Poland and to claim all the privileges for which their former service had been the sole justification. They enjoyed a monopoly of landowning. They exercised sovereign and unlimited power over the serfs on their estates. They could not be taxed without their consent, and in practice they paid none of the usual taxes, not even customs duties. They could not be arrested or imprisoned or deprived of their property without trial, nor punished for their speeches and opinions. They held a monopoly of the higher positions in the Church and of political rights and offices. Through their control of the Diet, the Dietines, and the courts of justice, they had in their hands whatever machinery of government existed. Finally, every nobleman, however indigent or insignificant he might be, had the right to attend and to participate in the elections to the throne, as a supreme demonstration of the fact that in Poland the sovereignty belonged to every *szlachcic* individually, as well as to all the *szlachta* collectively. It may be doubted whether any other class has ever obtained such unrestricted independence and such a fullness of power and privilege. The *szlachta* themselves were wont to boast that it was impossible to imagine a happier lot than that of a Polish nobleman, and they looked down upon all the other peoples of Europe as the "slaves of despots."

Naturally there grew up in the minds of the ruling class an idealization of this "golden liberty," purchased by "the blood and toil" of their "virtuous ancestors," which became a sort of religion, and a veritable obsession. One hardly knows whether to wonder more at the glorification of the *szlachta* as a caste or at the panegyrics lavished upon the constitution which the nobility had created. The *szlachta*, it was said, were exalted above all the other classes as the cedars of Lebanon above the common trees. They were the heart and hands of the body politic, as the king was the head and the commoners the feet. As they gave their lives to the defense of the Republic, it was meet that the lower orders should serve them. It was necessary to have in the state one class of people who, disdainful of all gain, sought only the dignity, honor, and advantage of the fatherland. Traders and artisans, absorbed in money-making, were incapable of lofty thought or deeds, just as the *szlachta*, living only for virtue, truth, and right, were incapable of any low action.

As for the constitution, it was defended with a great store of classical erudition, which testifies to the profound influence of Humanism upon Polish thought. With their minds full of political and legal ideas borrowed from antiquity, with the old phrases about "tyranny," "freedom," and "equality" ever upon their lips, the *szlachta* finally came to conceive of themselves as the reincarnation of the Roman Republic. The analogy was useful in a dozen ways. Did not history show that in the ancient republics political rights had also been confined to one class of well-born, wealthy, and leisured citizens, below which stood a servile proletariat? Was not a deputy exercising the Liberum Veto merely a tribune of the people? Was not a Confederation simply a new form of the Roman dictatorship? Nowhere else, perhaps, was the ideal of a democratic republic of the ancient type so popular—or so potent in shaping political theory and practice.

Religion also added its sanction to the apotheosis of the *szlachta* state. In order to assure the victory of the Counter-Reformation, the Jesuits had not hesitated to make themselves ardent champions of "golden liberty," and to proclaim that the free constitution of the Republic was peculiarly adapted to Catholic principles and teaching. Under the influence of the clergy, the Poles came to regard themselves as under the special protection of Providence, as a chosen people; and confirmation for this belief was found in the many signs and wonders of the seventeenth century, especially in the miraculous deliverance of the country from the Swedes in the time of John Casimir.

Extravagant as such theories were, they took deep root in the minds of the nobility. Combined with material interests, class egotism, and the instinct of self-preservation, they produced in the *szlachta* a blind conservatism, a horror of all innovations, a fierce determination to maintain the existing state of things, which long rendered reforms almost impossible.

The constitutional development of Poland from the end of the fourteenth down to the middle of the seventeenth century had been continuous, consistent, and logical. Unfortunate as that evolution had been, there had at least been life and movement. But in the seventeenth century growth ceased. The constitution had taken on fixed forms, and now entered upon a period of petrifaction during which all the disastrous effects of the preceding evolution made themselves increasingly and appallingly felt. The seventeenth century was marked by intellectual and moral retrogression, economic decline, growing political anarchy, and continual, exhausting, and on the whole disastrous conflicts with the neighboring powers. Then followed the dullest and dreariest period of Polish history, the reigns of the two Saxon Kings (1697–1763), an age in which patriotism, public spirit, energy, and initiative seemed to have deserted Poland. After the incessant wars of the preceding period, amid which the nation could still produce heroes like Czarniecki or Sobieski, the *szlachta* laid aside their swords and abandoned themselves thenceforth to the joys of life on their estates, enhanced by constant and exuberant festivities and varied by the excitements connected with the Diets, the Dietines, the law courts, and a sordid and senseless party strife. This age of materialism, selfishness, apathy, and stagnation brought Poland to the depths of degradation. Her impotence was now well known to all the world, her anarchy proverbial, and her complete downfall a matter of common discussion.

THREE

The Secularization
of Eastern Europe
(1789–1918)

The meaning of "Liberty, Equality, Fraternity" varied from region to region in Eastern Europe according to the level of socio-economic development and the political consciousness of the people. The message of the French Revolution had its most powerful impact on Greek merchants and intellectuals, whose exposure to French revolutionary ideas had been the most intense. The various sectors of Greek society rallied, according to their particular socio-economic and political interests, to the call of revolution against the Turk. But the Greek

Revolution of 1821 showed that the French message had lost something in translation: The revolutionaries were seeking liberty for all Greeks, but not necessarily equality and fraternity. The drive for social equality, in the Greek lands and elsewhere, was subsidiary to the attainment of the nationalist goal of independence (or autonomy).

In Eastern Europe, nationalism was indeed the immediate offshoot of the French Revolution: the nationalism of elites opposed to Habsburg and Ottoman imperial rule. National self-assertion was feared by the Sultan and the Kaiser; its containment, as best expressed in the Holy Alliance and the covenants of the Congress of Vienna, was essential for the maintenance of the empires' internal security and of the European balance of power.

Social revolution, too, was opposed by Habsburg, Turk, Russian, and Briton; by the conservative landowners of the two empires; and, for that matter, even by some of the vigorous exponents of the nationalist message. "Liberal" Magyar and Rumanian aristocrats, Greek merchants, and Croatian and Bohemian intellectuals all assigned a secondary place to social reform throughout most of the first half of the nineteenth century. But the forces favoring containment of the nationalism of the elites and the social aspirations of the masses were repeatedly challenged during those years, most belligerently in 1848.

In the Ottoman Empire, the need to placate the forces of political and social change was recognized by 1830. The establishment of an independent Greece, an autonomous Serbia, and self-governed Rumanian provinces appeased conservative leaders. But the legalizing of conservative nationalism in constitutional forms—allegedly imitative of French prototypes—did not obscure the reality that Greece, Serbia, and the Rumanian provinces were protectorates of conservative powers bent on containing social and political manifestations that threatened the stability of the European state system. The Hatti-Sherif, promulgating oligarchic boyar constitutionalism in Moldavia and Wallachia, was typical of the compromises derived from the instability of the Ottoman Empire, the revolutionary challenges of its subjects, and the political interests of the European powers.

There was considerably less toleration of national and social manifestations in the Habsburg Empire and in isolated, partitioned Poland. Cultural nationalism was tolerated in its nonpolitical forms if it served the purposes of the imperial court. In the medieval sense of the monopolistic privileges of the aristocratic "nation," it was also tolerated if—and often because—it served the political purposes of the arch-conservative, feudal, aristocratic empire. In its other manifestations, however, especially if linked with demands for social reform, nationalism was ruthlessly suppressed. The demands of 1848, whether they were as modest as the proposals of the Slavs or as radical as those of Kossuth, were rejected or militarily suppressed by the defenders of traditional imperial and aristocratic values.

The most powerful defender of the political and social status quo was imperial Russia. Tsar Nicholas I, the "sergeant of Europe," was equally prepared to suppress the Polish independence uprising of 1830, the Rumanians' revolt in Moldavia in 1848, and Kossuth's revolution in Hungary in 1849. Revolution in any form, but particularly if it involved peasant emancipation, was intolerable to the Russian autocrat.

The failure of the revolutions of 1848 was only relative in East-Central Europe. The frustrations of defeat were compensated by the recognition of a common purpose between leaders and masses. The emancipation of the peasantry, as envisaged by Kossuth in Hungary and Balcescu in Wallachia, was not immediately realized. But the need for social reform penetrated into even the most reactionary circles in Vienna, Budapest, and St. Petersburg. Within fifteen years after the defeat of the revolutionaries of 1848, serfdom was de jure abolished in all lands that had been exposed to revolutionary action. Inadequate as the land reforms were, they temporarily defused the countryside and ensured the neutrality of the peasantry as the East European empires sought to adapt themselves to the realities of the 1850's and 1860's.

A dramatic alteration of the balance of power in Eastern Europe took place during the decade of adjustment and compromise that began with the unification of the Rumanian provinces in 1859 and ended with the Austro-Hungarian Compromise (*Ausgleich*) of 1867. Following his defeat in the Crimean War, the Russian Tsar, formerly the principal oppressor of disruptive nationalism and social change, became the "Tsar Emancipator," the supporter of Balkan nationalism. Alexander II, unlike his father, recognized the need for modernization of the Russian Empire. He adopted the principle of encouraging the formation of national states —albeit conservative in their political and socio-economic structure. Russia's support of national causes permitted the unification of Moldavia and Wallachia into an autonomous Rumania in 1859, prompted the emancipation of the Rumanian peasantry in 1864, and precipitated the removal of the Turks from Serbia. It also inflamed the aspirations of Bulgarians and other Southern Slav intellectuals and politicians, who sought to emulate the Rumanian gains.

But it soon became evident that the tsars favored the dissolution of the Ottoman Empire into client states of Russia. This reality was acceptable to national conservative leaders to the extent that it limited or retarded the process of socio-economic change, but not insofar as it encouraged the attainment of true national independence. It was rejected outright by Francophile and reformist Rumanian liberals, as well as by Rumanian and other Balkan radicals who regarded 1848 as the failure of "bourgeois democracy" and "bourgeois nationalism." Social revolutionaries seeking to destroy all feudal empires and bourgeois states were few in number in Southeastern Europe. Such revolutionary agitators as there were, particularly among the Bulgarian emigration in Russia and Rumania, viewed the annihilation of the Polish revolutionaries by Russian armies in 1863, the removal of the "emancipator" Alexandru Ion Cuza by "reactionary" Rumanian landlords in 1864, and indeed all other social injustices in the

Balkans as a reflection of Russian-supported, if not imposed, conservatism. But these were the views of a minority. The politically conscious, particularly in Serbia and Rumania, were more apprehensive about developments in the Habsburg Empire, both before and after the Compromise of 1867.

The Habsburgs' repression of militant nationalism after 1849 indicated that they were aware of the multiple social and political threats to the integrity of the empire posed by the revolutionary manifestations. The regressive Schwarzenberg and Bach systems proved as successful as the Metternich system in containing nationalism and social change; but they were unable to meet the external challenges of Napoleon III, the Italians, the Russians, and later, Bismarck. The ensuing search for compromise—which began with the appeasement of the oppressed through peasant emancipation and the offer of national equality in a supranational federal empire—posed a serious threat to both the aristocratic imperial Austrian order and the aristocratic Magyar nation. Emperor Francis Joseph may have commanded the loyalty (*Kaisertreue*) of his subjects in the 1860's, but he did not seek to modernize his state or to arbitrate the disputes and conflicting interests of "inferior" or "nonhistoric" nations. The Hungarian magnates shared his views, at least insofar as the aspirations of the Slavs and Rumanians were concerned. But following Austria's humiliating defeat by Prussia in the Seven Weeks War, even Vienna understood that the stability, if not the very survival, of the imperial order required compromises by the dominant Austrians and Hungarians in the face of the demands of the majority of socially and nationally underprivileged Slavs and Rumanians. The *Ausgleich* of 1867, however, rejected federal solutions and socio-economic reforms commensurate with the seriousness of the situation and the requirements of a secular-industrial age; instead, it confirmed the supremacy of the aristocratic Magyar and Austrian oligarchies in the renamed Austro-Hungarian Empire. Rejection of change paved the way for dissolution of the other multinational empire, the Ottoman. In both cases, the force was nationalism, in a variety of forms, all of them lethal.

The reaction of the underprivileged nations to the Austro-Hungarian Compromise transcended the frontiers of the empire. Although the forces favoring dissolution were still small in number and, as yet, unprepared to precipitate the debacle, East European nationalism became a more formidable force to contend with for all those who favored the maintenance of the Habsburg Empire and the peaceful and orderly dissolution of the Ottoman. But the policy of containment became more and more difficult to enforce as nationalist leaders sought the support of the increasingly dissatisfied masses in both empires.

In the Habsburg Empire, the peasant soon learned that emancipation from serfdom did not automatically guarantee him economic security, social mobility, or political rights. The restlessness of the peasantry was exploited by nationalist politicians and socialist agitators. National injustice (the persecution of minority nationalities) and social injustice (the lack of economic and social opportunities) became the battle cry of all opposed to the Compromise. The divide-and-conquer policies of Vienna, however, prolonged the life of the empire as the Emperor remained above politics, invoking the *Kaisertreue* of his subjects to placate their discontent.

A more serious threat to the ruling elites in Eastern Europe came from the nationalist and social revolutionary agitation in the empire of the Sultans. The Serbs, pressing for a Greater Serbia, fanned discontent among fellow Slavs in Bosnia and Herzegovina, where an impotent Porte was unable to prevent the exploitation and oppression of the peasantry by venal pashas and avaricious feudatories. In Serbia proper, social revolutionaries sought the support of the Serbian peasantry against the ruling dynasty and a corrupt political establishment bent on substituting nationalist agitation for genuine social reform. Bulgarian radicals, operating from Rumanian bases, sought to arouse the Bulgarian peasantry against an ever more abusive Porte, while Pan-Slav agitators, encouraged by Russia, held out the promise of liberty, equality, and fraternity to all Slavs in the Peninsula. The turmoil reached explosive proportions in the mid-1870's, as the Bosnians, Herzegovinians, and Bulgarians rebelled against the growing oppression of the Porte and its representatives. The violent repression of the Bulgarian uprising led to Russia's military intervention and victory over the Porte, but also to its severe diplomatic defeat at the Congress of Berlin, in 1878.

Russia's humiliation by the Germanic powers and Great Britain temporarily stayed the hand of the nationalists, socialists, and all who sought the dissolution of both multinational empires, but it did not stop them altogether. Beginning in the 1880's, Serbian, Rumanian, Bulgarian, and even Albanian nationalists increasingly thought in terms of territorial aggrandizement. But the Balkan "empire-builders" were faced with a serious internal and external problem—the disaffection of the masses, exposed and exploited by such radical social reformers as Svetozar Markovich and Dimitar Blagoev. They tried to placate the masses with minor concessions and extravagant promises contingent on the attainment of the "supreme goal" of total national unification, at the expense of Habsburgs or Turks. But these panaceas generally fell on deaf ears, both in the home countries and among their Balkan neighbors. Such was the case in Macedonia, where many of the inhabitants—whether Slavs, Greeks, or Turks—wanted a Macedonia for the Macedonians and not a Macedonia for Bulgaria, Greece, or Serbia. It was also true in the Austro-Hungarian Empire, where many Croats, Slovenes, and Rumanians would have preferred an *Ausgleich* to union with Serbia and the old Rumanian Kingdom.

The Habsburgs and, particularly, the Hungarians were alert to possible internal changes caused by nationalist demands, and most certainly to the possibility of internationalization of the empire's nationality problems. Political, cultural, and socio-economic repression was used to attain the denationalization, if not homogenization, of the population of the multinational state. The Austrians' efforts were partly successful because of the masses' allegiance to the Emperor and the empire's relative prosperity, derived from gradual industrialization and the secularization of society. But the Hungarians' repression of the nationalities under their domination, particularly the Rumanians and the Slovaks, jeopardized the reconciliation efforts of the Habsburgs and inflamed the passions of East European nationalists everywhere.

Social and political ferment in Eastern Europe reached a near boiling point in the first decade of the twentieth century. The repression of such violent social manifestations as the Rumanian peasant revolt of 1907 and the rejection of the political demands of the nations of the Austro-Hungarian Empire exacerbated internecine and international frictions. Nationalist agitation, encouraged by Russia and opposed by the Central Powers, threatened to destroy the traditional balances of power in Southeastern Europe. The Bosnian crisis of 1908 was the prelude to the total unleashing of Balkan nationalism and the at least temporary fusion of the conflicting imperialist interests of the Balkan states. The Balkan Wars and the subsequent internationalization of the nationality problems of the Habsburg Empire destroyed the forces of stability in Eastern Europe and led directly to World War I and the ensuing radical transformation of the East European state and social systems.

Nationalism, Revolution, and Compromise (1789–1867)

14

THE FRENCH REVOLUTION AND SOUTHEASTERN EUROPE

N. IORGA

[The impact of the French Revolution of 1789 on the history of Eastern Europe remains a matter of dispute among historians. This is partly because of lack of agreement on the character of the Revolution itself, and partly because of disagreement over the nature of the societies of Eastern Europe that were exposed to revolutionary ideas and, subsequently, to military action. The Rumanian historian N. Iorga was among the first to perceive the significance of the French Revolution in Eastern Europe in terms of modern historical scholarship. The following section, originally presented as a paper before a conference on the French Revolution, in February, 1933, analyzes the bases for the reception of the message of the French Revolution in the Ottoman Empire and the Rumanian provinces.]

It is necessary first of all to define Southeastern Europe, which is entirely different from Eastern Europe (that is, Russia, Poland, and the area that

---

Translated by Margaret Logun from N. Iorga, *La Révolution Française et le Sud-Est de l'Europe* (Bucharest [n.p.], 1934), pp. 3–14.

comprises more than what is called the Balkan Peninsula). For those who are acquainted with the geography and history of these regions, the Balkan Peninsula stops, without any doubt, at the Danube. This does not mean that there is a difference between the civilizations of the countries on the left bank of the Danube and those on the right, but geography is geography and the Peninsula stops there. But Southeastern Europe does not stop at the Danube; it also includes what in the eighteenth century were the Danubian Principalities, Moldavia and Wallachia—the two sections of Rumania that were later reunited to form one state—as well as a large part of what was previously the kingdom of Saint Stephen, Old Hungary.

Southeastern Europe, therefore, as it shall be used here, includes all of the Balkan Peninsula; Turkey—that which is genuinely Turkish, or Ottoman, but in a special way, because of its immunity to influences like those of the French Revolution until the great events of the nineteenth century; and also the Rumanian principalities and Transylvania.

In order to facilitate the presentation of such a new and complex subject, I shall not distinguish among the different nationalities. This is not to say that in the eighteenth century a Turk was at the same stage of development as a Greek; or that there was much similarity between Greek and Turkish elements, on one side, and Slavic elements, as represented by the Serbs and Bulgarians, on the other; or that there was any equivalence between regions that lie to the south of the Danube and the Danubian Principalities; or even that the situation of the Rumanians in Transylvania was anything like that of the free Rumanians, who paid a tribute to the Sultan but were governed by their own princes, had their own army, obeyed laws that were not interfered with by the Turkish imperial legislation, and led a life completely apart from the Turkish provinces in the eighteenth century.

Between the Rumanians of Wallachia and Moldavia, on the one side, and those of Transylvania on the other, there were tremendous variations, and I have no intention of ignoring these or the other differences that existed during this period. But in order to study and resolve the problem at hand, it would seem best to consider the large social classes over and above racial differences and provincial boundaries. These classes must be presented as a whole, as *the* factor that was influenced by the French Revolution.

We must now look at the manner in which the French Revolution influenced the different classes as a whole, regardless of national limits and state boundaries.

I shall begin with the peasant class.

The peasant class in the Rumanian countries, in the Balkan Peninsula, and also in Transylvania enjoyed a standard of living not inferior to that customary in the West, which explains why the revolutionaries never had any appreciable success with the rural masses. These masses asked for nothing and hoped for nothing; where there were any movements, they were determined by motives entirely different from those that brought to life the French Revolution.

The Serbian revolution, which was a peasant revolution, and the corresponding revolution of 1821 in Wallachia, brought about the establishment of the Serbian state. The Wallachian revolution of 1821 had some influence on the history of the Rumanians in the nineteenth century, but that influence was very remote, very tenuous, and, as expressive of the ideas of the French Revolution, very questionable.

All this is easy to explain, since in the provinces in the Balkan Peninsula that were subject to the Sultan's authority, where were stationed his soldiers, his *sipahis*, and for some time his *janissaries*, as well as his administrators of varying importance, the peasant remained master of his plot of land; he lived as a free man. There was no servitude in the Ottoman Empire, which explains why that foreign regime was supported.

There were certainly some movements in the Ottoman Empire in which the peasants participated, but these stemmed from or were provoked by the rapacity of the large Christian states neighboring Turkey. Thus it was outside agitation, or else religious sentiment, that caused the fundamental and irrevocable opposition that existed between the Christian population of Southeastern Europe and the population of the dominion of the Sultan. The Sultan was, without doubt, an emperor, a continuator of the Byzantine, and consequently of the Roman, emperors, but he nevertheless belonged to another religion—and between the two religions there was an antagonism impossible to surmount.

The situation of the Rumanian peasants in the Principalities was different and not as favorable as that of their neighbors in the provinces ruled by the Sultan. Their inferior status can easily be explained by the fact that in the provinces directly subject to the Sultan, payment was made only to the Turkish master—the *sipahi* stationed in the village—and to no one else, since there was no longer an aristocracy or a native master. On the other side of the Danube, however, where the Rumanians of the Principalities lived, payment was made first to the Sultan, in the form of an an annual tribute sent by the ruling princes to Constantinople in order to fulfill their duty to the Empire; next to the noble or landowner (*boyar*); and finally to the prince, of Wallachia or of Moldavia, who represented himself to his subjects as the successor to the Christian emperors of Eastern Europe and who demanded great luxury and false splendor.

It should be noted, however, that this peasant from whom a great deal was taken to support three different masters—the Sultan, the *boyar*, and the prince—lived on extensive, very rich land, the administration of which was, as yet, somewhat undetermined. There were at this time no active officials with power over the peasant. Not having to put up with officials, dependent on his own initiative, free to extend his work over the land that he either had legally annexed or owned through inheritance, the peasant felt little disposed to revolt.

The eighteenth century records the beneficial influence of Western Europe on the princes, which can be measured in terms of their popularity in the West: the princes' names were mentioned in a book published in Paris, which satisfied their vanity (as it did that of Catherine II), for they liked nothing better than to be regarded as reformers. Well before the French Revolution, the *philosophes* exerted a tremendous influence in the two principalities as well as in the Christian sections of Constantinople—that world of Phanar from which came the rulers of the two Rumanian countries—and the princes thought first and foremost of the poor subjects they would win over, against the nobility, to their imperial master, the Sultan. Thus the legislation of the Phanariote princes includes measures forbidding the *boyars* to demand more than ten to twelve days of work per year from the peasants. (The Western serf would probably have been extremely satisfied had nothing more than that been asked of him.) Despite all the attempts by the noble landlords to obtain more, there was continual opposition from the Phanariote princes, *philosophes* and reformers alike. Nothing more was ever to be wrested from these so-called foreign despots, who became, despite their Greek origin, more or less integrated with the Rumanians, only to become weak rulers, preoccupied with trying to win over public opinion and terrified of any kind of movement on the part of their subjects. When any complaints against the prince arose at Constantinople, the "poor *rayahs*" were blamed, but never the local master and his agents.

In Transylvania, the situation was entirely different. That is why, in 1784, a revolutionary movement originated among the Rumanian peasants, represented by the masses who attacked the castles of the Magyar nobility (but not the towns); the leaders of this movement were finally hunted, caught, and executed by the Emperor's soldiers, though they believed to the end that their action had been approved by Vienna and that the Court would not take drastic measures against their *jacquerie*.

About twenty years earlier, there had been a far more widespread movement. In the movement of 1784, only those peasants who lived on the Emperor's land, in the mining areas, participated. In the 1760 movement, which also had a religious character (the Orthodox opposed reunion with the Church of Rome of Rumanian Transylvania), the territory occupied by the revolutionaries was much larger. Thus, in Transylvania there were two peasant revolts, but in the Principalities only one (1821).

The first revolt of the peasants on the other side of the Carpathians was that of the Serbs (1804). It took a very different form from the peasant movements elsewhere in Central Eastern Europe. The Serbs complained that the Sultan—whom they recognized as the legitimate emperor, despite the religious difference—had appointed officials in Serbia who were abusing their powers. What the revolutionaries under Karageorge demanded, therefore, was the correction of the abuses.

To explain insurrection for such a cause—not against the Sultan but against his representatives—requires an understanding of influences extending, in some cases, quite far back in history. In the Balkan Peninsula, a sense of freedom and peasant initiative had survived all changes in government. There, it was never wise to lay so much as a finger on the peasant. The rural dweller was far more thin-skinned than the bourgeoisie or the nobility. If his ancient privileges were abused, there was a revolt, as Byzantium learned more than once, e.g., in the time of Isaac the Angel at the beginning of the thirteenth century. And, doubtless, at other times, too, law-abiding peasants had suddenly risen in revolt.

It sometimes happened that the peasant's rights entailed sacrifice. The peasant accepted this, because sacrifice was a part of his tradition and a condition of his privileges. But once either was threatened, once a new demand was made, however insignificant, transcending the long-accepted set of demands, he would not put up with it, and he revolted. Thus did the Rumanian peasants of Pinde revolt against Isaac the Angel in the thirteenth century, and thus did the Serbian peasants under Karageorge revolt against the Turkish administrators at the beginning of the nineteenth century.

Historical memory, therefore, combined with Austrian incitement, contributed to the eruption of this popular movement. It was a uniquely peasant movement, because, as we shall see in our discussion of the middle and merchant classes in Serbia, there was no national bourgeoisie at the time. The majority of the people who performed the bourgeois economic functions in Serbia were from Macedonia and were more or less graecicized. In Bosnia and Herzegovina, there was also an aristocracy which, however, was Muslim and thus separate from the rest of the nation. In 1790 or in 1804, "Serb" always meant "peasant."

Karageorge, a former Austrian noncommissioned officer, who maintained ties with the large neighboring state and bore the historic consciousness of his people's past on his shoulders, responded to the incitements coming from the other side of the border. When Karageorge came on the scene, there was also a local revolutionary outburst in a neighboring region, Vidin, that was neither Christian nor Serb but appeared to be a phenomenon of the disintegrating Ottoman Empire at the end of the eighteenth century: the revolt of the great Pasha of Vidin, Pasvant-oglou, who had maintained relations with the French government. There was also some encouragement of Karageorge on the part of the rebellious Pasha, as well as from many other provincial governors.

Karageorge's army was not a casual army, ill defined and lacking in political direction. It was called the "national assembly," of which Karageorge was the "great leader" (*veliki vojd*). Was there any influence of the concepts of the French Revolution in the Karageorge revolt? It is impossible to say, for although the idea of a popular assembly's becoming an army was far removed from Southeast European tradition, one should take into account the complex character and peculiar psychology of the leaders and soldiers of the movement.

The Wallachian insurrection of 1821 was influenced by the Karageorge revolt. The Russians had intervened after 1806, during their war against the Turks, in order to defend the Serbian revolution. They made certain Rumanians march beneath their flag, particularly Rumanians from Oltenia, where the people were much more warlike than in other Rumanian areas. One of the Russian auxiliaries—Tudor Vladimirescu, who became an officer of the imperial army—witnessed the Serbian revolt, and he later aroused his countrymen in the same way. He also called his troops, which advanced on Bucharest, the "national assembly," and he was regarded with the same respect that Karageorge commanded from the Serbs. But Karageorge had encountered only the commanders of the Turkish armies; Tudor Vladimirescu, who had started both a national and a social revolution, was forced to distinguish between the *boyars*, he associated himself with those he considered would be useful to him—and it is immediately apparent that his movement was doomed to failure. For one does not make deals at such a time; it is a question of victory or death. To abandon one's principal objective can only lead to an uncertain if not a shameful end.

Let us now consider the middle class, the merchants. These merchants were in general Greek, or graecicized, since a distinction cannot be made between one who is Greek-born and one who, though Rumanian, uses the Greek language, lives in a Greek society, and has Greek interests. Nor can a distinction be made between the Slav of Macedonia, who has a different origin from that of the Greek, and the Greek with whom, out of necessity, he must associate in business. This Greek merchant class had a tremendous influence in spreading French revolutionary ideas because of the extensive scattering abroad of the Greek peoples, who were to be found everywhere.

There were also Greeks in Constantinople, but they existed alongside a Western colony, Levantine, frenchified, in which the Greeks did not play the principal role. The Greeks had, doubtless, a very important religious role. Constantinople was the seat of the Patriarch, a sort of substitute Byzantine emperor, who was surrounded by a Court and served by outdated yet very prestigious offices. He did not relinquish all his influence over other non-Greek, Orthodox regions.

But the active Greek bourgeoisie was not formed in Constantinople; it was to be found elsewhere: in Bucharest and Jassy, the two Rumanian capitals, and also in Transylvania and Eastern Hungary where, since the beginning of the eighteenth century, Greek companies had enjoyed, and were eager to extend, privileges from the emperor. Those people had relatives everywhere—from Kronstadt-Brasov to Tokay—and they enjoyed business relations with Trieste and with Philadelphia, not to mention the great European capitals of Vienna, Paris, and London.

Vienna was a great Greek center for all of Southeastern Europe, for in that city initiative as well as wealth belonged to the Greeks. It must not be forgotten that the first Greek newspapers, which contributed to the creation and development of the national consciousness of the Greeks, were published in Vienna; the Greek *Savant Mercury* and *Hellenic Telegraph* were founded in Vienna, and the first periodicals written for the Slavs of the South were published there. It was from Vienna that the brothers Poullio, Rumanian printers from Macedonia, sent French revolutionary propaganda into the Principalities, such propagandistic works as *L'histoire de la convocation et des élections aux Etats généraux en 1784, L'histoire politique de la révolution en France, Lettres du Père Manuel, Sur la souveraineté du peuple, Histoire de la Belgique républicaine, Essai historique sur la vie de Marie-Antoinette d'Autriche.*

Trieste, through the implantation of a fairly large Greek population, became what it was to be in the eighteenth and nineteenth centuries under the wings of the "Austrian eagle." In 1720 or 1730, Trieste was nothing; half a century later, it was flourishing, thanks to the efforts of the Greeks. (In fairness, however, it should be said that the inhabitants of Trieste were also concerned with intellectual pursuits and that from ancient times Trieste had always exhibited an insatiable curiosity, a desire to learn, and a love not only for scholastic training but for all kinds of religious doctrine, a phenomenon seldom encountered among happier and more privileged nations.) These Greeks were, in general, favorable to the French Revolution: it is through them that the Prince of Wallachia learned, in December, 1794, the (premature) news of the peace concluded between the French Republic and Prussia.

Finally, in addition to the bourgeoisie, there was also an aristocracy, an intellectual and ideologically oriented aristocracy at that. This aristocracy was composed of both Greeks and Rumanians. It is sometimes very difficult to differentiate between the two, because behind the Greek there is often a Rumanian background, and in the same aristocratic family some members would take one side and others the opposite. In the Rumanian countries, there was no aristocratic family that did not have a little Greek blood, and in this society one found oneself, sometimes most unexpectedly, belonging to a distant family in Constantinople or Athens, for in this Greek world, and in that of Southeastern Europe generally, there were many family ties.

These intellectuals lived in the Phanar, but they also lived in Bucharest and in Jassy. They traveled in Western Europe, despite a ban forbidding young people to pursue their studies there, for fear they would be won over by subversive ideas; thus to obtain a passport from the prince to go abroad and participate in a much more active intellectual life was difficult indeed.

These, then, were the elements that were exposed to French revolutionary propaganda.

15

THE ORIGINS AND ACTIVITIES OF THE HETAIRIA IN THE RUMANIAN PRINCIPALITIES

GHEORGHE CANTACUZENE

[French "bourgeois" revolutionary ideology appealed to Greek intellectuals, merchants, and bourgeois-oriented political leaders who sought the complete reorganization of the Ottoman system. The leading advocates of revolutionary change in the Ottoman Empire were the Phanariotes, who were centered in Constantinople and in the Rumanian provinces of Wallachia and Moldavia. The Greek secret revolutionary organization Philike Hetairia (Society of Friends) was patterned on French prototypes and expounded a revolutionary ideology derived directly from the French. The contradictions between French revolutionary doctrine and the realities of Southeastern Europe, evident to many at the time, were confirmed by the Hetairia's failure to stage a successful uprising against the Turks. A reasoned judgment on the activities and organization of the Hetairia is provided in the following contemporary account by the Rumanian Prince Cantacuzene, the military commander of the pro-Hetairia forces in Moldavia.]

When Prince Alexander Ypsilanti arrived at Odessa, Prince Gheorghe Cantacuzene asked him to explain the origins of the Hetairia and how he became the head of it. Price Ypsilanti gave the following account.

In 1816, certain low-class individuals decided to establish a patriotic society. It was based on Freemasonry, in spite of the religious superstitions and grievous prejudices of the Greeks, particularly those from the Morea, Epirus, and Thessaly. They therefore made some doctrinal changes, called the organization simply Hetairia ("Society"), and sent messengers to all parts to tell new recruits that heading the group would be: as founder, His Majesty the Tsar of Russia; as leader, the Count Capo d'Istria; and as

Translated by Margaret Logun from *Documente privind istoria Romaniei: Rascoala din 1821* (Bucharest: Editura Academiei), IV, 329–35.

members, several individuals from prominent families and certain archbishops. Thus the missionaries, or propagators, of this society had little
trouble in attaining the goals they proposed. It was even easier for them
to create enthusiasm and win converts, as they relied on a "big name"
and on the most righteous of causes. The "big name" was that of Rhegas,
who was admired too late by the Greeks but whose memory remains
strong in their hearts. Rhegas was made the progenitor of all the operations of the Hetairia. His compatriots were aware of the fact that he had
given his life to a society designed to liberate his unfortunate native
country. Some members of that society survived, and when the founders
of the present Hetairia began their underground activities, they did their
best to win them over, as well as to rally to their side the majority of
Greeks, who held Rhegas in high esteem. The earlier Hetairia had not
been regarded by Greek patriots as a means of deliverance from the
oppressive yoke of the Turks. It had not set its sights on the government,
and it bore little resemblance to the present demagogic organization,
which has wrought such havoc in Europe and has alarmed the religious
simplicity of the Greeks; by so doing, it would have failed to achieve its
goal.

As long as there were few initiates, the leaders of the Hetairia collected
money from the new recruits and remained completely unknown to all
the "brothers," and all went according to plan. But the number of apostles
swelled enormously. Among them were some true patriots, who considered
that such a society, were it ably led by a select few, could bring about a
change for the better in the destiny of Greece. But if the opposite were
true, if the Hetairia was only the creation of certain opportunists (as the
unfortunate events that followed proved it to be), and if its existence became known to the Porte, it could only spell ruin for the Greeks.

The brothers began to follow the progress of the Hetairia and sent several persons to Russia to find out the true purpose of the organization;
thereafter, a certain distrust appeared to spread among the proselytes.
Souliote deputies and representatives from different parts of Greece began
to arrive in Russia, striving, on some pretext, to see the Count Capo
d'Istria and to reassure themselves that Greece could rely on the protection of Russia. The leaders of the Hetairia, perceiving too late their inability to control matters, risking an eventual unmasking, and forced to
give an account of their conduct, of monies they had spent, and of mur-
ders they had committed in the name of that "venerable authority"
(which the Greeks supposed were those distinguished Greeks heretofore
mentioned), decided to entrust the supreme power of the Hetairia to a
man who, by virtue of his rank and privileged status, could deceive those
intent on uncovering the roots of the society; by making use of such a
personage, they could deceive the brothers and step aside themselves,
thus placing all responsibility on the one person of their choice. They
therefore sent to St. Petersburg one of their fellow members, Xanthos, a
merchant from Ismail, to get the Count Capo d'Istria to declare himself
the representative of the leaders of the Hetairia and of the nation, in
order to secure full authority for the society. Prince Alexander Ypsilanti

had indicated that the Count would decline this title, being a Minister of the Russian Imperial Majesty and therefore unable to accept without compromising him. Xanthos therefore addressed himself directly to Ypsilanti, saying that in view of the fact that the membership of the Hetairia had increased enormously and the enthusiasm and desire to get rid of the Turkish yoke had inflamed the hearts of all Greeks, an outbreak would be impossible to stop and that unless Ypsilanti consented to become the representative of the society and of the nation, the latter, having no leader, would end up as the victim of internal discord and of the Turks. Ypsilanti had therefore been called upon, in the name of those members of the Hetairia who could bestow full authority upon him, to become the head of this society in order to save the homeland from inevitable doom. Prince Alexander Ypsilanti did not want to accept without the consent of His Imperial Majesty [of Russia]. It was not until receiving this consent, and after having received instructions from the advisers of Count Capo d'Istria, that he accepted the title Representative of the Nation. Thus endowed with full authority, he went to Odessa to act accordingly.

This is how the Hetairia was envisaged in the formative stages. Let us say something about the effect that this must have had on the Greek nation. It was led to believe: (1) that Prince Ypsilanti became head of this enterprise with the consent of His Imperial Majesty of Russia; (2) that this was through the delegation of the supreme authority to him by the leaders of the Hetairia (assuming they were the distinguished persons already mentioned) and the invitation of all the "notables" from Morea, the Islands, and Thessaly, and the capitans of Epirus; (3) that there were already more than 80,000 Hetairists and Greeks armed and ready to declare themselves for revolution; (4) that Prince Brancoveanu and several Wallachian boyars sought the protection of Prince Ypsilanti, the representative of the Hetairia, to reclaim their ancient rights; (5) that the revolution of Tudor Vladimirescu in Wallachia was brought about on the orders and under the direction of the Hetairia; (6) that there were large sums of money in the coffers at Constantinople and Smyrna; (7) that once the signal was given, all the brothers would unite, each putting a little of his wealth into the national coffers; (8) that a large supply of arms—cannons, sabers, and ammunition—had already been acquired; (9) that as soon as the Greeks declared themselves, Russian troops would cross the border and come to their aid.

The plan of Prince Ypsilanti had been to embark at Odessa and at Kishinev for the Morea, where all operations would be started. But the evidence he received led him to abandon this plan. The false notions that the aspostles of the Hetairia had conveyed to him—the repeated assurances that Bulgaria and Serbia were ready to take up arms, and letters from the ephors of Constantinople urging him to start his move from Moldo-Wallachia—affected his decision. Unfortunately, he revealed his plans too soon to the enemy.

In view of everything that has been said, it should be apparent that the homeland did not take any part in the planning being done for it. Individuals with ulterior motives, having no aim or purpose other than to make a fortune at the expense of those they duped, and a Greece unaware and uninformed of the events, lacking resources and the arms necessary to stage a coup, awakening abruptly to the sound of her sons being massacred—that is what we have seen! If she took up arms, it was only in her own defense. Threatened by a terrible enemy, she was inspired by only one feeling—that of self-preservation—and it is most unfair to accuse her of deliberately provoking an enemy she had much reason to fear.

The Greek Revolution was accidental; the nation did not intend to take up arms against the Turks, knowing full well their strength. Far from trying to conceal the difficulties of such an undertaking, she knew that it was not in her power to succeed alone, and that the slightest step in the wrong direction could send her to her doom. A few individuals established the Hetairia—was it for the good of the homeland or for opportunistic reasons of their own? What followed gave us the answer! The word had been passed that all the primates of Greece and more than 80,000 men belonged to the Hetairia, whereas it was only after the admittance of Prince Ypsilanti that a large number of brothers were admitted in Morea, in the Islands, in Epirus, in Thessaly, and even in Russia.

We can further see that a large number of Greek villages are entirely ignorant of the purpose and results of this undertaking and, moreover, do not understand the fighting and what brought about the present crisis in Greece; if they do take up arms, it is solely to defend their lives, their wives, and their children against the Turks, who indiscriminately slaughter every member of the Greek nation. Hence the lack of unity, of submission, and of administrative principles, and the resulting anarchy. Hence each sector or district will rise up in it own defense, and not for common cause (not having heard of the Hetairia); moreover, it will be self-directed and will not wish to submit to anyone. It is only too evident that the revolution was not national by definition, but that the fatal consequences and the sphere of agitation into which it was thrown made it into a patriotic war. However, one cannot hide from the fact that the bitter memory of so many centuries of slavery, the hideous tyranny of the Turks, and the unsurmountable oppression inflicted upon the unfortunate Greeks by all administrative branches played their part, too.

We also see that the makers of this crisis were not very much concerned with strategy and tactics. Had the Turks not been obliged to focus all their attention on Moldo-Wallachia, in the belief that the coup would come out of Russia, and had they, instead of reddening the dagger of vengeance with the blood of the unfortunate inhabitants of Constantinople, dispatched some forces to the Peloponnesus, as they did to Greece (for the majority of the Greeks—all of them, in fact—were, as we have seen, very ignorant of what was going on and lacked the arms and munitions necessary for their defense)—what then would have happened to the leaders of the Hetairia who claimed that there were 80,000 Hetairists ready for anything?

Even more impressive proof of the incompetence of the instigators of the Hetairia can be found. When, by necessity, the war became a national one, all active branches of the leadership, unable to exercise further influence without incriminating the guilty ones, were rendered powerless, and now that their influence is at a low ebb, they seek to persecute those who can unmask their deceitful conduct.

The Greek crisis cannot be regarded as either a national revolution or a voluntary insurrection, for a society consisting of a few individuals does not make a nation. The nation, rightly said, only defended herself. But at this stage, the Greeks can no longer depend upon the Turks, since they have taken up arms against them. Even if Europe remains indifferent to this struggle, even if the Greeks are denied permission to receive arms and munitions from the Continent, they will die to the last man rather than fall again under the [Turkish] yoke, which has become even heavier for them, and this unhappy nation will be obliterated. What guarantee do they have for the future? Will they be able to ward off the vengeance of such a barbaric enemy? Soon, on various pretexts, the heads of the surviving leaders will fall—the lords, the principal merchants, learned men, and even the bishops—and there will be left only the lower classes; terrorism will result in slavery, which will spread throughout the vast empire. Where will the fury of a fanatical people against the children of Christ end? Spreading its destructive hand over religion, it will deny to our unfortunate descendants the faith of their fathers. One is surprised at those who are unaware of the influence a despotic government can exercise on a nation when its weapon is ignorance and its guide, fanaticism.

Even if the governments of Europe were to mediate in this crisis—not to save the Greeks but to return them to servitude—what assurance could they give regarding their future existence? One could argue that if the Turks do not strictly observe the articles of the convention, the whole of Europe will side with the Greeks. But once the Greeks lay down their arms, the Turks, delivered from the perilous situation in which they find themselves, can if they wish consolidate their power, and despite the assurances of Europe will further abuse the Greeks; the nation will be annihilated before the governments of the Continent can send aid. One may contend that the Turks will suffer for this. But of what use will vengeance be to a people who no longer exist?

Thus this Christian nation faces its doom, should the governments of Europe regard this involuntary and unforseen crisis as a revolution and suppress it in the name of international well-being and tranquility. For it is evident that had the Porte, instead of indiscriminately slaughtering the people, publicly disgracing the Father of the Church and the Clergy, prostituting and selling the wives and daughters of innocents, and desecrating the saints at the altar, conducted itself with moderation and prudence, the Hetairia, because of its poor organization, would never have achieved its goal; or better said, it would appear that the Hetairia had no purpose, for it neither thought of nor took the steps necessary to guarantee anything, and the national war need not have taken place. Now that the Christian religion has been forced to yield to that of Muhammad, the Greeks can no longer lay down their arms but are willing to risk everything in the hope of a brighter future.

16

THOURIOS: WAR HYMN

RHEGAS PHERRAIOS

[Many Greek intellectuals—who were perhaps even less perceptive than the Hetairia of the differences between the bourgeois West and the Ottoman East—were carried away by the nationalistic fervor generated by the French Revolution. Of the three major poets on the eve of the Greek War of Independence—Athanasius Christopoulos, John Velaras, and Rhegas Pherraios—Rhegas Pherraios would certainly be ranked third. But his great enthusiasm and, particularly, the widespread popularity of his "Thourios" ("War Hymn") secured him first place in the feelings of his countrymen. The spirit of the French Revolution and of Greek nationalism fills his verses.]

How long, brave men, shall we live in the straits,
Alone, like lions, on the crags of mountain ranges?
How long shall we live in caves, see bushes,
And flee from the world because of our bitter enslavement?
How long shall we leave our brothers, fatherland, and parents,
Our friends, our children, and all our relatives?
Better an hour of free life,
Than forty years of slavery and imprisonment.
What does it profit you to live and be enslaved?
Think how they sear you each hour in the fire.
Even if you become a dragoman, a vizier, an effendi,
The tyrant unjustly tries to destroy you.
You work all day at whatever he tells you,
Yet he still tries to drain your blood.
Soutsos, Mourouzis, Petrakis, Skanabis,

Excerpts translated by Byron C. P. Tsangadas from the original Greek text contained in Ap. Dascalakis, *Les oeuvres de Rhigas Velestinlis* (Paris [n.p.], 1937), pp. 63–71.

139

Gikas, and Mavrogenis* are mirrors for you to see.
Brave captains, priests, laymen,
Were unjustly killed, with an unjust sword.
And countless others, including Turks and Greeks,
Who lose life and wealth, without reason.
Come now with fervor at this time
To take the oath on the cross,
To choose able, patriotic men
Who can give us advice about everything.
The law should be the first and only guide,
And only one should become the leader of our country.
Because anarchy is similar to slavery,
And to live like wild animals is a harsher fire.
Then with hands raised to the heavens
Let us say this to God from our hearts:
"O king of the world! I swear to Thee,
Never to agree with the tyrant's opinion,
Neither to be a slave for him, nor to be beguiled by him,
Nor to yield to his promises.
As long as I live in this world, my sole and steadfast aim
Will be to make him vanish.
Faithful to my country, I will break the yoke,
Ever standing at my leader's side.
And if I break my oath, may lightning strike
And burn me till I vanish like smoke."
In East and West, and North and South,
All must be of one heart for our country
In the faith of each, freedom shall live,
To the glories of warfare we must run together.
Bulgarians and Albanians, Armenians and Greeks,
Negroes and Whites, with one common ardor,
Use our swords for liberty,
So that it will be heard everywhere, that we are courageous.

.   .   .   .

That way, brothers, together we will seize
Arms and liberate ourselves from bitter slavery.
To butcher the animals who keep us in bondage,
And who tyrannize both Christians and Turks.
The cross shall shine from land to sea,
And the enemy will bow to justice.
The world will be saved from this terrible wound,
And we will live in freedom, as brothers in the world.

* The names of famous Phanariote families, whose members were Princes of the Danubian Principalities; they were known for their tyranny over the Greeks of those lands.—ED.

17

SUPPLEX LIBELLUS VALACHORUM

[The Supplex Libellus Valachorum, the Rumanian "bill of rights," was submitted to Emperor Leopold II in 1791. Inspired by the reforms of Joseph II rather than by French revolutionary ideology, the petition reflects the general lack of awareness of the Revolution that characterized much of the Habsburg Empire prior to the Reign of Terror in France. Thus, with respect to Transylvania (and, as we shall see in the following selection, Bohemia), the validity of Iorga's thesis may be questioned.]

The supreme purpose and best intention of Your Majesty, in the government of this empire, is that human rights as well as the rights of citizens must be extended equally to all members of society, who support it through the sacrifices of their blood, sweat, and tears, and that no sector of the citizenry may deprive others of their rights through oppression. That is why the Rumanian nation of the Great Principality of Transylvania makes a public request before the throne of Your Majesty, urgently beseeching that you give back to her those ancient rights which belong essentially to each and every citizen and of which she was stripped in the last century, for no just cause, by the wickedness of the men at that time (as we shall see later).

The Rumanian nation is the most ancient of the Transylvanian nations, as she has her origins in the Roman colonies established in Dacia by Emperor Trajan at the beginning of the second century A.D., when a large number of soldiers settled there for the purpose of securing the province.

The successors of the Emperor Trajan kept Dacia in their possession for several centuries. During their reign, and particularly in the fourth century, the Christian faith was spread throughout the province, according to the rite of the Eastern Church, thanks to the help of the bishops

Translated by Margaret Logun from George Moroianu, *Les luttes des roumains transylvains pour la liberté, et l'opinion européene* (Paris: Gamber, 1933), pp. 62–66.

141

Prothogene, Gaudentzius, Nichita, and Theotim, as the universal history of the Church tells us.

Meanwhile, and even before the second century A.D., barbarian peoples were threatening this rich Roman province; in certain areas, they succeeded for a while, although they were never able to erase Roman names and domination. For it is certain that in the fourth century several fortified Eastern cities, particularly on the banks of the Danube, were subject to Roman emperors and that the province was inhabited by so many Romans that in the seventh century, after throwing off the yoke of the intruders, they founded a state of their own. Verily, it was this area of Dacia that we today call Transylvania.

The Rumanian inhabitants, upon ridding themselves of the domination of other races, were subject to appointed princes chosen from their own nation, until the arrival of the Magyars. As proof of the domination by foreign peoples who have invaded Dacia, we have kept until this day the appellation Vlachs, or Wallachs, which the Slavic people use for all Rumanians, Italians, or Latins; and, as attested by the historians Lucius Dalmata and Cromur Polonus, this appellation has been used for a very long time with respect to the Rumanian inhabitants of Dacia.

According to the ancient Hungarian chronicler, the Anonymous Notary of King Bela, their absolute ruler was their own Duke Gelu. But in the struggle to defend his country against the Magyars, he was unfortunate enough to lose both his crown and his life. After this misfortune befell their prince, the Rumanian residents of the province, known as Vlachs, no longer opposed the Magyars but, on the contrary, when they saw the death of their reigning prince, chose in his place, by a show of hands, Tuhutum, Duke of the Magyars, and by their oath affirmed their loyalty.

That is why the Rumanian nation respectfully approaches the throne of Your Majesty, beseeching and requesting the following:

1. That such hateful and contemptuous terms as "tolerated, "admitted," "not admitted," among the Transylvanian estates, and others like them that have been bestowed, with no right or justice at all, upon the Rumanian nation, like external blemishes, be retired henceforth as unworthy and injurious names. Thus, by the grace of Your Most Imperial Majesty, the revived Rumanian nation must be re-established and allowed to exercise her civil and political rights.

2. That the clergy of this nation loyal to the Eastern Church, regardless of whether they accept fully or not at all the creed and authority of the Roman Catholic Church, as well as the common people, the townspeople, and the villagers, must be considered and treated in the same way and enjoy the same benefits as the clergy, the nobility, and the common people of the Magyar, Szekler, and Saxon nations.

3. That in nominating and electing officials, rightful consideration should be given to Rumanians in accordance with their proportion in the population.

4. That counties, seats, departments, and all those communities in

which Rumanians form the majority, must henceforth carry Rumanian names, and that all the inhabitants of the Great Principality of Transylvania must enjoy, regardless of race or religion, according to their material situation and station in life, the same liberties and privileges and be subject, according to their ability, to the same fiscal obligations.

18

CULTURE AND SOCIETY IN BOHEMIA

ROBERT J. KERNER

[That the political and social attitudes of the Bohemian aristocracy were
conditioned more by the Josephinian experience than by the French is
made clear in the following excerpt from Professor Robert J. Kerner's
classic study, *Bohemia in the Eighteenth Century*.]

Bohemian society in 1790 presented many resemblances to our own times.
There was the same cry of the high cost of living, the "high-hat" question,
painted women, and inflated manners. In a ball in Prague where six hundred people amused themselves in dancing, during the course of the evening only three or four women could be found unpainted, the rest looked
like "painted" masks. The women wore hats which could not go through
the doors, and their choice of colors in dress was as shocking as their taste
in hats.

Society adhered closely to the lines laid down by the political Estates
and congregated in exclusive balls and in coffee and wine houses. The
upper Estates, namely the great magnates, the counts, and a few of the
barons, moved in the highest society, whose chief sin was extravagance in
all conceivable lines and especially in the breeding of horses. There were
some who maintained more than forty horses and were willing to ruin
themselves to secure more. As a result, Prague was overfilled with equip-
ages, which made the night hideous as they rattled over the cobblestones
of its hilly streets. Militarism held the upper Estates entirely in its grasp.
To be an officer in the army admitted one into the highest society and
made possible such unthinkable miracles as that "the son of a butcher
could lead a countess under his arm." The feeling of caste was so strong
that only militarism could overcome it. The pride and the vanity of the
Bohemian noble was as far-famed as his irreligiousness, which he took
as a sign of freedom from bigotry. To show this, he would talk long and

Reprinted, by permission, from Robert J. Kerner, *Bohemia in the Eighteenth Century*
(New York: Macmillan, 1932), pp. 77–80.

loud. As a matter of fact, no one could be more bigoted than he nor more responsible for his subjection to the usurer, than he himself. The lower nobility, a few barons, the knights, and the higher state officials composed the second grade of society. The third consisted of the petty officials, the educated elite, both scholarly and professional, and the better merchants. The final and lowest grade consisted of the rest of the urban and all of the agrarian population, although a real peasant was always a little lord in miniature in his miscroscopic domain. All loved to eat well and to drink their fill, and extravagance was as much in evidence with the insignificant peasant or tradesman as it was with the prince.

In such a society everyone, whether German or Czech, who did something for Bohemia was a "patriot." He might build a theater, found a library, write a book about the country's glorious past or in defense of its ancient rights, or praise it with pen or brush. German domination was complete and unquestioned, therefore it was liberal. Herein also lies the explanation of the fact that the Germanization of the eighteenth century was not of the kind that the nineteenth century was to know. German was spoken poorly even by the higher society, but Czech was not banished and under Leopold II it was heard very audibly in the antechambers during the coronation ceremonies. Joseph II had spoken Czech poorly, but Leopold II had studied it with diligence and had no hostility toward it. The theater which Governor Nostic built in Prague presented Italian operas, for Prague, above other European cities, had an especial taste for music, and the Czechs are a people noted for musical talent. The Casino in the Palace of the Thuns was a happy meeting place for the nobles. Here, in the winter of 1786, a company of actors played several dramas in Czech, *"in der nationalen Sprache,"* and thereafter in this theater and in others, Czech plays were on the billboards, and theaters were for once really full and became profitable investments. The mass of the population was Czech, and the mere business acumen of the theater promoters led them to see that it was "better for the people to express themselves freely in their own language than stiffly in another." One contemporary remarked, "I know no land where a national drama would be easier to present and where it would find a higher support." That was saying much for 1787, just at the time when Joseph II had about completed the official Germanization of Bohemia. These two forces, the Bohemian revival and autocratic Germanization, met in the last years of the reign of Joseph II, and in the reaction the revival triumphed.

Political discussion busied itself with the terrific slaughter caused by the Turkish war, the fall of the Bastille, the serail of the Turks, and the like. Stories of Turkish harems outnumbered disputes over the Bohemian Constitution. The age was too material, too practical to think of abstract political theories; it was indeed too lazy to think at all. Nevertheless Voigt wrote in the spirit of Montesquieu about law and the Bohemian Constitution, and Pubička and Dobner and Dobrovsky* and a group of others

* These men and their works were characteristic of the Bohemian cultural renaissance of the eighteenth century, with its definite national-historical orientation.—ED.

were busy composing the history of Bohemia or of its literature or trying to show in more ways than one that the Czech nation, although it had fallen low, was a nation with a proud historic past. They were furnishing the fuel to a future generation, which would catch fire from a Slavophile Russia and a romanticist Germany.

In cultured circles, the French Encyclopedia was a prize preserved and used with great care. A native thought it one of the proudest moments of his life to be able to show some intimate friend a Voltaire or a Rousseau or a Hussite Bible which had escaped the Jesuits or the censors. Czechs often wrote in German rather than in Czech, because they were sure to get a reading public, which after all was not small. Prague had two newspapers, bi-weeklies, a German and a Czech. Both were typical of the journalism of the day. As they existed only on the grant of a government license, patriots were often constrained to write in the manner of Montesquieu in the *Lettres Persanes* or of Havlíček, the nineteenth-century journalist, in his letters about Ireland. Nevertheless it may be truthfully asserted that many of the scribblers of that day deserved even a stricter censorship than Joseph II provided. That hardly applies, however, to the average Bohemian, who was ready to honor a Maria Theresa, to worship a Joseph II, and to respect a Leopold II.

In the country, the role of justice of the peace was a source of inspiration to the peasants. His "learning" and often his personality caused him to be much admired, and he was generally the natural leader of peasant revolts. Many of them were loyal patriots, like [Frantisek] Vavak, whose memoirs are the best individual source for the social life of the Bohemian peasant in the eighteenth century. Social unrest, when it occurred, was usually caused by famines, the result of bad harvests. It is clear, however, from the evidence that has been handed down to us, that except for several years, such as 1770, 1771, 1775, and 1780, the peasants lived quietly and even in a rude splendor. Vavak's memoirs show that in spite of the terrible harvest of "King Robot," merriment and even comfort were not lacking. The Bohemian peasant was a lord in comparison to the average Polish or Hungarian peasant, and if he was restless it was rather because he was better off than anything else. In years when famine or drought struck Bohemia, misery was quickly apparent. Bohemia's population grew so very rapidly that production of grains did not keep up with consumption, and the government had not as yet carried through any definite plan for the storage of grains nor perfected a complete system of transportation and of good roads.

It was a strange coincidence that, together with [a] political crisis, the year 1790 witnessed a great drought and a partial famine. This must be kept in mind when making an estimate of the conditions under which Leopold II came to the throne.

19

CATECHISM OF THE SECRET SOCIETY
OF REFORMERS IN HUNGARY

[Not all the nations of the Habsburg Empire displayed the same lack of comprehension of the French revolutionary message as did the Rumanians and the Bohemians. In the 1790's, the majority of the Hungarian aristocracy was still reacting to Josephinism by seeking restoration of its privileges on the basis of traditional contractual obligations and through traditional channels of redress. But there was also a handful of racial members of the lesser nobility who sought to bring about a revolutionary change in the imperial order. The so-called Secret Society of Reformers of Hungary was influenced by Jacobin ideology and practice. The most interesting feature of the Society's catechism, written by the Hungarian Jacobin Martinovics, was its adaptation of French revolutionary ideology to the needs and interests of a single class and its rejection of "bourgeois democratic" principles. Although the ideas and program of the Reformers were not tested during the period of the French Revolution, they constituted the prototype for the revolutionary manifestation in Hungary in the days of Louis Kossuth, fifty years later.]

CHAPTER I

OF THE PERNICIOUS RULE OF THE HOUSE OF AUSTRIA
OVER THE HUNGARIAN PEOPLE

Question: Is the Hungarian nation happier under the Austrian scepter than formerly under its own kings?

Answer: No. The Hungarians were indeed divided under their kings, which gave rise to factions, but they preserved their strength and energy of mind, the freedom of the nobility flourished intact, and the Hungarian

---

Reprinted, by permission, from R. R. Palmer and Peter Kenez, "Two Documents of the Hungarian Revolutionary Movement of 1794," *Journal of Central European Affairs,* XX, No. 4 (January, 1961), 426–33.

nation remained independent in the manner of all the leading nations of Europe. Under the Austrian scepter the Hungarian militia, which formerly constituted the national strength, is in the hands of the Germans; the Hungarian nobility has wholly lost its vitality, sells its patriotism to the Cabinet of Vienna in exchange for vain titles, and has retained the liberty of the nobleman in name only.

Q. In what way is the Hungarian nobility sold to the Cabinet of Vienna?

A. Since the counties, outside the Diet, dare no more than to submit petitions and humble representations to the King, the Cabinet of Vienna neglects to convoke the Diet and leaves the nation to be duped by its own factions. Maria Theresa refrained for many years from holding elections in the kingdom. Joseph avoided them. Leopold evaded them by his Machiavellianism and corruption. Francis, ignorant and incapable of ruling, has solemnly promised, under instigation of his ministers, that elections shall never be held. This assertion is secret, but quite true.

Q. What means does the court of Vienna employ to put down the patriotic representatives of the countries?

A. Commissions of inquiry, the army, and penalties. Joseph used his army against the landed nobility and the counties. Leopold and Francis appoint commissioners to search out the authors of patriotic representations, that they may be punished.

Q. How does the Cabinet of Vienna maintain this slavery of the Hungarians?

A. It keeps Hungarians away from the ministry and council, lest they oppose the enslavement of Hungary. All princes of Austria, except Joseph, in getting Hungarians to sell their freedom have made use of Hungarian prelates, who by their celibacy have ceased to be citizens of their country, and who owe their Church preferments to these Austrian rulers. The magnates of Hungary, created by Austria, are induced to live in Vienna, where they slowly develop habits of fawning on the court, and where German women and Viennese courtesans extinguish all love of country in them. Thus influenced by the court of Vienna, the magnates hold the highest dignities and sell their country, elude its laws, and spend their Hungarian revenues in Vienna. Since these magnates began to be corrupted by the court of Vienna, the Hungarians have been unable to raise another Rakoczy, or Tokoly, or Bercsenyi. So love of country remains only in name.

Q. What evil did the house of Austria bring upon Hungary by the Seven Years War with Prussia?

A. Five hundred thousand Hungarians fell in this war. Subsidies drawn from Hungary by the cabinet of Vienna reached almost 400,000 florins during this war. Hence Hungary suffered depopulation and loss of its substance.

Q. Did Hungarian soldiers gain any rewards after the war?

A. None at all. Nadasdy, disgraced, had to return to Croatia, because he had spoken out with Hungarian firmness against the drunkenness of Duke Charles of Lorraine and his ignorance in military matters.

Hungarian troops were always in places of greatest danger, the first to be exposed to the enemy, and yet were despised by the German Austrians. The only military leader to benefit was Hadik, who received the domain of Futak as a royal gift and so was made into the slave of the Cabinet and of the Austrians.

Q. How is the Hungarian soldier treated by the court of Vienna today?

A. Most ungratefully. As in the past, Germans and Italians now obtain Hungarian commands, together with most other military ranks, while the Hungarian officer is put off.

Q. Why does the nefarious court do this?

A. Because it is afraid that a homogeneous Hungarian army, made up of Hungarians only, would punish its crimes against the Hungarian people.

Q. Why did Maria Theresa introduce German normal schools in Hungary?

A. Because she wished to open the way to absolute despotism for Joseph. She hoped that the Hungarian nation would give up its language and in adopting the corrupted language of Austria would also accept the manners and despotism of Vienna to the ruin of Hungarian liberty.

Q. Why did Joseph wish to elevate the common people under the pretext of humanity?

A. Because he wished thoroughly to destroy the nobility and its resistance.

Q. Can Joseph be regarded as a defender of humanity in his relation to the Hungarians?

A. No. A king, who should work for the happiness of all, does wrong if he opposes one class on the plea of elevating another; for with one class depressed he wishes to subjugate the other, in order to put both beneath his yoke, like beasts. Even the best actions of a king, if they have a bad end, are evil.

Q. Why does the Cabinet of Vienna always have a German, not a Hungarian, as its ambassador to Constantinople?

A. Because it fears that a Hungarian would enter into an alliance with the Turks for the good of his own people and so shake off the heavy Austrian yoke.

Q. Why does that Cabinet so readily declare war on the Turks?

A. Because the Hungarian nation has no representative at Constantinople who might prevent this evil accord with the laws of his own country.

Q. Did Leopold give satisfaction to the Hungarian nation in sending Eszterházy to Sistova to make peace with the Turks?

A. Obviously not. The ambassador, a German [Austrian], Herbert, received the real instructions for negotiating with the Turks, while Eszterházy was only allowed to show ostentatious pomp, in contempt for Hungary, at the Congress. By such action the Machiavellian Leopold shamefully prostituted the Hungarians before Europe.

Q. Of what advantage to Hungary was the last war with Turkey?

A.   None. It did her harm. A hundred thousand Hungarians and eighty millions in Hungarian subsidies disappeared in the war.

Q.   Is it true, as alleged by the Viennese Germans against the Hungarians, that the court of Vienna was forced by tumults in Hungary to make peace with the Turks?

A.   It is altogether false, The court of Vienna made a secret agreement at Reichenbach and Pillnitz for the partitioning of Poland, and for the subjugation and extermination of the French with the aid of the other kings. Hence peace was made with the Turks, and the fruits of the Turkish war, which might have been to the advantage of the Hungarians, were brought to nothing.

Q.   Is it true, as asserted by Francis in the coronation Diet, that the French had declared war on him against his will?

A.   It is altogether false. The Treaty of Pillnitz was prior to the French declaration of war. In this treaty it had been concluded that the allied kings should take military action against the French under the leadership of Vienna, and therefore a large army, beyond all necessity, was being sent into Belgium. So, Hungarians, you may see the clumsy imposture and gross untruth of Francis!

Q.   What gain can the Hungarian nation expect from the war with France?

A.   None, only the utmost evil. For if the French should triumph, nobility perishes in Europe, and consequently in Hungary. Already, 135,000 Hungarians have gone off to this war, and 56 million florins, in cash and in kind, have been taken out of the kingdom. Hungarian soldiers in the war against France are bringing home democratic principles, which undermine the nobility. The absence of soldiers from the kingdom is causing great scarcity of money, and the kingdom is exposed to Turkish incursions. The export of grain to France is forbidden.

Q.   Are the laws of the country being violated during the war with France?

A.   Certainly. The ingenious way of taking revenues out of Hungary without [consent of] the Diet is a true evasion of the laws of the country, which Hungarian laws prohibit. This project was conceived by the primate of the kingdom, and by the [chief] justice and chancellor.

Q.   What penalty do they deserve for this?

A.   Death. Whoever violates the law and deceives a whole nation is a traitor to his country and deserves the penalty of death.

Q.   How has King Francis so far deceived the Hungarian nation?

A.   He interferes with the freedom of the press assured by the laws. He secretly threatens the county meetings, which defend this freedom according to law. When his [Hungarian] minions return from the French war, he wishes (as he himself declared despotically in a certain audience given to his agent Bujanovics) to cut off their heads, for fear that they might later resist or oppose him.

Q.   Why did King Francis take the oath according to Hungarian laws?

A. So that, once crowned and the oath taken, he might violate the laws of the country with impunity and treat the Hungarian nation as an ignoble colony.

Q. Would Hungary in this way be a true colony of the court of Vienna?

A. Yes. (1) The King of Hungary does not dream of residing in Hungary, just as the kings of England, Spain, and Portugal and the stadholder of Holland have no desire to reside in their colonies. (2) As kings levy intolerable taxes on goods of the colonies belonging to them, so the Cabinet of Vienna burdens all Hungarian products with a tax of almost 50 per cent. (3) As Mexican gold is continuously and freely taken out by the Spaniards, so are gold, silver, copper, and iron carried from Hungary to Vienna. On some of our coins the Cabinet of Vienna deigns to put the phrase "Protectress of Hungary," but the protectress counsels only ruin under the German [Viennese] Cabinet.

Q. Has the recent lot of the Poles under the Russians and Prussians been more shameful than that of the Hungarians under the Austrians?

A. It is the same. As the Russians and Prussians are foreign people in relation to the Poles, so are the Austrians in relation to the Hungarians.

Q. What then must be done by the Hungarians to liberate themselves from political nullity and from the Austrian yoke?

A. Like the Poles, they should raise up a holy insurrection, wrest the royal dynasty from the hands of Francis, and introduce a republic and good laws by which both nobles and non-nobles might be happy.

Q. Is the Hungarian people under any obligation to recognize the archducal family of Austria as legitimate?

A. No. Because the unjust and usurping Joseph broke the line of succession. Because the nation made no solemn contract with Leopold, and never accepted him as the first of a new line. Hence his son Francis cannot be the true heir to the kingdom. Even if he were, he has lost the right by breaking and violating the laws and is a true usurper of the Hungarian scepter and tyrant over the people.

Q. Among what nations should Hungary be placed, in view of its political situation?

A. Among the Wallachians [or Vlachs] and Moldavians. For the Poles are a hundred years ahead of the Hungarians in civilization [*cultura ingenii*]. Recently the Sardinians threw off the yoke of Piedmont, but Hungary still bears its yoke.

Q. Can Hungary subsist alone?

A. Very well. Nine million people living on the best of soil could, by introducing a proper order, resist Turks and Germans.

Q. In that case, should Francis be allowed to remain on the throne, if he consented to live in the kingdom and rule well?

A. Not even in that case, because royal promises are always false. On the first occasion, every king breaks his word and deceives his people without shame, and, if he can, puts them under the yoke without mercy. The system of a single king is arbitrary and leads to tyranny. Infants need a nurse, children a father, orphans a guardian, but only stupid nations need a king. Intelligence is not lacking to the Hungarians, if only the national educational institutions can be improved. A good king is a useless animal for the mass of the nation, consuming its wealth, perverting its moral character, fomenting misery for the people. A perfidious king is a traitor to his country and should be put to death. King Francis in his stupidity is guided by other men's lies; he is unfit to govern and is himself to be put rather under perpetual tutelage. Why then should he be allowed to rule, when by his lack of judgment and discretion he should be perpetually ruled himself?

CHAPTER II

ON THE POLITICAL REFORM OF HUNGARY

Q. In what way, then, should the Hungarians improve their political lot, and shake off the yoke of the infamous Cabinet of Vienna?

A. By adopting a new and better form of government, more suited to the genius of the nation.

Q. What should this consist in?

A. Let the Hungarian nation take back the supreme power from the King, and declare the country a free and independent republic.

Q. What should be the form of this republic?

A. Since under the name of the Hungarian nation are comprised all the peoples who inhabit the provinces belonging to Hungary and who are in effect different nations, each nation ought to constitute a province by itself, have its own particular constitution, and be united by a close bond with the others. That is, the Hungarian republic should be federal; each nation freely enjoying its own language, its own manners and customs, and its own freedom of religion. It is enough for the welfare of the republic if each nation is joined in a union with every other.

Q. What should be the basis of the republican union?

A. There are two kinds of security in any society: external and internal. The former guards against usurpation and injury by outside powers, the latter restrains domestic tumults against public order. All the Hungarian provinces should constitute a unified indivisible republic so far as external security is concerned, but a confederated republic in matters of internal security.

Q. How should the Hungarian republic be organized according to these mixed principles?

A. (1) Let the Hungarians adopt a twofold classification of citizens. Let one class contain the greater and lesser nobility, with no distinction between magnates and [other] nobles. Let the second class include all non-nobles, both urban and rural. (2) Since the population of the Hungarian provinces is about 9 million, the deputies or representatives in a general congress may number 248, of whom half, or 124, should be elected from among the nobles, the other half from among non-nobles. (3)

From 30,000 to 40,000 non-nobles shall elect one representative. For the nobles, however, as many as have, taken together, annual incomes from real and personal property of 100,000 to 130,000 florins shall combine to elect one deputy. Alternately, for periods of a fortnight, a noble or non-noble shall be chosen to preside. Special committees, e.g., for public safety, public instruction, etc., should have an equal number of representatives from each class of citizens. Each congress should last one year, except that the first or convention-congress should sit until the reform is completed. Let the convention-congress then form a constitution in which two chambers are adopted and the following principles accepted. The entire executive power should depend on the legislative body. Each federated province is to use its own language and be obliged to make its provincial constitution consistent with the fundamentals of the general constitution. Freedom of religion, thought, and writing should be complete, commerce unrestricted, justice administered gratis to all, the militia purely national, the arts and sciences cultivated.

Q. What will be the difference between the noble and the non-noble?

A. The noble alone will be the proprietor of [rural] land. The cities, formerly called royal, will be called national, and in them even the non-noble will have the right to real property. Non-nobles who are peasants and villagers will be tenants of the landowners and, in accord with the agreements with the landowners, will pay an annual amount either in money, or in kind, or in labor services. Since the noble is the same as the landowner, he should receive his customary revenues either by way of the feudal system or through rents. The noble may also use armorial bearings and will have the first right to command in the cavalry.

Q. What does the noble gain by this reform?

A. Much. For the noble is freed from three tyrants by this reform: the king, the magnates, and the estate of the upper clergy. Moreover, the nobles, since they would be raising the non-nobles to a second chamber and declaring them free from slavery, by being perpetually joined with them and in mutual support would themselves be invincible.

Q. What commerce could a reformed Hungary carry on?

A. A considerable amount, both internal and external. The peoples neighboring on Hungary, poorer than we in many products, would carry on trade and bring money into the republic. Hungary could most especially develop two ports, at Fiume and Zimony; since, after a commercial treaty with the Turks, there could be navigation from Zimony to the Black Sea. The huge forests of Slavonia and Croatia, suited for ship-building at Zimony, would bring great riches to their owners.

Q. But the funds necessary for this reform are lacking in Hungary?

A. Upon abolition of the useless royal dignity, Hungary would receive the royal and crown lands, the Palatine lands, the payments made by nobles to the crown for their mineral lands, the salt revenues, the postal fees, and the income from taxes, lotteries, and lesser sources. If the property of the clergy were added, then by an accurate calculation it is certain that annual revenues of 40 million florins would be available. And

since Hungary has no public debts, it cannot be doubted that these revenue would grow through wise administration and provide for all needs of
the republic, the army, the political offices, etc.

Q.   In that case, would it be necessary to pay any tax or subsidy?

A.   No, since these revenues are sufficient for public needs, except for
an occasional urgent necessity, in which event each man for his own welfare should pay a slight tax.

Q.   The bishops and prelates say that it is dangerous to convert Church
properties to profane use. For if these should be taken for that purpose,
then even the noble properties would be endangered.

A.   That is false. For the nobles are true owners of their goods, because they have obtained them by gifts, inheritance, or purchase, in a
word, by means admitted in the law. The nation on such a question uses
intelligence, observes the rights of humanity, and will never violate property. It is different with the Church's wealth, which the nation long ago
conquered by arms from the Romans and entrusted to King Stephen as
the first representative of the nation. He, in turn, with consent of the
estates, turned over the usufruct to the bishops and other churchmen to
advance the Christian religion. This aim has been achieved, and the
bishops who propagated the Christian religion made sufficient use of this
wealth. The modern ones use it to enrich whores and concubines or their
own relatives, worship God only with the lips, immerse their minds in
worldly arts, and so spend great riches on corruption. Hence the nation
ought to take back from these men both the incomes so perversely ex-
pended and the goods themselves.

Q.   But can the nation convert these goods, destined for spiritual use,
to profane ends?

A.   The nation has always retained these goods by proprietary right,
having only granted, through the king, the usufruct to the prelates. In any
case, it would be a more spiritual end for the nation to use these goods
to relieve poverty, help needy parish priests, and aid or relieve mendicity
than for the prelates to waste them on feasting, on luxury and extravagance, and on concubines and other perverse creatures of their own.

CHAPTER III

ON THE INSURRECTION OF THE HUNGARIANS

Q.   How can the Hungarians accomplish this reform?

A.   By insurrection against the Austrian depotism and against the
magnates and prelates.

Q.   How should this insurrection be arranged?

A.   If the Society of Reformers gains enough strength and understanding from this catechism, and numbers among its members some of the
more influential nobles in each county, then even the non-nobles may
be invited to join, and the whole of this catechism may be revealed to
them. When this is done, two or three neighboring counties should
print and publish an act of insurrection against the house of Austria,

the magnates, and the prelates and invite the other counties to accede to it.

Q. What should the act of insurrection contain?

A. It should list the crimes of the Cabinet of Vienna against Hungary, from Ferdinand to Francis [1526–1794], proclaim the insurrection, and conclude with these words: "To arms, citizens! Let us swear to lose life rather than liberty, to seek death rather than admit dependence on the house of Austria, to endure any extremes before ceasing to uphold the integrity of the Hungarian republic with all our strength."

Q. In this event, what must we do with the Hungarian armed force?

A. That part which is absent will be called home under penalty of being declared in a state of emigration. The rest, which is in the country, will rally to the national standard and take the oath to the nation.

Q. Is this insurrection an easy matter?

A. Very easy. The French have declared that they will defend all regenerated nations that are their friends. The Poles, in their present troubles, will be friendly to us, and it will be agreeable to the Turk to see the House of Austria weakened. Styria can hardly wait for Hungary to throw off the Austrian yoke and will desire admission into a union with Hungary. The only difficulty lies in throwing a few German regiments out of the kingdom.

Q. In that case, what will the Cabinet of Vienna do?

A. It will bewail its fall, but too late, and will return to its original status as an archduchy. For the Bohemians, too, have ideas of separation from the perfidious Austrian Cabinet, which, thus attacked will expiate its inveterate crimes.

To arms, citizens, noble and non-noble! Vindicate the innocent blood of our brothers who have perished in German wars fatal to us! Establish a more sound form of government, that our people at last, at the end of our century, may be blessed with a truly free constitution!

20

MANIFESTO OF THE FIRST PAN-SLAVIC CONGRESS

[By 1848, the message of the French Revolution was understood by all East European intellectuals, aristocrats, and merchants who sought to alter the status quo. Although the reaction against the Metternich system varied in form and intensity in each national group within the Habsburg Empire, the common denominator was nationalism.

The demand for change was voiced in its most moderate form by the intellectuals assembled at the First Pan-Slavic Congress, held in Prague in 1848 under the presidency of the Bohemian historian and national leader Francis Palacky. The Manifesto issued by the Congress made liberal use of French revolutionary slogans but ultimately sought only national equality for the Slavs of the Habsburg Empire. For the first time, however, the concept of the unity of all the Slav peoples of Eastern Europe was invoked. The traditional geographical boundaries separating the Ottoman, Habsburg, and Russian empires were regarded as artificial, if not yet obsolete.]

The Slavic Congress in Prague is something unheard-of, in Europe as well as among the Slavs themselves. For the first time since our appearance in history, we, the scattered members of a great race, have gathered in great numbers from distant lands in order to become reacquainted as brothers and to deliberate our affairs peacefully. We have understood one another not only through our beautiful language, spoken by eighty millions, but also through the consonance of our hearts and the similarity of our spiritual qualities. The truth and sincerity that have guided all our deliberations have persuaded us to make our demands known before God and the world.

The Latin and Germanic peoples, formerly famous in Europe as powerful conquerors, have for millennia guaranteed their independence by their

---

Translated by Max Riedlsperger from I. I. Udalzow, *Aufzeichnungen über die Geschichte des nationalen und politischen Kampfes in Böhme im Jahre* 1848 (Berlin: Rutten & Loening, 1953), pp. 223–26.

swords and have satisfied their lust for power in many ways. Their state-craft, based mainly upon the right of greater strength, gave freedom to the upper classes alone, who ruled with the help of privilege while only imposing duties upon the people. Only recently, owing to the strong influence of public opinion, which like the spirit of God has suddenly spread throughout all lands, has it been possible to break the fetters of feudalism and to return to the individual, everywhere, the eternal and inalienable rights of man.

The Slavs, on the other hand, who in the past loved freedom most fervently when it was least attended by a lust for power and a thirst for conquest, and in whom the longing for independence always hindered the creation of a higher central authority, fell one after another to domination. As a result of a policy that the world had for a long time judged to be appropriate, our noble brothers, the heroic race of the Poles, were also robbed of their state; it appeared that the whole, great Slavic world had fallen forever into slavery and that its compliant subjects did not hesitate to surrender even their capacity for freedom.

But this foolish opinion perished eventually, with the aid of God, Who in this time of intense upheaval speaks to the heart of every man. The spirit finally won. The magic of the old curse is destroyed, the thousand-year-old structure, which was built and defended by raw power, together with cunning and malice, is laid in ruins before our eyes; the fresh spirit of life, which blows over broad meadows and creates new worlds, the free word, and the free deed have finally become truth. Now even the long oppressed Slav lifts his head again, throws off domination, and raises a powerful voice to claim his ancient heritage of freedom. Strong in numbers, still stronger in determination and the newly won brotherly unity of its races, he nevertheless remains faithful to his nature and to the principles of his forefathers; he demands neither domination nor conquest but freedom, for himself as well for others, and he demands that freedom be generally recognized, without exceptions, as the most sacred right of mankind.

We Slavs therefore reject and abhor every domination by mere force that tramples upon these claims; we condemn all privileges and special rights, as well as all political class distinctions; we demand, without exception, equality before the law and equal rights and responsibilities for everyone. Wherever one person among millions is born into oppression, there true freedom is still unknown. Yes, liberty, equality, and fraternity for all who live in the state is our watchword today, as it was a thousand years ago.

It is not only in behalf of the individual within the state that we raise our voices and make known our demands. The nation, with all its intellectual merit, is as sacred to us as are the rights of an individual under natural law. Even if history allows men to develop more fully in some nations than in others, it always shows that the capability of development of those other nations is in no way limited. Nature, which knows neither noble nor ignoble nations, has not called upon any of them to dominate another, nor has it appointed any nation to serve another in attaining

its particular goals. The same right of all to attain the optimum development is a law of God, which no nation may transgress without punishment.
It is a sin, however, when such a law is neither recognized nor, as would
seem proper, observed by the most advanced nations of our times.

That which they have already willingly renounced, namely authority
and guardianship vis-à-vis individual persons, they still claim vis-à-vis
individual nations: They indiscriminately claim the right to dominate in
the name of freedom. Thus, the free Briton refuses to recognize the
Irishman as being of equal birth; thus, the German threatens the Slavic
nations with force if they should refuse to contribute to the political
might of Germany; thus, the Magyar claims for himself the exclusive
right to nationality in Hungary. We Slavs condemn absolutely all such
claims and refuse them the more emphatically, the more unjustifiably
the freedoms are disguised. We remain faithful to our nature; we do not
wish revenge for past injustices, and we extend our hand to all neighboring peoples who are prepared with us to recognize and to protect the
complete equality of all nationalities, without regard to their political
power or their size. Similarly, we attack and abhor that policy by which
nations and peoples are treated as conquests that can be acquired to
one's heart's content, traded and divided without regard to the origin,
language, customs, and preferences of the people or to their natural
ties, their proper *nationality*. The sheer brute force of the sword alone
decides the fate of the conquered, who frequently have not even taken
up the fight and who, generally, are required to provide soldiers and money
for the securing of despotisms or, at best, adulation for the despot.

In the belief that the powerful spiritual stream of today demands
new political forms and that the state must be re-established upon altered
principles, if not within new boundaries, we have suggested to the Austrian
Emperor, under whose constitutional government we, the majority, live,
that he transform his imperial state into a union of equal nations, which
would accommodate these demands no less fully than would a unitary
monarchy.

We see in such a union not only salvation for ourselves but also freedom,
culture, and humanity for all, and we are confident that the nations of
Europe will assist in the realization of this union. In any case, we resolve,
by all available means, to win for our nationality the complete recognition of the same political rights that the German and Hungarian peoples
already enjoy in Austria. In addition, we have confidence in the powerful
support for justice that is found in every truly free heart. The enemies
of our nationality have succeeded in frightening Europe with the specter
of political Pan-Slavism, which allegedly threatens with universal destruction everything that has been gained in the name of freedom, culture, and
humanity. But we now know the magic word that alone can exorcise
this specter and promote freedom, culture, and humanity. We do not want
to conceal that magic word from the people or from ourselves: The word
is justice! Justice for the Slavic peoples in general and for its oppressed
people in particular.

The German boasts that he is superior to the other races and that he is qualified to judge the particular characteristics of other nations fairly. We hope that he won't be caught in a lie when talking about the Slavs. We raise our voices vigorously in behalf of our unfortunate brothers, the Poles, who were robbed of their national identity by insidious force. We call upon the governments to rectify this curse and these old onerous and hereditary sins in their administrative policy, and we trust in the compassion of all Europe. We further protest against the arbitrary division of a country, especially as this applies today in Posen. We expect the Prussian and Saxon governments to desist from pursuing their systematic denationalization of the Slavs in Lausitz, Posen, and East and West Prussia. We demand that the Hungarian Ministry abolish without delay the use of inhuman and coercive means toward the Slavic races in Hungary, namely, the Serbs, Croats, Slovaks, and Ruthenians, and that they promptly be completely assured of their national rights. Finally, we hope that the inconsiderate policies of the Porte will no longer hinder our Slavic brothers in Turkey from strongly claiming their nationality and developing it in a natural way. If, therefore, we formally express our opposition to such despicable deeds, we do so in the confidence that we are working for the good of freedom. Freedom makes the peoples who hitherto have ruled more just and makes them understand that injustice and arrogance bring disgrace not to those who must endure it but to those who act in such a manner.

As the youngest, but in no way the weakest, we enter again into the political arena of Europe and suggest that we summon a *peoples' congress* of all European nations for the purpose of advising on international questions. We are convinced that free peoples can agree more easily than paid diplomats. May this suggestion be considered, lest the reactionary policy of individual courts again provoke the anger and hatred of nations to the point where they will destroy one another.

In the name of the liberty, equality, and fraternity of all peoples!

21

DECLARATION OF INDEPENDENCE BY THE HUNGARIAN NATION

["Liberty, Equality, Fraternity" did not have the same meaning for the Hungarians that it had for the Slavs in 1848. Under the leadership of Louis Kossuth, the Hungarian aristocratic "nation" sought to attain political independence for Hungary on the basis of principles enunciated by the Secret Society of Reformers half a century earlier. The radical Declaration of Independence by the Hungarian Nation was adopted by the Hungarian Diet in April, 1849, in response to Austrian measures designed to prevent the assertion of Hungarian separatism and the attainment of Kossuth's revolutionary goal. The Declaration, however, failed to realize the dream of the revolutionaries: an independent Hungarian Republic. Two months after the Declaration, in June, 1849, military intervention by Russia cut short the life of the Republic and forced Kossuth into exile. It also paved the way for the Austro-Hungarian Compromise of 1867.]

We, the legally constituted representatives of the Hungarian nation assembled in Diet, do by these presents solemnly proclaim, in maintenance of the inalienable natural rights of Hungary, with all its appurtenances and dependencies, to occupy the position of an independent European state; that the house of Lorraine-Habsburg, as perjured in the sight of God and man, has forfeited its right to the Hungarian throne. At the same time, we feel ourselves bound in duty to make known the motives and reasons which have impelled us to this decision, that the civilized world may learn we have not taken this step out of overweening confidence in our own wisdom or out of revolutionary excitement, but that it is an act of the last necessity, adopted to preserve from utter destruction a nation persecuted to the limit of the most enduring patience.

Reprinted from Francis W. Newman (ed.), *Select Speeches of Kossuth* (London: Trübner & Co., 1853), pp. 10–21.

Three hundred years have passed since the Hungarian nation, by free election, placed the house of Austria upon its throne, in accordance with stipulations made on both sides, and ratified by treaty. These three hundred years have been, for the country, a period of uninterrupted suffering.

The Creator has blessed this country with all the elements of wealth and happiness. Its area of one hundred and ten thousand square miles presents, in varied profusion, innumerable sources of prosperity. Its population, numbering nearly 15 millions, feels the glow of youthful strength within its veins, and has shown temper and docility which warrant its proving at once the main organ of civilization in Eastern Europe and the guardian of that civilization when attacked. Never was a more grateful task appointed to a reigning dynasty by the dispensation of Providence than that which devolved upon the house of Lorraine-Habsburg. It would have sufficed to do nothing to impede the development of the country. Had this been the rule observed, Hungary would now rank among the most prosperous nations. It was only necessary that it should not envy the Hungarians the moderate share of constitutional liberty which they timidly maintained during the difficulties of a thousand years, with rare fidelity to their sovereigns, and the house of Habsburg might long have counted this nation among the most faithful adherents of the throne.

This dynasty, however, which can at no epoch point to a ruler who based his power on the freedom of the people, adopted a course toward this nation, from father to son, which deserves the appellation of perjury.

The house of Austria has publicly used every effort to deprive the country of its legitimate independence and Constitution, designing to reduce it to a level with the other provinces long since deprived of all freedom and to unite all in a common sink of slavery. Foiled in this effort by the untiring vigilance of the nation, it directed its endeavor to lame the power, to check the progress of Hungary, causing it to minister to the gain of the provinces of Austria, but only to the extent which enabled those provinces to bear the load of taxation with which the prodigality of the imperial house weighed them down; having first deprived those provinces of all constitutional means of remonstrating against a policy which was not based upon the welfare of the subject but solely intended to maintain despotism and crush liberty in every country of Europe.

It has frequently happened that the Hungarian nation, in spite of this systematized tyranny, has been obliged to take up arms in self-defense. Although constantly victorious in these constitutional struggles, yet so moderate has the nation ever been in its use of the victory, so strongly has it confided in the king's plighted word, that it has ever laid down arms as soon as the king, by new compacts and fresh oaths, has guaranteed the duration of its rights and liberty. But every new compact was as futile as those which preceded it; each oath which fell from the royal lips was but a renewal of previous perjuries. The policy of the house of Austria, which aimed at destroying the independence of Hungary as a state, has been pursued unaltered for three hundred years.

It was in vain that the Hungarian nation shed its blood for the deliverance of Austria whenever it was in danger; vain were all the sacrifices which it made to serve the interests of the reigning house; in vain did it, on the renewal of the royal promises, forget the wounds which the past had inflicted; vain was the fidelity cherished by the Hungarians for their king, and which, in moments of danger, assumed a character of devotion; they were in vain, since the history of the government of that dynasty in Hungary presents but an unbroken series of perjured deeds from generation to generation.

In spite of such treatment, the Hungarian nation has all along respected the tie by which it was united to this dynasty; and, in now decreeing its expulsion from the throne, it acts under the natural law of self-preservation, being driven to pronounce this sentence by the full conviction that the house of Lorraine-Habsburg is compassing the destruction of Hungary as an independent state; so that this dynasty has been the first to tear the bands by which it was united to the Hungarian nation and to confess that it had torn them in the face of Europe. For many causes a nation is justified, before God and man, in expelling a reigning dynasty. Among such are the following:

1. When the dynasty forms alliances with the enemies of the country, with robbers, or partisan chieftains to oppress the nation;

2. When it attempts to annihilate the independence of the country and its Constitution, supported on oaths, by attacking with an armed force the people who have committed no act of revolt;

3. When the integrity of a country, which the sovereign has sworn to maintain, is violated, and its resources cut away;

4. When foreign armies are employed to murder the people and to oppress their liberties.

Each of the grounds here enumerated would justify the exclusion of a dynasty from the throne. But the house of Lorraine-Habsburg is unexampled in the compass of its perjuries, and has committed every one of these crimes against the nation. . . .

In former times, a governing *council,* under the name of the Royal Hungarian Stadtholdership, the president of which was the Palatine, held its seat at Buda, whose sacred duty it was to watch over the integrity of the state, the inviolability of the Constitution, and the sanctity of the laws; but this *collegiate* authority not presenting any element of *personal* responsibility, the Vienna Cabinet gradually degraded this council to the position of an administrative organ of court absolutism. In this manner, while Hungary had ostensibly an independent government, the despotic Vienna Cabinet disposed at will of the money and blood of the people for foreign purposes, postponing our commercial interests to the success of courtly cabals, injurious to the welfare of the people, so that we were excluded from all connection with the other countries of the world, and were degraded to the position of a colony. The mode of governing by a *ministry* was intended to put a stop to these proceedings, which caused the rights of the country to moulder uselessly in its parchments; by the change,[1] these rights and the royal oath were both to become a reality. It was the apprehension of this, and especially the fear of losing its control over the money and blood of the country, which caused the house of Austria to resolve on involving Hungary, by the foulest intrigues, in the horrors of fire and slaughter, that, having plunged the country in a civil war, it might seize the opportunity to dismember the kingdom, and to blot out the name of Hungary from the list of independent nations, and unite its plundered and bleeding limbs with the Austrian monarchy.

The beginning of this course was (after a Ministry had been called into existence) by ordering an Austrian general [Jellachich] to rise in rebellion against the laws of the country and nominating him Ban of Croatia, a kingdom belonging to the Kingdom of Hungary. . . .

The Ban revolted, therefore, in the name of the Emperor and rebelled openly against the King of Hungary, who is, however, one and the same person; and he went so far as to decree the separation of Croatia and Slavonia from *Hungary*, with which they had been united for eight hundred years, as well as to incorporate them with the *Austrian* empire. Public opinion and undoubted facts threw the blame for these proceedings of the Archduke Louis, uncle to the Emperor; on his brother, the Archduke Francis Charles; and especially on the consort of the last-named prince, the Archduchess Sophia; and since the Ban, in this act of rebellion, openly alleged that he acted as a faithful subject of the Emperor, the Ministry of Hungary requested its sovereign, by a public declaration, to wipe off the stigma which these proceedings threw upon the family. At that moment affairs were not prosperous for Austria in Italy; the Emperor therefore did proclaim that the Ban and his associates were guilty of high treason and of exciting to rebellion. But while publishing this edict, the Ban and his accomplices were covered with favors at court and supplied for their enterprise the money, arms, and ammunition. The Hungarians, confiding in the royal proclamation, and not wishing to provoke a civil conflict, did not hunt out those proscribed traitors in their lair, and only adopted measures for checking any extension of the rebellion. But soon afterward the inhabitants of South Hungary, of Serbian race, were excited to rebellion by precisely the same means.

These were also declared by the King to be rebels, but were nevertheless, like the others, supplied with money, arms, and ammunition. The King's commissioned officers and civil servants enlisted bands of robbers in the principality of Serbia to strengthen the rebels and aid them in massacring the peaceable Hungarian and German inhabitants of the Banat. The command of these rebellious bodies was further entrusted to the rebel leaders of the Croatians.

During this rebellion of the Hungarian Serbians, scenes of cruelty were witnessed at which the heart shudders; the peaceable inhabitants were tortured with a cruelty which makes the hair stand on end. Whole towns and villages, once flourishing, were laid waste. Hungarians fleeing before these

[1] The change was solemnly enacted in the Parliamentary Law of March, 1848, which King Ferdinand V sanctioned by his public oath in April, 1848.

murderers were reduced to the condition of vagrants and beggars in their own country; the most lovely districts were converted into a wilderness. . . .

The greater part of the Hungarian regiments were, according to the old system of government, scattered through the other provinces of the empire. In Hungary itself, the troops quartered were mostly Austrian; and they afforded more protection to the rebels than to the laws, or to the internal peace of the country. The withdrawal of these troops, and the return of the national militia, was demanded of the government, but was either refused, or its fulfillment delayed, and when our brave comrades, on hearing the distress of the country, returned in masses, they were persecuted, and such as were obliged to yield to superior force were disarmed and sentenced to death for having defended their country against rebels.

The Hungarian Ministry begged the King earnestly to issue orders to all troops and commanders of fortresses in Hungary, enjoining fidelity to the Constitution and obedience to the Ministers of Hungary. Such a proclamation was sent to the Palatine, the Viceroy of Hungary, Archduke Stephen, at Buda. The necessary letters were written and sent to the post office. But this nephew of the King, the Archduke Palatine, shamelessly caused these letters to be smuggled back from the post office, although they had been countersigned by the responsible ministers; and they were afterward found among his papers when he treacherously departed from the country.

The rebel Ban menaced the Hungarian coast with an attack, and the government, with the King's consent, ordered an armed corps to march into Styria for the defense of Fiume; but this whole force received orders to march into Italy. . . .

The rebel force occupied Fiume and disunited it from the Kingdom of Hungary, and this hateful deception was disavowed by the Vienna Cabinet as having been a *misunderstanding;* the furnishing of arms, ammunition, and money to the rebels of Croatia was also declared to have been a misunderstanding. Finally, instructions were issued to the effect that, until special orders were given, the army and the commanders of fortresses were not to follow the orders of the Hungarian Ministers but were to execute those of the Austrian Cabinet. . . .

The King from that moment began to address the man whom he himself had branded as a rebel as "dear and loyal" (*lieber Getreuer*); he praised him for having revolted and encouraged him to proceed in the path he had entered upon.

He expressed a like sympathy for the Serbian rebels, whose hands yet reeked from the massacres they had perpetrated. It was under this command that the Ban of Croatia, after being proclaimed as a rebel, assembled an army and announced his commission from the King to carry fire and sword into Hungary, upon which the Austrian troops stationed in the country united with him. . . .

Even then the Diet did not give up all confidence in the power of the royal oath, and the King was once more requested to order the rebels to quit the country. The answer given was a reference to a manifesto of the

Austrian Ministry, declaring it to be their determination to deprive the Hungarian nation of the independent management of its financial, commercial, and war affairs. The King at the same time refused his assent to the bills submitted for approval respecting troops and the subsidy for covering the expenditure.

Upon this the Hungarian Ministers resigned, but the names submitted by the president of the council, at the demand of the King, were not approved of for successors. The Diet then, bound by its duty to secure the safety of the country, voted the supplies and ordered the troops to be levied. The nation obeyed the summons with readiness.

The representatives of the people then summoned the nephew of the Emperor to join the camp and, as Palatine,[2] to lead the troops against the rebels. He not only obeyed the summons but made public professions of his devotion to the cause. As soon, however, as an engagement threatened, he fled secretly from the camp and the country, like a coward traitor. Among his papers a plan, formed by him some time previously, was found, according to which Hungary was to be simultaneously attacked on nine sides at once—from Styria, Austria, Moravia, Silesia, Galicia, and Transylvania.

From a correspondence with the Minister of War, seized at the same time, it was discovered that the commanding generals in the military frontier and the Austrian provinces adjoining Hungary had received orders to enter Hungary and to support the rebels with their united forces.

This attack from nine points at once really began. The most painful aggression took place in Transylvania; for the traitorous commander in that district did not content himself with the practices considered lawful in war by disciplined troops. He stirred up the Wallachian peasants to take up arms against their own constitutional rights and, aided by the rebellious Serbian hordes, commenced a course of vandalism and extinction, sparing neither women, children, nor aged men; murdering and torturing the defenseless Hungarian inhabitants; burning the most flourishing villages and towns, among which, Nagy-Igmand, the seat of learning for Transylvania, was reduced to a heap of ruins.

But the Hungarian nation, although taken by surprise, unarmed, and unprepared, did not abandon its future prospects in any agony of despair.

Measures were immediately taken to increase the small standing army by volunteers and the levy of the people. These troops, supplying the want of experience by the enthusiasm arising from the feeling that they had right on their side, defeated the Croatian armaments, and drove them out of the country. . . .

The defeated army fled in the direction of Vienna, where the Emperor continued his demoralizing policy and nominated the beaten and flying rebel as his plenipotentiary and substitute in Hungary, suspending by this act the Constitution and institutions of the country, all its authorities,

[2] The Palatine was a high officer elected by the Diet, as its organ, and the defender of its Constitution. In fact, they always elected a prince of royal blood. He was virtually a viceroy.

courts of justice, and tribunals, laying the kingdom under marital law and placing in the hand of, and under the unlimited authority of, a rebel the honor, the property, and the lives of the people; in the hand of a man who, with armed bands, had braved the laws and attacked the Constitution of the country.

But the house of Austria was not contented with the unjustifiable violation of oaths taken by its head.

The rebellious Ban was taken under the protection of the troops stationed near Vienna, and commanded by Prince Windischgratz. These troops, after taking Vienna by storm, were led as an imperial Austrian army to conquer Hungary. But the Hungarian nation, persisting in its loyalty, sent an envoy to the advancing enemy. This envoy, coming under a flag of truce, was treated as a prisoner and thrown into prison. No heed was paid to the remonstrances and the demands of the Hungarian nation for justice. The threat of the gallows was, on the contrary, thundered against all who had taken arms in defense of a wretched and oppressed country. But before the army had time to enter Hungary, a family revolution in the tyrannical reigning house was perpetrated at Olmutz. Ferdinand V was forced to resign a throne that had been polluted with so much blood and perjury, and the son of Francis Charles (who also abdicated his claim to the inheritance), the youthful Archduke Francis Joseph, caused himself to be proclaimed Emperor of Austria and King of Hungary. But no one can by any family compact dispose of the constitutional throne without the Hungarian nation.

At this critical moment, the Hungarian nation demanded nothing more than the maintenance of its laws and institutions and peace guaranteed by their integrity. Had the assent of the nation to this change in the occupant of the throne been asked in a legal manner, and the young prince offered to take the customary oath that he would preserve the Constitution, the Hungarian nation would not have refused to elect him King in accordance with the treaties extant and to crown him with St. Stephen's crown, before he had dipped his hand in the blood of the people.

He, however, refusing to perform an act so sacred in the eyes of God and man, and in strange contrast to the innocence natural to youthful breasts, declared in his first words his intention of conquering Hungary (which he dared to call a rebellious country, whereas it was he himself that raised rebellion there), and of depriving it of that independence which it had maintained for a thousand years to incorporate it into the Austrian monarchy. . . .

But even then an attempt was made to bring about a peaceful arrangement, and a deputation was sent to the generals of the perjured dynasty. This house, in its blind self-confidence, refused to enter into any negotiation, and dared to demand an unconditional submission from the nation. The deputation was further detained, and one of the number, the former President[3] of the Ministry, was even thrown into prison. Our deserted capital was occupied and was turned into a place of execution; a part of

[3] Louis Bathyanyi.

the prisoners of war were there consigned to the axe, another part were thrown into dungeons, while the remainder were exposed to fearful sufferings from hunger and were thus forced to enter the ranks of the army in Italy.

Finally, to reap the fruit of so much perfidy, the Emperor Francis Joseph dared to call himself King of Hungary in the manifesto of the 9th of March [1849], wherein he openly declares that he erases the Hungarian nation from the list of the independent nations of Europe, and that he divides its territory into five parts, cutting off Transylvania, Croatia, Slavonia, and Fiume from Hungary, creating at the same time a principality for the Serbian rebels and, having paralyzed the political existence of the country, declares it incorporated into the Austrian monarchy.

The measure of the crimes of the Austrian house was, however, filled up when, after its defeat, it applied for help to the Emperor of Russia; [4] and, in spite of the remonstrances and protestations of the Porte and of the consuls of the European powers at Bucharest, in defiance of international rights, and to the endangering of the balance of power in Europe, caused the Russian troops stationed at Wallachia to be led into Transylvania for the destruction of the Hungarian nation.

Three months ago, we were driven back upon the Theiss; our just arms have already recovered all of Transylvania; Klausenburg, Hermanstadt, and Kronstadt are taken; one portion of the troops of Austria is driven into Bukovina; another, together with the Russian force sent to aid them, is totally defeated and to the last man obliged to evacuate Transylvania and to flee into Wallachia. Upper Hungary is cleared of foes.

The Serbian rebellion is further suppressed; the forts of St. Thomas and the Roman entrenchment have been taken by storm, and the whole country between the Danube and the Theiss, including the country of Bacs, has been recovered for the nation.

The commander in chief of the perjured house of Austria has himself been defeated in five consecutive battles and has with his whole army been driven back upon and even over the Danube.

Founding a line of conduct upon all these occurrences, and confiding in the justice of an eternal God, we, in the face of the civilized world, in reliance upon the natural rights of the Hungarian nation and upon the power it has developed to maintain them, further impelled by that sense of duty which urges every nation to defend its existence, do hereby declare and proclaim, in the name of the nation legally represented by us, the following:

1. Hungary, with Transylvania, as legally united with it, and the possessions and dependencies are hereby declared to constitute a free, independent, sovereign state. The territorial unity of this state is declared to be inviolable and its territory to be indivisible.

---

[4] The Russian army entered Transylvania on January 3, 1849. This is the army which was driven out again. But the main Russian armies were only on the move in April and took two months longer to enter Hungary. These were applied for late in March.

2. The house of Habsburg-Lorraine having, by treachery, perjury, and levying of war against the Hungarian nation, as well as by its outrageous violation of all compacts, in breaking up the integral territory of the kingdom, in the separation of Transylvania, Croatia, Slavonia, Fiume, and its districts, from Hungary; further, by compassing the destruction of the independence of the country by arms, and by calling in the disciplined army of a foreign power, for the purpose of annihilating its nationality, by violation both of the Pragmatic Sanction and of treaties concluded between Austria and Hungary, on which the alliance between the two countries depended—is, as treacherous and perjured, forever excluded from the throne of the united states of Hungary and Transylvania, and all their possessions and dependencies, and are hereby deprived of the style and title, as well as of the armorial bearings belonging to the crown of Hungary, and declared to be banished forever from the united countries and their dependencies and possessions. They are therefore declared to be deposed, degraded, and banished forever from the Hungarian territory.

3. The Hungarian nation, in the exercise of its rights and sovereign will, being determined to assume the position of a free and independent state among the nations of Europe, declares it to be its intention to establish and maintain friendly and neighborly relations with those states with which it was formerly united under the same sovereign, as well as to contract alliances with all other nations.

4. The form of government to be adopted for the future will be fixed by the Diet of the nation.

But until this point shall be decided, on the basis of the foregoing and received principles which have been recognized for ages, the government of the united countries, their possessions and dependencies, shall be conducted on personal responsibility, and under the obligation to render an account of all acts, by Louis Kossuth, who has by acclamation, and with the unanimous approbation of the Diet of the nation, been named Governing President (Gubernator), and the ministers whom he shall appoint.

And this resolution of ours we proclaim for the knowledge of all nations of the civilized world, with the conviction that the Hungarian nation will be received by them among the free and independent nations of the world, with the same friendship and free acknowledgment of its rights which the Hungarians proffer to other countries.

We also hereby proclaim and make known to all the inhabitants of the united states of Hungary and Transylvania, their possessions, and dependencies, that all authorities, communes, towns, and the civil officers, in both countries and cities, are completely set free and released from all the obligations under which they stood, by oath or otherwise, to the said house of Habsburg; and that any individual daring to contravene this decree, and by word or deed in any way to aid or abet anyone violating it, shall be treated and punished as guilty of high treason. And by the publication of this decree, we hereby bind and oblige all the inhabitants of these countries to obedience to the government, now instituted formally, and endowed with all necessary legal powers.

22

CONSTITUTION OF THE THIRD OF MAY

(EXCERPTS)

[The ideas of the French Revolution, as they applied to an aristocratic society, were first adopted in Eastern Europe by the Polish nobility. Influenced by the principles of constitutionalism that had rendered the French absolute monarchy into one compatible with the interests of the dominant class in France, the Polish *szlachta* consented to the modernization of the Polish state system to the extent that Poland became an aristocratic constitutional monarchy. The celebrated Constitution of the Third of May, adopted in 1791, was designed to reform the obsolete political order in Poland. The motivation of the *szlachta* was self-preservation within a national political framework, following the first partition of Poland by Russia, Prussia, and Austria. The new Constitution, however, was found unacceptable by Russia and its conservative supporters in Poland, and that opposition played a major part in the events leading to the second partition of Poland, in January, 1793.]

Stanislas Augustus, by the grace of God and the will of the Nation, King of Poland;

Unitedly with the confederated states, doubly reunited and representing the Polish nation;

Convinced that the perfection and the stability of a new national Constitution alone can assure our existence; taught by long experience of the inveterate vices of our political organization; determined to take advantage, given the present situation in Europe, of this fleeting moment that has left us on our own, free from the shame of foreign domination; placing well above our individual happiness, and even above life itself, the political existence, internal liberty, and independence of the nation with

Translated by Margaret Logun from Daniel-Charles Niewenglowski, *Les idées politiques et l'esprit public en Pologne à la fin du XVIIIe siècle* (Paris: Goupy, 1901), pp. 220–23, 230.

whose destiny we have been entrusted; wanting to be worthy of the vows and of the gratitude of our contemporaries and of posterity—we lift ourselves above those obstacles that arouse passions, having nothing in view but the public well-being, and wanting to secure for all time the safety of the homeland and the integrity of its frontiers.

After much consideration, we are firmly resolved to enact the present Constitution, which we declare sacred and unalterable until such time as it will become obsolete, the will of the people having expressly recognized the necessity of making some changes therein; and we wish all subsequent regulations of this Diet to be conformed to.

I

RELIGION

The dominant national religion is and remains the saintly Roman Catholic faith with all its rights. The solemn renunciation of Catholicism in order to embrace one of the other confessions is forbidden under previous penalties for apostasy. However, love of one's fellow man being one of the most sacred precepts of that religion, we owe to all men, regardless of the faith to which they belong, peace and liberty in their beliefs, under the guarantee of the State. We therefore guarantee, throughout the Polish territory, complete liberty to all religions and creeds, in conformity with the given laws in this respect.

II

LANDHOLDING NOBILITY

Full of reverence for the memory of our ancestors and honoring in them the creators of a free government, we guarantee most solemnly to the nobility all its immunities, liberties, and prerogatives, as well as the pre-eminence that belongs to it in private as well as in public life; and especially we irrevocably declare, confirm, and guarantee all the rights, statutes, and privileges that Casimir the Great, Louis of Hungary, Wladyslaw Jagellon and his brother, Witold, Grand Duke of Lithuania, Wladyslaw and Casimir Jagellon, Jean-Albert and his brothers Alexander and Sigismund I, as well as Sigismund Augustus, the last of the Jagellons, legally and legitimately accorded it. We declare the Polish nobility equal in dignity to the nobility of all other countries; and we recognize the most perfect equality among the members of this body not only regarding the qualifications for duties and for all public offices, which confer honor, glory, and profit, but also for the pleasure of privilege and prerogatives attributed to the *szlachta*. Above all, we wish that [the member of the *szlachta's*] individual liberty and safety, his entire property, both chattels, and fixtures, will remain forever as sacred and inviolate as they have been from time immemorial. We solemnly guarantee that in the laws that are to be enacted we shall not tolerate any change or restriction that might carry the slightest prejudice regarding the property of any individual, and that neither the supreme authority of the nation nor the government established by it, under pretext of royal rights, or any other, will be able to formulate any claim to these properties in their entirety or in part. That is why, in considering individual liberty and the legal property of all citizens the true bonds of society and the foundations of civil liberty, we confirm, ensure, guarantee, and desire that they will always be respected and considered inviolate.

Recognizing that the members of the *szlachta* are the principal defenders of liberty and of the present Constitution, we appeal to the patriotism and honor of every gentleman and request that he respect and preserve the sacred character of this Constitution, which alone can be the bulwark of the homeland and the guarantee of our independence.

III

Town and Bourgeoisie

We want the law, decreed in the present Diet and entitled "Our Royal Villages Declared Free Throughout the Length and Breadth of the Domains of the Republic," to be fully enforced; this law, which gives a truly new and effective basis regarding the liberty of the *szlachta*, as well as the independence and integrity of our common homeland, should become an integral part of the present Constitution.

IV

Peasants

Country people, whose hands produce the largest source of the nation's wealth, constitute the largest sector of the population and, consequently, the most imposing force in the country. It is as much through justice, humanity, and Christian duty as in our own interest that we place them under the protection of the law and the government, declaring that all authentic agreements and arrangements that the landlords have made or are making with their peasants and which favor the latter, including certain franchises or concessions, shall be deemed to have been concluded with the entire community and assume the character of contractual, communal, and reciprocal obligations, and that their stipulations, sincerely interpreted in mind and spirit, shall be placed under governmental guarantee. All agreements and similar arrangements, and the obligations that proceed from them, once consented to by a landlord, are strictly binding upon the latter and his heirs, as well as upon his beneficiaries, no matter what their title, and none of these by his own authority alone shall be justified in modifying them. Reciprocally, the peasants, according to their possessions, once contracts are accepted, arrangements concluded, and obligations freely agreed to, cannot free themselves by unilateral action but only in accordance with the terms of the agreements, which must be faithfully carried out, whether they are permanent or temporary in character.

As we have guaranteed to the landlords all the rights and privileges they enjoy with regard to their peasants, and as we are seeking to increase the population of the country in the most effective manner, we grant complete freedom to all individuals of all classes, including foreigners who have settled in Poland and all those who have left their homeland and wish in their hearts to return. Thus, all men, foreign or native, once they have trodden upon Polish soil, can freely and without hindrance follow their pursuits where and when they please; they shall be able, at their own will and for as long as they wish, to make such agreements as they see fit according to the kind of business they intend to do, and shall pay either in cash or by doing manual labor; they shall be able to settle down in town or country; lastly, they shall be able to remain in the country or to leave, should they consider it appropriate, on condition that they have carried out completely the obligations they voluntarily agreed upon.

V

Government, or the Nature of Public Power

In society, everything is derived from the will of the Nation. Therefore, in order that integrity of the domains of the Republic, the liberty of the citizenry, and civil administration remain forever in perfect equilibrium, the Polish government, by virtue of the present Constitution, shall comprise three powers: legislative authority, which shall rest in the assembly of the estates; supreme executive power, in the person of the King and in the council of surveillance [*straz*]; and judicial power, in magistrates who have already or shall be invested.

VI

National Army

The nation must rely solely on itself to repulse all attacks and to safeguard the integrity of its territory; all citizens are therefore born defenders of the rights and independence of the homeland. The Army must be one organized defensive force, coming from the heart of the nation. The country must honor its troops and give proportionate compensation for their devotion in the defense of the State; the troops must guard the safety of the country's borders and must maintain the public well-being; in a word, they must be the mighty shield of the Republic.

But, in order to fulfill these varied obligations unflinchingly and in conformity with the prescriptions of the law, the Army must remain under civilian control and, on oath, must remain loyal to the nation, the King, and the Constitution.

23

THE HATTI-SHERIF OF AUGUST 29, 1830

[Revolutionary manifestations, whether or not they were influenced by French ideology, were sometimes capable of resolution within the existing imperial framework. Compromise was in fact a characteristic feature of East European political life throughout the nineteenth century, even though the compromise agreements benefited only a few members of society and were more often than not ignored in practice. In the Ottoman Empire, compromise often took the form of an arrangement between the Porte and "revolutionary" leaders whose real aim was personal gain rather than the liberation of the masses from Ottoman rule. The following decree, issued by the Sultan Mahmoud in resolution of the demands of the Serbian nation, is characteristic of such agreements.]

Sultan Mahmoud Khan, son of Sultan Abdul-Hamid Khan, always victorious! May the contents be carried out! The treaty concluded at Adrianople between my Sublime Porte and Russia, containing the clauses of the Convention of Ackermann, stipulating: that the Porte will reach an understanding with the Serbian deputation at Constantinople in order to attend to the interests of Serbia; to give them freedom of religion and internal administration, incorporation of "breakaway" districts, assessment of taxes, the administration of the properties and fiefs belonging to Muslims, permission to travel with proper passports, the ability to found hospitals, schools, and printing presses; to prohibit Muslims from living in Serbia except in fortresses; and, finally, to grant them permission to have some sort of representation at Constantinople of such character, however, as not to alter the subject relationship.

Seeing that the Serbian nation, which has given proof of its loyalty to my Sublime Porte, is the object of my benevolence and that I wish to do right by her requests in a just and convenient manner, in order to in-

Translated by Margaret Logun from Gregoire Yakchitch, *L'Europe et la resurrection de la Serbie (1804–1834)* (Paris: Hachette, 1907), pp. 497–500.

crease domestic security; consequently, having agreed with the Serbian deputies at Constantinople, the following was resolved:

1. The said nation shall have complete freedom of worship in her own churches.

2. Prince Miloš Obrenovič, here present, by virtue of the imperial diploma that he carries and in return for his loyalty to my Sublime Porte, is confirmed as First Prince of the Serbian nation, a position that shall hereafter be considered hereditary in his family.

3. He shall continue to administer (in the name of my Sublime Porte) the internal affairs of the country in agreement with the assembly of Serbian nobles.

4. With regard to the six districts that are to be reunited with Serbia, we have agreed to comply with reports made by the commissioners named by Russia and My Sublime Porte, and in this respect shall make the exact inquiries.

5. The *haraj* [head tax] and other taxes shall be set at a fixed amount. The administration of military fiefs owned at the moment by Zi'ams and Timariotes, except those of Nis, shall be entrusted to the Serbs, and the revenues, like those from the districts that are to be reunited with Serbia, shall be subject to taxes, which shall be payable to the treasury at Belgrade.

6. In future, the officers and employees of my Sublime Porte shall in no way meddle in the administration of the country, nor in disputes among Serbs, nor shall they take from them one *para* [penny] more than the agreed-upon tax.

7. My desire being that the said nation should above all enjoy the advantages of commerce under my imperial protection; every Serb who wishes, on receiving a signed passport from his prince, shall be allowed by the authorities of my Sublime Porte to travel in all regions of my vast empire and to do business there like other subjects of my Sublime Porte, without having to pay an *aspre*, my will being that he be aided and protected throughout, and with the exception of customs, no one shall take from him *Avaid* or *Zevaid* or anything in violation of state regulations; care should be taken not to commit punishable offenses in this respect.

8. Goods presented to customs at Belgrade, to be forwarded to Constantinople, shall be given Serbian approval for clear passage and shall be subject to the required customs fee.

9. Customs rights for goods leaving the Belgrade customs for other points shall be collected by the Serbs, who shall pay the total tax amount to the treasury at Belgrade. Prince Miloš shall establish the measures required for the exercise of these rights. The proportionate prices of the goods shall be examined every seven years, and the fixed amounts shall be increased or decreased proportionately.

10. The Prince shall maintain such armed forces as may be required to prevent troubles and disorders and to police the country.

11. The Serbs shall be allowed to establish hospitals, printing shops, and schools for the public education of the young;

12. Turkish *voevodas* and *musselins* shall no longer function except in fortresses, the jurisdiction of the country being hereafter entrusted to the aforementioned Prince;

13. Those Turks who own real estate in Serbia and who no longer wish to maintain relations with the country have one year in which to sell it at a fair price to the Serbs, according to appraisals made by the commissars.

14. Produce from homes, vineyards, gardens, land, and other possessions of Muslims who do not wish to sell them shall be deposited, along with the tribute, in the treasury at Belgrade, to be forwarded to the respective owners.

15. Muslims who are not concerned with the upkeep of fortresses are forbidden to live in Serbia.

16. The Serbian nation shall contribute to the said Prince the amount necessary for his maintenance, in a manner commensurate with his rank, without, however, placing too heavy a burden on the people;

17. As soon as the position of Prince becomes vacant, the successor shall pay, on receiving official investiture, the sum of 100,000 piastres to the imperial treasury, and that out of his own pocket.

18. The archbishop and bishops elected by the nation must be invested by the Greek Patriarch of Constantinople, without, however, having to come to the capital city.

19. The members of the Senate, so long as they are not guilty of any crime against my Sublime Porte or the laws of the country, cannot be removed from their functions and deprived of their employment.

20. If the said nation, in its own interest, sees fit to establish a postal service, the authorities of my Sublime Porte shall not pose any obstacles in that respect.

21. If a Serb refuses to serve a Muslim voluntarily, he shall not be forced in any way to do so.

22. With the exception of the imperial fortresses that have existed in the country since antiquity, all other fortresses, more recently constructed shall be demolished.

23. Since Serbia is part of my well-protected states, my Sublime Porte shall not be hindered from securing from Serbia cash, cattle, provisions, and other commodities of all kinds as may be needed and when she sees fit.

24. Finally, there shall be Serbian agents at Constantinople to discuss with my Sublime Porte matters concerning their country.

These are the points upon which we have agreed and which have been resolved. For these reasons I deign to bestow this most gracious *hattisherif*, which shall be promulgated and solemnly read to the Serbian people.

You, my vizier Hussein Pasha, and you, *mullah* of Belgrade,* upon having acquainted yourselves with the notable provisions of the present

---

* Regional and local officials.—Ed.

most gracious *hatti-sherif*, shall make known to the Serbian nation that as long as she proves herself grateful, as she must be, for all my gracious acts in her regard she shall always be the object of my benevolence and shall enjoy our imperial security as long as she remains loyal and obedient.

You, vizier and *mullah*, endeavor to impress upon the Serbs the necessity to fulfill their duties as subjects and to take care not to do anything that might be contrary to these duties.

You shall act according to my commands; and having published this noble firman and registered it in the acts of the Mehkeme of Belgrade, you shall return it to Prince Miloš Obrenovič, who shall then keep it.

24

THE OUTLINE OF THE FUNDAMENTAL LAWS

[Compromise assumed more sophisticated forms in the Habsburg Empire, where the emperors not only displayed magnanimity toward their subjects but also appealed to the people's *"Kaisertreue."* Moreover, unlike the Turkish sultans, who refused to accept even the concept of revolution by the Christian *rayahs*, the Habsburg emperors were on occasion prepared to provide relief and redress in terms meaningful to revolutionary leaders. The Kremsier Constitution of March, 1849, granted, albeit tentatively, the fundamental rights demanded by the revolutionaries of 1848. An early draft of the fundamental laws (September, 1848), reproduced below, reveals the limited objectives of those seeking constitutional guarantees from Vienna, which the court was willing to consider under duress.]

1. All men have the same innate and inalienable rights. Of these, the most important are: the rights of self-preservation, of personal freedom, and of integrity, and the right to advance one's own spiritual and material well-being.

The exercise of rights finds its natural and necessary limitation only in recognition of the same rights for others.

2. It is the task of the state effectively to protect and advance these rights. The individual citizen consigns, from the totality of his rights, only so much to the state as is necessary for its purposes.

3. The totality of the citizenry is the *Volk*. All executive powers emanate from the *Volk* and will be exercised in the manner stipulated in the Constitution.

4. Austrian citizenship will be acquired, practiced, and lost according to the provisions of this constitutional charter and a special law.

5. All citizens are equal before the law. All privileges of class and all types of designations for nobility are hereby abolished and may no longer

Translated by Max Riedlsperger from Karl Schneider, *Der Reichstag von Kremsier* (Prague: Haase, 1927), pp. 98–104.

be granted. All citizens have an equal right to all public appointments. Only personal merit justifies public distinctions or rewards; no commendation may be inherited.

6. The freedom of the individual is guaranteed. No one may be deprived of a proper judge against his will. Privileged and exceptional courts may not exist. No one may be arrested other than by power of a judicial warrant that includes the reasons for arrest, except in the event that the culprit is caught in the act of committing a crime. The warrant of arrest must be delivered to the arrested individual immediately, or no later than twenty-four hours after the arrest. Each person arrested by agencies of public security must be taken before the proper court within twenty-four hours or released. If no palpable evidence of a serious crime is presented against an accused, then he is to be investigated while at liberty, under bond or bail as determined by the court according to law.

7. Court proceedings shall be public and oral. In criminal procedure, the rules of assize courts apply to the prosecution. The exceptions to this rule are determined by special laws. No one may be tried a second time for the same crime if he has been found innocent by a jury, and no one may be sentenced twice for the same violation; by the same token, no one shall be required to testify against himself or to bear witness against his parents, children, brothers and sisters, or spouse.

8. A punishment may be pronounced only upon a judicial verdict according to a law already in existence at the time of the crime. The death penalty is abolished. Penalties of public labor, public humiliation, corporal punishment, branding, or confiscation of property may not be imposed.

9. Domestic rights are inviolable. A search of domicile and papers, or a confiscation of the latter, can be undertaken only by judicial order in cases and in a manner determined by law. The inviolability of domestic rights shall stand as no obstacle to the arrest of a fugitive from justice.

10. The privacy of letters may not be violated, and the confiscation of letters may be undertaken only on the basis of a court order and according to the provisions of law.

11. The right of petition and assembly of petitioners is not limited.

12. The individual freedom of domicile, travel, and study, and of property within the boundaries of the state, is subject only to the stipulated limitations of the community laws. Emigration may not be limited by the executive power; specifically, no departure tax may be levied.

13. Austrian citizens have the right to assemble peacefully and unarmed without prior administrative permission. Open-air assemblies may be prohibited only in cases of imminent danger to public order and security.

No armed corps may advise upon or consider political questions or resolutions.

14. Freedom of association of citizens is guaranteed and may not be made contingent upon any administrative permit. This right may not be limited by law except where it stands in opposition to the equal exercise of the rights of others, to public customs, or to the purposes of the state.

15. Each person has an inviolable right to honor God according to his

convictions and his freely chosen denomination. Each religious sect is to be treated according to the established principles of association, as stipulated in Article 14.

16. There is no state church. No one may be forced to take part in the affairs, ceremonies, and duties of a cult he does not profess or to observe the sabbath of the same.

17. Religious differences are no grounds for differences in the rights and responsibilities of the citizen.

18. The legality of a marriage is determined by the formal assent of the bridal couple before the bureau designated by the state for the acceptance of the marriage contract. A church wedding may take place only after the civil marriage has taken place. Difference of religious denomination shall be no hindrance to civil marriage.

19. Education is free; any measure encroaching upon the freedom of instruction is prohibited. The suppression of this abuse shall be regulated solely by law. Public instruction is to be imparted free of charge and shall be regulated by law. No religious sect may be allowed to exercise control over educational institutions.

20. Everyone has the right to express his thoughts freely, to write them down, to express them pictorially, and to publish them in any way or form he chooses. This right may not be curtailed, suspended, or canceled under any circumstances and in any way, namely, by censorship or by license, by measures for security or by authorization fee. An abuse of this right shall be punished according to general laws and only by judgment rendered by an assize court. When the author of a publication or the creator of a pictorial representation is known and has his official residence in the state. Until the enactment of a revised penal law, the provisional press regulations apply to the abuse of the press.

21. Every race has the inviolable right to the protection and preservation of all aspects of its nationality, and of its language in particular. The state accepts responsibility for the equality of all customary languages in schools and in official and public life.

22. Property is under the protection of the state. No one may be dispossessed of his property except (a) in execution of a judicial decision, or (b) by expropriation for reasons of the public well-being. The latter may be undertaken only according to the provisions of a special law and in exchange for appropriate compensation, which usually precedes expropriation.

23. Property may be limited neither by vassalage nor by the institution of entailment. The dissolution of feudal bonds shall be determined by a special law. Entailed family property becomes indivisible property in the hands of that person to whom the same had fallen on the day of notification of this Fundamental Law.

24. The citizen is not otherwise limited in the free disposition of his estate than by the provisions of civil law and the special laws concerning the division of property.

The division of property into patrimonial and usufruct estates is forever prohibited.

25. Everyone shall bear a share of taxation by the state in proportion to his property and income.

26. Every citizen and every piece of land must belong to a local community. The basic laws of each community are (a) the election of its administrator and its representatives; (b) the independent administration of its affairs and the management of the local police (community regulations shall include the limitations on the alienation or disposition of capital); and (c) the publication of its budget and, as a rule, publication of proceedings.

27. The *Volkswehr* exists for the protection of the state and the Constitution and shall be divided into an Army and a National Guard and regulated by special laws. The *Volkswehr* shall swear an oath to the Constitution and may be used for the suppression of internal disorder only by command of the civil authorities and in a manner and in cases determined by law.

28. Each citizen is personally responsible for service in the Army. Exceptions shall be specified by the Military Law.

29. The Army is subordinate to civilian courts and laws. Military courts are to have jurisdiction only in time of war or in disciplinary proceedings.

30. All able-bodied men who do not serve in the Army have as a rule the same right and obligation to serve in the National Guard. More precise stipulations and exceptions to this rule are included in the National Guard Law. Everyone not specifically exempted from service in the National Guard by this law has the right to bear arms.

25

THE AUSTRIAN COMPROMISE LAW OF 1867

(EXCERPTS)

[The Austro-Hungarian Compromise of 1867 was more representative of the political mentality and interests of the Habsburg emperors than was the Kremsier Constitution of 1849. Although Emperor Francis Joseph would have preferred to continue to rule as absolute monarch over his empire, Austria's defeat by Prussia in 1866 prevented further resistance to Hungarian demands for equality. The *Ausgleich* precluded the democratization of the imperial order by safeguarding the conservative interests of the dominant Austrian and Hungarian aristocracies, at the expense of reformist and revolutionary "have-nots" in all parts of the Austro-Hungarian Empire.]

I

The following matters are declared common to the kingdoms and provinces represented in the Reichsrat and to the provinces of the Hungarian Crown:

1. foreign affairs, including diplomatic and commercial representation with foreign countries as well as dispositions that may be necessary with regard to international treaties; however, in cases where constitutionally required, the ratification of international treaties remains reserved to the representative bodies of both halves of the Empire (the Reichsrat and the Hungarian Reichstag);

2. military affairs, including the Navy; with the exception, however, of recruitment and legislation concerning the method and manner of fulfilling the military obligation, and of orders relating to the movement and maintenance of the Army; also excluding the regulation of civilian relations and the rights and duties of nonmilitary employees of the Army;

Translated by Max Riedlsperger from Ivan Zolger, *Der staatsrechtige Ausgleich zwischen Osterreich und Ungarn* (Leipzig: Duncker & Humboldt, 1911), pp. 298–306.

3. finance, with regard to those expenses to be commonly defrayed, especially the confirmation of the budget and the examination of the appropriate accounts.

II

The following matters, while not actually administered in common, should be dealt with according to common principles to be agreed upon from time to time: (1) commercial matters, especially customs legislation; (2) legislation concerning indirect taxes closely related to industrial production; (3) the establishment of a coinage system and monetary standard; (4) orders relative to those railway lines that affect the interests of both halves of the Empire; (5) the establishment of a defense system.

III

The expenses of common affairs (Section I) are to be borne by both halves of the Empire according to a ratio to be determined from time to time by an imperially sanctioned agreement of the representative bodies (Reichsrat and Reichstag). Should no agreement be reached between the two representative bodies, then the Kaiser determines this ratio, *but only for the duration of one year*. The financing of programs for either part of the Empire according to this provision is, however, exclusively the affair of each part.

A common loan may, however, be taken out for the defraying of the costs of common affairs, in which case also, everything that pertains to the contracting, application, and repayment of the loan is to be managed in common.

The decision whether to take out a common loan remains reserved to the legislatures of both halves of the Empire.

IV

Payment of the burdens of the present state debt is regulated by an appropriate agreement between the two halves of the Empire.

V

The administration of common affairs is performed by a common responsible ministry, which, however, is not permitted to conduct the specific governmental business of one of the two parts of the Empire in addition to the common affairs.

Orders relative to the administration, leadership, and internal organization of the joint Army are the exclusive prerogative of the Kaiser.

VI

The right of legislation of the representative bodies of both halves of the Empire (the Reichsrat and the Hungarian Reichstag) is to be exercised

by the same, insofar as it is concerned with common affairs, through delegations of representatives. . . .

XV

The agreement of both delegations is required for all laws concerning
the affairs within the area of jurisdiction of the delegations; failing an
agreement, a resolution framed and accepted in a common plenary session of the two delegations and in every case sanctioned by the Kaiser is
necessary. . . .

XXIX

As a rule, sessions of the delegations are public. In exceptional cases
the public can be excluded on the motion of either the President or at
least five members, passed by the delegation after the departure of the
audience.

A resolution, however, may be passed only in public session.

XXX

Both delegations shall communicate their resolutions to each other, as
well as necessary explanations thereof.

With respect to the delegation from the Reichsrat, such communication
is to be written and in German; regarding the delegation from the Reichstag, it is to be in Hungarian; in both cases, it shall be accompanied by an
authoritative translation in the language of the other delegation. . . .

XXXVI

Agreements with respect to those subjects that are not actually treated
as common but are regulated according to common principles shall be
effected either by the responsible ministry, which works out a bill of common consent and submits it to the appropriate representative bodies of
both sides for passage and, if agreed upon by both sides, submits it to the
Kaiser for his sanction, or by the selection of deputations of equal size
from both representative bodies, which shall work out a proposal under
the guidance of the appropriate ministry; which proposal shall then be
communicated by the ministry to each representative body, which then
shall submit it to the normal process. A resolution adopted by both representative bodies is then submitted to the Kaiser for sanction. The second procedure is to be followed especially with regard to an agreement
on contributions toward the costs of common affairs. . . .

26

THE PROBLEMS OF BOURGEOIS TRANSFORMATION IN EASTERN AND SOUTHEASTERN EUROPE

E. NIEDERHAUSER

[Historians have generally accepted the thesis that the dissolution of the Austro-Hungarian and Ottoman empires became inevitable in the period of general European crisis that began with the unification of Germany. The debate continues, however, over which factor was primarily responsible for the disappearance of the empires: nationalism, obsolete socio-economic orders, imperialism, or World War I. If no agreement has been reached on this point, it is because historians have tended to concentrate on specific national problems, which varied considerably in the different countries of Eastern Europe. The following article, by the Hungarian economic historian E. Niederhauser, attempts to analyze the characteristics common to all the East European countries in the second half of the nineteenth century. His Marxist analysis assumes the inevitability of both revolution and war, and concentrates instead on the difficulties of modernizing the underdeveloped countries of Eastern Europe.]

Reprinted from *Nouvelles études historiques* (Budapest: Akademiaia Kiado, 1965), I, 565–80.

It is generally accepted that the bourgeois transformation took place in the nineteenth century [in Eastern and Southeastern Europe], whether viewed as a definite temporal event or as the culmination of a longer historical process. This period is, therefore, the one dealt with in this paper. . . .

Both [Eastern and Southeastern Europe] exhibit many common features but there are also marked differences between them. However, their striking similarities and actual relationship clearly distinguish their development from that of Western Europe, and so a comparative and chronological treatment appears justifiable.

At the period under consideration one area, Eastern Europe, comprised that part of Germany which lay to the east of the Elbe, i.e., the original Prussian territories and Mecklenburg, the Empire, and the Habsburg European part of Russia, including the so-called Polish Kingdom. That is it embraces those territories where the "second edition" of serfdom, seigneurial domestic economy, appeared and where the capitalist development of agriculture followed the Prussian pattern after the bourgeois transformation.

The other area was the Balkans, where, under Turkish rule, the Turkish pattern of feudalism was implanted, resulting in considerable differences between the conditions of the peasantry of this area and those in the Eastern European countries mentioned above.

Between the two areas there were provinces, country regions, or even whole countries representing a certain transition between the two types, such as the two Rumanian Principalities, Dalmatia, or Bosnia and Herzegovina. In fact, the separate treatment of each country can lead to the discovery of many local peculiarities, of numerous versions of transitory states, not only in those countries we have just designated as transitory but elsewhere, too, and not between the two types—the Eastern and Southeast European—only, which we are to treat here, but also between these and other patterns of European social development.

We cannot enlarge upon these peculiar features here, of course, as the scope of our article will not allow us to give more than a sketch. It will be a sketch also in the sense that, instead of presenting detailed documentation, it will give an enumeration of these only, declarations instead of convincing analyses. And it will be a sketch also in the sense that it will not endeavor to grasp more than the general outlines, and to draw the main contours.

Whichever aspect of the development to be outlined here we try to scrutinize, we shall find countless data contradictory to the proposed thesis. Still, the over-all picture will emerge from these many transverse lines just when looked at from a certain distance. And this is, at the moment, the important thing for us. It is from this point of view that we would now like to pick out some important aspects of Eastern and Southeast European development and to point out, through them, some problems of bourgeois transformation.

The first and incontestable common peculiarity was the agrarian character of the whole area, the preponderance of agricultural production over other branches of economic life, a fact so well known that it hardly needs to be borne out particularly. Agricultural production was backward as compared with the European standard of the day, and the rule of the three-course rotation could be taken as universal. Exceptions pointed much more toward the presence of a more primitive than toward more developed forms of husbandry. This statement is valid for both areas, those where big land estates based on seigneurial domestic economy were to be found and those where large estates actually consisted of peasant plots, or where not more than the very beginnings of seigneurial domestic economy could be found (we have here in mind the area under Turkish rule and the appearance of what was called the *Çiftlik* estate).

The second peculiarity was the weakness of industrial development. Handicraft of medieval origin still pursued in medieval forms was widespread everywhere (in the more backward territories it was expressly predominant). In the East European territories manufacture (a result of eighteenth-century development) played a prominent part which, to a great extent, was due to the economic policy of enlightened despotism. Industry, too, had appeared, yet manufacture was, in a great measure, of feudal character, as it was owned by landlords of big estates who resorted to forced peasant labor. Trade, at that time, was for the most part intermittent and external and was just about to yield ground to internal trade, which came to play a positive role in the development of national markets. In the Eastern European area, merchants' domestic trading capital had an important part in the ensuing industrial development, while in the Balkans, Greek merchants' capital could form no national market. In all areas, capitalist credit service appeared only sporadically and not earlier than toward the mid-century.

Everywhere, old feudal husbandry was in the process of disintegration; production for the market had long since broken through the frames of economic regions formed by autarchic big land estates or by the towns and their zones of influence. The barriers against economic development erected by the feudal social system could be felt ever stronger. These hindrances, beyond making an objective appearance in the difficulties of agricultural production (the impossibility of introducing more developed agronomical methods because of the resistance of the peasants), not to speak of medieval conventions impeding industrial production, appeared also in the *minds* of contemporaries, even more so because the realization of the fact that production under prevailing economic conditions would advance only with difficulty had already been recognized by the enlightened despotism of the former century and not only in the period in question.

In the first half of the century, the problem of bourgeois transformation had already come to the fore in the Balkans. The peasants' production for the market or the industrial production of manufactured goods and factories began to strain the existing frames, and ways were sought to get free of restrictions. As Engels had stated in 1847 concerning the Habsburg

Empire, machines and railways would, sooner or later, strain the rotten frames.

The situation had been, to a certain extent, similar in the Russian Empire, too. Still, the position was not quite the same in Russia: Forces acting against feudalism were, at the given moment, weaker than they were in the Habsburg Empire, especially in the territories of the Turkish Empire, with the exception of the Greek territory proper.

There was no direct correlation between the disintegration of the feudal system and the appearance of new capitalist conditions as far as the intensity of the two was concerned; disintegration, the failure of feudal relations of production, was more obvious than the appearance of capitalist elements, the old was disintegrating more rapidly than the new was appearing. The examination of class relations can supply new explanations for this.

Again, we have to refer to a cliché: the weakness of the bourgeoisie. Dissimilarities, of course, were considerable in this field, too. Even more so, as in the Habsburg Empire the Austrian or Czech bourgeoisie were already a powerful element; it was much stronger and much more self-conscious than the new bourgeoisie of the Russian Empire. To some degree even the Austrian bourgeoisie, and the Russian bourgeoisie to an even greater degree, did not firmly oppose the feudal state power. On the contrary, they kept close contact with it and expected from it, not without reason, that some of their economic claims would be satisfied. They expected protection from the state against the competition of more developed Western industrial countries. Thus, one of the basic classes of the capitalist society to come had, to a certain extent, an interest in maintaining the feudal state power, because, beyond what had been said, in a multinational empire this class would have to fear for its hegemony in the case of bourgeois transformation. The bourgeoisie of the nationalities was not bound by such considerations, as this class was very weak everywhere. Until 1848, the Czech bourgeoisie had been the only power of importance. If we examine the other basic class, the working class, the proletariat, we can see that it existed only in the western provinces of the Habsburg Empire at best, that is to say, a working class really numerically important was to be found only there or, to some extent, in the Polish Kingdom, i.e., the Polish territory belonging to Russia. There, and even more so in Turkish territories, urban plebian strata, at best, could be found—strata which could supply only fighters in a bourgeois revolution (and they did supply in 1848, and in other territories at a later date), and even their number was rather restricted, even in Austria.

Society had yet another factor: peasantry, a social stratum largest in numbers everywhere, one that experienced most directly the disadvantages of feudalism. This was potentially the great reservoir of the struggle fought for bourgeois transformation. This was valid for the East European territories as well as for the Balkans. The difference was that in the Balkans (in Montenegro and Albania) remnants of a primitive communal system, of tribal and clan systems, could still be found among the peasantry.

In addition, and also as a result of the peculiarities of Turkish feudalism (especially in territories where the elimination of the sipahi system had been accomplished, or at least begun), the peasantry of the Balkans had to oppose and resist state power much more directly than in East European territories. Here, the landlord stood to the peasant as his direct enemy, and the peasant was attached to the faraway Emperor by an often powerful, although groundless, illusion.

Society had yet another stratum, which also felt the disadvantages of the prevailing system: This was, paradoxically enough, the ruling class of the feudal system itself, the nobility. This, of course, could be observed only in those areas where disintegration had progressed further, where the faults and absurdities of the system became more obviously apparent, i.e., in the Habsburg Empire, and is valid for only a small minority of the nobility in Russia. A still narrower stratum, partisans for some sort of change, could be found in the Rumanian Principalities. This feature in the development of the two latter countries apparently showed the transition toward the Balkan area. Here, in the Turkish Empire, the local feudal ruling class was still resisting reforms, even such as would remain within the bounds of feudalism; and as to more far-reaching reforms of a bourgeois character, not even the central government would foster the idea of introducing them, since the disintegration of the feudal system—even though examined in the dimension of the whole Empire and not of the Balkans only—had not yet come to a stage where the question of the necessity of such reforms could have arisen at all.

A greater demand for bourgeois transformation existed in the East European area proper, i.e., for the liquidation of the feudal system, within the ranks of the basic classes of feudal society than within those of the basic class of the capitalist system, i.e., the bourgeoisie. The working class (where it existed at all), and the plebeian urban strata supported, as a matter of course, the bourgeois transformation (although very few in their ranks had in fact realized this task objectively). However, owing to their weakness, the position they held was not decisive. This shows that from the social aspect as from the economic one outlined above, the disintegration of the old elements, at least outwardly, was stronger than was the integration of the new ones.

These were, of course, basic factors in the bourgeois transformation. This black and white picture drawn on the basis of class relations must, however, be colored by another rather complicated Eastern European feature which had developed in the course of centuries—the multinational character of the area, which made it very difficult, often even impossible, to draw precise ethnical frontier lines between nationalities. The social structure of the various nationalities was rather divergent. Some nationalities had their own feudal ruling class (Poles, Hungarians, and Croats), while among others there was no feudal ruling class, only the beginnings of the bourgeoisie could be found (let us mention a characteristic example of this, the Ukrainians, Slovenes, or Bulgarians). The overwhelming majority of the Eastern European nationalities in this era did not live in a state of their own but were forced to live within the frame of multi-national empires and subject to those empires. This was a point of strong similarity between the Eastern European and the Balkan areas. This is, in our opinion, the main factor that makes it possible and desirable to treat these two areas together and comparatively.

The above situation was not improved by the fact that certain differences existed: The Habsburg Empire had taken formal cognizance of the existence of the nationalities (within feudal frames stretching back into the past), at least of those led by a feudal ruling class, while Russia, e.g., would not recognize them (the Poles excepted, at least before the late thirties of the century), nor would Turkey. To emphasize the complicated state of the problem, we only mention that it would be impossible to state the number of nationalities or to mark them off with certainty in either area, as the level of their self-consciousness also varied according to the differences in their economic and social status. The Macedonians furnish one well-known example, as at this period they did not consider themselves a separate nationality but Bulgarians. The development of these nationalities was very diversified, and, no doubt, dissimilarities could be found in their economic and social conditions. There was, however, one common feature that, sooner or later, appeared with more or less vigor: the development of a national bourgeoisie, or (in the minority of cases) that of a ruling class of noblemen who, obviously, within rather narrow bounds, were ready to undertake certain of the tasks of a national bourgeoisie.

Thus, the inner development of nationalities, too, pointed toward bourgeois transformation. This inner development, which has been fairly well exposed by research concerning individual countries, has generally and aptly been named as the process of national rebirth. Its peculiarities and stages are well known, beginning with the appearance of linguistic followed by cultural demands in a broader sense, leading to the appearance of certain political claims. These last might be restricted to the level of demanding a kind of autonomy within the framework of a multinational empire or might go as far as the logical conclusion of such a movement, claiming an independent bourgeois national state and the acceptance of an armed struggle for this cause. (It would be worth while examining separately whether this concept of national rebirth, conditionally extended to all Eastern and Southeast European countries, was to be found among the suppressed nationalities of multinational empires only, or whether it was a phenomenon to be observed in the development of ruling nations also.)

Almost without being aware of it, we have come here to a very fundamental question. We have been speaking about a bourgeois national state, which necessarily implied national independence (or at least many attributes of national independence in the form of a comprehensive autonomy). Consequently, we have commuted certain basic interrelations (and this commutation did actually take place, in these rebirth movements): Our starting point was the bourgeois transformation. We have surveyed the economic and social preconditions of this development, look-ing for such forces as would be ready to back a bourgeois transformation. We have not, however, examined the fundamental principle of this trans-formation. There is no need, of course, to discuss this in detail, as there is actually no great difference between Marxist and bourgeois historio-graphy on this question: On both sides, the attainment of power by capi-talism, the liquidation of feudal conditions, and the consolidation of bour-geois proprietorship have been accepted.

When the oppressed nationalities of Eastern and Southeastern Europe arrived at the stage of bourgeois transformation and national rebirth and at the process of becoming a bourgeois nation, these processes had already reached completion in Western Europe. There, bourgeois nations had al-ready been established. They were developing within the framework of bourgeois national states, at least so it seemed when looked at from East-ern Europe. Hence, a bourgeois national state seemed to be the final goal, for the very reason that such states existed in Western Europe, and the West, or more precisely France, was the model and the standard. Who could have imagined, even in the middle of the last century, that a prob-lem of nationalities could exist in France, too? Thus, bourgeois trans-formation had become intertwined with national independence, a bour-geois national state comprised a claim for bourgeois transformation and an aspiration toward national independence. The first can, of course, be considered fundamental, as the claim for a bourgeois national state was included in the problems of bourgeois transformation.

In the national movements of Eastern Europe, however, this relation had become commuted, (i.e., that one of the aims of bourgeois transfor-mation would be the establishment of a bourgeois national state, where this state would thus be a subordinate category of bourgeois transforma-tion as a whole): A bourgeois national state (and here the word *national* has to be stressed and not the word *bourgeois*) had become the main category, the major task, and bourgeois development itself had become a part-problem of the latter. This was quite obvious in those cases where the rebirth movement was led by the feudal ruling class or, at least, by the majority of that class. But even in those cases where the movement was, in fact, led by national bourgeoisie, and where its essential point, i.e., an aspiration toward becoming master in the respective areas of the national market (as has been clearly exposed by research concerning individual countries) had been or was to be developed, even in these cases, the move-ment took the shape of a fight for national independence (by fight we understand here, of course, not armed insurrection alone). And these na-tional movements, as a consequence of the repartition of nationalities in the area concerned, were bound to turn against one another, too; one and the same territory was claimed by at least two, if not more, pretenders. Was this to mean that the fight for bourgeois transformation in Eastern Europe was solely or mainly a struggle for national independence? It seems that this question must be answered in the affirmative.

As has been referred to, one of the potential elements (numerically the most important element) of this struggle was the peasantry. Peasant movements were to be encountered everywhere throughout the period, and in some places they were of considerable proportions (the uprising, e.g., that broke out in Russia and in some countries of the Habsburg Empire in connection with the cholera epidemic of 1830–31, or the peasant movement of 1850 in Turkish territory). We could not find, however, in this era, peasant wars similar in scale to those that had agitated whole countries more than once in the feudal age. The reason for this was of no account in the given situation; it is inessential whether a struggle of such proportions was made hopeless from the outset by the increased strength of the state machinery or whether a concentration of forces was impossible owing to the internal development of and differences among the peasantry. The important fact was the lack of nationwide peasant wars, which might have shaken, if not overthrown, feudalism.

We could not say, of course, that the peasantry was on the whole passive. Surely, it played an important part in various revolutionary movements, independence wars (in the Balkans, for example) as the main army of these movements; in other cases it was the element endeavoring to make the revolution swing into a more radical direction. Yet, in these cases the peasant movement was part only of the general revolutionary rebirth, the slogan of which was national independence, and only within such limitations were these movements willing to solve certain problems of bourgeois transformation.

The historical events in Eastern Europe were, in fact, a series of national-liberation wars. The 1848 revolution in the Habsburg Empire had consciously aimed at solving social problems, but here, too, the question of national independence came first, even with the German-speaking population of the empire. Here, however, the problem showed up in a particular form, namely, the movement aimed at the establishment of a united German state.

Whether we examine the Polish insurrections of 1830–31 and 1846, the 1848 revolutions spreading over the greatest part of Eastern Europe, or the 1863 Polish uprising, we shall find everywhere that these were national independence wars. This was their basic and, in fact, only common feature. For the bourgeois content of the various movements was rather divergent, i.e., the measure of their willingness to solve the problems of bourgeois transformation varied. In some cases the uprisings led by the nobility did not even raise the problems of bourgeois reforms (as, for example, the 1830 Polish insurrection, where it was of no importance that some *had* realized the necessity of attaining aims beyond the achievement of national independence; the movement as a whole was a conservative revolution). For the most part, the movements in question *did* raise the problems of bourgeois reforms. They were bound to do so in order to mobilize the peasant masses (it was mainly the 1830–31 Polish experience that taught them to do so). The scope of bourgeois transformation aimed at had been narrow, and the conservation of the power of the feudal ruling class was much more important than consistency in carrying out all the aims of bourgeois transformation.

It was the 1863 Polish uprising, the latest among these events, which broke out under the most developed conditions and went furthest in solving the peasant problem, the most important social problem inherent to bourgeois transformation in Eastern Europe; but the abolition of big land estates was not attained by this uprising, nor did it give the whole land into the hands of peasants.

These uprisings, which allied the fight for independence with bourgeois transformation and with social revolution, failed. Reactionary forces (let us use, for the sake of generality, this rather neutral, expression, which may, and must, imply many things) gained the upper hand.

. . . The inherent contradiction of these movements, initiated under the leadership of the feudal ruling class, eliminated the possibility of the victorious outcome of independence wars waged for *bourgeois* transformation and led by *feudal* elements. To make the peasantry as a mass force interested in the struggle, a radical suppression of feudal conditions, a comprehensive liquidation of big land estates would have been needed. The nobility as a leading class had not, of course, brought itself to take such measures and was bound, therefore, to lose, sooner or later, the support of its masses (if such masses existed at all from the outset). Consequently, the solution could be nothing but ambiguous. National independence could not be attained in full, in the best case semi-independence could be gained (such as that gained by the Hungarians, e.g., in the Compromise of 1867). As far as bourgeois reforms were concerned, here too, the conditions remained ambiguous, as big land estates continued to exist and were supported by the state. This was the case with the 1848 movements in the Habsburg Empire and the 1863 Polish insurrection. True, there were nationalities within the Habsburg Empire that could not produce a feudal ruling class, and thus their struggle for independence was not hindered by this burden (we have to consider here, primarily, the nationalities in Hungary and the Ukrainians in Galicia, where, in both cases, the fight for independence was directed against a nation which itself led an independence fight under the leadership of its nobility). However, these nationalities were so weak numerically and at such a low level of economic and social development that, sooner or later, they were bound to look for allies, and these they found in the reactionary forces of the Habsburg Empire.

Whether we take the Serbian insurrection of 1804 (which lasted for a very long time), or the uprising of the Bulgars, which broke out in 1876 but was soon defeated, we find that the independence wars of the Balkan people were different in their character. Neither the national feudal ruling class nor the bourgeoisie, which was making and maintaining certain relations with the feudal state power, took part in these fights; these were peasant movements where the antifeudal fight coincided with the struggle for independence: The expulsion of the Turks also meant the banishment of feudalism. Consequently, bourgeois transformation in these places could be much more radical, and could liquidate the big land estates. In Greece, this struggle had been led in a somewhat similar manner, although it had not been as successful in liquidating the feudal land estates. We must not forget that foreign intervention by Russia and the Western pow-

ers greatly assisted the victory of the insurrection, the success of bourgeois transformation, which here took the form of national independence
wars. This was shown by the fact that the 1875 uprising in Bosnia and
Herzegovina led, as a consequence of foreign intervention, to anything
but bourgeois transformation and national independence: Austro-Hungarian occupation had conserved feudal characteristics here up to the beginning of the twentieth century. Nor was independence or bourgeois
transformation attained, in a different international situation, by the 1903
Macedonian revolt, which was similar in character but with a stronger
social element. Rumania, again, provided a transitional case: Formally,
its independence was due to Russian intervention. But in the case of Rumania, or formerly the two Rumanian Principalities, the question was
only formal, as these were, throughout the period, independent of Turkish
power (and if any great power had any influence on their internal affairs,
this was, at least in the first half of the century, Russia much more than
Turkey). Here too, bourgeois transformation meant a series of reforms
coming from above, just as in other East European countries.

Here we have, however, come to bourgeois transformation itself. The
transformation in the Habsburg Empire and in the Polish Kingdom was
forced out by the 1848 and the 1863 revolutions. The fundamental social
measures taken by these revolutions could no longer be invalidated by reactionary forces gaining the upper hand. In Prussia, too, it was the 1848
revolution that brought bourgeois transformation after the first steps
forced out by the Napoleonic wars. (We consider here, of course, the
development of the old Prussian territories only—that of the territories lying to the East of the Elbe—which, by their entire social structure, fitted
into the mold of East European development. Within this framework, we
are not in a position to examine the development of other German territories, and the problems of Prussia and German unity.) In Russia, no
such revolution broke out. If we examine thoroughly what has been said,
the following conclusion may follow as a matter of course: The revolution
failed to break out because there was no nationality inside the empire
strong enough to launch an independence war (gauging strength here by
the state of economic and social development rather than by the number
of inhabitants). Nor can the fact be disregarded that here, unlike the case
of the Habsburg Empire, the nation in power had, by its more numerical
preponderance, disabled, if not ruled in advance, the action of nationalities. By the end of the 1850's, internal development had brought about a
revolution situation, and this very revolutionary situation forced out bourgeois transformation.

Whether we take the Habsburg Empire, Prussia, Russia, or Rumania,
bourgeois transformation had been a transformation accomplished from
above, by the representatives of the feudal ruling class. Revolution in the
Habsburg Empire and in Prussia had, no doubt, brought into existence the
essential elements of this transformation, which could no longer change
(only that in the Habsburg Empire the ruling classes of the nationalities
had played a decisive role in the calling forth of these elements, whereby

this transformation had been kept, from the outset, within certain bounds). Whereas in Russia, the 1859–61 revolutionary situation had confined certain limits to the transformation (limits somewhat narrower than in the Habsburg Empire) and reforms coming from above could not give less than what had been granted by the revolution. The 1863 Polish uprising had a part in this transformation, as did the revolutions of the Habsburg Empire. Moreover, here bourgeois reforms coming from above had even added to the results of the revolution, in order to guard against new uprisings.

What, then, did this bourgeois transformation mean? From the social aspect it meant one essential change, which however, considering the agricultural character of the East European area as a whole, was of decisive importance. This was the abolition of serfdom or, more precisely, the granting of bourgeois landed property to former serfs (or to peasants, as in the Polish Kingdom the institution of serfdom had ceased to exist as early as 1807). It also meant (in some areas) the creation of a large landless peasantry, part of which at least could already find employment, without any restriction, in developing big industry. This transformation was important mainly from the angle of the capitalist progress of agriculture, as it gave an impetus to this development, even though it meant the Prussian course (as Lenin named it). Nor had this transformation been indifferent from the aspect of industrial progress, as it made possible the influx of some of the peasantry into industrial production in the towns. Concerning this, it was a peculiar feature that the abolition of serfdom was most complete in those areas where progress had been less hampered by feudal fetters (in the Habsburg Empire). Whereas in areas where, even prior to the introduction of reforms, the peasants' confinement to the land had been a serious obstacle to industrial development (in Russia and in Rumania), the reform itself maintained in some way or other the peasants' confinement to the land (though this land was now owned by them) and, consequently, maintained certain difficulties in the way of industrial progress.

The abolition of feudal rights was merely a concomitant symptom of the liberation of serfs and had contributed, as a matter of course, to clearing the way toward capitalist progress. Still, it did not contribute to this development in the same measure as the liberation of serfs did. The liquidation of guilds and the granting of free practice of trade, too, were very important reforms but did not reach, at that time, the importance of the emancipation of serfs.

Other reforms were also introduced in the course of bourgeois transformation: the modernization of public administration, the introduction of a kind of self-government, the elmination of the feudal shackles of the juridical system (and, consequently, the introduction of equality before the law), and the reorganization of public education. These reforms were introduced in the Habsburg Empire, in Prussia, in Russia and in Rumania. At the same time, we can see the legal buttressing of bourgeois property and the progressive development of a modern bourgeois legal system. It is very characteristic, however, that when listing these reforms we cannot begin by mentioning the fundamental change in the form of the constitution. We cannot do this for the simple reason that such change did not take place; even in the 1848 revolutions, it can be traced only sporadically. The drawing of political conclusions of bourgeois transformation and the establishment of a bourgeois republic did not take place in Eastern Europe. Monarchic form survived, and in the Habsburg Empire and Russia, even feudal despotism continued to exist for a while (in Russia this was, in fact, a rather lengthy period). The constitutional monarchy that succeeded despotism carried many a remnant of this latter. It will not be difficult, of course, to understand after what has been said that reforms coming from above were introduced by the feudal ruling class; a class that, in the political field at least, sought to maintain its former power to the fullest possible measure, once it had been forced to make so many concessions in the economic and social fields. This class endeavored to maintain its power, as long as possible, by the form of despotism, and after the constitutional transformation, by keeping control of the leading positions in the government. In the Habsburg Empire, this constitutional transformation took place at a time when the structure of the social system was even more feudalistic; in Rumania, the intermezzo of despotism, at least in the formal sense, had not taken place at all after the bourgeois transformation; consequently, in these countries the ruling class of feudal origin did, in fact, succeed in maintaining leadership for the most part, and only step by step did it cede certain positions to the bourgeoisie. In the western section of the Austro-Hungarian Monarchy this happened earlier, as there capitalist development and the progress of the bourgeoisie took place more rapidly. In Prussia, too, the representatives of the old feudal ruling class retained government positions.

In Russia, despotism was able to maintain its position for a long time and, consequently, was able to leave the actual government of the state in the hands of the old nobility and gentry. In fact, this was the situation even after 1905.

The reforms introduced in the course of bourgeois transformation—beginning with the reorganization of local administration and going as far as the establishment of constitutional monarchy—had brought about certain political and legal frames for the progress of capitalism, all this originating, we have to emphasize again, from above. The progress of capitalism went on within these frames and was supported, to a certain extent, by the government. In the Balkan countries, more radical results had been achieved, regarding serfdom, as we have already pointed out, which was the fundamental question of bourgeois transformation. More radical results were achieved concerning national independence. This is not surprising, as the Balkan countries that had once belonged to the former Turkish Empire had de facto become independent, or, more exactly, independent of Turkish power. Transformation had also been more radical concerning the political and legal structure. The 1879 Bulgarian constitution elaborated one of the most democratic European state organisms of the day. Although the constitution of the Greek Kingdom did not go so far, it established frames more democratic than had the Austro-Hungarian and the Russian monarchies.

In Serbia alone, this progress had been slower; in fact, it lasted for long decades. Formally, the country had twice been given a constitution of a relatively democratic character—one similar to the Greek constitution— still, the absolute power of the sovereign was left intact as far as, we may say, 1903; only for short transitory periods could the bourgeoisie attain the de facto enactment of one or the other constitution. This also bears upon the fact that, in this country, the fundamental processes of bourgeois transformation came to unfold much more slowly than the rate at which the country gained political independence.

Yet, external factors, too, had played a certain part in gaining ground for the political frames of bourgeois transformation, just as they played a role (and here an important one) in acquiring political independence. This was especially obvious in the case of Bulgaria, where the constitution had been elaborated, for the main part, by the Russian occupying forces and sanctioned by the Russian government. In Greece, there was a similar interference as far as the establishment of political institutions was concerned. In the Serbian state alone, there was no external influence to be observed in the organization of governmental institutions. Thus, in the Balkan countries, unlike the East European development, the frames within which capitalist progress could take rise had been established, for the most part, as the result of an internal revolutionary movement. Accordingly, these frames were, over and above warranting national independence, considerably more democratic than the ones in the East European monarchies (this was national independence in the formal sense at least, and, as such, it held good even for Bulgaria, where the Turkish protectorate was implicity considered by everybody as nominal only).

The more important question was how capitalist progress could fill up these frames, what possibilities bourgeois transformation offered for the free flow of capital. It is impossible, of course, to give here even an outline of the history of the development of capitalism in the East European countries or empires. Anway, the phenomena in question are well known in the broad outline concerning each and every country. We have to content ourselves with mentioning a few general characteristics only.

The agricultural character of the East European area had not been considerably changed by bourgeois transformation. Thus, the question is what possibilities were left to capitalist progress in the field of agriculture, first of all. Again, we have to refer to a well-known and often discussed phenomenon: In Prussia, Russia, the Habsburg Monarchy, Rumania, and, within more limited frames (and under feudal conditions that still survived to a certain extent), Bosnia-Herzegovina capitalist progress followed the Prussian course. This meant the survival of big landed estates and was a course painful for peasant farming. The size of peasant farms was kept, after the emancipation of serfs, within more or less exactly fixed limits, and their expansion was made rather difficult or, in some places, even impossible by the existence of large landed estates. It was under such poor conditions that peasant farms set out for capitalist progress, and the rise and consolidation of a rich peasant stratum (employing hired wage-workers, too) started. Feudal land estates rode out the difficulties of transition by resorting to various transitional forms, e.g., paying off in labor and métayage; in some areas, big land estates went back to these forms even though earlier they had already switched over to wage work. In the end, however, these latifundia became transformed into estates of a capitalist character. In other cases (nor was this a unique phenomenon), they could not tide over the hardships of transition, fell apart, and from their parts the new bourgeois-type big land estates (owned, as a rule, by urban or village bourgeoisie) came into existence in the course of the capitalist concentration of land.

As to the Balkan area, here we encounter another occurrence. In this area bourgeois transformation abolished Turkish feudal estates (it is indifferent here whether this big land estate was in the hand of a landlord or was owned—after the liquidation of the sipahi system—by the state), and from under the big land estate, covering the peasant farm, this latter rose to the surface (here again, it is indifferent that, in some places, former serfs had to pay redemption to the landlord while, in other places, they became owners of the land without any encumbrance whatever). The one-time *Çiftlik* estates, even though they survived, could not be compared with the latifundia of the Monarchy, Russia, or even Rumania, as far as their size was concerned. For the most part, they had the same role here that rich peasant estates had in other territories. Thus, with the disappearance of big land estates in this area a kind of free progress became possible for the peasantry. There was an obstacle, however, to this development: Here the expansion of peasant farms was not restricted by big land estates but, in a much more decisive way, simply by the size of arable land. Soon after bourgeois transformation, peasant farms reached everywhere the limits of cultivability under existing agrotechnical conditions, and, in the time to follow, peasants had to face here a shortage in land, just as in the non-Balkan areas. No land distribution whatever could be hoped for there to solve the land question, with the exception of some very limited possibilities (certain estates owned by the state, etc.). While in other areas, big estates at least, but rich peasant farms almost no less, could avail themselves of the possibilities of mechanization, the poor farmers of the Balkan area were bound to cultivate land with the most primitive tools.

If we examine the progress of industry, we find similar differences, and again to the injury of the Balkan countries. In both the Austro-Hungarian Monarchy and Russia, industrial revolution took place simultaneously with the introduction of bourgeois reforms (reforms which were, more or less, of a political character), and in the two empires there was a very rapid progress of big industry to be observed. (As a matter of fact, this took place in certain areas only, which, in the case of the Monarchy inevitably coincided with the territories of certain nationalities and, consequently, caused national offenses; whereas in Russia, even where this process took place on the territories of nationalities, e.g., in Ukraina, both the bourgeoisie striving for the development of big industry and the workers drudging in the factories were mainly, or at least to a great part, Russians.)

On the territories which originally belonged to Prussia, the classical land of the Prussian course, there was no large scale industrial progress, and this territory remained, much more than the others, an agricultural area (this holds good for Mecklenburg as well). The enormous industrial progress of the Western Prussian territories and of united Germany, generally speaking, cannot be neglected here.

In the Balkan countries, the beginning of this development could be encountered at a much later date only, and even at the time of the turn of the century the industrial level of these countries lagged far behind that of the two great monarchies. It is another question that even the development of these latter fell far behind the speedy advancement of the Western countries including Germany, and there was no essential change in their agricultural character either, although both the relative and absolute number of agricultural population rose at a rather quick pace, while in the Balkan countries this took place at a very slow speed only.

Still, the optics of this comparison, drawn to the injury of the Balkan countries, is rather misleading. Namely, at first glance—if the matter is simplified to the extremity and put in a rather rough way—it may seem that the quicker progress of capitalism in the Austro-Hungarian Monarchy and in Russia was due to the fact that feudal remnants, i.e., the survival of big estates, first of all, had created conditions advantageous for capitalist progress. Big land estates had undoubtedly contributed in a certain measure to the development of big industry; the accumulation of capital within the latifundia and, even more so, the possibilities of state accumulation deriving from the rich sources of these empires promoted the development of big industry. This circumstance, however, will not give a full explanation of the quick and successful capitalist progress of these nations. The basic reason lay in their former development, that the economic standard of these empires had been—at the time of bourgeois transformation, or rather during the decades preceding this transformation—at a much higher level than that of the Balkan countries. The reasons for this lay even deeper; they were to be found in their former development as a whole. We could refer here to the fact that, in these countries, enlightened despotism had set the progress of industry on its way as early as the eighteenth century, while the Turkish Government, at the same time and later, had done its best to impede this progress. And, in all probability, when looking for reasons, we could reach back to earlier periods as well. As far as our subject is concerned, however, the important thing is that here the conditions advantageous for capitalist progress were not created by bourgeois transformation.

On the contrary, bourgeois transformation introduced relatively less advantageous conditions. The more advantageous possibilities, resident in the Balkan development, could—as a consequence of the considerably lower starting point—make their effect felt only much later; on the whole, they began to act at the time when, after World War II, the possibilities of a radically new development emerged in practically the whole Eastern European area.

27

THE IMPERIAL OTTOMAN FIRMAN RELATIVE TO THE ESTABLISHMENT OF THE BULGARIAN EXARCHATE

[Although the disintegration of the Ottoman Empire was accelerated in the 1860's and 1870's by nationalism, imperialism, and incipient capitalism, the sultans remained impervious to the forces of change. Their attitude was most evident with respect to the Bulgarians, the Christian subjects of the Porte who had been most isolated from the political currents of the nineteenth century. In the Bulgarian areas of the Ottoman Empire, the principal exponent of nationalist doctrine was the Church, whose aim, as late as the 1860's, was to gain administrative autonomy from the Greek Patriarchate in Constantinople. The Porte, for political reasons, was prepared to consider this demand for religious autonomy, and in 1870 it established a Bulgarian national church (Bulgarian Exarchate). It is noteworthy that the Bulgarian demands were strongly supported by Tsarist Russia, which at the time was willing to recognize the validity only of a religiously based, conservative nationalism.]

It has at all times been My Imperial desire that all faithful peoples and subjects dwelling in My Empire should enjoy to the full extent such order and security as are necessary to them for the professing of their religions, as also in all their social relations; that they should live in peace and humanity, in order that they may by so doing aid Us to the utmost of their ability in Our incessant efforts for the furtherance of Our Empire and of civilization.

But inasmuch as there have of late arisen—contrary to Our Imperial wish—certain misunderstandings and misinterpretations as to how far the Bulgarian metropolitans, bishops, priests, and churches be dependent upon the Patriarchate—which misunderstandings and misinterpretations have

Reprinted from Balkanicus, *The Aspirations of Bulgaria* (London: Simpkin Marshall, Hamilton, Kent & Co., Ltd, 1915), pp. 245–49.

greatly grieved Us—it has been found necessary to institute an investigation into the causes which have led up to the said misunderstandings and misinterpretations and to submit them to a thorough examination. The results of this investigation are embodied in the following articles, which have been adopted and approved as being the definite solution of the controversy.

ARTICLE I

A separate ecclesiastic district shall be established under the official name of "the *Bulgarian Exarchate*," the same to include certain districts over and above the metropolitanates and bishoprics hereafter to be mentioned. The administration of the spiritual and religious matters in these districts to be entirely vested in this Exarchate.

ARTICLE II

The chief Metropolitan of these districts shall bear the title of "Exarch." He shall also be the canonical president of the Bulgarian Synod.

ARTICLE III

The internal spiritual administration of this Exarchate shall be established by a supplementary law, which must be in accordance with the fundamental canonic and religious regulations of the Orthodox Church and which must be previously subjected to the approval of My Imperial Government.

This supplementary law must preclude the possibility of any interference, either direct or indirect, on the part of the Patriarch, with religious matters, or with the elections of bishops and exarchs. As soon as the Exarch is elected, the Bulgarian Synod shall inform the Patriarch of the fact; and the Patriarch, on his part, shall immediately grant his approval, in accordance with religious law.

ARTICLE IV

The Exarch, having been appointed through Our sublime firman, shall mention the name of the Patriarch in the prayers in accordance with the rubric of the Church; but previous to his election, the person considered worthy of the office of Exarch must be personally presented to My Government.

ARTICLE V

In matters pertaining to his jurisdiction, the Exarch will have the right to negotiate directly with the local authorities and, if need be, even with Our Sublime Porte. The approval must be obtained before *berats* [investiture] may be granted to such persons in holy orders as come under his jurisdiction.

ARTICLE VI

All matters concerning the Orthodox faith and necessitating mutual consultation must be referred by the Bulgarian Synod to *Vasseljenski* Patriarchate and Synod; and these shall be bound to render assistance without delay and to answer without hesitation such questions as may be put to them.

ARTICLE VII

The Bulgarian Synod shall receive the Holy Oil from the Patriarch of Constantinople.

ARTICLE VIII

Such bishops, archbishops, and metropolitans as are subject to the Vasseljenski Patriarchate shall be at liberty to approach the Bulgarian Exarchate, in the same manner as the Bulgarian bishops and archbishops holding office in Greek eparchies; they will also be permitted to sojourn in the capitals of vilayets and other centers of administration; but they must not convoke synods outside the limits of their own diocese, nor interfere in the affairs of such Christians as are not subject to them, nor officiate without the permission of the bishop of the diocese in which they happen to be.

ARTICLE IX

Even as the metoch of Jerusalem, which is situated in Phanar, is dependent upon the Patriarch of Jerusalem, so the Bulgarian metoch and church situated in the same suburb shall belong to the Bulgarian Exarchate. And whenever the Exarch shall require to come to Constantinople, he shall be allowed to reside in his metoch; as to such Divine Service as he may have to celebrate during his sojourn in the capital, he shall be subject to the same ecclesiastic rules as apply in similar cases to the Patriarch of Alexandria, Drenopolje, and Jerusalem.

ARTICLE X

The jurisdiction of the Bulgarian Exarchate shall extend over the eparchies of Sofia, Vratsa, Tulcea, Vidin, Nis, Pirot, Kiustendil, Samokov, Veles, Plovdiv, Mute-Sariflik Islimne, and the *"casa"* of Sosopolie, with the exception of about twelve villages on the shores of the Black Sea, between Varna and Kustendje [Constanta], which are inhabited by a non-Bulgarian population. The following towns shall also be excepted: Varna, Anhial, Mesemvria, Plovdiv, and Stanimaka, together with the villages of

Kuklen, Voden, Arnaut-Key, Panagia, Novo Selo, Leskov, Ahman, Batchovo, Belashtitsa, and the monasteries of St. Anargirius, St. Paraskeva, and St. George. The monastery of St. Panagia and the interior of the Plovdiv district shall belong to the Exarchate, but such inhabitants of the eparchy as may not wish to be under the Exarchate shall be free. The details in this matter shall be arranged between the Patriarchate and the Exarchate in accordance with canonic and ecclesiastic law.

If the population of any other places besides those enumerated above, and professing the Orthodox faith, should wish unanimously, or if at least two-thirds of them should wish to be subject to the Bulgarian Exarchate, and if subsequent investigation should prove this to be so, their desire ought to be gratified; but as such desire must be expressed either by the whole of the population, or at least by two-thirds thereof, such persons as would attempt to spread discord among the population shall be held responsible to the law.

ARTICLE XI

Such monasteries as are situated in the Exarchate and which are, by canonic law, subject to the control of the Patriarchate shall continue to be governed as they have been hitherto.

28

THE SOLE SALVATION LIES IN REVOLUTION

KHRISTO BOTEV

[The conservative nationalist demands of the Church were not palatable to all Bulgarians who sought to change the existing order. This was particularly true of the radical émigré intelligentsia working for the liberation of the nation from Ottoman rule. Khristo Botev, a Bulgarian nihilist revolutionary, advocated revolution as the only way to attain Bulgaria's independence. The following article, published in Rumania in January, 1875, is characteristic of the views of Bulgarian radicals of the period.]

The savage, barbaric, and inhuman Turkish yoke, which in the course of almost five centuries has pressed and today, more than ever, presses down upon the neck of our impoverished and oppressed but vital and as yet unspoiled nation, has brought this nation to such a low social level, in comparison with the other nations of Europe, that many of our perhaps even sincere patriots have come to the servile and already outdated conclusion that our nation first needs science, education, knowledge, and mental development, and that only after these are achieved can one think of its political liberation; only then will the nation be able to take its place in the history of mankind.

Although this problem has been studied by our émigré journalism for the past half-dozen years, and although it has been resolved—both by the advocates of human freedom and by the aspirations of the nations themselves—in favor of common sense and in favor of that section of oppressed humanity into whose midst no true science can penetrate, this opinion has, nevertheless, become so widespread that it is ready to block all revolutionary ideas and even to engage in open warfare against them. We have therefore resolved to avert the blow and to point out as clearly as possible the weak and outdated aspects of this position.

In the first issue of our newspaper, we touched on this problem, stating

Translated by Nonna H. Carr from Ivan Undjiev, *Khristo Botev* (Sofia [n.p.], 1956), pp. 194–98.

that "as for an individual man, so for an entire nation—in order that it develop and reach a certain level of moral and material well-being—one condition, above all others, is necessary. That condition is freedom; and since that condition is absent in our country, one can say that no progress is possible." But now, as if to illustrate the groundlessness of our conviction, an announcement appears, under the very noses of our émigrés, regarding a literary-scientific newspaper to be called *Znanije*, in which the "Society for the Dissemination of Useful Knowledge" tells us simply and clearly that until a nation reaches a certain level of development and education and acquires a certain body of knowledge, it does not deserve to be regarded as a nation. In other words, our nation does not need, nor is it capable of, freedom. We shall agree, for the moment, with this sensible, clear, and convincing sermon on science, but we shall ask the Society: How does it intend to disseminate science and education in our nation when the conditions are so unfavorable and forbidding? Is it possible for our nation, under the existing barbaric despotism, the terrible persecutions and restrictions, to apprehend anything of sound and useful science, and with its aid to lighten the burden of its present situation? Is it possible that this could occur before these conditions are eliminated and before the nation receives complete political freedom?

We can see that, from its rebirth to the present day, our nation has traveled a long way thanks to education; but if we take a closer look at the economic situation and at our long-suffering people, then we must conclude either that there never has been (nor is there now) any education, or that if it has existed (or does exist) it is totally unnecessary, for it brings no essential benefits to the nation. Indeed, we do have schools, reading rooms, newspapers, bookstores, and literature. But all this has led our nation to such a degree of human happiness that we are now able to record accurately in writing when there was famine in Turkey, when there was pestilence, when there was a fire, when the tsarist armies came, when the Circassians came, when even infants were burdened with a tax, when. . . . But tell us, please, does this represent progress for a nation that has the same right to exist as any other nation in the world? Let others say what they will, we insist that if such "progress" continues in the future, the existence of our nation is unthinkable. Turkey has already stretched its deadening hand over all its life forces, and nothing will deflect this hand except fire and the sword.

But let us assume that the China of Europe [Turkey] will be able to start on the road to progress, and that even our nation will be given at least those tokens of freedom of which our gluttonous and complacent compromisers dream. Even in that case, we again ask: Will this safeguard the existence, the development, and the future of the Bulgarian nation? You might, but we would not, under any condition, wish our nation the progress of the Czechs, the future of the Poles, or the good fortune of the Croats. We cannot compare those nations with the Bulgarian nation, which has forgotten its past, hates its present, and places all its hopes on the immediate future. This nation awakened half a century ago, and all its activity consisted of striving to throw off that inhuman double yoke that had brought it to the point of forgetting its own name. The nation ridded itself of the *kamilavka* [Church vestment], which prevented it from acquiring any new human ideas, and of the [Church] hierarchy, which the nation had grown to hate to such a degree that even now it does not enjoy any respect. The nation has seen what was necessary for emancipation from slavery, and it has come to the conclusion that to exist it must throw off the barbaric Turkish yoke.

Of course, for the nation to do this it is necessary for science and literature, poetry and journalism, in other words, for all the spiritual activity of its leaders, to take on the nature of political propaganda, i.e., all of the above must conform with the life, the desires, and the needs of the nation and must cease to be science for science's sake, art for art's sake, or journalism that chews over and over again the old, decayed, and long-discarded European dung. But there are those who say that science, literature, poetry, etc., are products and reflections of the very life of the nation; therefore, if they provide us with some guidance, this shows that they meet the requirements and reflect the strivings of the nation. Yes, this could be meaningful to us, but only in the event that our nation could enjoy even that illusion of freedom now enjoyed by the Czechs, Croats, Serbs, Poles, Irish, and others. Shall we then wait until we too are granted such freedom? Wait, gentlemen, wait, lead the nation along the road of your stupid peaceful progress, and the nation will soon resemble that famous cartoon in which the holy fathers of the second French Revolution ridiculed their own deeds. It depicted the animal called an ass (may the nation forgive us this expression), and extending from the saddle past its head a stick with an armful of hay tied to it—tied in such a manner that the animal's head could not reach the hay. The ass attempted without success to take a bite of hay, and, suffering, hungry, thirsty, and deceived, it walked ahead, moving along the road of progress. We are directed along the same road by the advocates of that peaceful progress being preached today to our nation, but with this difference: The French ass walked alone, while atop ours sits the Bosporus idiot; it is led by the Exarchate and driven forward by our freedom-loving and progressive slaves. But we have had enough.

From all that has been said so far, we can draw no other conclusion than that the sole salvation for our nation lies in revolution. Let those who have ears listen. Our revolutionary party will soon indicate where it stands, what it represents, and what it strives for.

29

THE PROPOSAL OF FIFTEEN FOR THE ORGANIZATION OF THE YOUTH OF SERBIA

SVETOZAR MARKOVICH

[Radical solutions to national problems were also proposed in nations other than Bulgaria. In Serbia, socialist ideas were expounded by opponents of the corrupt and regressive Serbian dynasty and its political leaders. In the eyes of the reformers, the Serbian ruling clique was no better than those that ruled the Ottoman and Habsburg empires, to which the Serbian establishment was ostensibly opposed. However, the solutions to the problems of Serbia proposed by the leading Serbian socialist Svetozar Markovich, although radical, were not revolutionary in Botev's sense. The following selection (dated 1870) presents Markovich's ideas on the role of youth in the modernization of Serbia.]

Four years ago, the youth of Serbia joined together and worked, on the foundation of freedom and with the aid of education, to free and morally unite the Serbian people.

By now, the youth have met four times in general assembly; the sons of Serbia have gathered from all the Serbian lands; they have become acquainted and have affirmed that they are brothers, the sons of one people; the youth of Serbia, Hungary, and Austria have expressed clearly and openly their wish that the Serbian people unite in spirit, and this wish has spread throughout all the lands of the Serbian people. It is time that we met together to decide upon a course of action by which we may become free and united.

The youth have declared that their task is to develop the national consciousness of the Serbian people, and that once the people have become conscious they will, as a natural consequence, be free and united. But, if the youth truly want to put their words into action—if they truly want to develop a national consciousness—they must fix their eyes upon a clearly

Translated by Donald M. Yengich from Svetozar Markovich, *Sabranani spisi* (Belgrade [n.p.], 1965), pp. 125–29.

defined goal. The political and social institutions, the economic situation, education, literature, and religion are all closely related and all influence the development of the national consciousness. It has become apparent from the program of the youth thus far that they aspire to develop a national consciousness only through literature and oral communication. But if one looks at all the factors that influence national consciousness, it is quite apparent that the influence of literature on the national consciousness can be lessened and even destroyed by other influences, such as the political and social institutions, the economic situation, the schools, and the Church. If, for example, the political institutions are contrived in such a way that they derive their optimum strength from the state and use that strength not to the advantage but actually to the detriment of the people, in order to keep them in bondage and ignorance, then those political institutions smother national consciousness; against such institutions a literary struggle is not enough, but rather every legal means within the reach of the united Serbian youth is needed. It is imperative for the development of the state that the people themselves have control of all their resources and set up their own institutions. Only then can the people set up institutions that will develop a national consciousness, such as those that will support a rich literature, open good schools, set up institutions for the improvement of the economic situation, and so on. The development of the national consciousness depends on the establishment of political and social institutions that will advance the freedom and material well-being of the people; it depends on schools and literature; but all this is impossible if the people themselves are not in control.

To work for the development of the national consciousness means to work for the improvement of all aspects of national life and to open up all the channels we have enumerated. The youth must work not only in literature but also in education and in the communal schools, in congresses and general assemblies, and in community planning for bettering the economic condition of the people, for the protection of health, for the development of the people's strength—in short, the youth's work must extend into all that embraces the life of the people. But the youth have stated that they will work on the foundation of truth and knowledge. Truth and knowledge must remain the foundation of the youth's work and must become the bond that will unite all the youth, in their various endeavors, into one whole. The youth must have one basic belief: that truth, insofar as it concerns the social and political institutions of the state, the economic situation, the schools, and the Church, is gained through education.

We therefore suggest that the united Serbian youth reorganize on the following basis:

I. BASIC PRINCIPLES

1. The youth think that the Serbian nation must control its own development and that this will occur if all the institutions in the Serbian nation are based on democratic principles. The Serbian nation cannot

establish its institutions on democratic principles until its neighbors do likewise, and that will be possible only if the nationality question in Austria-Hungary and the Eastern question itself are settled on the principles of the freedom of mankind.

2. Science tells us that the state must be a union of people for the achievement of the goals of individuals, as they themselves stipulate. The form of the state is communal, and the state is considered a gathering of free communes.

3. In every people's state it is understood, it is self-evident, that the people themselves enact all laws. In a true democratic state the laws are enacted by direct vote of the people, and those who enforce the laws are responsible to the regular courts.

4. In the interest of society, the material independence of every member must be guaranteed. Without material independence there can be no honor, order, nor freedom among the people. Accordingly, the state has the right to take all measures it finds necessary to assure the material independence of each member.

5. In every society there are no rights without obligations, nor any obligations without rights. That which gives rights to each member of society is his work: Each member of society who works and earns a living must enjoy all rights without distinction. In accordance with this, the youth recognize the absolute equality of men and women and consider it essential that women be given the same rights in education and vocation as are men.

6. Schools for the education of the people must be so constructed as to turn out not only educated citizens of the nation but also educated laborers; therefore, in addition to schools for general education there must be schools for special education and for education in agriculture, trade, industry, and commerce. Education is to be financed by the state.

7. Our people are divided into three religious groups (if we except the Uniates). The goal of the youth is to unite the Serbian people through learning, through the development of a common awareness; religion therefore stands outside the sphere of the youth's activities. A man may believe what he likes, but the principles of truth and honor, and moral principles in general, must be the same for all people who live in the same society.

II. THE YOUTH ORGANIZATION

1. Every Serb is a member of the Omladina [Youth] if he professes its principles and agrees to work according to them. Every member of the Omladina is obliged to work according to these principles in the community, through the congress and the general assembly, through the press and at public meetings—in a word, everywhere in public and private life.

2. Every member is obliged to enroll in one of the local committees; he is also to pay yearly one florin, or ten groši, for which he will receive the Omladina calendar and books.

3. In order to carry out the Omladina's business, the general assembly shall select an annual central committee, which shall set up local committees wherever possible.

4. It is the responsibility of the local committees to assemble the members and collect suggestions for the Omladina, to circulate the Omladina's books, to organize the people, to raise the living standards of the people, to protect health, to keep the people informed, etc. The local committees shall also arrange public lectures, meetings, and speeches and in general do all that will further the achievement of the goals of the Omladina. . . .

5. The work of the annual central committee is divided into three main divisions: the administrative division, which sets up the local committees; the financial division, which manages the finances of the society; and the literary division, which puts together the written records and calendars of the Omladina and publishes books for the people. The local committees shall also engage in all of these activities.

6. In the local committees and the general assemblies, every member has the right to offer suggestions on the Omladina's activities, which may be accepted or rejected by a majority of the members. . . .

7. One-fourth of the total income of the Omladina shall go into a central educational fund, which shall be used to assist those working according to the Omladina's principles who have suffered hardship and are in need of help. The annual central committee shall decide who is to receive this aid and how much. . . .

30

THE BULGARIAN CONSTITUTION OF 1879

[In Southeastern Europe, the "establishment," whether Ottoman or national, invariably responded violently to demands for change. The brutal suppression of the Bulgarian uprising of 1876 led first to war and then, in 1878, to the creation of an autonomous Principality of Bulgaria. The rulers of the principality were almost as unsympathetic to radical challenge and democratic rule as their Turkish overlords and the guarantors of their autonomous status, the Russians. But they used the same democratic formula for legalizing their rule as had been used elsewhere in the Balkans, a "liberal" constitution. The Bulgarian Constitution of 1879 was typical of these constitutions in the rights and obligations it set forth for the subjects and in the political organization of the state. Implementation of the provisions, however, was of secondary concern to the rulers, whose primary interest was the dismemberment of the Ottoman Empire through the incorporation of Bulgarian-inhabited areas into a Greater Bulgaria.]

I
REGARDING THE TERRITORY OF THE PRINCIPALITY

Article 1. The territorial limits of the principality of Bulgaria may be neither extended nor diminished without the consent of the Grand National Assembly.

Article 2. Rectifications of the frontier, if they regard uninhabited districts, may be made by the ordinary National Assembly (see Article 85).

Article 3. The territory is divided, for administrative purposes, into counties, districts, and parishes. The organization of this administrative division on the basis of parochial autonomy will be determined by special legislation.

Reprinted, by permission, from C. E. Black, *The Establishment of Constitutional Government in Bulgaria* (Princeton, N.J.: Princeton University Press, 1943), pp. 291–99.

II

The Prince's Authority and Its Limits

Article 4. The principality of Bulgaria is a heredity and a constitutional monarchy, with a national representation.

Article 5. The prince is the chief representative of the state.

Article 6. The prince of Bulgaria bears the title of Excellency; the heir-apparent that of Serenity.

Article 7. The prince of Bulgaria may not simultaneously rule over any other state without the consent of the Grand National Assembly.

Article 8. The person of the prince is sacred and inviolable.

Article 9. The legislative power resides in the prince and in the national representation.

Article 10. The prince confirms and publishes the laws that have been passed by the National Assembly.

Article 11. The prince is commander in chief of all the military forces of the principality alike in time of peace and in time of war. He confers military rank and office in accordance with the law. Every one who enters military service must take an oath of fidelity to the prince.

Article 12. The executive power is vested in the prince. All organs of this power act in his name, and in virtue of his order.

Article 13. The judicial power, in its entirety, belongs to the persons and legal tribunals that act in the name of the prince. The relative positions of the prince and of the tribunals and persons referred to will be determined by special regulations.

Article 14. The prince has the right of modifying or commuting sentences according to the law of criminal procedure.

Article 15. The prince enjoys the right of pardon in criminal cases, but the right of amnesty belongs to him conjointly with the National Assembly.

Article 16. The prince's rights, as expressed in Articles 14 and 15, do not extend to the sentences of ministers condemned for violation of the constitution.

Article 17. The prince represents the principality in all its relations with foreign states. In his name, and with the approval of the National Assembly, special conventions may be made with the neighboring states regarding matters dependent on the administration of the principality, and for which the reciprocal action of the governments in question is required.

Article 18. Ordinances and regulations emanating from the prince have force only after being countersigned by the appropriate ministers, who assume the entire responsibility for them.

III

The Prince's Residence

Article 19. The prince is bound to permanent residence within the principality. Should he absent himself, he must name a substitute for the period of his absence, who shall be invested with rights and duties determined by special legislation. Before quitting the principality and appointing a substitute, he must give public notice by proclamation.

Article 20. The heir-apparent is similarly bound to reside within the principality, which he may leave only with the consent of the prince. . . .

V

The Law of Succession to the Princedom

Article 24. The dignity of prince is heredity in his eldest male descendant. The succession shall be regulated by a special law.

VI

The Prince's Coming of Age, Regency, and Guardians

Article 25. The reigning prince, or heir-apparent, is considered to be of age at eighteen years.

Article 26. Should the prince succeed to the throne before coming of age, a regency or guardianship is appointed until his majority. . . .

Article 31. The prince, on coming of age, takes on himself the government of the principality, after taking the oath and giving notice by public proclamation.

Article 32. The education of the prince while a minor, and the management of his property, are entrusted to the dowager princess and to guardians nominated by the ministerial council, with the consent of the princess.

Article 33. The members of the regency cannot at the same time be the personal guardians of the prince minor. . . .

VIII

The Civil List of the Prince and of His Court

Article 35. The National Assembly assigns, for the maintenance of the prince and of his court, 600,000 francs yearly. This sum cannot be augmented without the consent of the National Assembly, nor diminished without that of the prince. . . .

IX

Religion

Article 37. The state religion of the principality of Bulgaria is the Eastern Orthodox confession.

Article 38. The prince of Bulgaria and his descendants are restricted to the exclusive profession of the Orthodox religion, but the first elected prince of Bulgaria may, exceptionally, profess his original religion.

Article 39. The principality of Bulgaria, as, from an ecclesiastical point of view, forming an inseparable part of the jurisdiction of the Bulgarian

Church, is subject to the Holy Synod, which is the highest spiritual authority in the Bulgarian Church, wherever that may exist. Through the same authority, the principality remains united with the ecumenical Eastern Church in matters regarding dogma and faith.

Article 40. Christians of other than the Orthodox faith, and those professing any other religion whatever, whether Bulgarian-born subjects or naturalized, as well as foreigners permanently or temporarily domiciled in Bulgaria, have full liberty to profess their religion so long as the performance of their rites does not violate the existing laws.

Article 41. No one can, under pretext of religious scruples, exempt himself from conformity with the general laws, which are binding on all in common.

Article 42. The ecclesiastical affairs of non-Orthodox Christians, and of non-Christians generally, are managed by their own ecclesiastical administration, subject, however, to the ultimate superintendence of the competent minister, according to the special laws to be promulgated in this regard.

X

LEGISLATION

Article 43. The principality of Bulgaria is governed in strict accordance with the laws enacted in the manner prescribed by the constitution.

Article 44. No law may be enacted, extended, modified, or annulled until it has been examined and passed by the National Assembly, which also alone has the right of its authorized interpretation.

Article 45. A law passed by the National Assembly must be submitted to the prince for confirmation.

Article 46. After a law has been confirmed by the prince, it must be promulgated in full, and in promulgation distinct mention must be made that the law has been approved by the National Assembly. No law is valid or enforceable until after such promulgation.

Article 47. If the principality is threatened by an imminent danger from without or within, and it be at the same time impossible to convene the National Assembly, the prince may, solely under such circumstances, on the advice of the ministerial council and on the collective responsibility of the ministers, issue ordinances and make dispositions having the force of law. But such ordinances and dispositions must be subsequently submitted to the approval of the first National Assembly convened, in order to retain force.

Article 48. Ordinances of the kind above stated (Article 47) may in no case regard the imposition of taxes or other dues within the principality, which can be affected only after the sanction of the National Assembly.

Article 49. The National Assembly alone has the right of determining whether the conditions imposed by this constitution have been duly observed before the proclamation of any given law.

Article 50. The ordinances by which a law is actually given force, and the measures necessary to that effect, depend on the executive.

XI
STATE PROPERTY

Article 51. All state property belongs to the principality of Bulgaria, and neither the prince nor his relatives can derive any personal profit from it.

Article 52. The manner after which state property can be alienated or mortgaged, as also the management of the proceeds derived from it, will be determined by law.

Article 53. State property is under the management of the competent minister.

XII
THE SUBJECTS OF THE PRINCIPALITY OF BULGARIA

Section 1. General Regulations

Article 54. All those born in Bulgaria, and who have not adopted any other nationality, as also the children of Bulgarian subjects born outside the principality, are regarded as subjects of the principality of Bulgaria.

Article 55. Foreigners can, at their own request, be admitted to Bulgarian citizenship, but the assent of the National Assembly is requisite for that purpose.

Article 56. Any subject of the principality may give up his citizenship after having completed his military service and discharged his remaining obligations toward the principality, according to a special law to be enacted for this matter.

Article 57. All Bulgarian subjects are equal before the law. There exists no privileged class in Bulgaria.

Article 58. Titles of nobility or rank, as well as orders and decorations, cannot exist within the principality of Bulgaria.

Article 59. The prince, however, enjoys the right of founding a recognized mark of distinction for the military on active service.

Article 60. Subjects of the principality alone have the enjoyment of its political rights, but all residents whatever within the principality share its civil rights, according to the law.

Article 61. No one can buy or sell slaves within the limits of the Bulgarian principality. Any slave of either sex, and of whatever religion or nationality becomes free upon setting foot on Bulgarian soil.

Article 62. Laws concerning public order and police regulations are binding on all who reside within the principality.

Article 63. All real property within the principality, not accepting that held by foreigners, is subject to the action of Bulgarian law.

Article 64. In every other respect the condition of foreign subjects resident in Bulgaria is defined by special law.

Section 2. Public Service

Article 65. Only Bulgarian subjects may hold office, civil or military, in the public service.

Article 66. Foreign subjects may also be employed in the public service, but for each separate appointment the approval of the National Assembly is required.

Section 3. Rights of Property

Article 67. The rights of property are inviolable.

Article 68. Cession of property may be obligatory only when required for the public advantage or for state purposes, and then only in accordance with equity, and after the payment of compensation. The manner in which such cession is effected will be determined by special legislation.

Section 4. State Taxes and Dues

Article 69. Every subject of the principality of Bulgaria, without exception, must pay the state taxes and dues determined by law and must bear the fines imposed on default.

Article 70. The reigning prince and the heir-apparent are exempt from all taxes, state dues, and fines.

Section 5. Military Service

Article 71. Every subject of the principality is obligated to military service, according to the law to that effect.

Article 72. Military persons can be tried for criminal offenses in military courts only when they are on active service.

Section 6. Rights of Person, Domicile, and Correspondence

Article 73. No one can be punished without having previously been sentenced by a competent court having legal authority.

Article 74. No person can be imprisoned, and no house searched, except under the conditions provided by law.

Article 75. No one can be subjected to any form of punishment except such as is specified by law. Torture and confiscation of goods may not be inflicted for any crime whatsoever.

Article 76. Should disturbances occur of a character to endanger the public safety, the prince may suspend the action of Articles 73 and 74 within particular districts, and even throughout the whole principality, but he can do this only under condition of submitting his decrees to that effect to the approval of the first National Assembly convoked afterward.

Article 77. Private letters and telegrams are secret and inviolable. A special law will determine the responsibility of those to whom letters and telegrams are confided.

Section 7. National Education

Article 78. Primary education is gratuitous and obligatory for all subjects of the principality of Bulgaria.

Section 8. Freedom of the Press

Article 79. The press is free. No censorship may be instituted, and no caution may be required from authors, editors, or publishers. If the author be well known and resides within the principality, no action may be brought against the editor, the publisher, or the salesman.

Article 80. The Holy Scripture, prayerbooks, and catechisms destined for use in the churches of the Orthodox rite, as also treatises of ecclesiastical law destined for use in Orthodox schools, must be submitted for the approval of the Holy Synod.

Article 81. Offenses in whatever concerns the press can be tried only under the law and by the ordinary courts.

Section 9. Freedom of Assembly and of Association

Article 82. Subjects of the Bulgarian principality have the right of meeting together, peaceably and without arms, to discuss any topic whatever, without requiring any previous permission to that effect. Public meetings held in the open air are subject to the ordinary police regulations.

Article 83. Bulgarian subjects have the right of forming associations without any previous authorization, on condition that the object pursued and the means employed by these associations be not prejudicial to public order, religion, or good morals.

Section 10. Right of Presenting Petitions

Article 84. Every Bulgarian subject has the right of presenting petitions to the several authorities, signed either by one person or by several collectively. Legally established corporations have the right of presenting petitions through their representatives.

XIII

NATIONAL REPRESENTATION

Article 85. Representation in the principality of Bulgaria is expressed by the National Assembly, which is either (1) Ordinary, or (2) Grand.

31

INSTRUCTIONS CONCERNING THE FORMATION OF SECRET BANDS

[Macedonia was the focus of imperialist and national conflict in South-eastern Europe in the late nineteenth and early twentieth centuries. The Balkan states, and Bulgaria in particular, sought to "liberate" conationals in order to increase their territory at the expense of the Ottoman Empire. Reformists and revolutionaries in Macedonia, who included socialists and nationalists, opposed this Balkan imperialism and advocated social reform and political autonomy for the Macedonians. Their most effective organization was the Internal Macedonian Revolutionary Organization (IMRO), whose goal of "Macedonia for the Macedonians" was to be attained through a "war of national liberation" against all imperialists. The goals of the IMRO and the organization of the "war of liberation" in Macedonia are described in the following IMRO document of 1903.]

Chapter I

In each *kaza* [district], a band shall be created for the purpose of revolution. These bands shall be regarded as constituent parts of a total organization, sometimes called the "entire organization." These bands shall undertake secret raids, each within its *kaza*, with such previous knowledge of the appropriate committee as may be necessary.

Chapter II

1. Since the bands are parts of a higher entity, they shall occasionally instruct the population about their raids and the fundamental ideas, purpose, duties, and content of the statutes of the entire organization.

2. In places where the organization is established, the bands shall work to educate the members of the organization to be serious fighters for

Translated by Max Riedlsperger from Tomo Tomoski, *Dokumenti od Vienskata Arhiva za Makedonija od 1873–1903* (Skopje: 1955), pp. 91–101.

the nation and shall endeavor to prepare them for opportunities for the activity of the organization and to teach them the necessity of obedience; in places where the organization is not established, but exists only in rudimentary form, the bands will seek formal organization, and this task must be carried out in a manner corresponding to the instructions and the statutes; the bands are to give reports of their undertakings to the appropriate *kaza* committee and are to obtain from it directions and commands when necessary.

3. Through persuasion and moral influence, the people shall be induced to procure weapons voluntarily.

Chapter III

4. The bands shall establish, with the support of the *kaza* and village committees, a police force and secret postal communications; they shall also prepare the membership list of the village committee together with curricula vitae of the same. In short, they shall closely examine all articles of the Instructions and execute those parts that so far have not been implemented.

5. The bands, since they prescribe force of arms in support of the committees for the purpose of bringing about armed resistance in cities and villages, shall instruct the people in the art of war, in drill, and in such additional information as may be necessary.

6. The bands shall endeavor to procure the munitions demanded by the *kaza* committee and ordered by the *kaza*, either by themselves or by offering protection to those who do so for them. It is also their duty to distribute weapons to those inhabitants who are members of the organization, to take care of the weapons cache, and to ensure that the members' weapons are kept clean.

7. Whenever a compulsory requisition of funds occurs, the bands shall support the *kaza* committees. When such a requisition is deemed necessary by the leaders, they shall marshal their material and mental influence to explain this necessity both to members of the organization and to those not belonging to the organization at the time of the collection.

8. Upon the command of the committee, the death penalty shall be inflicted upon persons when it appears necessary in order to prevent them from doing any further harm.

9. Weapons that fall into the hands of enemies are to be recovered whenever possible. With regard to the Muslim and Christian rebels outside the organization, it must be made certain that they do not work against the bands. Those who do so are to be destroyed upon the unanimous decision of the central or *kaza* committee, or their activity is to be rendered harmless.

10. The bands shall undertake plundering and confiscation of money for political purposes in the name of the squad occupied with liberation according to the unanimous decision of the central or *kaza* committee. Funds from this source are secured by the treasury of the entire organiza-

tion; they shall in fact be delivered, with the prior knowledge of all the members of the bands, to the local committee in exchange for a receipt and then transferred to the central committee.

In unusual cases, the money shall be delivered directly to the central organization.

The Four Highest Duties

11. At the time of the rebellion in their *kazas*, the bands shall form a cadre ready for self-sacrifice, which, on command from the central committee, will first unfurl the flag of revolt. In the most difficult moments and in time of conflicts, its members will strive not to allow the courage of the guerrillas to falter and will rouse them; they also must not neglect the performance of the following duties:

a. In order to ensure the assistance of the inhabitants when matters become serious, they must win the affection of the inhabitants and lead them by setting a worthy example.

b. They must show great zeal in upholding the work of freedom by word and deed, must prove themselves to be true fighters for the liberation of the land, and must in this way bind the inhabitants to the cause and continue to rouse them.

c. They must endeavor to win as many true friends as possible among the members of the organization, who will persevere in the battle to the utmost.

d. They must, when selected to do so, take upon themselves the most dangerous tasks, or else effect the accomplishment of such tasks by the force of their propaganda.

CHAPTER IV

GENERAL RULES FOR THE BANDS

12. The bands must endeavor to carry out their raids and other ventures with the utmost secrecy and must refrain from acts that could bring great harm to the local inhabitants and to the entire organization.

13. Since the bands are members of the rebelling organization, they must at all times observe the statute of the central committee and of the entire organization.

14. It is the responsibility of the bands to maintain the Articles of the Organization Statutes in strictest secrecy: (a) what is undertaken in one village should not become known in another; (b) not one word about one's own ventures or about matters concerning the entire organization may be spoken in the presence of others; (c) along the roads as well as in the villages one should endeavor to remain hidden from the eyes of people outside the organization; (d) members of the bands are strictly forbidden to raise questions about matters unrelated to their duties.

15. The bands of neighboring *kazas* may unite under the leadership of the local band in order to carry out tasks for the benefit of the entire organization as well as for defense against an overwhelming enemy. The

unification can be accomplished on the suggestion of the head of the administration committee of the local band, or, if necessary, of the leader of the band. The band of a *kaza* may, in order to avoid pursuit, cross the boundary of another *kaza*. For the duration of its stay, however, its members are to be considered guests and must therefore obey the regulations of the local band's leader and of the local board of directors of the administration committee. Just as the bands may enter other *kazas* in the interest of the entire organization and to resist the enemy, they may also recruit outsiders to their side if necessary or may enter the service of another *kaza* committee; with these exceptions, it is absolutely forbidden to enter another *kaza*.

16. It will be considered inexpedient and therefore a crime if the entire organization is involved in the struggle prematurely as a consequence of an attack on a village or the incitement of village inhabitants to revolt before the consolidation of the entire organization. The culprits will be prosecuted and subjected to punishment as enemies of the people.

17. The bands are not authorized to carry out an execution without the decision of the head of the local administration committee, with the following exceptions: (a) in the case of those convicted of spying and whose elimination does not involve great sacrifice; (b) when it is necessary in order for a band either to avoid public exposure or to protect the entire organization; (c) when it becomes necessary to eliminate another band that does not belong to the entire organization and that stands in its way.

18. The bands must precisely investigate, in their own and, if possible, in neighboring *kazas*, the geographical and topographical conditions, roads, footpaths, the locations of mountains and valleys, all important places in general, safe hiding places, suitable invasion points, armaments of the revolutionaries and Muslims, the number of revolutionaries, revolutionary situations, strength of the enemy, and all other important aspects.

CHAPTER V

RELATIONSHIP OF THE BANDS TO THE COMMITTEES

19. The bands are usually under the command of the *kaza* administration committees and must carry out the orders of the chief of the same; they must also secure his consent for each undertaking and render a report after successful execution. Moreover, the regulation of further interrelations shall be by mutual agreement.

20. The bands will take every precaution in executing the commands imparted by the central committee and the local administration bodies. They will also take care that no friction occurs between the towns and villages of the *kaza*. The bands shall write a monthly report on their activities and send it to the local central committee.

21. The local administration committees are obliged to acquire weapons, food, clothing, and other necessary material for the bands. Just as they give orders for the movement and undertakings of the bands, they must secure the means for the quick and certain movement of the bands and,

if necessary, also provide hiding places. Just and reasonable demands of the bands will be taken into account by the administration committee.

22. The bands may elect people whom they want to use as receivers of stolen goods, etc., from among members of the organization. These people shall be informed about every aspect of the organization that is pertinent to their work. A band shall not shrink from any sacrifice to rescue others in danger.

23. If the heads of the administrative committees and the leaders of the bands must consult one another, they are to accomplish this either orally, through especially responsible people, or in writing, according to the stipulations of the entire organization. In very important cases, commands will be set down on paper and will remain in the hands of the bands as documents of evidence. This applies also in regards to more important matters, such as executions and the forcible confiscation of money.

24. Disputes between the bands and the village committees will be arbitrated by the administration committee of the *kaza*, and disputes between the latter and the bands, by the central committee, either personally or by sending a commissar to the village or town. The bands are obliged to use the prescribed way of correspondence, not only in matters concerning the *kaza* administration committee, but also in such general matters as the institution of a complaint by the central committee.

25. Upon command of the central committee, the bands may leave or change their headquarters.

26. If a band leaves the *kaza* without command, it will be construed as an act of recklessness. The dissolution of the bands is effected by decision of the central committee.

27. Depending upon the situation in the *kaza*, the bands will consist of seven or more people and will be under the command of a leader named by the central committee.

28. The members of the bands must be strong and capable people and must be ready to divide those difficult tasks among themselves, risking their lives in the mountains and in hiding places. They must have sworn an oath to the entire organization and should be chosen, as far as possible, for their qualities as intelligent fighters. They should be capable and not lacking in perseverance and stability. In short, the whole band must be inspired with self-abnegation and perseverance. People who give way to personal desire for revenge may not be admitted into the bands.

29. Admission into the bands is determined by unanimous decision of the local administration committee. The bands may admit no one without its approval. On the other hand, the administration committee may not force any persons upon the bands who incur the displeasure of the latter.

30. Members of the committee who are pursuing a matter that lies in the interest of the entire organization and whose arrest is sought by the local government temporarily enter the service of the bands; the leaders keep such people, as well as others who temporarily join the bands in some other manner, with them until consultation with the administration committee is possible.

31. (a) Forcible requisitions of food and clothing, as well as demands for protection and shelter, are strictly forbidden, unless absolutely necessary, as is everything that could bring about condemnation by the inhabitants, such as drunkenness and brawling in houses where a band is situated; the lightest punishment for this is expulsion from the band and exclusion from the entire organization, in addition to confiscation of weapons. (b) The members must love one another like brothers and must be ready to sacrifice themselves for one another and to rush to the aid of a comrade in danger; this will be made generally known as the duty of every member of a band.

32. If a guerrilla deserts a comrade in danger, even to save himself, then he is considered a coward and will be excluded from the entire organization.

33. It is the duty of each guerrilla to disregard and foreswear any undertaking of which his comrades disapprove. Plotting and intrigue within the band is not allowed, and those so engaged shall be punished by their comrades.

34. Since the members of the bands are in the service of a sacred cause, they must fraternally share food and such things as are given to them or fall into their hands. The leader in no way has priority in the sharing of the above. Avarice and consideration for one's own advantage is considered dishonorable.

35. Members of the bands who serve in their home territory must endeavor not to meet their relatives and family. No guerrilla may separate himself from the band and go to his house without the permission of the leader.

36. No one may leave his own band and join a different one without special permission. Whoever attempts this or leaves the band without sufficient reason will be excluded from the organization.

37. Since the weapons of the bands belong to the committee, they must be returned by the leader to the committee when members leave.

38. The sustenance, movements, and other activities of the band are regulated by the leader. He also determines where the bands are based, where they spend nights, and when they should arrive at a given destination. He regulates guard duty and determines measures necessary for the security of the band. He is responsible for the acquisition and distribution of food and other necessities and arbitrates quarrels between members of the band and between the band and the populace.

39. The plan for a mission will be determined by consultation between the leader and the members; the command for the execution of the plan, however, is reserved to the leader. He gives the members orders, supervises them, and determines when and where each is to complete his task. If the head of the administration committee demands a man from the band for any purpose and the leader feels that the loss will leave the band incapable of accomplishing its task, he is free to surrender the man or not.

40. The members of the band owe obedience to the leader in all designated cases. Therefore, the leader must on his part endeavor to be sin-

cere. He may not give his commands in a rude manner. He must take the opinion and wishes of the people into consideration and avoid everything that could damage the proper execution of an undertaking.

41. If there is a difference of opinion among the band members about an article or a plan, the opinion of the leader is decisive. If a dispute cannot be settled in this way, the administration committee must be called. Either the committee or a delegate will investigate the matter, and upon this basis a decision will be made. The leader must give ear to the complaints of the members and must submit them to the local or central committee. Until an answer is received, a plaintiff may not disturb the harmony of the band.

42. The members of the bands have a great opportunity to fulfill their duties faithfully. By deeds worthy of imitation they can easily win the affection of the population. Furthermore, they must strive to set a good example by zealously observing the leader's commands, which are aimed toward achieving internal order, and in other connections by exhibiting harmonious cooperative living. If all the commands of the leader are obeyed exactly and zealously, everything will proceed happily. The leaders and members of the bands and the committee are responsible to one another for mistakes ensuing from failure to heed the foregoing regulations.

43. Provided that rapport is maintained, and in all cases of "undertakings for the purpose of incitement," the leaders and members have the same freedom of speech and the same rights.

44. Complete understanding must prevail within the band and is the responsibility first of the leader and then of each individual member. Suitable remedies will be used against dissension and ordinary transgressions, as well as against lack of discipline within the band. Brutality is to be guarded against.

45. Those guilty of lack of discipline in the performance of entrusted duties, of acts against the opinion of the leader or the entire band, and of acts—be they in word or deed—against the interests of the entire organization will be punished in sight of the whole band. Those guilty of failure to improve, of acts against the opinion of the entire organization, of self-willed preservation of personal interests, of bad character or repeated drunkenness, of inability to get along with comrades or members or other committees, and finally, of arbitrary departure from the band will be summarily excluded from the entire organization.

32

THE TASKS OF THE BULGARIAN SOCIAL DEMOCRATIC PARTY

DIMITAR BLAGOEV

[The Balkan socialists were in general critical of the imperialism of the small and great powers in the Balkans. Within the socialist movement, the Bulgarian socialists played a dominant role because of their exposure to the radical ideas of the Russian intelligentsia in the second half of the nineteenth century. Among the socialist solutions to the problems of Bulgaria (and of Southeastern Europe in general) were those propounded by Dimitar Blagoev, the head of the "narrow" wing of the Social Democratic Party of Bulgaria. The following selection from his works was published as the lead article in the first issue of the party's organ, *Rabotnik*, in 1892.]

The socialist movement in Bulgaria dates from as early as 1885. Seven years have passed since that time. At first, the socialist movement appeared in a very indefinite form. Until two years ago, Bulgarian socialism was a negation, a mixture of revolutionary phrases, utopian socialism, Russian nihilism, and Proudhon-Bakunin anarchism. The reasons were our undeveloped economy and our lack of knowledge of the contemporary socialist movement in Europe.

Yet, the economic development that is taking place in front of our eyes, along with our acquaintance with the European socialist movement, has modified the Bulgarian socialist movement, too. About two years ago, a new socialist movement, known as social democracy, made its first appearance. This movement does not restrict itself to the so-called intelligentsia but penetrates among the workers as well. The diffusion of the ideas of scientific socialism strengthened the movement and united

Translated by L. A. D. Dellin from Dimitar Blagoev, *Prinos km istoriata na sotsialisma v Bulgaria* (Sofia, n.p., 1954), pp. 152–56.

most socialists in the organization that presents itself today in this newspaper. Thus, the Bulgarian Social Democratic Party has been in existence and in operation for at least one year. The publication of the Bulgarian Social Democratic Library and the literary and material assistance rendered to the periodical *Den* [*Day*] attest to this fact.

The Bulgarian Social Democratic Party considers it most natural to work openly and legally. The party considers any other activity unnatural, as it may give rise to misinterpretations of the ideas and goals of the Social Democrats. Perhaps there are socialists in Bulgaria who do not share these views, but the Social Democrats who belong to the Social Democratic Party consider open and legal work a major condition for the success of socialism in Bulgaria. That is the reason for publishing this newspaper. However, the word "party" is associated with peculiar notions. When one says "party," one immediately thinks of partisan struggles; many will recall Bulgaria's traditional political parties; others will think we are looking for ministerial portfolios, demanding power, etc.

All this could be true of a bourgeois party, but not of the Social Democratic Party. The latter does not aim at power by any means. For it to obtain power would mean to proclaim a socialist coup, which is the final goal of social democracy. Yet it cannot gain power until the majority of the population embraces its ideas and the program that it seeks to implement. Until that time, it will work by all legal means in order to develop the consciousness of the working class and to attract it to the ideas of social democracy.

It should be clear from the above that the Bulgarian Social Democratic Party is the direct opposite of a bourgeois party. The Bulgarian Social Democratic Party is part and parcel of world democracy. It is an alliance of all Bulgarian Social Democrats who accept its program and its tactics.

The Bulgarian Social Democratic Party represents a separate and independent entity from the workers' associations and unions, which aim at the mutual assistance of their members or the defense of their interests. The Social Democratic Party defends the general interests of the working class. Its immediate task is to attract to its program and tactics all workers, whether or not they are members of associations and unions. Being composed of the most conscientious working forces in Bulgaria, the Bulgarian Social Democratic Party is the vanguard of the workers' movement, the organized militant force of the working class. To propagandize among the workers the ideas, programs, and tactics of social democracy; to develop their class consciousness; to point to the class struggle as the truest means for improving their condition and liberating them from exploitation—such is the task of this newspaper.

From the above, it is not difficult to determine the relation of the Bulgarian Social Democratic Party to the other political parties. The principles that it expounds determine these relations. It sees that small-scale manual labor cannot prosper in Bulgaria, because it is being ruined by the competition of foreign machine-made goods. Our crafts and agriculture are declining from year to year, machines are being introduced, and large farms are being developed. In other words, our country is marching on the road to capitalism. It could not be otherwise. We will pass through capitalism inevitably. Everything contributes to its development in Bulgaria. Our state assists in the development of capitalist production by means of giving aid for factories and machines and by protecting the interests of the capitalist class. In Plovdiv today, an agricultural-industrial congress is taking place that will recommend to the state various means for developing capitalist production. The National Assembly is about to debate legislation having the same object. All in all, the leaders of our state and of our national development find no other road but the development of capitalism. This road will be followed by our people as well, in order to reach socialism. For capitalist production leads to none other than the socialist order. By introducing machines, it ruins small-scale production and concentrates factories, land, machines, and trade in the hands of a few. The majority of the population is coming to consist of hired workers, a working class whose situation deteriorates from day to day. Finally, capitalist production, with its merciless laws, leads to the point at which it destroys itself and pushes humanity toward the socialist order. Yet in spite of all this, the transition to socialism and the liberation of the working class cannot occur without the public and political education of that class, without its cognizance of its purpose.

The Bulgarian working class grows from year to year. As capitalist production develops, the situation of the working class will grow steadily worse, for capitalist production can prosper only when there are workers to exploit. The interests of the capitalists and those of the workers are directly opposed. Until the workers realize their condition and the great tasks they have as a class, they cannot expect any party to liberate them from their economic yoke. *The liberation of the workers is the task of the workers themselves.*

The Bulgarian Social Democratic Party, operating on these premises, cannot but be sympathetically inclined toward any party that assists our people to survive more easily the sufferings caused by capitalism and that, at the same time, does not prevent the socialists from developing the consciousness of the working class today and in the future or from indicating the conditions under which it may free itself from the yoke imposed by capitalism. In general, the Bulgarian Social Democratic Party will operate completely independently of all other political parties that recognize the existing bourgeois order.

Finally, we consider it our duty to point out that the newspaper *Rabotnik* [*Worker*] expresses the ideas, opinions, and tactics only of those Bulgarian socialists who are members of the Bulgarian Social Democratic Party. The Bulgarian Social Democratic Party is not responsible for opinions, ideas, and actions expressed or performed outside and without the approval of this newspaper, even when such is done in the name of social democracy and of the Party.

As may be seen from this article, which constitutes a declaration of principles, the Bulgarian Social Democratic Party expounds the same principles embraced today by all other social democratic parties and by the Workers' Social Democratic Party. It is worth noting how clearly the "Partyists" ["the Narrows"] were able, fourteen years ago, to grasp the socialist movement in Bulgaria on solid ground. They perceive the Social nature and the tasks of the Social Democratic Party and to put the Democratic Party as a political organization of the "most conscientious working forces in Bulgaria," as a vanguard, a front-line detachment of the workers' movement, an "organized military force of the working class." They see the Social Democratic Party as something separate from and independent of the workers' associations and unions or, in other words, as independent of the workers' economic organizations. It is the Social Democratic Party that *defends the general interests of the entire working class.* "Its immediate task is to attract to its program and tactics all workers, whether or not they are members of associations and unions." "To propagandize among the workers the ideas, the programs, and the tactics of social democracy, to develop their class consciousness, to point to the class struggle as the truest means for improving their condition and liberating them from exploitation"—such is the task of the Party and of its organ, *Rabotnik.* In other words, to separate the workers and the working class, which "grows from year to year" in step with the capitalist development of the country, into an independent political or- ganization that operates "completely independently of all political parties that recognize the existing bourgeois order"—such was the task of the "Partyists." Their means were socialist propaganda and agitation.

The *Social Democratic Library,* which the Party continues to publish zealously, as well as the newspaper, served the first purpose, the workers' clubs, rallies, speeches, and participation in political and social life served the second purpose: agitation. All in all, the Bulgarian Social Democratic Party, although giving the "political class struggle" an importance out of proportion to its membership, remained an *association for propaganda and agitation* then and for a long time thereafter. If [Karl] Kautsky has called such a strong party as the German [Social Democratic Party] an *association for propaganda and agitation,* then it is obvious that the Social Democratic Party of Bulgaria cannot be anything else.

33

THE SECOND BOHEMIAN LANGUAGE LAW
PROPOSAL OF 1903

(EXCERPTS)

[The Habsburg emperors used the "carrot and stick" approach to contain the political demands of the leaders of the various national groups constituting the Austro-Hungarian Empire. The national leaders were first of all seeking cultural autonomy, albeit as a prelude to political autonomy or independence. The Habsburgs were less adamant in the face of the demands than were their Hungarian partners. However, despite the occasional concessions made by Vienna, the policy of Germanization, or Magyarization, of the territories and peoples under Austro-Hungarian domination was relentlessly pursued. The following document, prepared by Austrian Prime Minister Ernst von Körber, in January, 1903, is typical of the Austrian language laws. It reveals the continuing insistence on the use of German in official transactions of more than routine importance. At the time the document was considered, the end of the policy of Germanization was not in sight.]

SECTION TWO. RULES OF LANGUAGE USE AND LANGUAGE AREAS

10. Three language areas are designated by the sovereign authorities in the Kingdom of Bohemia for the regulation of language use: (1) unilingual Bohemian territories; (2) unilingual German territories; (3) bilingual territories.

The jurisdictional boundaries of the *Bezirke* [regional] and *Kreise* [district] courts are to be reshaped . . . in such a way that, as a rule, the court's jurisdiction encompasses only unilingual communities.

Similarly, the political boundaries of the *Bezirke* are also, taking into consideration the tasks of administration, to determine as much as possi-

Translated by Max Riedlsperger from Alfred Fischel, *Das österreichische Sprachenrecht* (Brünn [Brno]: Irrgang, 1910), pp. 346–56.

ble the language of the inhabitants. In both cases, the wishes of the population, as well as commercial relationships, are to be taken into consideration.

By this demarcation, every *Bezirke* in which the minority of people speaking the second language is 20 per cent or more is to be regarded as bilingual.

In future, after every second census, a revision is to take place, based on changes in this percentage. . . .

A. OFFICIAL LANGUAGE
IN EXTERNAL SERVICE COMMUNICATION

I. Authorities of the Unilingual Areas.

11. In unilingual areas, the authorities are to employ, as a rule, the language of the appropiate areas as their official language in external service communications, that is, in oral and written communications with external parties.

12. Oral negotiations and requests for reports and written petitions in other vernaculars are permissible for the authorities of the unilingual areas.

Parties are not obliged to supply translations of documents or other written depositions drafted in other vernaculars to supplement, expedite, or otherwise clarify official actions.

A petitioning party shall receive an official copy of the written disposition of his suit in the language of the petition; oral petitions shall be similarly negotiated in their language.

13. In oral negotiations, participation is assured to the parties who employ the other vernacular.

Particularly, it will be ensured that full knowledge of the substance of proceedings, as well as the testimony of witnesses, expert testimony, and decisions and rulings pronounced at the proceedings, shall be conveyed to all parties involved.

14. In cases where the wording is of importance, the testimony of witnesses and expert testimony are transcribed and recorded in the language in which they are given.

15. The provisions of Articles 12, 13, and 14 shall also apply to proceedings in criminal cases.

If a defendant uses the other vernacular, then he is to receive simultaneously official copies, in his language, of pertinent instructions, decisions, rulings, and, especially, the bill of indictment. The presiding officer of the proceedings is to take care that no disadvantage accrues to the accused from his ignorance of the language.

16. Official announcements in a unilingual *Bezirke* are published in the official language; if, however, there are communities that use a vernacular other than the official language, the announcement is to be made in that language as well.

The same applies to such communities with respect to official orders.

17. The language of official publications, official seals, and stamps is to conform to the official language of the authorities.

18. The entries in the public records (land register, water register, mining register, etc.), as well as the trade, guild, and other public registers, are to be made by the unilingual authorities in the official language. . . .

II. Authorities in the Bilingual Areas

19. With respect to the authorities in the bilingual areas, the language of external service communications is fundamentally to be determined by the language of the party addressed.

In external service communications, an official action that serves as the final disposition or ruling of an oral request or a written petition is to be conducted in this language. If the said action deals with official proceedings, requests, or petitions involving several parties who do not use the same language, then both vernaculars are to be used simultaneously, and the requests or decisions are to be recorded in both vernaculars.

20. Proceedings before bilingual authorities are to be carried out in the language of the party concerned. If several parties who use different languages take part, then the proceedings shall take place in one of the languages, if this can be agreed upon, or, if not, they shall be conducted in both vernaculars.

The above rules of conduct shall determine in which language the official declarations, decisions, and rulings are to be published and, on the basis of the rulings and decisions ensuing from the proceedings, the language in which they are to be executed.

If the proceedings are carried out in both vernaculars and if an understanding is not reached between the parties concerning a common suitable language, then the declarations and statements of either party, insofar as they are not reproduced in the language of the other party, are to be documented in the court record. For the rest, the details entered in the record of the proceedings and, furthermore, the dispositions and decisions of the authorities are to be recorded in the original language.

It is to be officially assured that, in bilingual proceedings, the party who uses the other language be fully apprised of the substance of the explanations and pronouncements of the proceedings in his language.

21. In official proceedings that are not instituted by a concerned party, as well as in official orders that are not initiated by the parties to whom they apply, or indeed in any similar actions, the officials must use the language of the person with whom the official proceedings are concerned or to whom the orders are issued. This does not apply to persons who have instituted proceedings.

If the proper choice of language is not known, or if the language is not known, or if the language is neither of the vernaculars, then officials must use whichever vernacular can be assumed to be understood by the party concerned, as determined by his place of residence or by other circumstances known to the officials.

If a decision or decree is issued simultaneously to several persons who do not use the same language, then the order must be in both vernaculars.

A party is justified in demanding that an order be repeated in his desired vernacular within three days after the issuance of the order. In this case, however, the date of issue is the day the first order was issued.

22. Witnesses and experts can use either of the two vernaculars in proceedings before officials of bilingual areas. Their testimony is to be transcribed and recorded in the language used.

23. In criminal court cases, the regulations of Articles 20–22 apply. The indictment and all other written orders are always to be presented to the accused in his language; in the case of the participation of several people who do not use the same vernacular, they are to be presented to each of the accused in his own language. . . . Deviations from the stipulations concerning the language to be used in main proceedings may be made only if they are feasible; in case of disproportionate difficulties resulting from special circumstances, namely, with respect to the selection of the jury; or when the accused himself agrees to the use of the other vernacular. . . .

24. Official notices in bilingual areas are issued in both vernaculars.

The official publications, official seals, and stamps are to be furnished with bilingual texts in these areas. The local language of the majority of the population within the jurisdiction of the authorities shall determine the order of the bilingual texts.

25. Entries in the public books are registers mentioned in Article 18 are to be made by the bilingual authorities in the language of the oral or written application or of the decree on the basis of which the application was submitted. . . .

B. Official Language in Internal Service Communications and Official Correspondence

26. In the internal service, the unilingual authorities in the Kingdom of Bohemia shall use their official language for all official proceedings.

In bilingual bureaus, the language of the internal service communications conforms to the language in which the case discussed was submitted to the office. In matters initiated by the authorities, the bilingual bureaus must use vernaculars, if necessary, in the internal service communications; the circumstances determine the appropriate language.

The German language is to be used: in the establishment and direction of all lists, credentials, and bookings of the police authorities in matters related to the armed forces; in the reports, legal advice, business, and statistical statements attached to proposals to the central offices, insofar as summary reports or provincial summary statements are not prepared by the provincial offices from these business papers for their own use; in information, reports, memoranda, and statements in state police matters or in matters of state security; and in qualification lists of government officials.

27. In communications with all sovereign nonmilitary authorities, as well as with provincial authorities not subordinate to Vienna, the authorities of the unilingual areas use their official language.

In communications with unilingual authorities, the authorities of the bilingual areas use the official language of the former; in communications with authorities of bilingual areas, as well as with those of the court of the second instance, the language in which the matter has been introduced is used. . . .

30. The German language is to be used in communications with officials outside the area of application of this law, to the extent to which it has been used previously.

I. Provincial Authorities

31. The sovereign provincial authorities in the Kingdom of Bohemia have authority if they are not divided into separate language divisions, i.e., bilingual, and they must exactly follow the stipulated regulations for the authorities of the bilingual areas.

In communications between higher and lower authorities, the official language of the lower authorities is the one to be used.

If the lower authority is bilingual, then the higher authority must use the language determined by the state of affairs. . . .

II. Regulations for Revenue, Postal, and Telegraph Offices

33. All sovereign revenue offices and other offices concerned with money in the Kingdom of Bohemia are to use the German language in the keeping of revenue journals, revenue vouchers, registers, audits, and all other revenue records insofar as they are used by the central organs for the exercise of control or for auditing.

The same applies to the internal service communications and the operation of postal and telegraph offices, to fiscal establishments directly subordinate to a central office that carry out state functions, and to mutual communications of the appropriate organs and offices.

The stipulations of this law are applicable, as much as possible, to nonmilitary post offices with a large volume of business.

III. Language Facility of Officials

34. The authorities of the unilingual areas are to appoint, as a rule, officials whose own colloquial language is the official language of authorities concerned.

-- However, where necessary, it is to be provided that, for the most propitious handling of communications with parties speaking other languages, such officials as have exhibited a complete oral and written command of another language are to have responsibility.

It is incumbent upon the authorities of the bilingual areas to provide a suitable number of officials who know both vernaculars for service requirements.

IV. Final Stipulations

35. The stipulations of this law are to be applicable to court and state agencies, as well as to subordinate officials of the Ministries of Interior, Finance, Trade, and Agriculture in the Kingdom of Bohemia. . . .

34

SOCIALISM AND NATIONALISM IN POLAND

[The Russian tsars shared the concern of the Turkish sultans and the Habsburg emperors with respect to "revolutionary" actions, particularly in the case of Poland. The Polish Revolution of 1863 was put down in blood by the armies of Alexander II. Undaunted by the crushing of their national aspirations, the Polish intelligentsia renewed their demands for the restoration of political rights and even for independent statehood. Nationalists made up a majority of the Polish revolutionaries, but the socialists, who established a Polish Socialist Party in exile in France, in 1892, also voiced comparable demands. The following two documents, "Aims of the Polish Socialist Party," set forth at the party's first congress in 1892, and "Poland's Claim to Statehood," by the editor of the nationalist paper *New Reform*, disclose both the similarity between the goals of the socialists and the nationalists and their different reasons for advocating Polish statehood.]

AIMS OF THE POLISH SOCIALIST PARTY

The Polish Socialist Party, as the political organization of the Polish labor class, struggling for liberation from the yoke of capitalism, strives above all to overthrow the present political slavery and to obtain power for the proletariat. In this striving its aim is: *an independent Democratic Republic*, based on the following principles:

POLITICAL

1. Direct, universal, and secret suffrage, a people's legislation conceived as both sanctional and initiative.

Reprinted, by permission, from Manfred Kriedl *et al.*, *For Your Freedom and Ours* (New York: Frederick Ungar, 1943), pp. 166–67, 142–44.

2. Complete equality of the rights of the nationalities forming part of the Republic on the basis of voluntary federation.

3. Community and provincial self-government with the election of administrative officers.

4. Equality of all citizens, irrespective of sex, race, nationality, or creed.

5. Complete freedom of speech, press, meeting, and association.

6. Free court procedure, election of judges, and responsibility of officers before the court.

7. Free, obligatory, universal, complete education; students are to be supplied with means of livelihood by the state.

8. Abolition of a stable army; general arming of the people.

9. Progressive income and property tax; similar inheritance tax; abolition of all taxes on food and other prime necessities.

ECONOMIC

1. Labor legislation: (a) an eight-hour working day, regular thirty-six-hour interruption every week; (b) minimum wages; (c) equal pay for women and men for equal work; (d) prohibition of work for children up to fourteen years of age; limitation of the work of juveniles (from fourteen to sixteen) to six hours per day; (e) prohibition of night work as a matter of principle; (f) factory hygiene; (g) state insurance in case of accident, unemployment, sickness, and old age; (h) factory inspectorate elected by the workers themselves; (i) labor exchanges and workers' secretariat; (j) complete freedom of workers' strikes.

2. Gradual nationalization of land, instruments of production, and means of communication.

POLAND'S CLAIM TO STATEHOOD

KONSTANTY SROKOWSKI

The loss of political liberty has placed a new and very important problem before us, the consideration of which should not be passed over lightly. The problem is how to regain our lost independence. Although a practical solution may not be reached, the demand for political independence will last as long as humanity in its biological evolution does not replace its ideals with some higher concepts of cooperative work. At the present level of development the national state is the best ground for the cooperation of all the life-giving forces. For that reason the desire for political liberty among the Polish people will endure as long as these forces persist. They would, however, automatically disappear with the death of the people themselves.

All other conceptions and representations result either from ignorance or from tactical reasoning, which, however, cannot withstand logical criticism.

It is clear that the Polish people, because of historical factors and because their very existence is chained to so great and tragic a problem, had to reduce all justifications for statehood to one principle: to regain or reconstruct a nation as a foundation of collective energy and the sole source of all justifications for statehood. The Polish state crumbled in only one internal part—the physical. The moral and intellectual, rooted in the character of the people, their conceptions, traditions, and customs, has outlasted the physical. They submit to the destructive and changing influences of other nations only very slowly. Therefore, we can say that the Polish state has a potential power to exist—that it in fact has never ceased to exist and, let us hope, will never cease to exist. It follows then that where there is a potentiality there is obviously a possibility for the actual realization of this potentiality.

As the Polish nation approaches the moment of the realization of its dreams, so the justification for statehood changes from abstraction and theory to the unassailable and practical imperative. Peace will not come like the *deus ex machina*—nor will it come by the power of a decree. Rather it will be a gradual process by means of cultural evolution created by life itself. As it makes itself more apparent, so greater masses of people will gather around this idea. Only the vulgar can call this idea of universal peace "utopia," but among these poverty of thought is coupled with overabundance of words. It is very sad that there should be so many of the ignorant among us.

When a natural and lasting balance is attained, humanity will release a living and creative energy, which is now being used to maintain the temporary and unnatural balance. What humanity will do then, what it will achieve, is difficult to imagine today. Until that time, we are living in a prehistoric era, and real history—the history of the free spirit of humanity —will start only when all people of this earth have enough to eat. . . .

We know that a short period of balance, merely among some social classes and not whole nations, resulted in the Renaissance. We, with all our culture and our hell of social contrasts, will have to wait a long time for such a manifestation.

In the natural and permanent balance of the future, nationalities as such will lose the reason for being. To the fortunate children of this future golden age, nationalistic struggles will be as foreign as religious battles are to the majority of people today. Nationality will become an innocent cult, deprived of any practical meaning. The so-called national ideals will become fetishes for which humanity once spilled oceans of blood. National tolerance will be as universal as religious tolerance is among better Europeans today. All this will come because nations will no longer be economically important. The syndicate of consumer-producer, for whom the highest good is: "I have, he does not have"; the greatest evil: "He has and I do not have"—will disappear. Organizations for fire insurance lose the reason for their existence when forced insurance is imposed on all. The same reasoning may be applied to nations. They lose the reason for existing as aggressive and defensive organizations when it is unnecessary to defend and impossible to attack.

Messengers of the desired balance are here now, but the balance itself is hidden behind the horizon of time. Contrasts between nationalities, particularly in Central and Eastern Europe, where culture began its work of liberating man several ages late, are still great. Nationalities as economic groups are just approaching the role of aggressor-defender, individuals are just attaining social consciousness and lifting themselves with difficulty to the rung of national solidarity. They are still far from the top of the ladder of social balance. Here, more than anywhere in Europe, strict and implacable reality places them farther from the future happy state. Here competition and mutual repression of separate nations must first pass the phase of sharp competition, here realistic politicians—not in the vulgar sense of the word—must first come to understand the opposites: human egoism and fraternity; illiteracy and culture; regression and progress, before the balance can be realized.

35

THE CAUSES OF WORLD WAR I

INTRODUCTION TO THE AUSTRO-HUNGARIAN REDBOOK

[Francis Joseph was willing to reach some accommodation with national groups in order to maintain the integrity of the Austro-Hungarian Empire. But he was totally uncompromising with respect to Serbian aspirations to incorporate the lands inhabited by the Southern Slavs into a Greater Serbia. The Southern Slavs question was the Achilles' heel of the Empire; the Habsburgs regarded any change in the East European status quo that might result from Serbia's attainment of her goals as ipso facto grounds for war. One month after the murder of Austrian Archduke Francis Ferdinand by a Serbian nationalist in Sarajevo, Austria's declaration of war on Serbia marked the beginning of World War I. The Austro-Hungarian analysis of the causes of the war, justifying the Empire's reaction to the events at Sarajevo, is contained in the Introduction to the Austro-Hungarian Red Book, an official report published in 1915.]

Since the dynasty of Karageorgevic ascended the blood-stained throne of Serbia and surrounded itself with those who had conspired against the life of King Alexander, the Kingdom has continually, though by different paths and with varied intensity, pursued the aim of undermining, by hostile propaganda and revolutionary plots, those territories of Austria-Hungary which are inhabited by the Southern Slavs, in order to tear them away from the Monarchy, whenever the general political condition might be favorable to the realization of the Great-Serbian claims.

To what a pitch the hopes of the kingdom on the Sava had been raised, and how near she thought herself to the attainment of their aspirations, appeared in the embittered animosity and the deep disappointment which

---

Reprinted from E. von Mach (ed.), *Official Diplomatic Documents Relating to the Outbreak of the European War* (New York: The Macmillan Company, 1916), pp. 525–30.

were created in this crazy and deluded country by the annexation of Bosnia and Herzegovina and which brought her to the verge of war.

Left in the lurch by Russia, the protecting power, who did not at the moment consider herself sufficiently prepared, in the spring of 1909 the Serbian Government found themselves compelled to give a solemn declaration before Europe, that they recognized the new political and international conditions which had been created by the annexation, and to acknowledge that the interests of Serbia had not been affected thereby. They were also compelled to dissolve the gangs of armed men which had been raised against the Monarchy, and to undertake for the future to maintain friendly relations with Austria-Hungary.

The expectations were not fulfilled that it would now be possible for the Monarchy to live in peace and good neighborly relations with Serbia, as she had lived during the rule of the Obrenović dynasty, and, as was then the case, to show good will to, and further the interests of the State, which owes to Austria-Hungary the recognition of her independence at the Congress of Berlin. The Serbian Government who, by their promise, were under an obligation to maintain friendly and neighborly relations with Austria-Hungary, permitted their press to foment hatred against the Monarchy in an unprecedented way; they permitted associations formed on Serbian territory under the leadership of high officers, civil servants, teachers and judges, publicly to pursue their aims with the object of stirring up revolution in the territories of Austria-Hungary; they did not prevent prominent members of their military and civil administration from poisoning the public conscience in such a way that common assassination was regarded as the best weapon in the struggle against the Monarchy. From the atmosphere created by this malicious agitation there sprang up a whole series of murderous attacks on high functionaries of the Monarchy, which ended in the execrable crime against the exalted person of the heir to the throne, the Archduke Francis Ferdinand, which had been carefully prepared in Serbia. However, the sacrifice of his life for the Fatherland, by which our enemies in their mad folly expected that the downfall of the Monarchy would be accelerated, brought all the peoples of Austria-Hungary together in fiery unanimity around the dynasty. The whole world learned how unshakable were the foundations on which the Monarchy rests, and how firmly and loyally her sons cling to one another. All felt it; there was no room for any doubt that our honor, our self-respect, and our deepest interest peremptorily demanded that we should deal with the criminal conspiracies of Serbia and obtain guarantees for the security of Austria-Hungary.

The unhappy experience which the Imperial and Royal Government had had with this dishonest neighbor showed us the only way by which our interests could be secured.

It was necessary to present to Serbia all such demands and to require from her such guarantees as would ensure the punishment of the accomplices in this shameful outrage and the suppression of the Great-Serbian projects. Since the unparalleled patience of Austro-Hungary had been interpreted as weakness by Serbia, the Belgrade Government must be made to understand that the Monarchy was determined if necessary to go to the utmost limit in order to maintain her prestige and the integrity of her territories; and that she could not tolerate any longer the intrigues of the Sava Kingdom, which were meant to deceive the Powers, by an apparent agreement to the demands of Austria-Hungary, while at the same time she kept open the possibility of continuing her underhanded attack against the Monarchy as she had done after the solemn promise of 1909. Against the usual Serbian tactics of using the most reprehensible means to work for the separation of the Southern Slav territories of Austria-Hungary, and then, when the Monarchy called her to account, of seeking protection and impunity from the Powers, there was only one way open to the Imperial and Royal Government of protecting their territory, and making an end of the injury done to their commercial life by the constant repetition of the intolerable attacks engendered by Serbian aspirations, if they were to avoid endangering the peace of Europe. From the beginning, the Imperial and Royal Government met the apprehensions of the Powers with the assurance that the Monarchy would not go beyond what was necessary for the protection of her own interests, and did not propose any annexation of territory. Within these limits, which she had imposed upon herself, she must, however, insist that the controversy with Serbia should be carried through as a question directly concerning Austria-Hungary and this state. The request made by Russia for an extension of the time given to Serbia for answering our demands would have given the Belgrade Government an opportunity for new subterfuges and for further procrastination, and would have opened the door to the interference of single powers in the interests of Serbia. It was therefore necessary to refuse any prolongation of the time limit. Although before sending her crafty and evasive answer, Serbia had ordered general mobilization, and thereby publicly proclaimed her hostility, the Monarchy waited two days before proceeding to a declaration of war. The suggestion of the British Government that the settlement of the Serbian controversy should be entrusted to a conference of the Powers did not reach Vienna until after the opening of hostilities, and was therefore outstripped by events. This proposal was, however, in itself, not well suited to securing the interests of the Monarchy. Nothing but the integral acceptance of the Austro-Hungarian demands on the part of the Belgrade Government would have given a guarantee for a tolerable relationship with Serbia. The Entente Powers, however, were guided by the desire of substituting for the effective demands of Austria-Hungary, which were painful to Serbia, a method of compromise, by which every security for a future correct attitude on the part of the Sava Kingdom would have been lost, and Serbia would have been encouraged to continue her endeavors to bring about a separation of the Southern territories of Austro-Hungary.

When the Imperial and Royal Government demanded from Serbia that she should punish those accomplices in the crime of Sarajevo who were in Serbian territory, and fulfill the duties which are a necessary condition for friendly relationships between neighboring states, their only object was to protect our dynasty from outrage and the territory of the Monarchy from criminal intrigues. They were representing the common interest of the civilized world that murder and outrage should not be used with impunity as a weapon in political controversy, and that Serbia should not continue incessantly to menace the peace of Europe by her aspirations.

The Entente Powers were guilty of a serious wrong when, under the spell of their own political interests, they closed their ears to these postulates of public morality and humanity, and ranged themselves beside the kingdom with its load of guilt. Had they listened to the assurances of the Monarchy which, by her conservative policy and her love of peace during the violent changes which had taken place in the Balkan Peninsula, had gained full right to their confidence, and had they maintained a waiting attitude toward the Serbian conflict, the world war would have been avoided. It is they who must be made answerable before history for the immeasurable suffering which has come upon the human race.

There can be no doubt that the small Serbian state would never have ventured, with an animosity which was scarcely concealed, to work for the separation from the great neighboring Monarchy of the territories which were inhabited by Southern Slavs, if she had not been sure of the secret approval and protection of Russia, and if she had not been able to depend on the powerful pan-Slavist tendency in the Empire of the Tsar forcing the Russian Government, if necessary, to come to the aid of the kingdom in her struggle for the realization of the Great-Serbian projects.

In the course of the two last centuries the Russian Empire has extended over gigantic areas with the elemental force of a glacier, and has, again and again, subdued fresh races under the Muscovite rule, suppressing their culture, religion, and language. As the supreme and inflexible aim of this restless pressure toward universal dominion there stands before her the possession of the Dardanelles, which would secure to the Russian Empire predominance in the Near East and in Asia Minor, and gain for Russian exports an opening independent of the will of other countries.

As the realization of these plans would injure important interests of Austria-Hungary and Germany, and as it was therefore bound to encounter the inevitable opposition of these powers, it was the endeavor of Russian policy to weaken their power of resistance. The powerful central European union which barred the way to the universal dominion of Russia must be shattered, and Germany must be isolated. The first step was to hem in the Habsburg Monarchy by the creation of the Balkan Union, and to undermine its authority by the pan-Slavist and Serbian intrigues in its frontier territories. A necessary condition for carrying out this plan was the overthrow and expulsion of the Turks in order that the increased power of the Christian Balkan states should be available against the two Central Powers.

When the Balkan Union broke up owing to the quarrel over the territory which had been torn from Turkey, and the Russian plans were threatened with failure, "the protector of the Slavs" [Russia] allowed Bulgaria to be overthrown, humiliated, and deprived of the largest share of the territory which she had won. The Balkan Union which, after the overthrow of the Turks, could now be directed rather against Austria-Hungary and Germany, and could be used by Russia and France for changing the relations of the European powers, was to be set on foot again by the prospect of the acquisition of fresh territories, planned at the cost of the Monarchy, through a successive pushing forward of frontier from east to west. In this criminal game of Russian diplomacy, which threatened the existence of the Monarchy and the peace of the world Serbia was a cat's paw which Russia would not give up even in order to avoid general war.

The Imperial and Royal Government—and the documents provided in this collection give ample evidence of this—again and again almost up to the outbreak of war assured the Cabinet of St. Petersburg that they would not violate any Russian interest, would not annex any Serbian territory, and would not touch the sovereignty of Serbia, and that they were ready to enter into negotiations with the Russian Government on Austro-Hungarian and Russian interests. Russia, however, had not expressed herself as satisfied with the solemn declarations of the Imperial and Royal Government; as early as July 24, in the communiqué of that date, she assumed a threatening tone, and on July 29, although Austria-Hungary had not mobilized a single man against Russia, she ordered the mobilization of the military districts of Odessa, Kiev, Moscow, and Kazan; this was a threat to the Monarchy; on July 31 she ordered general mobilization, disregarding the repeated warnings of the Imperial and Royal Ambassador, and the declaration of the German Government, which had been made on the 26th, that preparatory military measures on the part of Russia would force Germany to counter-measures which must consist in the mobilization of the army, and that mobilization meant war.

On July 24 the Imperial and Royal Ambassador, in conversation with the Russian Minister for Foreign Affairs, laid stress on the peaceful disposition of the Monarchy. Her only object was to make an end to the menace to our dynasty from Serbian bombs, and to our territory from the revolutionary machinations of Serbia.

The attainment of this end was a vital question to the Monarchy. She could not, therefore, allow herself to be terrorized by the possibilty of a conflict with Russia, in the event of that country's taking Serbia under her protection; she must make an end of the intolerable situation, that a Russian charter should give the Serbian Kingdom continued impunity in her hostility to Austria-Hungary.

On July 30, the British Secretary of State again suggested that Austria-Hungary, in her conflict with Serbia, should avail herself of the mediation of the Powers. Guided by their desire to do the utmost in their power to maintain general peace, the Imperial and Royal Government declared themselves ready to accept this mediation. The honor and the interest of Austria-Hungary, however, required that this should not take place under the pressure of the threatening measures of Russia. It was, therefore, a paramount necessity for her to require that the hostile measures of mobilization in the Empire of the Tsar should, first of all, be revoked. This demand the St. Petersburg Cabinet answered by mobilizing the whole of the Russian forces.

In alliance with the self-seeking policy of Great Britain, and the desire for *revanche* [revenge] of the French Republic, the St. Petersburg Government disdained no means of securing predominance in Europe to the Triple Entente and paving the way for their boldest schemes.

Russia's unscrupulous hands tried to weave the threads of her policy into a snare to be cast over the head of the Monarchy. When Austria-Hungary, following the dictates of self-preservation, determined to tear the web to pieces, Russia attempted to stay the hand of the Imperial and Royal Government and to humiliate the Monarchy.

Exposed to the greatest danger in their vital interests, Austria-Hungary and Germany saw themselves confronted with the choice of protecting their rights and their safety, or of giving way before the threats of Russia.

They took the road pointed out by honor and duty.

FOUR

The Modernization
of Eastern Europe
(1918–41)

The collapse of the imperial order at
the end of World War I and the re-
drawing of the political map of East-
Central Europe into one consisting of
a large number of historical and non-
historical national states compounded
rather than simplified the long-standing problems of the area. The succession states, offshoots of the prostrate
Habsburg, Ottoman, and Russian empires, were established theoretically on
the principle of self-determination of
nationalities. In practice, however,
that principle was tempered by the
strategic considerations of the nation-

states and the interests of the victorious European powers. National self-determination in itself was not a guarantee of political and socio-economic viability; often, it merely exacerbated the problems of the area without providing meaningful solutions.

The fact is that neither the emerging countries nor the historical states of Eastern Europe were able or willing to face up to the political and socio-economic realities of the postwar world. The beneficiaries of the largesse of the great powers—Rumania, Yugoslavia, Czechoslovakia, and Poland—were confronted with the problem of maintaining their states against the revisionist claims of the nations at whose expense they had been created. The East European political leaders were so preoccupied with furthering, or opposing, territorial revisionism that they tended to ignore the basic problems of modernization of the state order.

The overriding need of the region—harmonious co-existence among the various nationalities populating the area and, in the case of the multinational nation-states, internal political order as well—was relegated to a secondary position in all the East European countries (with the possible exception of Czechoslovakia). National reconciliation was subordinated to chauvinism, revisionism, and generally discriminatory if not hostile manifestations toward neighbors and minorities. Such unhealthy manifestations by both the have and the have-not nations, and by the dominant nationalities in the multinational states, were excused on the grounds that they protected the interests of the nation. Regrettably, the political elites showed little understanding of the true interests of the nation; if anything, nationalism served as a substitute for realistic solutions to the enormously complex socio-economic problems of the succession states.

The most serious difficulties were encountered in the nationally diverse states of Southeast Europe: Yugoslavia and Rumania. The assumption of the ruling elites in these countries—the Serbs and the Wallachians, respectively—that the socio-economic and political aspirations of the inhabitants of the newly incorporated provinces would be satisfied by national integration alone was indeed fallacious. It is not altogether certain that most Croats, Slovenes, Bosnians, Dalmatians, Transylvanians, or Bessarabians had actually sought national integration, although the attainment of the "supreme national goal" was, presumably, the occasion for rejoicing among the general populace in the two integrated nation-states. What is certain, however, is that the attainment of that goal was no substitute for equality of opportunity and the satisfaction of other economic and cultural needs.

In Bulgaria, enlightened social and economic policies obscured an underlying irredentism. Under the leadership of Aleksandr Stamboliski, the masses enjoyed political and socio-economic rights commensurate with their interests and the political realities of postwar Eastern Europe. The modernization of the villages and the granting of political power to the peasantry—realistic, if unsophisticated, solutions to the problems of an agrarian state—were short-lived, however, for in 1923 the irredentist forces in Bulgaria assassinated Stamboliski and assumed power themselves.

The subordination of the interests of the peasantry was not limited to

Bulgaria. It was also the case in Hungary and Poland, where postwar agrarian reforms were at best nominal; in Rumania, where, despite a major agrarian reform, political power was retained by the urban bureaucratic, industrial-bourgeois, and landowning classes; and even in Greece, Yugoslavia, and Czechoslovakia. This did not necessarily mean that the socio-economic and political status of the peasantry declined from pre-war standards, but it did mean that the peasants' expectations, or at least their hopes, of progress were not fulfilled.

The disgruntled peasantry was soon joined by disgruntled industrial workers, intellectuals, and professional groups who could not be absorbed into the political and economic life of the static East European countries. The primary exception was Czechoslovakia, where a bourgeois-democratic industrial state functioned despite its multinational composition. Elsewhere in Eastern Europe, the ruling elites soon resorted to authoritarian forms of government. In the 1920's and 1930's, collective or individual dictatorships sprang up to preserve national unity as they saw it.

In the 1920's, the succession states were threatened by both Bolshevik imperialism and Italian Fascism. The Communist threat provided the rationale for the establishment and perpetuation of the conservative Horthy regime in Hungary. It also provided the justification for Rumania's and Poland's posture as bastions of anti-Bolshevism, and for the suppression of Communism in Bulgaria after Stamboliski's assassination. The threat of Fascist imperialism was invoked less frequently, most notably in Yugoslavia.

But the 1930's tested the viability of the East European states more rigorously than did the 1920's. The Russian Communists and the Italian Fascists, and their supporters and followers in Eastern Europe, were too weak to undermine the stability of even the most vulnerable states of Eastern Europe; but the effects of the Great Depression were not so weak, nor was Nazi Germany. It is true that there was not always a direct correlation between the rise of the Third Reich and the consolidation and expansion of authoritarian regimes and outright dictatorships in Eastern Europe. Nor could the failure of the "democratic experiment," or at least of the multiparty system, be ascribed wholly to the effects of the Great Depression. Nevertheless, the Depression did aggravate the economic plight of the peasantry and of other social classes, with the resultant exploitation of disaffection by both the right and the left. Communist solutions were generally rejected because of their dogmatism and because their exponents were persecuted by the regimes in power. Socialist and Social Democratic programs were also less than effective, because they ignored the plight of the peasantry. The solutions offered by the extreme right were more palatable, particularly when they called for Christian peasant "crusades" against the ruling establishments and Jewish commercial interests.

But the agitation from right and left was used as an excuse to abolish political activism by all parties and to consolidate unitary, suprapolitical rule by monarchs, regents, and military juntas. Such "protectors of the national destiny" as King Carol of Rumania, King Boris of Bulgaria, Prince Paul of Yugoslavia, Regent Horthy in Hungary, the Polish colonels, Zog of Albania, and Metaxas of Greece all invoked the need for stability in assuming the role of defenders of their countries against internal and external foes.

The external enemies varied from country to country. Communist Russia was the universal foe; Nazi Germany and Fascist Italy were generally in the same category. But even in the search for neutrality and continuing independence, the revisionists and irredentists of Eastern Europe never fully abandoned their own territorial claims and counter-claims. There was little change in these alignments until Munich and World War II, when the East European nations chose sides according to the interests of their rulers or the military realities of the period.

It would be erroneous to assume that the authoritarian regimes of the 1930's did not provide partial solutions to the problems of the East European societies, or that their state forms were incompatible with the historical traditions of the area. Partly through choice but mostly through necessity, the process of modernization was accelerated in all countries in the decade preceding World War II. The economic realities brought on by the Great Depression had to be faced by all the regimes and made German economic penetration difficult to resist. But Hitler's economic imperialism was actually beneficial to the countries' economic growth, and so was the war, at least in the case of Germany's allies. Nor is it possible to deny that internal reforms and the containment of extremist nationalist, irredentist, and revisionist manifestations permitted a temporary reconciliation—or at least camouflaging—of national vendettas. The political and socio-economic maturation—albeit in an authoritarian framework—of the countries of Eastern Europe (with the exception of Czechoslovakia) was a definite achievement, until the Axis powers sought total control over the region and used the traditional policies of divide and conquer to achieve their ends. The destruction of the Czechoslovak state at Munich, with the resulting exacerbation of the muted antagonism between Czechs and Slovaks, and the disintegration of Yugoslavia through the *Sporazum* of 1939 and of Rumania through the Vienna *Diktat* and the Molotov-Ribbentrop agreement, rekindled national hatreds and facilitated Germany's conquest of Eastern Europe in World War II. But the policy proved to be a two-edged sword in that it strengthened the determination of the peoples of Eastern Europe to recoup the violated national boundaries and, in most cases, to rid themselves of the conqueror. These attitudes, aided by destruction of property and the general economic progress recorded either before or during the war, were to be exploited by the Communists and their external supporter, the Soviet Union, as a new concept of national and social liberation began to emerge from the ruined German empire. Thus, a new era was to be ushered in in 1944.

36

THE POLITICAL SYSTEM OF EASTERN EUROPE
BETWEEN THE WARS

HUGH SETON-WATSON

[The problems facing the nation-states of Eastern Europe after World War I were, to a considerable extent, a reflection of the general crises of the twentieth century. The inadequacies of the peace settlements, the failure of the Western allies to recognize the significance of the Bolshevik Revolution, the abandonment of Europe by the United States, and all the other factors that eventually brought on World War II were not necessarily related to—certainly they were not determined by—specific East European problems. The precarious position in which the East European countries found themselves during the interwar years was not always of their own making. But the failure of the rulers of those countries to cope with their problems contributed to the political and socio-economic instability of the area. Hugh Seton-Watson's analysis of the political system of Eastern Europe between the wars focuses on the narrow class policies generally pursued by the ruling establishments in the years following World War I.]

Reprinted, by permission, from Hugh Seton-Watson, *Eastern Europe Between the Wars, 1918–1941* (Cambridge, England: The University Press, 1945), pp. 123–56.

THE RULING CLASSES

In 1918 the states of Eastern Europe had reached different stages of social evolution. In some the aristocracy of earlier centuries still retained considerable power. In others a modern bourgeoisie was already established. Others again possessed neither aristocracy nor bourgeoisie, and their ruling class was in process of formation. A few words on these differences are necessary as an introduction to a discussion of the political systems of the East European countries.

In Hungary, during the second half of the nineteenth century, a large part of the landowning aristocracy was ruined by the agricultural crisis, sold its lands, and found employment in the civil service and free professions. Thus was formed a Hungarian middle class, which occupied the social position of a bourgeoisie but retained the mentality of an aristocracy. The commercial bourgeoisie remained at first mainly Jewish. After 1918, however, the second generation of the Hungarian middle class began to enter trade and industry on a considerable scale, challenging the position of the Jews. The political ruling class of Hungary between the world wars was a combination of the remaining great families and the aristocratic middle class.

In Poland a similar process had taken place earlier. Already in the eighteenth century the *szlachta*, or country gentry, the basis of Poland's strength in her great days, had been impoverished. Its members first became penniless hangers-on of the magnates. Under the Partitions they drifted, like their Hungarian counterparts, into the civil service and free professions. In the Prussian territory they also entered trade and industry, and during the period of "denationalizing" pressure from Berlin there first appeared the beginnings of a Polish commercial class. In the Russian and Austrian territories, the Poles left trade to the large Jewish population, which played a prominent part in the rise of a modern industry at the end of the century. Thus, the ruling class of Poland, as of Hungary, comprised a landowning aristocracy and a mainly noncommercial middle class of aristocratic origin. In both countries after 1918, the middle class grew more powerful and paid more attention to economic affairs, while the influence of the landowners declined. But the rising middle class kept the mentality of the aristocracy and still remains different in character from the bourgeoisies of either Western or Southeastern Europe.

In Rumania the aristocracy had lost ground since the beginning of the century. The land reform dealt it a mortal blow. Its place was taken by the new Rumanian middle class, which consisted partly of people of similar origin to the Polish and Hungarian gentries, partly of elements risen from the lower classes. It contained a majority of civil servants and intellectuals, but commerce was also represented in it. Although trade and industry were little developed and were mainly in the hands of Jews, Rumanians were already, before 1918, beginning to take some interest in them. The Rumanian middle class therefore had a more bourgeois character than those of Hungary and Poland. This character was reinforced by the union of Transylvania and Banat with Rumania. These provinces had virtually no Rumanian aristocracy, and their highest social stratum consisted of the rural and small-town bourgeoisie formed from the peasantry.

A similar situation existed also in Croatia. Here, too, the aristocracy lost its material power with the land reform, and the middle class, formed partly of commercial elements from the Dalmatian coast and partly of recruits from the peasant class, took on a definitely bourgeois character. The Croatian aristocracy ceased to play an active part in public affairs, and all that it left to the middle class was a vague yearning for the lost social glories of the old empire.

In the Czech lands, the ruling class was a strong bourgeoisie, in which the commercial, intellectual, and bureaucratic elements were well balanced. It was recruited from the peasantry during the following years, and also from the industrial working class, already well developed by 1918.

The ruling class of Greece was a strong and wealthy commercial and intellectual bourgeoisie, also reinforced during the nineteenth and twentieth centuries from the peasantry.

In Serbia, Bulgaria, and Slovakia, there was no native aristocracy and no old commercial class. The Serbs and Bulgarians were essentially peasant peoples. When they attained independence, a ruling class was quickly formed of army officers, small-town shopkeepers, artisans, and rich peasants. In 1918 the process was not yet far advanced. The Slovaks had a similar rural bourgeoisie, still less developed. The lack of political experience was made up during the following years with the help of the Czechs, who made great efforts to train a Slovak middle class.

In Albania, there existed a tribal society based on loyalty to the chief of the clan. There were few literate people, and commercial civilization had hardly set foot even on the coastal strip facing Italy, still less spread into the mountains. The Albanians were peasants, soldiers, and artisans. Their ruling class was an aristocracy, which had once played a large part in the affairs of the Ottoman Empire and had thereby come into contact with the greater world, but had not felt to any notable extent the influence of the new society of nineteenth- and twentieth-century Europe.

The task of the ruling classes of the East European countries after 1918 was to attract to themselves new elements in order to strengthen themselves against possible revolutionary forces. They needed greatly to increase the number of people interested in the preservation of the existing regime but had to guard against being swamped by the influx of new recruits.

In Hungary and Poland, middle class and aristocracy had to be combined into a new ruling class. A compromise must be found between the interests of each, and the traditional spirit of the aristocracy be passed on to the middle class. Moreover, the ruling class, although more numerous and more experienced than those of the Balkan countries, needed to be recruited from below. In both countries there was, during the interwar period, a regular, if not very large, stream of recruits from the wealthier strata of the villages. This stream was both absolutely and proportionately greater in Poland than in Hungary.

In the other countries, the problem was the creation or enlargement of a bourgeoisie. In Czechoslovakia and Greece, where a substantial bourgeoisie already existed, the task was easier, and less hurried and drastic methods were required, than in Rumania, Yugoslavia, and Bulgaria, where this class was only beginning to appear.

The new bourgeoisie was formed from the villages. Sons of rich peasants obtained higher education in the small towns and came back to the village as teachers or priests. The children of schoolmasters, Orthodox priests, and Calvinist and Lutheran pastors could begin with an advantage over the other peasants' children. If they showed ability, they reached the university, the most important step toward social advancement. The main goal of East European university students of humble origin was the public administration. It was assumed that every student who passed his examinations had the right to a job in the state apparatus. The job might be of little importance, but it conferred great prestige on the son of a peasant or village priest. Other graduates of the universities, of greater ability and ambition, entered the free professions, set themselves up as lawyers, doctors, or engineers, and became absorbed in the town population.

The commercial class was formed partly from the same source. During the last years especially, the number of young men who have entered trade and industry after higher education has increased. Other sources were the village and small-town shopkeepers and the artisans, whom the state supported in order that they should replace Jews, Armenians, Greeks, or other foreign elements which enjoyed a dominant position in commercial life.

By this process, which had begun in the nineteenth century and developed very rapidly after 1918, was formed in Yugoslavia, Rumania, and Bulgaria a bureaucratic, intellectual, and commercial bourgeoisie which has constituted the ruling class of those countries during the last twenty years. The same process operated more slowly to strengthen the existing bourgeoisies of Czechoslovakia and Greece and the traditional ruling classes of Hungary and Poland. The political history of the Eastern European countries from 1918 to 1941 is the history of these classes.

THE BOURGEOISIE

It was already obvious in 1918 that industrial states are stronger than agrarian, and in a world of national states it was understandable that each nation should wish to have an industry of its own.

There were a number of reasons for industrialization in the East European countries. A new industrial system would give the state a greater degree of international prestige, security, and independence. It would offer the ruling class a means of enriching itself. It would provide employment for a considerable number of young men of the ruling class, in various business offices, commercial enterprises, and managerial posts. It would produce within the state's frontiers a number of commodities purchased by the ruling class, formerly imported from the West. Lastly, it would give employment to a part of the labor overflow from the countryside. The last consideration did not play a big part in the calculation, but all the factors enumerated above contributed to convince the East European governments of the desirability of increased industrialization.

As we have seen, the commercial bourgeoisie did not constitute the predominant political factor in all the East European states after 1918. But in all these states the main economic aims of the commercial bourgeoisie were served by the ruling classes and the governments.

In Poland, during the first years after World War I, the middle class was the strongest element, and as a part of it was already engaged in trade and industry, and the reconstruction of the devastated country required a large measure of industrialization, an economic policy suited to the interests of the commercial bourgeoisie was adopted. When, after 1926, the great landowners obtained more influence, they accepted this policy.

In Hungary, the strongest element from 1920 onward was the big landowners, and the commercial class was mainly non-Magyar—Jewish or German. Yet here, too, the economic policy that was followed was entirely acceptable to the commercial class. The landowners were, already in 1918, extremely dependent on the banks, with which the most eminent representative of the landowning class, Prime Minister Count Bethlen, had close relations. Moreover, it was hoped by interesting foreign capital in the development of Hungarian industry to win sympathy for Hungarian political aims. Industrial protection was adopted from early in Bethlen's premiership, and the landowners, whose interest in the export of grain might have been expected to cause them to oppose it, were placated by protection and subsidies for their own products.

In Czechoslovakia, industry was firmly established already and continued to grow during the following twenty years. The existence beside a prosperous and experienced bourgeoisie of a trained and disciplined working class and a reasonably well-educated and organized peasantry made possible a more balanced state economic policy than was pursued in the other East European countries.

In Rumania, Yugoslavia, and Bulgaria, the agricultural interest was represented after the land reforms by a backward and unorganized peasantry, while political power was concentrated in the hands of a newly created ruling class, which was beginning to take an interest in industry and trade and was encouraged therein by Western interests. Consequently, the economic policy of these three states was dictated by the interests of the bourgeoisie, which had little need to consider the desires of the other classes.

Thus, although the situation of each country differed in some respects from that of its neighbors, it can be said that in all the interests of the commercial class took first place in state economic policy, compromising where necessary with those of the landed oligarchy. This does not mean that state economic policy was directed constantly and consciously against the interests of the small peasants and industrial workers. At times the interests of all coincided. The bourgeoisie, influenced during the first years by liberal ideology, believed that by its generous land reforms, or by the support which it gave to land reforms where these had not been carried out, it was defending the interests of the peasantry. Moreover, it could point out the great interest of both peasants and workers in the creation of an industry which would supply them with employment and commodities. Yet in fact, if the interests of bourgeoise, peasantry, and working class were not always opposed, they were always different. Industrialization certainly benefits the peasantry in the long run, but this long-term utility is obscured, for the first years at least, by the burden which it puts upon the poorest classes of the population. During the pre-Depression years, the peasantry was neglected by the East European governments, which devoted themselves to such economic activity as directly interested the ruling class.

The most striking example is to be found in the export taxes levied by the Liberal Party in Rumania on agricultural products between 1919 and 1928.[1] It is calculated that these cost Rumanian agriculture 120,000 million lei. They prevented an accumulation of wealth by the Rumanian peasantry, which would have lessened the impact of the Depression. But during these years the peasants seemed to enjoy prosperity. Agricultural prices were little lower than industrial, and the export taxes, though resented, were supported.

When the Depression brought the peasantry throughout Eastern Europe to the verge of ruin, the governments were obliged to take steps to help them. Conversion laws were passed, and institutions, such as the grain monopoly in Czechoslovakia and the privileged export company in Yugoslavia, were formed to secure better agricultural prices. But during and after the Depression, as before it, the interests of the commercial and industrial bourgeoisie took precedence over those of the peasantry and working class. This is clearly seen in the statistics of the agricultural-industrial "price scissors." This disparity was not caused by the governments, but they did little to mitigate its effects.

Foreign capital played a large part in the economic development of the East European countries after 1918. Its importance was relatively smallest in Czechoslovakia, where native capital predominated. In Rumania, the commercial class, represented in the all-powerful Liberal Party of the Bratianus, attempted a policy of economic nationalism, creating obstacles to the investment of foreign capital and hoping that Rumania could industrialize herself by her own resources. This policy caused great hardship, as its burden was shifted onto the poorest class. When, in 1928, the Liberal regime was succeeded by that of Maniu, the national peasant leader, the barriers were removed, and foreign capital poured into the country. In the other East European countries, foreign capital was welcomed from the beginning. In 1932, it was shown at the Stresa Conference, which discussed Danubian problems, that the greatest value of investments of foreign capital in this region during the fourteen years following World War I was in Hungary and the least in Bulgaria. It is a

---

[1] The Liberal Party was not in power for the whole of this period, but the two Averescu Governments (1919–22 and 1926–27) were under the influence of its leaders and pursued a similar economic policy.

fact, which may or may not be connected with this, that Bulgaria has the most egalitarian social structure in Eastern Europe, and Hungary the least.

The influx of foreign capital undoubtedly assisted the process of industrialization. From the point of view of the East European states, however, foreign capital has its disadvantages. It is a source of constant annoyance to the nationalist commercial bourgeoisie of the states, for it feels that it does not own its own country's resources, and this hurts its pride. This is particularly the case in the countries where the native commercial class finds itself in conflict with a Jewish commercial class—Hungary, Rumania, and Poland. Resentment against the Jews leads to resentment against all "interfering" foreign interests. Secondly, the foreign capitalists are able to influence the character of the industrialization and to prevent the execution of a careful plan. The foreign capitalist will invest in what industries interest him, not in those whose creation the interest of the state requires. Of course, these are often the same, but they are not necessarily so. Thirdly, the interest payments are a heavy burden on the resources of the states. In order to maintain good political relations with the creditor countries, the governments find it necessary to pay regularly, but this means that they cannot spend their revenue on large-scale public works for the benefit of the masses, even if they should wish to do so.

The supply of foreign capital came to an end with the Depression. Payment of interest was suspended in Hungary and other countries. During and after the Depression the East European governments began not only to interfere in industry but to found enterprises of their own. Such action was dictated by the general need to assist depressed industry and by the particular desire to eliminate Jews and other foreign elements. In Hungary and Poland, industrial and commercial enterprises were filled with young men of the national middle class, many of whom had no special training and who performed the functions of a state industrial bureaucracy rather than of independent businessmen. The governments increased their control over cartels and took over completely a number of industries, particularly those connected with war production. The most ambitious venture in state enterprise in Eastern Europe was the Polish Central Industrial Region, where a considerable beginning was made with the creation of vital war industries in an area where it was hoped that they would be out of reach of potential enemies. In Yugoslavia, the government played, under Milan Stojadinović, an active part in the improvement or creation of metallurgical and chemical enterprises. In Rumania, the place of state enterprise was taken by the activity of King Carol II and his close friends, who by various means concentrated in their hands a large part of the total industry of the country.

Whether organized by native private enterprise, by foreign capital or by the state, the new industries laid a heavy burden on the masses. Heavy tariffs protected articles whose price was from 50 to 300 per cent above that formerly paid for importing them from Western Europe. Many such "artificial" industries could certainly not be defended on grounds of strategic necessity. They benefited only a small number of persons directly interested in them, and their cost was borne by the poorer section of the town population and, to a lesser extent, by the peasantry.

The taxation system was calculated to make the poorer classes pay for the economic program of the ruling class. Here again, Czechoslovakia, whose political and social life approximated that of a democratic Western country, must be excepted. In the other countries of Eastern Europe, the main burden was supported by the people. Indirect taxes were especially unjust, being imposed on articles of popular consumption. In the last years before the outbreak of this war, the proportion of indirect to total tax receipts was over 60 per cent in Yugoslavia and Bulgaria and over 75 per cent in Rumania.

An important form of indirect taxation is the various state monopolies introduced in all the East European countries. The articles subject to these monopolies were those of most universal consumption, such as salt, tobacco, and matches. The monopolies were extremely important sources of revenue for the state, but this revenue was obtained at the cost of grave social injustice. A striking example is the Yugoslav Tobacco Monopoly, which sold tobacco to the public at a price more than twenty times higher than that which it paid to the producers. The tobacco-growers of Macedonia and Herzegovina, peasant smallholders of some of the poorest regions of the country, were compelled to sell their whole crop to the monopoly at prices arbitrarily fixed by it at a miserably low level. If they withhheld a part for their own use, they were liable to fines or imprisonment. The Tobacco Monopoly was therefore not only a most unjust indirect tax, affecting the whole nation, and thus particularly the poorest, but it was also a severe tax on production. It would be easy to quote other examples of unjust taxation from the state monopolies of Poland, Rumania, and Bulgaria.

The proceeds of these taxes were spent on objects of interest to the ruling class. They did not come back to the masses, who had paid them, in the form of social services, improved communications in rural areas, public works, greater security, or better administration. Payment of heavy taxes is bearable if the people feel that the money is being spent in their interest. But in the East European countries, a large part of it simply went into the pockets of ministers and high officials, and the remainder was used for the benefit of a small minority. And the people knew this.

The failure of the economic policy of the East European states to deal with their problems was largely due, as has been seen, to the lack of a thorough plan of industrialization, to the lack of coordination of industrialization with the natural products of the countries, and to the preoccupation of industrialists with the export market. It might appear obvious that new industries, artificially created in backward countries, could not compete in the great export markets with the industries of Western Europe and America. The hope of healthy industrialization lies in the development of the internal market. Only by raising the purchasing power of the masses, and in particular of the peasantry, could the East European governments hope to lay the foundation of a healthy industrial system. But this they were unable or unwilling to see, or, if they saw it, they did nothing about it.

Thus, although it would be possible to argue that the long-term interests of the East European ruling classes are identical with those of their peoples, this argument would have little more than academic importance. The fact remains that during twenty years their economic policies, representing what they conceived to be their interests, were in conflict with the interests of their peoples. This cannot be disproved by pointing to the numerous successful enterprises of national importance, for instance the creation of the Polish port of Gdynia, or by enumerating the superficially impressive palliatives to agrarian distress forced on the governments by the Depression.

There were three main conflicts of interest: between bourgeoisie and landowners; between bourgeoisie and industrial working class; and between bourgeoisie and peasantry. The most important was the last. The quarrels of the landowners and industrialists were solved by compromise in Hungary and Poland. The quarrels of employers and workers were solved by physical force, to the advantage of employers. But the working class, outside Czechoslovakia—to which, as already noted, this description hardly applies—does not represent a very large part of the population. The fundamental conflict in Eastern Europe is that between the ruling bureaucratic-commercial class and the peasantry.

This issue is usually confused by misplaced emphasis on the superficially intimate connection between the peasantry and the new ruling classes. It is pointed out that in Rumania, Yugoslavia, and Bulgaria, the majority of the ruling class consists of sons of peasants. This is true but unimportant. Few books have been written on Eastern Europe which do not point out that the minister or businessman of the Balkan states was in most cases born in a village, and could easily go back to his village tomorrow and live as a peasant. There are two answers to this. First, the peasant's son who has risen in society does not go back to the village, except to see his parents or a friend. He lives and works in the town, and his family grows up there. He may keep his house in the village or build himself a new and better one there, but he will go back there only for short spells on holidays, exactly as an English beer lord may spend his holidays in Inverness-shire. He no longer belongs there. Still less do his children. Second, the "sons of peasants" who become ministers or businessmen are almost always sons of big holders, schoolmasters, or priests, of the "rural bourgeoisie." Few are sons of one of the smallholder families which form 70 per cent of the agrarian population of Eastern Europe. And in 1944, it is still less likely that a member of this agrarian proletariat will rise to a high place than it was in 1918. Village-born politicians may visit the villages at election time and shake hands with the whole population. But the days of patriarchal beneficence are past. This hand-shaking may once have meant something. Today it is an empty demagogic gesture. The politicians, the businessmen, and the big bosses of the bureaucracy have no more in common with the village proletariat than has a Western industrialist with his workers. They speak the same language and live in the same geographical area, but their interests, aims, and outlook are wide apart.

The Western tourist can see this for himself by taking a motor trip of a few miles from any East European capital. He may enjoy an excellent lunch with a friend in a comfortable Bucharest flat, furnished with all the amenities of modern civilization, and then spend the afternoon in the countryside. Along the asphalt road to Sinaia on the weekend, the luxurious cars make an unbroken line. But if he turns off after ten miles onto a side road, the tourist will soon find himself in as primitive a village, with as many dirty, ill-housed, ill-clad, cheerless wretches as he likes. The ruling classes of Eastern Europe do not contain so many millionaries as those of the West. But the contrasts of wealth are more striking, for the bottom level is lower, and on it sit more than half the people.

THE WORKING CLASS

Since the end of the nineteenth century, an industrial working class has sprung up in certain areas of Eastern Europe. The oldest and most developed are those of Bohemia-Moravia, the Budapest district, and Western Poland (Silesia and Łódż). The railway workers of all the East European countries have by now a tradition of more than one generation. The Rumanian petrol industry has a considerable number of skilled workers, who already form a social class distinct from both bourgeoisie and peasantry. The same is true of parts of Croatia and Slovenia, where Zagreb, Ljubljana, Celje, and Maribor form industrial centers of some importance. Since 1918, the growth of industry in all the East European countries, particularly in the cities of the Balkans—Athens, Salonica, Sofia, Belgrade, Bucharest, Plovdiv—has led to a great increase in the number of industrial workers. This new Balkan working class has, however, not yet passed its first generation and is not always clearly differentiated from the peasantry from which it originated.

The problems of the industrial workers in Bohemia-Moravia, Silesia, Budapest, and Łódż are the same as those of their fellows in Western Europe. In Eastern Poland, Rumania, and the Balkan Peninsula, on the other hand, special problems exist, for which parallels could be found in the semi-industrialized countries outside Europe, but which hardly exist in the West. They are due to the close connection between the factory and the village.

Overpopulation in the villages sends the peasants into the towns in search of work. This constant influx of unskilled workers creates a permanent reserve of labor, which the employers can use to keep wages low. When times are good and wages rise, the influx is correspondingly greater, and the old level of wages is soon restored.

A large part of the influx consist of seasonal laborers, who spend only a few months in the factory and return to their villages with their earnings. These men have their house, and produce part of the food needs of their families, on their holding. They only need sufficient wages to cover their small cash requirements—town-made foodstuffs, clothing, and taxes. They are therefore content with a much smaller wage than is needed by a worker who lives with his family in the town. The employers naturally use these cheap workers for as many purposes as possible. Their presence is a factor permanently depressing wages. It affects all but the skilled industrial workers.

The unemployment statistics of the East European states during the last twenty years have not been very striking, even in the Depression years. The reason why they have been comparatively low is that when there is less employment in industry, most of the unskilled workers go home to their villages and sit there and rot. The state forgets about them, and they do not appear in the official statistics.

A better standard of living for the urban unskilled worker in Eastern Europe depends on the success of measures to deal with the agricultural overpopulation problem. It is unlikely that even with the best will in the world very big results could be obtained in this direction for a number of years. But until progress is made toward curing, or at least relieving, the misery of the village, the urban unskilled worker can have little hope.

It is possible to relieve the situation for a short time by restricting the liberty of the peasants to migrate to the towns. Such measures are only justifiable, however, if accompanied by real attempts to deal with the peasant problem. They are dangerous, for they usually lead to laziness on the part of the authorities. It is easy for a government to use the police to prevent the peasants from leaving their villages, refuse them employment unless they are furnished with a labor permit, and arrest them as "Bolsheviks" if they object. The classical description of this system is to be found in Silone's magnificent novel about Fascist Italy, *Fontamara*. Most of the East European states offer analogies.

The only solution is that governments should devote themselves principally to the solution of the peasant problem, reduce to some extent the influx into the towns, and establish a minimum wage for urban unskilled workers. But it is much easier to point to the desirability of this "solution" than to carry it out.

The skilled worker is not immediately threatened by the pressure from the village. He will only be threatened when a large number of unskilled workers learn skilled trades. And in view of the low standard of living and lack of technical education, this is not likely to be the case for some years.

The East European governments conformed with the recommendations of the International Labor Organization concerning hours and conditions of work, insurance, and social services, but many of the measures adopted remained on paper, and in all the countries under review the benefits of such measures were confined to the skilled workers. The condition of the workers was far better in Czechoslovakia than in any of the other East European states. In Hungary, it was fairly good for certain skilled trades. The situation of the Hungarian working class was improved by the fact that the pressure of the villages on industrial employment was much smaller than in neighboring countries to the north, south, and east. This was due partly to the absence of an acute overpopulation problem, partly to the fact that the landowners were interested in keeping the surplus agricultural population on the land. They profited from the existence of an agricultural labor reserve and were not disposed to let the industrialists take this from them. In Poland, there was a fairly numerous skilled working class in the old industrial centers, which enjoyed a reasonable standard of living. The Depression caused substantial unemployment in Poland, Czechoslovakia, and Hungary, but the development of state enterprise, particularly of the armaments industry, in the last years before the war greatly relieved, even if it did not completely cure, unemployment.

During the twenty years between the two wars, then, the skilled workers of Eastern Europe—who were almost entirely confined to the three most northerly states and constituted less than half the total number of industrial workers—had a tolerable existence, maintained to a large extent at the expense of the unskilled workers and peasants. Consequently, the skilled workers were not on the whole a revolutionary element in East European politics. The threat to the established order came far more from the peasant masses and the first-generation workers of peasant origin.

Trade unions prospered only in the three northerly countries, and in the skilled trades. In the metallurgical and textile industries, there were strong trade unions. Particularly important were the printers' unions. In all three countries, the trade unions were closely connected with the Social Democratic Parties, which had been founded on the model of the German and Austrian parties. In Rumania and the Balkans there were few skilled workers, and German influence was of small importance. In these countries, the trade unions were less connected with parties. Social Democratic Parties hardly existed. Left intellectuals were influenced by French and Russian rather than German ideas. Communist influence was much stronger than Social Democratic. The only part of the Balkan Peninsula where Social Democratic trade unions of the Central European type existed was Slovenia, where Austrian models had been imitated already before World War I.

Mention should also be made of Catholic and nationalist trade unions. The former were most important in Poznania and Polish Silesia, where they dated from the time of the national struggle under Imperial German rule, in which the Catholic Church had led all classes of the Polish nation. They were also of some importance in Czechoslovakia and Slovenia. The most important nationalist trade unions were those connected with the Croatian Peasant Party.

In the three northerly countries, the trade unions were able to resist pressure from outside the working class. The Czechoslovak trade unions played an active and constructive part in political life until the destruction of the democratic republic. In Poland, they survived the attacks of fascist elements until the end. In Hungary, the skilled workers were sufficiently strong and important to maintain their unions until the outbreak of war with Russia. They were helped in this by the difference of interests between the landowners and the industrialists.

In Rumania and the Balkans, the trade unions were never strong. The absence of a large body of skilled workers and the low cultural and economic level of the peasant recruits to industry made the task of organization almost impossible. Moreover, the governments were terrified of trade unions and "nests of Communism" and used every excuse to repress their activities, organizing strike-breakers, constantly backing up employers, and putting down strikes by armed force. Two examples of the latter are the "massacre' of the Jiu valley, carried out by the "progressive" Government of Iuliu Maniu in 1929, and the railway strike of Bucharest (Grivita workshops) in 1934, suppressed by Vaida Voevod and Calinescu at heavy cost of life, after complete violation of promises which had been made in order to secure the evacuation of the shops by the workers. The history of Yugoslavia and Bulgaria during the last twenty years contains more numerous and bloodier examples. In Rumania, independent trade unions were officially abolished in 1938 and replaced by "guilds" under the fascist system erected by King Carol II. In Bulgaria, they had no real power after 1923 but existed nominally until the *coup d'état* of 1934, when they were superseded by officially organized labor institutions. In Yugoslavia they continued to exist in theory until the invasion of the country, although they had long ceased to have any importance, and had been threatened by the official, uniformed "trade unions" created on the Italian model by Stojadinovič and Cvetkovič.

THE EDUCATIONAL SYSTEM

The importance of the educational system in the formation of the new ruling classes of Eastern Europe has already been briefly indicated. The East European states prided themselves particularly on the progress made in education during the twenty years between the wars. Enormous numbers of schools were built in regions where they had been quite unknown. Universal compulsory elementary education was introduced, and a genuine attempt was made to enable poor children of talent to obtain higher education.

The equality of opportunity was greater in the Balkan states, Rumania, and Czechoslovakia than in Poland or Hungary, where the remnants of a feudal society provided an obstacle, and in all the countries under review there is a difference between the pre-Depression and post-Depression periods. During the first years, at least in the "reformed" states, the possibilities of higher education were far larger than after 1932. The combination of the general economic trends with the special effects of the Depression widened the gap between the rich and poor peasants, and the masses sank back into the swamp of hopelessness from which they had emerged for a few years after 1918.

It would be unfair to underestimate the achievements of the East European states in education. During the twenty years illiteracy was enormously reduced. If it has not been eliminated, if there are still regions in Bosnia and Bessarabia, to take only two examples, where more than 80 per cent of the population cannot read or write, this cannot be blamed entirely on those in charge of educational policy. The peasants themselves were not always cooperative. Often, children needed at home for work in the fields were not allowed by their parents to go to school. A further, almost insuperable, difficulty was the absence of communications, particularly important for the mountain villages of the Balkan Peninsula and the Carpathians. Special problems existed in parts of Central Hungary, where the peasants live not in compact villages but in individual houses, separated by several hundred yards from their nearest neighbors. The situation of the school is bound to be unfavorable for some outlying families, whose children have to walk a number of miles. The truth is that education, like public health, is dependent on economic improvement and reform, and the deficiencies of the latter in the East European states constantly hampered their extremely praiseworthy efforts in the former.

Sufficient progress was made to stimulate a most striking appetite for knowledge. The word "intellectual" has perhaps greater prestige in Eastern Europe than anywhere else in the world. Merchants, soldiers, and public officials love to call themselves by this name. Books are in constant demand, and adults take great trouble to continue their own education long after leaving school or college. The East European universities have produced many distinguished scholars, and governments have spent large sums on the provision of modern scientific and medical equipment, generously assisted by the Rockefeller and other American foundations. The highest level of education and culture was undoubtedly to be found in Czechoslovakia, which could bear comparison with Western Europe. The ancient University of Cracow and the more modern ones of Budapest and Warsaw attained the highest level. In view of the slender resources at their disposal, it must be admitted that the Balkan universities and colleges made great progress. Such men as Professor Slobodan Jovanovič of Belgrade would have lent distinction to any university in Europe or the New World.

Yet, when all credit is paid to the activities of Ministers of Education and of a vast anonymous army of selfless and untiring men and women teachers, it must unfortunately be stated that there were grave deficiencies in the content and quality of the education provided. One reason for this was the lack of qualified teaching staff available. Even in Czechoslovakia, this defect made itself felt. Slovakia, and still more Ruthenia, had a very small number of educated men, and few of these were willing to devote their lives to educating their less fortunate compatriots. It was necessary to bring in Czechs to direct the schools, and this led to considerable ill-feeling. In Poland, Western Galicia and the Prussian territories could provide a substantial number of cultured and capable people, but these were in practice frequently overlooked in favor of less suitable persons from the Russian territory, who had won the gratitude of the government by political or military services. In Hungary, the teaching staff was somewhat more adequate, but this was partly because popular education was relatively less developed than in the neighboring countries. In the Balkan countries and

Rumania, the lack of staff was acute. Teachers were insufficiently trained, and education suffered accordingly.

The predominant ideology in East European, as in West European, educated circles in 1918 was that of liberalism. The two fundamental principles of this creed were the independence of national states and the liberty of the individual in society.

The conflict between romantic nationalism and individualist egalitarianism, already apparent in West European intellectual life in the nineteenth century, and especially in the contrast between French and German interpretations of liberalism, received still greater emphasis after 1918. The difficulties involved in this conflict were too much for the inexperienced teachers of the East European states. They continued to pay lip-service to the ideas of the French Revolution, but they understood little of their implications. In practice, they fell back on the safe and easily intelligible doctrines of romantic nationalism.

Emphasis was laid on history, and particularly on the heroic medieval periods in which each East European nation had for a brief span of years dominated its neighbors. Serbian children were taught to look back to the glories of Dushan, Bulgarians to the Empire of Simeon, Rumanians to the wars of Stephen the Great and Michael the Brave. Poles were reminded that their armies had once sat in Moscow, Hungarians that their forefathers had raided as far as Naples or Nîmes. The youth of each nation was taught to regard its neighbors as inferior to itself in culture, moral values, and courage.

Analytical historical study hardly existed. Such distinguished historians as the great Rumanian Professor Iorga confined themselves to erudite chronology, written in a highly romantic and bombastic spirit. Critical study of the development of social institutions and ideas was only beginning, and if it received some encouragement in Prague, Budapest, and Belgrade, in most East European centers it was frowned upon by the elder generation of professors. If this was true of the universities, it is hardly surprising that in the schools the poorly trained teachers were hardly able to give their pupils more than a grounding in the "three R's" and a conviction that chauvinism is the highest civic virtue.

The part played by university students in the lives of the East European states forms a sad chapter in the history of the last twenty years. The great majority of East European students are sons and daughters of poor families, enabled by the state to continue their studies. They should constitute the elite of these young nations. It is regrettably true that they did not do so. Only a comparatively small proportion were inspired by a love of learning or a desire to train their intellects for the service of their countries. Their idea of such service was rather that they had an automatic right to a place in the state administration after spending a given number of years at the university. A university diploma was considered a claim on the state for the rest of life. Moreover, a great part of their time was spent in political activities, not always of a very creditable kind, which detracted from their work. A number of excellent young men and women completed their training every year, but they seldom formed a very high percentage.

There are, of course, very great differences between different universities. The best universities were those of Czechoslovakia. The Hungarian universities have a fairly good record, and their faults may be said to be those of all European universities, including those of Great Britain. If too much of the time of the students of Belgrade University was spent on political meetings, it must be emphasized that they rendered an immense service to their own country and to the peoples of the Balkans by their devotion to the principles of political freedom and social justice. During the Yugoslav dictatorship, the only place where free discussion was possible was within the walls of the University of Belgrade, whose autonomy was respected by all governments; and the intellectual integrity and personal courage of many students and professors were a source of inspiration to their people.

The lowest level in Eastern Europe was that of the Polish and Rumanian universities. These words must not be understood to mean that there were not noble, disinterested, and industrious men and women among the professors and students of these two countries. The names of such people would fill many volumes. But in both countries, the impatient and discontented idealism of the younger generation and of the intellectual class were exploited by governments and politicians for the basest purposes.

In Poland bands of anti-Semitic and fascist students were used by the National Democratic Party to embarrass the government, and by the government against Socialists, Democrats, and national minorities.

In Rumania, the students were a simple instrument of the police. Numbers of students were hired for small sums to create disorders at opposition meetings, in order to provide the government with a desired excuse for the introduction of martial law and the suppression of inconvenient political organizations. In 1925, the liberal politician Tatarescu paid students and provided them with free railway transport to the frontier town of Oradea Mare (Nagyvárad), where the police authorities equipped them with stones to smash the windows of Jewish shops. Some hours of breaking, beating, and looting gave the Government what it needed. In the University of Jassy in Moldavia, the Iron Guard group grew up in the twenties among students who spent their time almost exclusively in anti-Semitic demonstrations, pogroms, strike-breaking, and outrages against "Communist" intellectuals and workers. The "hero" Codreanu, one of these students, murdered the police prefect of the town, was acquitted, and gained a reputation for patriotic courage on the strength of it. When the professors were rash enough to remind the students that they had come to the university to work, the students "went on strike," and refused to take their examinations. Many of the professors encouraged them.

It is obvious that the responsibility for this horrible state of affairs lies not with the students themselves but with the governments and ruling classes, who committed an unforgivable crime against their own peoples by their deliberate perversion of the morals of the growing generation.

The false educational system of Eastern Europe, which at the best encouraged chauvinism and at the worst helped to destroy all conceptions of morality, is one of the fundamental causes of the misfortunes of these peoples. Unhealthy romanticism, national arrogance, and intellectual and moral dishonesty were not confined to the schools and universities but extended to the press, publications of all sorts, and the theater—official propaganda in the widest sense. The ruling class formed in this atmosphere was hardly likely to make a success of its rule. It had no sense of responsibility toward other classes, no understanding of the principle of individual liberty, no knowledge of the fundamental problems of its country, and still less of the character and condition of neighboring countries. The young generation was brought up to hate and despise other nations, to fear its own people, and to see in any proposal for collaboration with other states a poisonous intrigue of "Reds," Jews, and Freemasons. It was deceived by any kind of demagogic anti-Semitic or antidemocratic agitation and fell an easy prey to Nazi propaganda. In view of the type of education that the East Europeans received, the surprising thing is not that Hitler and his minions found sympathizers among them, but that so many did not succumb to his blandishments.

There can be no hope of progress for the peoples of Eastern Europe without a radical reform of education. Unfortunately, "solutions" of this problem are not easy to find. Education in Western Europe and America is not so free from faults that we can quickly prescribe remedies for the misfortunes of Eastern Europe.

It is clear that more provision must be made for the training of schoolteachers. A much more extensive and efficient system of teachers' training colleges is required. In this respect it is certain that Western Europe can help, for it has undoubtedly reached a more advanced stage. If the East European states cannot at first find a sufficient number of professors for the training colleges, these could be provided from the West, on the understanding that they would be replaced as soon as possible by their own nationals.

The need for a more ambitious system of technical, medical, and agricultural education has already been indicated. There is room for enormous numbers of village doctors, engineers and agricultural experts in all the East European countries, especially in Rumania, Eastern Poland and the Balkan Peninsula. During the last twenty years the comparatively small development of these branches of study was the more striking in view of the overcrowding of the law faculties, whose students in many cases received no more than a training in chauvinism as a preparation for a bureaucratic post. Technical and medical training are of more importance to the backward countries of Eastern Europe than knowledge of the complicated concepts of French constitutional law. The overdevelopment of law study was largely responsible for the grave problem of "intellectual unemployment," which became most acute in Eastern Europe during the Depression and provided a generous supply of "Führers" for the various fascist movements of Eastern Europe. As long, however, as the social problems of the villages are unsolved, there will be no possibility, in a rationally ordered East European state, of "overproduction" of doctors, agricultural experts, or engineers.

Far greater attention should be paid to the study of neighboring nations. During the last twenty years, rich East Europeans would send their children to study in France, Germany, or even England, but no one ever took the trouble to study the language, social conditions, or history of neighboring peoples. Consequently, there were, for instance, hundreds of Rumanians who knew something about France, quite a large number who even intimately understood France, but hardly any who knew anything about Poland, Bulgaria, or Yugoslavia. Yugoslavia and Rumania were allies for twenty years, but the attitude of the educated classes of the two peoples to each other was marked by complete ignorance, indifference, and contempt. This lack of cultural relations between the East European states was one of the fundamental reasons for their failure to collaborate against common external enemies. It is of great importance that in the new Europe means should be provided for regular exchanges of students, teachers, and simple citizens and peasants between the countries of Eastern Europe.

The main object of a new system of education in Eastern Europe must be the removal of the pernicious spirit of romantic nationalism from the schools, press, and literature. This is no easy task, and one that does not concern Eastern Europe alone. It should be clearly understood that this is not a plea for the discouragement of ordinary ideas of patriotism. The truth is that the best way to stimulate patriotism is to prevent chauvinism. The chauvinist "nationalists" of Eastern Europe were mostly not patriots at all but acted as dupes and agents of Nazism in betraying their countries to Germany and Italy. The next generation of East Europeans must be taught to combine love of their own country with respect for the liberties of other nations. A new outlook must be built up which will avoid the extremes of romantic nationalism, on the one hand, and colorless and loquacious cosmopolitanism—of the type not uncommon in certain organizations of liberal tendencies in post-1918 Britain—on the other.

THE ADMINISTRATION

The administration of the East European states varied according to their past history. The best was to be found in the regions formerly belonging to Austria—Bohemia and Moravia. Hungary and the provinces formerly belonging to her had a rather more backward system. The worst administration was that of the former Russian and Turkish regions.

In the new states of 1918, regions of Eastern and Western standards were combined together, and this gave rise to special problems, of which more will be said later. In Yugoslavia, Rumania, and Poland, it may be said with little exaggeration that the Eastern methods prevailed over the Western. In Bulgaria, the Eastern system has never been challenged. In

Czechoslovakia, the Austrian tradition of honest and fairly efficient administration was continued, and in Hungary, conditions were, as before World War I, somewhere between Western and Eastern.

The old Russian bureaucracy was the offspring of Mongol and Byzantine traditions, while that of the Balkans owes its origin to a combination of Byzantine and Turkish conceptions. Both were essentially arbitrary and dictatorial, but their severity was always mitigated by inefficiency and corruption. The Balkan official regards himself as immeasurably superior to the peasants among whom he lives and from whose ranks he has sprung. To be an official is the fondest dream of every able young son of a peasant. The Balkan official does not like to work. He considers himself so fine a fellow that the state and the public should be proud to support him for life and should not ask him to make efforts that will tax his intellect or character. A visitor to a Balkan ministry or police headquarters in the middle of the morning will find the rooms filled with good-natured fellows comfortably enjoying a cup of Turkish coffee and a chat with their friends. The papers lie on their desks. Outside stand, sit, and squat patient queues of peasants awaiting their various permits and receipts. Foreigners and citizens with *"protekcija"* [2] obtain swift and polite attention, but the people can afford to wait. They have waited many hundreds of years already for justice, and few more hours will not make much difference. Time counts little in the Balkans.

Balkan bureaucracy involves obscure and complicated formalities and documents, the result of an accumulation of laws and taxes superimposed on each other since the beginning of time, which provide a constant source of revenue to the bureaucrat and of annoyance to the citizen. Everything which can be is centralized in the capital. The local official dreads above all responsibility. Everything must be referred to a higher quarter. Days pass before an answer is received, and the citizen may be summoned to the capital, at his own expense in time and money, to settle some trifling formality.

It would be absurd to suggest that contempt for the public, pompous laziness, love of formality, and fear of responsibility were the monopoly of Balkan bureaucracy. They are, however, perhaps more marked in the Balkans, Poland, and Rumania than in the West. What is more especially Eastern is the corruption of officialdom. Few books on Eastern Europe by tourist "experts" fail to express indignation at the railway official who let them off with half-price and put the half in his pocket or at the innkeeper or merchant who changed their money at an illegal rate. Petty corruption is widespread in the lower ranks of every branch of the bureaucracy in Eastern Europe. Its cause is very simple. The official is so badly paid that he cannot support his family without extra sources of revenue. These he finds in minor transgressions of the law and in the granting of minor illegal privileges to those willing to pay for them. As the laws are often

---

[2] This is the Serbian form of a word used, with different terminations, in all the languages and countries of Eastern Europe, to denote "special protection," "connections," "graft," or "pull." It is indispensable for the making of a career.

cumbrous, stupid, inefficient, and oppressive, there is seldom any lack of people ready to bribe an official to ignore or contravene them.

Although this corruption had a bad effect on both officials and citizens and caused unnecessary hardship to those who were too poor to buy exemptions or precedence, its importance should not be exaggerated. Most petty officials in Eastern Europe are not vicious men. They are kind-hearted souls who put their duty to their families before all else and whom economic pressure compels to take a "realistic" view of their duty to the nation.

Far more serious was corruption in high places. If petty venality can be cured by raising the salaries of government servants to a reasonable level, it is much harder to prescribe a cure for the more insidious upper-class corruption. This too is not an exclusively East European phenomenon, but it takes on in Eastern Europe forms comparatively rare in the West.

In Eastern Europe the greatest fortunes are made not in industry or banking but in politics. The Ministries of the Interior and of Foreign Affairs of most of the countries under review possessed large "discretionary funds," of which the ministers often embezzled part or all. Ministers of Finance enriched themselves by selling high protective tariffs to industrialists. Ministers of Trade (and even crowned heads of states) received generous allotments of shares from foreign companies anxious for concessions. High officials in ministries fared little worse than their ministers. Particularly lucrative was the job of Inspector of the Ministry of Labor. Many inspectors found factory owners extremely grateful for the omission in their reports of certain minor irregularities and deficiencies in the working conditions of their men.

Public officials showed respect to members of the ruling class, particularly to those who made it worth their while, but to the masses they were pitiless. This is true of Hungary and Poland quite as much as of Rumania and the Balkan Peninsula. Taxes were collected with ruthless brutality. This was particularly bad in the last few years, when the governments needed every penny for their military expenditure and, as usual, put the main burden on the masses. If a peasant owned arrears of taxes, the gendarmes would come to his house when he was working in the fields—or when he and all adult males in his household were serving in the army. If the women could not pay, the gendarmes seized the few belongings of the household. If the wife and children objected, they were beaten. Outrages of this sort were often committed for the sake of a few pennies.

The most striking example of this sort that came to the knowledge of the author is from Kishinev (Chișinău), capital of the then Rumanian province of Bessarabia, in the spring of 1940. The gendarmes of this province received orders to collect arrears of taxes from the peasants of the neighborhood. For two weeks they toured the villages, seizing what they could find, blankets, rugs, tools, any spare clothes. The spoils were sold on their return in the public market of Kishinev and realized the impressive sum of 800 lei (about 16 shillings). Quite apart from the injustice of the procedure and the brutality employed to carry it out, it should be stressed that the state cashed about as much as the salary of one of the gendarmes for the period of collection. To achieve this, many peasant households were deprived of everything but the clothes on the backs of the women at a time when the men were mobilized on the frontier, liable at any moment to be called upon to fight for their country.

Although cases of this kind may be regarded as rather exceptional, injustice, ruthlessness, and brutality were widespread all over Eastern Europe except Czechoslovakia, and even there they were not unknown. These abuses will only be eradicated by an entirely new spirit in education, but something could be more quickly achieved by the promulgation and enforcement of laws forbidding, with heavy penalties, the confiscation for nonpayment of taxes of indispensable household accessories and instruments and the use of physical violence by the gendarmes and police except for cases of violent crime. Such laws or regulations existed in the East European states during part or all of the interwar period, but no one took any trouble to enforce them, and they were, consequently, almost universally ignored.

The sufferings of the people were increased by the fact that there was no redress against administrative abuses. The legal experts of the East European states could show the foreign inquirer a most beautiful system of courts and appeals, which appeared, on paper at least, as advanced as that of France, Britain, or the United States. But all this remained on paper. A peasant who complained of an act of injustice was denounced as a "Communist," sent before a military court, beaten from time to time, and sentenced either to prison or to forced labor under military discipline. If the village mayor collected more than the legal communal tax and pocketed the difference, only "Communists" would think of protesting. A peasant who did not like to have his daughters raped or his property stolen by a gendarme must be a "Bolshevik." And in the courts, the word of a politically sound, patriotic gendarme was always taken against that of a subversive peasant.

DIFFERENCES OF CULTURAL LEVEL

Special problems were created in provinces which had been ruled by "Western" methods and, owing to the territorial settlement of 1918, came under "Eastern" administration, or vice versa. Czechoslovakia, Yugoslavia, Rumania, and Poland were states of mixed "Western" and "Eastern" provinces. The Austrian provinces of Bohemia and Moravia acquired Slovakia and Ruthenia, whose past administration might be described as "backward Central European." In this case, the more advanced dominated the more backward. Serbia acquired the Austrian provinces of Slovenia and Dalmatia, the Hungarian provinces of Croatia and Voivodina, the Austro-Turkish [3] province of Bosnia, and the Turkish province of Macedonia. Rumania acquired the Austrian province of Bukovina, the Hungarian provinces of Transylvania and Banat, and the Russian province of Bessarabia. In both these cases a primitive "Oriental" State acquired

---

[3] Bosnia had been ruled by Austria for forty years (1878–1918), but this period had been too short to obliterate Turkish habits and traditions.

large areas accustomed to more advanced standards of administration than it could provide, and at the same time other areas considerably more backward than it was itself. Poland was composed of a thoroughly Western, a semi-Western and a completely Eastern area. The three sections struggled against each other during the succeeding twenty years, without decisive results, although it might be said on balance that Oriental standards prevailed.

A few words are necessary at this point to illustrate the three types of problem created. These are Western superimposed on Eastern; Eastern superimposed on Western; Eastern superimposed on still more backward Eastern.

The only example of the first type is provided by Czechoslovakia. During twenty years, Czech officials and teachers did much to raise the economic and cultural level of Slovakia and Ruthenia. But they met with little gratitude. The leaders of the Slovak people in 1918 were the priesthood. The Lutheran Church represented the intellectual elite of the Slovaks, and both welcomed the union of Slovakia with the Czech lands and cooperated with the Czechs in the task of building up a progressive Slovakia. The Catholic priesthood, however, resented the cultural predominance of the Czechs. Slovak Catholic priests were mostly men of little education, brought up to regard all ideas more recent than the Middle Ages as inventions of the devil. The Czechs, with their emphasis on social services and modern education, were to them a "godless" folk.

The great influence of the Catholic priests over the Slovak masses was used to inflame violent nationalism, directed equally against Czechs and Hungarians. Obstruction by the Slovaks to reforms convinced the Czechs for their part that the Slovaks were a stupid and reactionary people. The young generation of Slovak intellectuals, brought up in the schools and universities founded by the Czechs, turned against their benefactors with fierce hatred. The antagonism created by the difference in cultural and political traditions of Czechs and Slovaks was a constant source of trouble to the young republic and helped to bring about its downfall. In Ruthenia, similar factors operated, but the very low level of national consciousness among the Ruthenes, their small numbers, and the hostility of the various Ruthene factions among themselves made the Ruthene question much less important than the Slovak.

Examples of the second and third types can conveniently be taken from Yugoslavia and Rumania. The difficulties of Poland in connection with this problem of different cultural levels will be briefly mentioned elsewhere.

The ruling class of the old kingdoms of Serbia and Rumania (known respectively as *Srbijanci* and *Regateni*) considered that they had "liberated" the new provinces and therefore had a right to the gratitude and respectful deference of their inhabitants.[4] The assumption of this superior

[4] A *Srbijanac* is a Serb from the pre-1918 kingdom, as opposed to a Serb from the new provinces across the Sava. These were known as *Prećani* (*preko* = across). A *Regatean* is a Rumanian of the *Regat* or old kingdom. These three words will be used below.

moral attitude caused intense resentment among Slovenes, Croats, Transylvanians, and Bukovinians, whose reaction was to declaim interminably about the superiority of their own culture and to denounce the newcomers as "Byzantine barbarians" or "Orientals." This, naturally, exasperated the "liberators" and increased their determination to maintain political and economic power in their own hands.

Having in fact suffered heavy casualties and having brought devastation on their homes in a war which they had entered principally in order to win these provinces, the "liberators" expected that the "liberated" would pay a large share of the expenses of reconstruction and gave practical shape to their desire by various economic measures directed against the new provinces to the profit of the old. Moreover, they too often regarded the new provinces as colonies, to be provided with new "nationally trustworthy" public officials, a convenient field for the employment of the sons of the rapidly forming ruling class. Srbijanci and Regateni officials flooded the new provinces, bringing with them the customs and morals of their Balkan ancestors, diluted with some smattering of French constitutional theory acquired from half-digested lectures by graduates of the Sorbonne.

The reactions of the different provinces to this policy varied. The most successful resistance was offered by the Slovenes. They were protected by their language, which is sufficiently different from Serbo-Croatian to make it impossible for large numbers of Srbijanci officials to colonize their country. Moreover, they showed themselves eager from the beginning to cooperate with the Serbs in the construction of their common state. Although there were troubles from time to time, it may be said that the Slovenes found a satisfactory place in the life of Yugoslavia. Many Slovenes obtained posts in the administration in other provinces besides their own, and in the Belgrade ministries, while retaining much of the substance of home rule in their own lands.

The Rumanians of Bukovina hardly constituted a serious problem. They continued, with much justification, to complain bitterly of the contrast between the methods of government employed by Bucharest and those to which they had been accustomed under Austria. But their loyalty to the Rumanian State was secured by the fact that they were faced in their own province by the hostility of a Ukrainian minority of numbers almost equal to their own, against which the help of Bucharest was essential. The least agreeable peculiarities of the Rumanian bureaucracy in Bukovina were concentrated against Ukrainians and Jews, and the Bukovinian Rumanians enjoyed tolerable conditions. In Transylvania, the problem was more serious.

Although strongly in favour of unity with the Regat, to which they were tied by fear of the large Hungarian minority in their midst and of the Hungarian state beyond their frontier, the Transylvanian Rumanians deeply resented the penetration of Regateni into their province. The battle for economic and administrative control was fought fiercely between Bucharest and Transylvania for more than a decade. In the end, the

Transylvanians probably more than held their own, for what they lost in Transylvania they gained in the form of important political, economic, and administrative posts occupied by Transylvanians in the Regat.

The most dangerous problem of this kind in Eastern Europe was the Croatian question, of which more will have to be said later. The Croats had not only regional patriotism and consciousness of superior culture but also a definite sense of separate nationhood. The antagonism of the Croats, first against the Srbijanci and then against all Serbs, only increased with the passage of time. The more the Croatian intellectuals prattled about their "thousand years of culture," the more angry the Serbs became, and the more Serbian officials and gendarmes Belgrade sent to "keep order" in Croatia, the more implacable became the hatred of the Croats.

Particularly wretched was the fate of the third category, backward areas annexed by "Eastern" States, such as Bessarabia, Macedonia, Polesia, and Volhynia. The peoples of these areas lacked the political and cultural standards of the advanced regions and had neither material nor moral weapons with which to defend themselves. They became the victims of merciless economic exploitation and police brutality. Examples of the "Raubwirtschaft" to which they were subjected have already been given in the Yugoslav tobacco monopoly (which affected above all the peasant of Macedonia) and the tax-collectors of Kishinev. The "liberating" officials could beat, rob, and rape as they pleased, using the well-worn slogans of "Bolshevik" and "enemy of the state" to justify their outrages. This was all the easier because all the areas in question were particularly insecure frontier districts. The result of exploitation and persecution was, however, to turn even the potentially loyal part of the population into real Communists and separatists.

The importance of these conflicts can hardly be exaggerated. In most of these regions, the sources of conflict are very old, but they were greatly intensified by the administrative abuses described above. A good and tactful administration would have softened and might even, with time, have eliminated them. The methods practiced had disastrous results, which affected not only the provinces in which they were applied but the whole political life of the states. The example of corruption, greed, and violence offered by the "liberating" bureaucracies had an unfavorable effect on the morals of the victims. When they have had the opportunity, the Croats, despite their much-vaunted "culture," have shown that they can rival and surpass the Serbs in all the unpleasant characteristics which they attribute to them. After twenty years of Great Rumania, the Transylvanians could compete in dishonesty with the Regateni. Moreover, the methods of "Raubwirtschaft" employed in the backward provinces had a degrading influence on the public life and morals of every part of the states, which cannot be overestimated. The Srbijanac or the Regatean suffered greater abuses from his own rulers, because they had tried them out with such success on his Macedonian and Bessarabian cousins. Oppression, robbery, discontent, and disunity were greater throughout Eastern Europe in 1939 than they had been in 1918.

The Political System

Peasant poverty, bad education, bad adminstration, and an ignorant and irresponsible ruling class destroyed all hope of real democracy in Eastern Europe between the wars. The prevalent political ideas in 1918 were those of the French Revolution—freedom, equality, and brotherhood for all. Their bearers were, however, the educated and semi-educated class, the quickly forming bourgeoisie, whose material interests were opposed, in the short run at least, to those of the peasant and workers, whom they kept in their place by police terror and mulcted by taxation.

In Hungary, the Red Revolution and White Counter-Revolution swept away all hope of democracy. In Czechoslovakia, the balance of social forces and the strength of the liberal tradition allowed the achievement of some measure of true democracy. In the other countries of Eastern Europe, a pseudo-democratic system maintained itself for varying periods of years, succumbing in the end to dictatorship well before the outbreak of war.

The pseudo-democratic surface of Polish, Rumanian, and Balkan politics bore little relation to reality. Exceedingly liberal constitutions existed side by side with exceedingly dishonest and unscrupulous police machines, which exercised various forms of most effective political pressure on the unprivileged classes. Elections were seldom more than a farce. Voters were bought or intimidated, votes were forged, ballot boxes were lost or stolen. A few elections of the interwar period are worth remembering, either because the electors were given some chance to express their views or because, despite police pressure, a government failed to obtain a large majority. But the great majority of elections were of no interest whatever, for everyone knew the result beforehand. Elections were always accompanied by the most extravagant promises. Freedom, justice, and prosperity would be established once and for all by each party. With each election, the number of voters who listened to these promises decreased. Words like "democracy" mean little to an East European peasant at the best of times. After some years of unfortunate experience, even the most simple-minded convinced themselves that all this was talk and nothing but talk. All parties and all politicians, they believed, were alike. All were dishonest, and all wanted to get something out of them without giving them more than they could help in return. The quarrels of the parties were just quarrels among the "gentlemen." They did not concern the people. An election was rather fun, because it was an opportunity, recurring every few years, to earn a little money and some free šlivovica, vodka, or tsuica by selling one's vote to the highest bidder. Outside Czechoslovakia, where the people had political education, and a few special areas like Croatia and Eastern Galicia, where national and political problems existed which interested every individual, party politics was viewed by the masses with increasing apathy.

As the world Depression deepened, social discontent grew. The peasants and workers sank deeper into the squalor of poverty and despair. Even the rich peasants were alienated by the increased abuses of the administration and the police. Disillusioned by the old parties, the people looked for new men. Extremist movements of left and right gained ground. The illegal Communist and persecuted Nazi organizations expanded their ranks. Observing the rising tide of misery and hatred, the ruling classes became more and more frightened of their own peoples. Every protest was a sign of "Bolshevism" and was met with brutal repression as such. One by one the last traces of "democracy" disappeared, and pseudo-parliamentarism gave way to police dictatorships or fascist regimes.

It would be a mistake to pretend that there was no difference between pseudo-parliamentarism and open dictatorship. Under the former, there were at least a few safety valves. The peasants of any given village might hope to obtain small material advantages through the local deputy when the latter's party was in power. Criticism of the government—often mis directed—was allowed to appear in the press. If the masses, even in the most "parliamentary" period, had little opportunity to express their views and little hope of receiving justice, at least intellectuals of the ruling class enjoyed some freedom.

With the establishment of dictatorships, these last trivial blessings were removed. Freedom, prosperity, and power were confined to members of the ruling gang. Fine proclamations were issued about national unity, moral regeneration, non-party objectivity, and strong hands, and foreign journalists could always be found to write sycophantic articles of praise in the world press. But all this fine talk was insincere. The dictatorships of Eastern Europe did some good things, no doubt. No government sets out deliberately to ruin its country. Great political, social, and economic problems were forced on their attention by the march of events, which they hoped to postpone by various palliative measures. But to deal seriously and radically with the tasks imposed by the national interest was beyond their power. Composed of stupid, timorous, dishonest, and pettily cunning men, confronted with internal and international situations that were too difficult for bigger men than they, they could only hesitate, temporize, and take the line of least resistance. These "strong governments" were no more than greedy, corrupt, and brutal class regimes, which did not feed but fed upon their peoples and whose only strength lay in the bayonets of their gendarmes.

37

NOTES TO THE COLLAPSE OF HUNGARIAN SOCIETY BETWEEN THE WARS

JOSEPH HELD

[Hungary was among the East European countries that were least success-ful in adjusting to the political realities of the post–World War I years, i.e., of the twentieth century. The following analysis of Hungarian society between the wars concentrates on the problems of class conflict and the built-in rigidity of the ruling establishment. As a case study, it bears out Seton-Watson's general analysis in the previous selection.]

On a bright Holy Saturday afternoon in the early 1930's, a strange and tragic event happened in Ozora, a small village in southern Hungary. After the traditional Resurrection celebrations, during which Christ's body was symbolically paraded throughout the village, the people of the *puszta* gathered around the village inn.[1] This was the place where the scores which had accumulated between the inhabitants of the *puszta* during the preceding months were usually settled. The fights proceeded according to unwritten laws, starting with the cowherds and ending with the partici-pation of the carriage drivers. It was a procedure accepted by both the village peasants and the authorities not to intervene until the fighters were exhausted. Then the gendarmes usually succeeded in calming the passions. On that day, however, a single gendarme appeared at the inn, probably by mistake, when the fighters were still in the possession of their full strength. He was subdued and crucified on the door of the inn! The peo-

[1] The generally accepted Hungarian meaning of *puszta* corresponds to plains or grasslands. But small settlements in the midst of large estates were also called *puszta*. These were inhabited by hired laborers and their families, permanently employed by the landlords. These laborers were traditionally called servants. The settlements were not villages; they were isolated from the outside world, totally dependent on the landowner for not only their livelihood, but also the everyday direction of their family affairs.

Reprinted from *East European Quarterly*, II, No. 3 (September, 1968), 303–13.

ple of the *puszta* inflicted upon the unfortunate gendarme all the cruelties which they had learned from the Bible. Half the people of the village of Ozora witnessed the deed, and not one soul lifted a finger to stop it.[2]

Even measured by East European standards, the circumstances of the "example of Ozora" were strange and thus provoked intriguing questions. We might ask: What motivated the people of the *puszta* to crucify the gendarme? Was their act simply an expression of accumulated resentment against authority represented by their unfortunate victim? Illyés believed, along with other Hungarian writers, that this was so. The peasants' nerves were very tense not only from the brutal treatment they had regularly received from their superiors on the large estates but also by their almost complete isolation from the rest of society for the greater part of the year. "They are told that the servants should open their mouths only when the soul leaves them . . . thus, the servants take their orders with stony faces as if they were Adam yet half-clay . . . consequently, they bear the punches all year around, and when the time of festivities arrives, they take it out of their system." Illyés maintained that these fights were just as necessary for the *puszta* people as food; without them they would have lost their sanity.

However, there may be another explanation; it is possible that the peasants acted according to age-old Asiatic traditions that survived from the period when the Hungarians were a nomadic people living in the steppes of southern Russia, reinforced by the Turkish occupation of Hungary during the sixteenth and seventeenth centuries. According to these traditions, human suffering was inconsequential. Manliness, which was expected above all from a representative of authority, was measured by the self-control of individuals in withstanding physical pain; and, by crucifying him, the peasants tested the competence of the gendarme and of the ruling stratum of society as well.

It is at least doubtful, however, that such Asiatic traditions would have survived so long in Hungary. My own doubts are strengthened by the observations of such historians as Professor Seton-Watson. He believes that it is but the language of the Hungarians which reminds one today of their Asiatic origins. Christianity, it is argued further, transformed Hungarian culture, which now conforms to values and standards of Western civilization. It is customary today to speak of the Hungarians as a deeply religious people.

But what kind of Christianity is presented to us by the problem of Ozora? What kind of morals and values did the people of the *puszta* cherish that made it possible for them to act this way? Why did the village peasants permit the murder? Was this action representative of the entire peasantry of the *pusztas* or of some special elements among them?

In order to answer these questions, we must re-examine Hungarian mentality and divorce it from the myths which have surrounded it in our times.

One such myth which we frequently encounter in dealing with Hungarians is that they are regarded as a deeply religious people. We must not

---

[2] Gyula Illyés, *People of the Puszta (Puszták Népe)* (Budapest: Nyugat Kiadó, n.d.), p. 141.

be misled by the frequent announcements confirming this view, originating, in most cases, from men representing the outlook of the former Hungarian aristocracy of the interwar period or from individuals not too well informed about Hungarian mentality.

In fact, the Hungarian masses had never really become Christian in the Western sense. Christianity introduced ideas of moral equality in the West; Hungarian individuals belonging to the lower classes, on the other hand, were never even permitted to feel morally equal with the upper stratum of society. Moreover, before 1945 they accepted their alleged inferiority with a sort of fatalism unknown in the Western world.

The Hungarian peasants did not understand the liturgy of the Catholic Church, since it was conducted in Latin; this was one of the possible explanations for the fact that a large number of Hungarians immediately embraced Calvinism when it reached the country in the sixteenth century. But even then, the new religion was used by every stratum of Hungarian society as a political tool rather than a spiritual force. Many of the towns, especially those in East Hungary and Transylvania, accepted Calvinism as a means of resisting the power of feudal nobles; towns, such as Debreczen and Sárospatak, acquired an atmosphere in which the new religion was assimilated with a strong sense of independent *bürgertum*. Members of the aristocracy used Calvinism in the sixteenth and seventeenth centuries as a means to defy the growing power of the Catholic Habsburgs. But the fact is that the majority of the peasants could not care less whether they were Catholic or Protestant; they were usually traded from Catholic to Protestant landlords or vice versa as cattle and were compelled to change their religion in the process. Both Catholicism and Protestantism have served mainly political purposes in Hungary ever since. *It is this aspect of Christianity which left a deep mark on Hungarian mentality.*

This explanation might be taken to account for the brutality of the people of the *puszta*, and for the village peasants' neutrality is the face of the murder in Ozora. Christian values existed only at the surface of the mentality of Hungarian peasants, easily dropped if they came into conflict with their passions.

Since the great peasant rebellion of 1514, at least, a cleavage existed also in the social field, the peasants remaining always passive in times of crises threatening aristocratic Hungary. This passivity made the Turkish conquest of Hungary easier; it contributed to the defeat of the first nationalist government in 1849. During the 1930's, Hungarian society retained its semi-feudal, aristocracy-dominated character, at least until the accession of Gyula Gömbös to power in 1932. Hence, the peasants felt little affinity with official Hungary. A feeling of aversion toward central authority, so well represented by the gendarme, therefore was probably the other most important reason for the murder in Ozora. The action of the people of the *puszta*, moreover, was representative of the growing radicalism of the Hungarian countryside.

Rapid industrialization in the twentieth century resulted in an equally rapid rise in the numbers of the Hungarian middle classes. However, the composition of these classes changed so rapidly that it lacked social, mental, or cultural homogeneity. While the Hungarian middle classes were, as late as 1900, composed of a large number of Jewish and German elements, after World War I they were reconstituted by the entry into their ranks of the poverty-stricken majority of the former Hungarian gentry.[3] The influx of this "new blood" changed not only the composition but also the basic mentality of these classes. Formerly occupying an intermediary position between the aristocracy and the peasantry, the Hungarian gentry had aspired to standards of aristocratic behavior which often reached the character of *extravaganza*. This group now dreaded assimilation into the merchant-trading classes, whose professions it deeply despised; the best solution for its members to retain the illusion of their national importance was to seek administrative positions. It was relatively easy for them to acquire degrees in law, one of the prerequisities, besides "protection" by a person of influence, for success, but they were still disoriented and dissatisfied. They cherished the pre–World War I regime which enabled them to live the life of leisure of a semi-aristocracy. They revived the atmosphere and the ideas of the nineteenth century in the 1930's. They often circulated myths, such as that of the Sumerian origins of the Hungarians, as a "scientific" explanation for the alleged superiority of the Hungarian "race" over its neighbors. One consequence of this twentieth-century neoromanticism was the emergence of secret gentry societies based on medieval notions. In the realm of foreign policy, the new romanticism led Hungarian gentry to the wrong choice of friends and allies, to the rejection of the new realities of interwar Central European life and politics.

Following the influx of gentry elements, the Hungarian middle classes became less homogeneous in character than ever before. Some of the older components of the classes preserved their values, among which thriftiness and love of work predominated. The merchantry generally rejected the predisposition of the gentry for violence. The majority of the gentry, on the other hand, drifted more and more toward fascism.

The advent of Gyula Gömbös as Prime Minister in 1932 brought the gentry element into actual political power, which was to lead Hungary along the road to political adventure. It was all the easier for them to obtain and retain control, as the urban masses had come under the influence of Josephinism in the previous century, and now the idea that the state was the instrument of progress was readily accepted. The impact of the Great Depression in 1931 contributed to the rise of the gentry to political predominance, because it was followed by the actual abdication by the aristocracy of its leadership. The abdication of power in the face of national emergency became, from this time on, a standard practice in Hungarian politics, and it was repeated by the gentry a little more than a decade later, in 1944, when the Hungarian gentry abdicated its political power in favor of a mob, with irreparable social and political consequences for Hungary.

[3] Many of the gentry lost their lands to newly rich capitalists. In addition, about 320,000 of them, mostly public servants, fled from the successor states in 1919.

The Hungarian proletariat rose to some importance toward the end of the nineteenth century. Its members were largely recruited from among the landless peasantry, attracted by the glitter of rapidly growing industrial centers, largest among them the capital city, Budapest. As late as the middle 1930's, however, this group was but a semi-proletarian class, manning the factories and work shops; these workers often returned to their villages in time of depression or unemployment. Many future permanent members of the class found jobs at construction sites, while the rest of their families were sharecropping on the large estates in the countryside. As a consequence, it would have been difficult to discover any sign of class-consciousness as a general characteristic of the Hungarian working class. The trade unions, organized in the 1890s, did everything in their power to promote a working-class mentality, but they had a difficult task. The leadership of the unions was mostly of middle-class origin and, therefore, had not entirely understood the difficulties of the membership. The Social Democrats had likewise little influence in Hungary until the late 1940's, and then only under artificially created political conditions in which the levers of power were controlled by the representatives of the Hungarian Communist Party.

The Communists were even less significant than the Social Democrats in promoting proletarian class-consciousness in the 1930's. The party was declared illegal after 1920, its leaders fled to Russia or were persecuted, its membership disappeared. Its existence was verified only in the dream-world of the Hungarian gentry; Communists became a convenient scapegoat for the social ills of Hungary, which neither the aristocratic nor the gentry regime had enough courage to tackle. In fact, however, the Communists remained spectators within and without the country, only to profit from the general collapse and disillusionment after 1944.

By the mid-1930's, the Hungarian middle classes were just as divided as the peasantry, with no unity of purpose in their ranks. Some of them criticized the gentry-controlled regime and turned Marxist; others turned fascist in their despair, with the object of making the dominant position of their class impregnable. The desire of both sections for separateness and distinction was one of the major motives behind their anti-Semitism.

Division within the ranks of the peasantry, divided middle classes, a working class without an ideology or strong party-organization, an aristocracy which had lost its self-confidence—such was the picture of Hungarian society on the eve of World War II. Hungary was utterly unprepared for this tremendous trial of strength. She was heading toward social and political collapse. In the impending catastrophe, many of the old values, already under attack for a considerable time, were doomed to disappear or to be altered. With them the dreamworld of the 1930's was also to go.

The old mental structure of Hungary began to decay, together with her social fabric, early in the twentieth century. Many of the causes were not peculiarly Hungarian; industrialization and the emergence of new classes, which complicated and aggravated the strained social relations of ancient date, strengthened the direction of the process. But the decay was immensely accelerated after 1932 by the premiership of Gyula Gömbös, which may be taken as one of the turning points in recent East European history. The rapidity of change to industrialization in the 1930's excluded the possibility of a gradual transformation of traditional values.

The advance of Gömbös to the premiership signaled a change of guards in the composition of the ruling elite. Before 1932, the Hungarian aristocracy controlled practically all important administrative positions; after that date, the gentry became predominant. Some of the consequences of this revolutionary change were corruption and graft in the administration on a large scale, growing thought control, and cooperation with Nazi Germany.

It is true that there existed graft and corruption in the administration before Gömbös's time, but large-scale scandals were usually confined to the immediate ruling circles. Now, former officers, friends of the Gömbös circle, and their friends and relatives, whose number continuously appeared [to be] rising, were placed in important positions. Here they sought "to make up" for the lean years, causing a serious decline in the standard of administration. Corruption reached alarming sizes, but the authorities closed their eyes to the evidence against their friends. But nepotism survived the system and remained, even after 1945, a familiar feature in Hungarian administrative life.

The political success of the German Nazis in 1933 encouraged the Hungarian gentry to devise a program similar to that of the German National Socialists. As one of the first steps in this direction, the Gömbös government began to sponsor anti-Semitic propaganda on a national scale. Militarism was also being encouraged. The paramilitary organization of youth, called *Levente*, provided one of the vehicles for both anti-Semitism and militarism in the countryside. Secret and open fascist societies promoted racial hatred and, at the same time, planted false notions of racial superiority in gentry minds.

Strong signs of moral decay appeared also among the Hungarian *intelligentsia*. A large number of these, for instance, not merely accepted thought control by the government but eagerly endorsed it. The few objectors were silenced by being labeled as Communists or, what was regarded by the gentry as even worse, Jewish dupes. English and French newspapers were banned from the newsstands; a vicious propaganda campaign was initiated against the broadcasts of the BBC and other Western radio stations; an efficient mail inspection system was introduced. It was as if a nationwide fog were descending over Hungary.

Professors at the universities openly falsified history, proving that even intellectuals of often high caliber were unable to assert their individuality against the currents of political hysteria. Theories were circulated about an imaginary Japanese-Hungarian common origin, and Finnish-Hungarian relationships were outright denied as derogatory for the nation. Ironically enough, this tendency also survived the political collapse of Hungary in 1945, providing for a "new" historiography that was viciously falsified even by Communist standards in East Europe.

Militarism was enforced at all levels, especially at the universities. Military chairs were established with wide authority to withhold diplomas if students were slow in exhibiting sufficient zeal in learning military discipline. This institution also survived the collapse and became an effective weapon in the hand of the Communist government after 1948 in enforcing conformity at the universities.

The collapse of the old values was accelerated by the anti-Jewish legislation of the late 1930's.[4] On the basis of the new laws, the despoliation of Jews became legal and official. Jewish factories and shops were either confiscated or placed under the direction of gentry supervisors. Such flagrant violations of the formerly much-respected property rights of Hungarian citizens could not fail to leave its mark on the mind of the masses. A chain reaction soon developed in the villages; after 1938, the peasants, instead of demanding land reform, began to demand confiscation of the large aristocratic holdings. Stealing became a large-scale phenomenon; all respect for private property—small or large—completely disappeared. When, a decade later, the Communist leadership was to assail lack of respect for "communal property" in Hungary, it was unwilling to admit the fact that it was confronted with an old phenomenon, a direct consequence of the collapse of the old values of Hungarian society.

The climax in the decline of the old system of values came during World War II. War always accelerated such changes in any event; now, robberies committed by Hungarian officers in Russia and other parts of German-occupied East Europe caused no public indignation; truckloads of furniture and other valuables were sent home by officers from Russia and Yugoslavia as booty. They were cheered by bystanders on Budapest streets; robbery thus became a generally accepted part of the values of society.

By 1943, the value structure of Hungarian society had been more or less completely undermined. In the process, the political structure was also undermined and finally destroyed. *But it was not the Germans nor the Russians who brought about the collapse of Hungarian society; it was the abdication of the gentry, its failure to find a remedy for the moral and social cleavages within the nation. Hungary collapsed under its own weight of an archaic, narrow political and social system.*

One major value that survived the catastrophe and aided the revival of Hungarian society after the war was the moral indignation of progressive elements against the system which had brought disaster to the nation. This feeling was, in fact, so strong that it outlived the initial enthusiasm of the indignant intellectuals for the Hungarian Communist Party in 1945 and expressed itself ultimately in 1956 for total revolution.

[4] The anti-Jewish laws of 1938 were introduced under Kálmán Darányi's premiership. These first laws were relatively mild, but their spirit was in contradiction to Christian values and were soon followed by more and more rigorous laws until they became legalized robbery.

38

REFLECTIONS ON DICTATORSHIP

JOSEPH PILSUDSKI

[The problems facing Poland after World War I were among the most complex in Eastern Europe. Poland's geopolitical position, aggravated by the reconstitution of a historical state that had ceased to exist following the partitions of the eighteenth century, has frequently been cited as the root cause of the Polish crisis of the interwar period. Characteristic of that crisis was the failure of the democratic process and the triumph of authoritarian dictatorial rule, first under Joseph Pilsudski and later under the Polish colonels. The failure of democracy, however, could also be ascribed at least in part to the inequities of the social order and to class rule. The several factors that brought on dictatorial rule in Poland were briefly analyzed by Seton-Watson. An explanation by Pilsudski himself, from a speech delivered in 1923, follows. Pilsudski's theoretical commitment to the democratic process and his opposition to dictatorship were discredited less than three years later, when he became de facto dictator of Poland.]

In November, 1918, occurred an ordinary, quite unhistoric event. A man whom we will call Joseph Pilsudski left the Vienna Station and, as happens to all of us, passed down the Ulice Marszalkowska, etc., to the Ulica Moniuszki.* He wore the same uniform in which you see me now, gentlemen. It was no ordinary journey from which he was returning, indeed: He was returning from Magdeburg. At the same time, others were also returning from various internment camps. In this, too, there was nothing extraordinary, nothing in the least historic. History begins later—an extraordinary history, on which I have often reflected in the course of the

* Streets in Warsaw.—Ed.

Reprinted, by permission, from Joseph Pilsudski, *The Memories of a Polish Revolutionary and Soldier* (London: Faber & Faber, 1931), pp. 366–71.

last five years, as I sought answers to questions which I suppose will trouble future historians still more, since they will no longer have eyewitnesses of these events. An extraordinary thing happened. In the course of a few days, without this man making any efforts, without any violence on his part, without any bribery, without any concession, timber or otherwise, without any so-called "legal" occurrences, something most unusual became a fact. This man became dictator. When I was preparing today's speech, I thought over this term "dictator." I don't wish to use any far-fetched term or coin any special title for myself; I only wish, as a historian, to define the phenomeon which cannot be otherwise described. For this man issued edicts universally obeyed; his orders were listened to passively; willingly or unwillingly, they were executed; he nominated the officials, both military and civilian. Whether he did well or ill I will not discuss at this moment, I am only concerned with the fact, the simple fact, the historical fact, which I cannot otherwise describe than by using the word "dictator."

To what are we to attribute it, gentlemen? Where are we to seek the cause of the surrender of this power to the man subsequently known in the index of history as Joseph Pilsudski? How did he become dictator of Poland without imposing his power by any violence, without making himself popular by any public activities? Whence this phenomenon? . . . This man was welcomed for one thing, for which he was considered extraordinary; one thing, I repeat, gave him the moral right to occupy this position, gentlemen: he wore this uniform, he was the Commandant of the First Brigade. The only value which men had at that time, the only moral force which compelled men to obedience, the only moral force which placed millions of men in his hands, was the fact that he was the Commandant of the First Brigade and returned from Magdeburg. . . . The new Poland as its first step chose, rightly or wrongly, a man dressed in a gray uniform, somewhat worn and stained in the prison of Magdeburg. . . .

From the history of dictatorships of every kind, inside and outside operettas, from the drama and tragedy of a humanity, I have reflected how dictatorships are formed. There are two usual ways. One, that of violence and the imposition of one's power. There are many examples of this in the history of the nations. The other is by free choice by men who, in a difficult moment, when an individual will is most needed and the public is frightened, seek one man to whom to entrust their fate. Here neither the first nor the second method was used. There was neither election nor violence. Here something quite different occurred, an achievement of the moral energy of the nation as it found itself in an exceptional situation.

Gentlemen, this fact of moral effort which the nation achieved at this time is not my history; it is the history of all those millions of people who then obeyed this dictator, who submitted to him even if it was with a shrug or an expression of ill-will. This actually occurred. It was like the denial of that melancholy, distant tradition, of that melancholy reputation which our nation had in the past. Even the Poles said that Poland existed by disorder. Poland was private greed, Poland was ill-will, Poland was anarchy. If we enjoyed sympathy after our downfall, we never enjoyed respect. We awakened not confidence but uncertainty, so that others wished to impose on us guardians for a nation of anarchy, weakness, and self-will, for a nation which could bear no government and came to its downfall through private greed. And it was in this nation that such an extraordinary thing occurred, and one so new to it. Gentlemen, I am proud of this fact, not only because the honor fell upon me, but for the reputation of my nation. Taking as the basis of the occurrence my earlier work in the First Brigade, I am proud of my work there.

Gentlemen, I was dictator for some months. It was my own decision—whether wise or foolish is irrelevant—to call the Diet, to surrender my power into its hands, and to create a legal form for the life of the Polish state. My decision was obeyed. The deputies, who have often attacked me since, were elected on my orders, obeyed that order, and accepted election; at a date fixed by me, they presented themselves at Warsaw. . . . The elections were free; no more than before did I seek for my own interests.

The Diet met on February 8. I opened it, gentlemen, in this uniform as Commandant of the First Brigade. I addressed the Diet in this uniform with the sword, given me by the officers of the First Brigade, at my side and was no more than I had been before.

A few weeks later a new historical fact occurred, a new act electing me unanimously in the Diet to the post of Chief of the Polish State and Commander-in-Chief of the troops then in Poland. After a few months, the wildest dream of any Pole in slavery was realized for me. . . . Everything was given into my hands. To beautify my work and my children, I was given the title which our children utter with respect almost as soon as they speak Polish. I was given the title of "Chief of State," a title which draws tears to the eyes, the title of a man who lives forever although he died, the title of Kosciuszko.* . . . Again gentlemen, I state that there was no violence, no corruption, no "concession," no attempt to compel anyone at that moment to raise his hand for me or give his vote for me.

I was set up higher than anyone had ever been set before, so that I cast my shadow upon all, standing alone in the light. Yet, there was a shadow which encircled me, which went before me, which remained behind me. There were many such shadows. These shadows surrounded me always, intangible, following me step by step, pursuing me and mimicking me. Whether on the field of battle, whether quietly at work in the Belvedere,† or caressing my child, this shadow pursued me inseparably. A monstrous dwarf on crooked legs, spitting out his dirty soul, spitting at me from every side, sparing nothing that should be spared, neither my family life nor my friends, following my steps, making monkey grimaces, distorting every thought—this monstrous dwarf crawled after me, an inseparable comrade, dressed in flags of various kinds and colors, now of a foreign state, now of our own state, crying aloud phrases, distorting its hideous

* Tadeusz Kosciuszko (1746–1817), Polish hero.—Ed.
† The presidential palace in Warsaw.—Ed.

mouth, imagining unheard-of tales! This dwarf was my inseparable companion, my inseparable comrade in good fortune and ill, in victory and defeat. Do not imagine, gentlemen, that this is only a metaphor. I will quote only a few facts so monstrous, so barbarous that it is difficult to understand into what sink of impurity it is necessary to dip the imagination in order to think of such things.

The representative of the nation chosen by all to represent all—is a thief. A commission of the Diet assembles to search for the royal insignia stolen by their representative.* . . . Can you imagine, gentlemen, anything more monstrous, more revolting? Can you have a representative of this sort? Imagine this anywhere else among the free nations; our representative a thief! Our representative betrays his country in time of war, enters into an understanding with the enemy! The Commander-in-Chief conducting the war is a traitor! Where is a punishment for him? Is there an attempt to remove him; is there an attempt to try him? Is there an attempt to make him responsible for his unheard-of crimes? There is none. It is only a question of spitting, of throwing mud, of which the mind, that can bring itself to such things, must be full. . . . This monstrous dwarf—was he hatched from our native marshes? Struck in the face by each of our conquerors, bought and sold from hand to hand, such are the men who wish to lower to their own level what has been raised up on high. . . . And this spitting was christened by lofty words, it was called national and patriotic! . . . .

At the moment when I left the Belvedere, the seat of the honor of Poland, another man entered it, legally chosen by an act to which the Marshal of the Diet had solemnly put his signature. I handed my power over to him in accordance with the constitution. Another man came to represent the whole nation and to enter upon that path which I had done a little to clear. I do not discuss his qualities or his failings, I do not estimate his value. This man had been raised above others, the duty of being our representative, the keeper of our honor and dignity had been laid upon him, as in my case, by a free choice. This rabble, this gang, which had set upon my honor, was now out for blood. Our president was murdered after street riots which lowered the prestige of those who work to represent us, by the same people who had formerly shown their hatred to the first representative, who was also freely elected. Now they had fulfilled a crime. Gentlemen, I am a soldier. A soldier is called to hard duties, which are often at variance with his conscience, with his ideas, with feelings that are dear to him. When I reflected for a moment that I, as a soldier, would have to defend these gentlemen, I hesitated in my conscience, and when I had once hesitated, I decided that I could not be a soldier. I resigned from the army. Those, gentlemen, are the causes and motives from which I leave the service of the state.

Gentlemen, in recalling these things to your minds, in sketching the history of the past five years, I do not in the least wish to make an im-

* A reference to one of a series of accusations made against Marshal Pilsudski in the Diet.—Ed.

pression of tragedy. I only wish to state that here is filth, and that it is given honor and power in Poland. I wish to say that if Poland succeeded in reforming the republic in the first period, it began subsequently to fall back into its old habits and that great efforts are necessary, gentlemen, to restore Poland again to the path of reform. I accuse no one; I am not a public prosecutor, I am not a *juge d'instructions*, I only seek the truth. As for myself, gentlemen, I ask you to remember me, and at the same time, I ask for a long, long rest so that I may breathe the air, so that I may be as free you, gentlemen, and gay as were the comrades of the First Brigade who, by their labor, secured me my greatest honors.

39

THE GERMAN PROBLEM IN CZECHOSLOVAKIA

EDUARD BENEŠ

[One of the recurrent problems in Eastern Europe after World War I was that of the national minorities. The nationality question was of paramount importance in Yugoslavia, Rumania, and Czechoslovakia. The rulers of Czechoslovakia, unlike those of Yugoslavia and Rumania, sought solutions to the nationality question, particularly with respect to the German population of the Sudetenland. In 1936, when Hitler raised the Sudeten-German question, the Czechoslovak government responded by affirming the validity of its nationality policy and the need for peaceful coexistence and collaboration among all the nationalities in Czechoslovakia. The following speech by President Eduard Beneš, delivered in August, 1936, sets forth the Czechoslovak position with respect to coexistence among nationalities in a democratic-industrial state.]

I have more than once in the past given my opinion on the relations of the German population to our state. What I say today will merely be supplementary and an emphasis of what I have already said.

1. In this land Czechs and Germans have lived side by side for centuries. In the Hussite struggles and in the Thirty Years War, which caused shifts in the areas of settlement of the two races, it was religious and social rather than national questions which were at issue. It was not until the nineteenth century that, with the evolution of the national idea, a nationality struggle in the modern sense of the term arose. That struggle, in addition to clash of ideas and politics, was in particular a fight for the soul of the individual. It would be interesting to ascertain what was the result of this struggle in the various periods. I shall hardly be wrong in asserting that during the last few decades the number of actually Czechized or Germanized persons was not such as to suggest any far-reaching

Reprinted from *The Problems of Czechoslovakia* (Prague: Orbis, 1936), pp. 9–28.

effect upon the general position of the two peoples in our state *inter se.* Official statistics provide no entirely reliable picture in this connection, as they had to take account of administrative conceptions which did not always allow of a precise presentation of the actual conditions of life. *Nationality conflicts are natural and inevitable on all ethnographical frontiers, but our two peoples are today mature enough not to allow themselves to be denationalized.*

The numerical proportion between our two nations can only change to an inconsiderable extent, even over very long periods, and today such changes are taking place only by way of natural processes as a result of sociological laws and the natural demographic conditions in the country. On these the political struggle has not, and indeed cannot have, any influence worth speaking of.

This is my first point, and the conclusion to be drawn is: Let us work together in the political and economic spheres, let us not exaggerate racial struggles and differences, let us keep them within reasonable bounds and reasonable forms.

2. *The questions of our national policy, and also the question of our Germans, have of late become a subject of attention both inside our country and beyond its frontiers. Let us say at once that the reasons for this are to be sought in the chaotic conditions prevailing in the international sphere, in the high tension of national sentiment in Germany, and in a certain radicalization of the racial minorities, not merely with us but in all countries.* On the part of Czechoslovaks this has aroused closer attention to these facts and resulted in a more serious study of them.

According to universally recognized international law, nationality questions are an internal concern for all countries without exception. Czechoslovakia adheres unconditionally to this principle, acts upon it, and will continue to act, without any deviation, upon it in future. *No European state has therefore any right to meddle in these questions, and Czechoslovakia,* as a sovereign state in complete consciousness of its dignity and its rights, *will in no wise suffer such intervention.*

The sole influence from outside which our state allows of in these matters is the supervision exercised by the League of Nations. Our state will in every case respect that. *Such supervision, however, applies to other states, indeed to all states.* Only by virtue of that do the nationality and minority questions in the various countries assume a certain international aspect. League of Nations control is carried out under the terms of treaties concluded by Czechoslovakia with other states, and by methods agreed upon with Czechoslovakia. *We permit of no other pressure, no other intervention in either the juridical or political sphere, and so cannot discuss our national questions with anyone else.* We voluntarily signed the minority treaties at the [Paris] Peace Conference with the express object of avoiding every other direct intervention calculated to be a hindrance to good relations between us and our neighbors, and in order to secure the existence of an objective, disinterested tribunal which, in case of a conflict in this connection, could step in and give its verdict.

If, in the past, Czechoslovakia has sometimes resolved to discuss this question with another state, such step was always taken on the basis of complete reciprocity and mutual equality. No state that enjoys respect can allow any unilateral discussion to take place concerning questions of its internal policy.

That is the purely juridical status of the nationality problem and the minority policy in Europe and also in Czechoslovakia. This status ensures for all nationalities in our country their own national and cultural existence. *I emphasize the fact that Czechoslovakia is a state in which no nationality is menaced in its national or cultural existence, and that the struggle of the minority nations here is not a fight for existence but merely a struggle for political power and co-rule in the state.* This state of affairs is expressed by both Czechoslovaks and Germans in the fact that the Germans are spoken of as equals among equals. I regard it as essential that no one, either here or abroad, should be led astray in this connection by any foreign propaganda or other political maneuver.

3. Here we arrive at the *internal political aspect* of our national problem. It was always my view that *Czechoslovakia should solve her national problems in her own way and by her own methods,* that the legal basis to which I have just referred should always—as is today the actual case with us—represent merely a certain juridical minimum, a basis which at all times—even in the worst days—would guarantee the minorities in our state their national existence, that our constitution and our practical internal policy should proceed further and regulate these matters according to the *internal needs of the state.* This is something over and above our international obligations; these are matters of exclusively internal consideration in which we allow no one to interfere from outside, and which depend *exclusively upon mutual agreement and cooperation between Czechs and Germans, upon direct, open, and loyal discussion, without pressure, without threats,* without nervousness and radicalism, without strong words and exaggerations, and without any tendentious representation of matters contrary to actual facts.

I have myself discussed these questions both last year and this on more than one occasion, at Most, at Ústí, at Teplice, and at Prague, with representatives of the Socialist Federation of Trade Unions and a delegation of the *Bund der Deutschen,* with all clarity and sincerity. I would expressly add that I entirely agree with what was recently said in Parliament and elsewhere by our Premier, Dr. Hodža, by our Minister of Foreign Affairs, Dr. Krofta, and by Cabinet Ministers Dr. Czech, Dr. Spina, and M. Zajiček concerning Czech-German relations and collaboration among the nationalities in this state.

At Znojmo I said: "My relationship to the Germans of this state is a human one: They are my compatriots, my co-workers, they are people suffering with me in days of need and rejoicing with me in the day of good fortune. In the search for the right way to fair collaboration, I have confidence in the Germans and in the Czechs, and in this matter I have special faith in my own efforts. I am convinced that the Czechs and the Germans will in the fairly near future come to a definitive political understanding in the state. I am in favor of the Germans in our republic receiving all that they require for their cultural and economic prosperity, and I am convinced that by a gradual and steady evolution and the maintenance of the democratic system of government this can be given them."

Addressing a delegation of the *Bund der Deutschen* last June 24 at Prague Castle, I supplemented the above with these words:

"Under the old regime we all grew up in an atmosphere of struggles, which we do not wish to revive, which are not necessary, and which cannot strengthen either of us. The way to mutual cultural and national respect, to collaboration and to a certain rivalry in good work is now open to both our nations."

You will not take it ill when I am candid enough to say that this work can only be successful if you follow in the footsteps of those classic figures of the German spirit, which are great and classic for the Czechs, too—in the footsteps of Herder, Lessing, Goethe, Schiller and their like—if we all do what we can to come close together in our ideal conception of the world, and if neither the one nor the other of us allow ourselves to be bewildered by the chaos of ideas of postwar Europe, by temporary ideologies which separate peoples instead of drawing them together, and which ere long will be ousted by the genuine ideals of humanity and a sensible Europeanism.

I will only supplement this by a few observations: *I am not afraid of the national differences in our state.* I am sure we shall solve and overcome them; we have also the necessary capacity, the essential energy, the good will. To overcome these difficulties was the wish of President Masaryk and one of the tasks which he set himself. I have taken over this task from him; I intend to support the government and all people of good will everywhere—wholeheartedly, sincerely, and indefatigably—in this work, and I am certain that I shall accomplish the task successfully. Of course, I cherish no illusions regarding the difficulties involved. There is need, frequently on both sides, of more courage to face and to comprehend these difficulties.

4. The Czechoslovak territories have, during the last two centuries, been the classical lands of nationality struggles. This is mainly because they border on states in which the awakening of the national consciousness and the formation of conscious national entities occurred in comparison with Western Europe—England, France, Belgium, Switzerland, etc.—some hundreds of years later, in fact, only in the course of the eighteenth and nineteenth centuries. A comparison between ourselves and the West of Europe in these matters is thus not feasible. *In the solution of national questions we may allow ourselves to be inspired by this or that people, but we cannot blindly imitate and adopt their systems.* The solution in our case must, as I have already said, be one that corresponds to our own particular conditions and springs from our own needs.

I regard it therefore as not the right thing to attempt to apply this or that ready-made formula to our conditions. I do not intend to be either the victim or the captive of any particular formula. In politics, that never leads to a good end. I therefore refuse to accept the slogan of autonomy or federative tendencies which spring from the application of fascist prin-

ciples, from totalitarian or Communist principles. I should like to leave
out of count all barren theories, doctrines, and formulae and *seek a course
demanded by a right practice, a practice duly answering to the life of the
country, a course called for by a correct, effective and quick-working administration, and by modern technical progress.*

For this there exists with us a single theoretical foundation, the only one
which provides a common meeting ground for us all. *Our Constitution is
of so liberal a character that it suffices to meet all these problems.* Our
political philosophy and morality takes the form of democracy, a democracy that provides us with the key to a solution of all our problems,
since it postulates in all political negotiations a respect of the human personality and complete civic equality, irrespective of diversity of class, nationality, or religion. If there is a general formula of concrete and practical
application to be noted with us as a trend of development, it is that which
I have more than once emphasized on previous occasions, that is to say:

*We stand for the principle of a reasonable decentralization combined
with an expedient economic and administrative regionalism.*

I am aware that today these views are regarded in some political circles
as out-of-date and no longer applicable and *that other principles are
sought, based on ideas of the totality of nation and state.* I keep calm,
however, in this matter. *It is sufficient for me to know that the views I
have expounded are truly human and that they have therefore survived
the ages and will outlast time.* Upon them, moreover—as I have already
said elsewhere on another occasion—rests our whole state. With them it
stands, and with them it will fall. It cannot therefore abandon them, come
what will.

5. I know that our Germans have complaints, desires, and demands of
a practical character. In the language and educational spheres these are
not matters of a fundamental character and are easy of disposal by reasonable practice. In economic matters, too, the question is substantially
one of reasonable practice. I do not hesitate to say that in these matters
mistakes have been made which must not be repeated, such as, for instance, that contractors and workmen have been called from Czech or
from Czech-German districts into German districts where unemployment
prevails. The German parties that support the government have already
discussed all these matters, and in the forthcoming activities—as Dr.
Hodža, the Premier, has declared—a right course of action will certainly
be pursued.

The greatest difficulties arise in matters concerning the state officials
and other employees. A number of the German wishes are in this connection justified. But precisely in this matter is it necessary to consider two
points. In the first place there is the question of confidence. It is compre-
hensible that a democratic state does not wish to entrust its administration to officials who profess fascist, totalitarian, or Communist principles.
That apples in all directions, equally for Czechoslovaks as for Germans.
This menace—as the situation presents itself today—is the greater from
the German side.

Let us further ask ourselves, in a candid and friendly spirit, whether perhaps just of late all kinds of things have not happened that have again necessarily justified the fears on the part of Czechs concerning the development of the state and of conditions in the state.

I am glad to state that in general the German officials and employees and the German soldiers fulfill their duties to the republic very satisfactorily, that the greater part of the German population are loyal to it as their fatherland, and that the German parties adhering to the government fulfill their duties to the state in self-sacrificing fashion. It needs only a fraction of the population, however, to come forward with alluring if impractical watchwords to provoke distrust on the other side. It then becomes very difficult to substitute confidence for that distrust, the confidence that is an essential primary condition wherever something of value is to be entrusted to the hands of another to be administered in common.

For this reason, I stress the fact of confidence, I stress the fact of patience and of time, and I should like to see that on the German side nothing should happen either in public declarations or manifestations or in private intercourse or in the course of the daily political discussions that is calculated with just cause to affect confidence on the Czech side, or that could serve as a justification for postponing the achievement of a reasonable settlement between Czechs and Germans.

I am speaking candidly and forthrightly. It is a friend who is addressing you, and one whose duty it is to deal with facts on all sides as they are, and in so fulfilling his duty toward the state, to seek in common with you a remedy for shortcomings.

6. I will close my answer to your references to Czech-German collaboration in our state *by asking on both sides for good will,* mutual trust, and a gradual closer approach one to the other. That implies patience, calmness, and composure on both sides. I would also ask, however, that we should all regard Europe in objective fashion and form an opinion as to how these problems are solved elsewhere, what is the position of the minorities in other countries, especially the big states, and thus compare conditions there with conditions in our country. *An honest man must admit that Czechoslovakia is, alongside Switzerland and Belgium, the most progressive in this respect.* An unbiased, unprejudiced politician who does not wish to do violence to the truth must agree that during the seventeen years of the highly tense and difficult postwar development in Europe and in a country which for centuries has been a classic region of nationality struggles it was not possible to solve all problems, but that, on the other hand, Czechoslovakia has in these questions done such work and achieved such progress, especially in Slovakia and particularly to the advantage of the Germans there, that no other country in Europe or in the whole world can challenge comparison with her. I have no objection to our discussing in common the shortcomings and the debit side of our policy, but I must ask that at the same time the asset side and the generally favorable balance of the seventeen-year policy of the Czechoslovak state in this sphere should be proclaimed. And therefore I object to the one-sided, biased, and untrue propaganda carried on abroad in this connection.

40

THE AGRARIAN QUESTION IN EASTERN EUROPE:
NOT CAPITALISM, NOT SOCIALISM

DAVID MITRANY

[The peasant question has historically been one of the most vexing problems facing the rulers of the agrarian societies of Eastern Europe. It became even more acute in the period of modernization that followed
World War I. In the interwar years, concessions were made to the peasants' land hunger, but little was done to modernize the village. There
were many reasons for official inaction, but basically they reflected an
unwillingness to face the economic and political consequences of rural
modernization. The peasant problem, it should be said, remains unsolved
today.

David Mitrany has studied the problems of East European peasant
societies for more than half a century. In the following selection, he
analyzes the agrarian structure of Eastern Europe in the twentieth century
and examines the reasons for the basic hostility toward the peasant displayed by political leaders and theoreticians, non-Marxist and Marxist
alike.]

The agrarian reforms enacted after 1917 took the general system of land
tenure in Eastern Europe far from the socialist idea of concentrated public
ownership and instead made the whole region overwhelmingly one of
small individual peasant holdings. Their effect on the organization of
production was equally distant from the Marxian purpose, but not in the
way or for the reasons assumed by various Western critics of the reforms,
who believed that the breakup of the large estates meant a change from
large-scale to small-scale farming. That was rarely true. The perverted
social evolution of those countries had been reflected also in the ways of

Reprinted, by permission, from David Mitrany, *Marx Against the Peasant* (Chapel
Hill, N.C.: The University of North Carolina Press, 1951), pp. 115–31.

their agriculture; even when they came to have a substantial corn export, this did not result from the spread of "capitalist" farming. Sometimes the accumulation of large estates served only to take them out of cultivation, their rich or aristocratic owners turning them into sporting estates. But in any case, at the turn of the century in Rumania, to give one instance, while the peasants were crying out for land only some 40 per cent of it was in cultivation. In the same country, properties over 250 acres, covering 49 per cent of the total area, were in the hands of only 0.46 per cent of all owners; but while they possessed half the usable land, these large owners had only one-tenth of the draft animals and less than one-tenth of the plows in use.

This discrepancy is explained by a peculiarity that lay at the core of the whole system. Of the huge area in the hands of large owners, only about one-sixth was farmed by themselves; the remainder was let to peasants or middlemen on leases running from three to five years, which meant that if they made any improvements they were likely to see their rent raised or lose their leases altogether. The middlemen were just middlemen, not farmers; all the equipment they brought with them, the peasants used to say, was a stick with which to drive them. In either case, the bulk of the land was worked mostly in sharecropping by the peasants, who provided their own teams and plows and carts and often also the seed. It was more like the system of domestic piece weaving at the beginning of the Lancashire cotton industry than modern factory production. That is indeed why, with a strong popular current behind it, the change on the practical side was easy in the Eastern countries, as both the nominally large-scale farming and peasant farming were carried on with the same means and methods, except for the drive. Estates run as well-organized capitalist farms were so few, except in the Vojvodina (Yugoslavia) and in Czechoslovakia, that people knew them by name and they were regarded as "model farms" —in Rumania, even on the eve of the recent war, there were only some twenty of them—and as such in many cases received privileged treatment under the land reforms.

That the general economic effect of these reforms was likely to be beneficial was admitted at the time, rather surprisingly, even by some of the Soviet experts. As Lenin had indicated years before, the immediate purpose of any agrarian reform was to remove obstacles that stood in the way of capitalist development, both from among backward smallholders and backward latifundia. But that was not exactly what happened. Economic changes undoubtedly followed the reforms; they were, however, the result of social not of technical factors. Some Western economists simply looked upon the fall in the production and export of cereals as proof of a decline in productivity. Production was bound to fall for a time; the war had caused losses in men, animals, and implements, neglect of the land, and human fatigue; and in any case the application of the reforms could not help upsetting things for a while. But these were incidents of the reforms, not necessarily their effects. The real change was not from large-scale to small-scale, from organized capitalistic to simple peasant farming, but rather from farming for the market to farming for subsistence. What distinguished the Eastern peasant from the Western large farmer or peasant farmer was that to him his land was first and foremost a means of raising food for his family and his animals. His production was accordingly diversified, and he took to market only the surplus, or perhaps something more if he were in need of cash. A freer use of their crops or even a larger yield meant first of all a higher consumption among the peasants themselves, who formerly had gone short of food or had been living on poor food. "I used to take my geese to market," was the way a Hungarian peasant put it, "and keep myself on potatoes; now I sell the potatoes and eat the geese." Some investigations undertaken in 1897 by two Russian professors, A. I. Chuprov and A. S. Postnikov, had found already then that "peasants in an economically stronger position satisfied first their own needs before they started producing for the market." That was the natural and immediate effect of the reforms as far as agriculture and its products were concerned. Hence the shifting of the land into the hands of small peasants could not, as things were, bring about a general improvement in supplies for the market or for export.

For the peasants, the land reforms proved beneficial even by economic standards. If one looked at trends rather than at particular figures, it was clear that the standard of living of the peasants was improving and, generally speaking, so was their production. Nevertheless, it is true that on the whole the outcome of the Eastern reforms has been disappointing, but other social reasons, of a somewhat negative nature, were responsible for that. The reforms themselves had little to do with matters of farming; they were never enacted as agricultural reforms but simply as measures for dividing up the land. Even in regard to land there were certain things the reforms could not do. One problem was that of rural overcrowding all over Eastern Europe; most peasant families were large, especially in Hungary, the average rural density being estimated at seventy people to one hundred hectares of farming land, when fifty people was taken as the limit of useful occupation. In spite of their sweep, the reforms could not give land to all. Again, five hectares was taken in the East as the minimum for a peasant family holding, or one hectare per member, but on an average the reforms could give them only half of that. Moreover, one of the worst and most stubborn features of peasant farming in that region was that many holdings consisted of several scattered strips, especially in hilly regions where each holding included strips of varying quality. The peasants held strongly to the idea that each villager should have a share of the better as of the worse soil, and the necessary give and take was all the more difficult when the peasants had so little confidence in governments and their officials.

All these were bad but also inevitable aspects of the division of the land. They made it all the more important to help the peasants to make the best use of it, to give them not merely the chance but the means to better their own lot and so agriculture in general. The transition had in any case to be a fairly long process, bound as it was to the accumulation of capital, but it could have been much shortened by providing capital from outside.

In this, the new measures and the policy that followed upon them were conspicuously deficient, and the reason for this offers a further, if indirect, proof that the land reforms were due to revolutionary pressure and not to any considered scheme for the improvement of agriculture. We have quoted Chayanov's saying that the Eastern statemen had to look at agrarian policy from the standpoint of population and so had to correct economic-technical with social considerations.* That no longer sounds very heretical now; since the Depression, the general outlook has shifted greatly, even in the West, toward ideas of "full employment" and "social security." But if that is how the problem had to be seen at all times, how much more was this so under the acute popular pressure that followed the Russian Revolution. Such indeed was the character of the ensuing reforms that to appraise them justly one would have to reverse the order of values suggested by Chayanov: The reforms left the Eastern statesmen with the task of correcting not the economic-technical with a social view, but the social with economic-technical considerations. Yet none of the governments concerned, though one might except that of Czechoslovakia, took steps to make the best of the new division of the land. They displayed an astonishing neglect of agriculture and its workers. The new peasant proprietors, except for a small minority, had not the means to acquire animals or implements or fertilizers; they were given neither credits nor guidance to replace the earlier compulsion, and for political reasons the cooperative movement was in most places kept chained to state controls. Improved communications to open up the village were vital, but public funds went into railways and elaborate motor roads while time and again in prolific areas, like Bessarabia, rich crops were left to rot because no transport could be found for them. In Yugoslavia in the early 1930's, in a period of many-sided agrarian reconstruction, the yearly public expenditure on agriculture amounted to less than forty cents per head of agricultural population.

On one point all experts were agreed, that peasant farming was not suitable for raising cereals. It was all the more suitable for dairy farming and market gardening, for industrial seeds and plants and similar crops, all of which brought in considerably higher returns in the market. That happened to be the kind of mixed farming the peasant knew best and which, in any case, he preferred, as meeting the varied needs of his own subsistence. Yet for one reason or another the Eastern countries strove rather to maintain cereal exports. The policy was so unnatural after the division of the land that in Rumania the government had to offer a bonus for growing corn while using freight rates and other means to make it difficult for the peasants to divert their new holdings to mixed farming. In general, the tendency was to leave agriculture to manage as best it could while granting favors to all sorts of industrial activities. Most of the industrial development depended on foreign capital and loans, and these were devoted to heavy and mineral industries, to armaments and such

* The quotation is not included in the extract reprinted here. A. Chayanov, an expert on Russian agrarian problems in the early twentieth century, was identified with the right wing of the Socialist Revolutionary Party.—Ed.

things; in no instance were they directed toward agricultural development, though the economic well-being of those countries depended in the first place on the strength of the agrarian sector.

There were, of course, variations between the several Eastern countries, but the general traits of that unnatural policy were closely alike in all of them, and there can be only one explanation for that. The dispossessed landed class had to seek refuge in civil and military positions, and in industry, trade, and banking, which were pushed artificially beyond the means and the needs of those countries. This could be done only with help from the state, some of it direct but most of it indirect, which made agriculture in general and the peasants in particular pay for these costly undertakings. At a time when the peasants needed help to organize their new holdings, their meager cash resources were instead drained by protective import duties and by taxes. Taxes being difficult to raise, the weight was thrown on indirect taxation; in the 1930's, this brought in 64 per cent in Bulgaria, in Yugoslavia 65.6 per cent, and in Rumania 72.5 per cent of the total tax receipts. After being given land cheaply, the peasants were made to pay for it several times over by such indirect means; they escaped the exploitation of the landlords only to fall into the stepmotherly tutelage of the mercantilist state. "The situation which before the reform existed on the land," wrote a Rumanian critic, "where a number of latifundiary owners retained the greater part of the agricultural revenue, has now been transferred to the domain of trade and industry." [1]

Strangely enough, this was actually admitted in an official document, namely in the preamble to the Rumanian fiscal law of 1923. "A state cannot be democratic," it said, "if at the moment when the large rural property disappears it allows a few people to accumulate fortunes from trade and industry while leaving the mass of the people in the state of the serfs of yesterday, who were unable to share in the benefits of our general prosperity." We have mentioned before the somewhat caustic argument of the Rumanian sociologist Zeletin,[*] that this was the only way to build up a reserve of national capital as a foundation for economic independence. However different the inspiration, the policy, it will be seen, was much the same as that which presided over the forced industrial development in Russia after the Soviet Revolution. At any rate, it is not surprising that, with all those faults of omission and commission, the Eastern land reforms did not provide the start of an economic advance and that agricultural output fell, though the area under cultivation had increased. The economic problem did not enter into their enactment or performance at all and could not stand out highly in their effects. The reforms were a series of revolutionary measures that were left to bear only their immediate and inevitable social results.

[1] D. I. Creanga, *"Veniturile si Averile Romaniei Mari"* (*"Incomes and Fortunes in Greater Rumania"*), published in *Buletinul Institutului Economic Romanesc* (Bucharest, 1927).

[*] Stefan Zeletin, whose main work was concerned with the formation and role of the Rumanian bourgeoisie.—ED.

That apparent neglect merely covered up the fact that the reforms marked a line of division between two social worlds, the feudal and the modern, and that the old having been demolished, the nature of the new, of the future economic and social organization, became the central issue in the countries of Eastern Europe. Two attitudes regarding it were face to face after the land reforms. Economists of the socialist and classical schools, especially in the West, doubted whether a fair standard of living could be achieved for the mass of the Eastern peoples unless industrial outlets were provided for a good many of them. In almost any peasant household, one working member, it was said, could have been spared, and that meant that all of them were underemployed. In earlier years, the pressure was eased by continuous emigration, but after the Depression the overseas countries had checked the flow, and the fear of Communist infiltration was likely to make them close their gates still tighter. For the time being, therefore, the problem could be dealt with only within the range of national policy. Its roots, apart from natural increase, were said to lie in the perverted agrarian conditions. The persistence of large estates or farms deprived many peasants of a chance to have a holding of their own; semi-servile conditions made many laborers redundant, one man being made to work as much land as could have provided a living for three; and women and children were still used too much for agricultural labors. Strip farming, together with extreme climatic conditions, in some parts also held back an excessive amount of labor. Nevertheless, the fact remains that between the wars there were registered in Southeastern Europe an absolute increase in rural population of nearly 30 per cent and hence but a slight decline in its proportion to total population, while there was little land left for subdivision.

While to a certain degree the excess of rural labor was therefore seasonal and technical, it was generally agreed that even a change to intensive agriculture could not find work for all and that substantial industrial development was necessary for both demographic and economic reasons. But there were wide differences of view as to the kind of industrial policy that was needed and as to ways and means. The industries set up after 1918 had done little to ease the population problem or raise the standard of living of the masses; they were mostly primary or heavy industries, depending on the interests of foreign investors or on the prospect of substantial profits through contracts or favors from the state, which therefore could establish themselves and survive only behind high protective tariffs. The whole trend had been haphazard or misdirected, without any regard to real needs and possibilities. One of the ablest Eastern economists, Virgil Madgearu, a leader of the Rumanian Peasant Party, had insisted that, unlike the old populists, the peasants in Eastern Europe were not opposed to industrial development as such. "If there is not in peasantism an inherent tendency against industrial development, it is, on the other hand, against protectionism, the breeder of hothouse industries, of trusts and cartels." Industries depending on high prices and tariffs and other restrictive measures could not offer an outlet for the surplus rural population.

To serve this essential purpose, any new industries had to meet two conditions above all: to produce things needed by the mass of the people and, using native materials in the process, to give employment to as large a number of them as possible. For this reason, the peasant movement wanted industries to be scattered widely in smaller units across the land to give the peasants additional employment during the slack seasons. All these conditions pointed in the first place to the development of domestic manufactures and processing industries, but in fact these were few and far between unless established, as in Poland, by the peasant cooperatives. The difference between the peasant and the capitalist views on industrialization was therefore one of ways and purpose. The peasant way might not relieve rural overpopulation in a direct way, by reducing numbers, but they believed that it would ensure better use of rural labor and so help in the diversification of agriculture; and it would have been an organic growth at comparatively little cost. Capitalist industrialization, that is, large-scale capital-goods industries in urban centers, might mitigate rural overpopulation, but the experience of the interwar period had shown that it could not relieve it greatly; and the accumulation of capital needed for such a type of industrial development would inevitably mean for the mass of the people, that is, for the peasants, for many years a still lower standard of living, a standard that, as in Russia—though it had the advantage of unlimited supplies of raw materials—could be imposed only by dictatorial methods.

Economists and others who had urged such industrialization by way of solving the social problem of Eastern Europe have been apt to overlook that the Western industrial revolution would not have been possible had it not been for the existence of less industrialized countries and of newly opened territories, together with the predominance of free trade. Internal markets in the West had been built upon an extensive trade with those vast external markets. It is true that, apart from those directly interested (and leaving aside the special case of Soviet Russia), certain groups in the East favored capitalist industrialization rather for reasons of state, as a foundation for national security and independence. But whatever the end, the means for such an artificial evolution could only come from the exploitation of the rural masses, and the policy was therefore up against the old Populist argument that it was bound to defeat its own ends. An industrial policy that could have no hope of thriving on external markets and that, in the process of growing up, impoverished the very people who made up the internal market was doomed to a hopeless vicious circle, always dependent on the state and all the time corrupting it.

But apart from holding a particular view on the nature of industrial development, there is no doubt that the Peasant leaders would have put their faith rather in agrarian development, and not merely from a sentimental attachment to the land. They firmly believed that this was the only road forward for their countries. In the West, the industrial trend had set in before the rural population had increased excessively, and since then any surplus had been continuously drawn away to the towns.

Eastern Europe having had no similar industrial expansion in the nineteenth century, the bulk of the people had to continue to seek their subsistence on the land; it was too late to change that division of labor altogether; any general social improvement would have to come above all from agrarian improvements. Therefore, it was a central question in the argument whether the poor results of the land reforms were due wholly to unnatural political and economic policies. Could the Eastern peasants under different conditions build up a productive and prosperous agriculture, as the Western peasants had done? A change in general conditions was, in their view, the crux of the problem, and the Peasant movement, as we shall see, had its answer to this. But even from an economic standpoint the issue was often misjudged by Western experts, who looked simply at figures of production and export. The question of large-scale versus small-scale in agriculture is a complex one and largely technical; in farming, the optimum size (apart from Thuenen's "concentric circles")* probably varies with soil, climate, and, above all, crops. In the context of this essay, it is necessary to take a somewhat wider view, and in its light the purely economic judgment would seem to rest on three fallacies—historical, economic, and social.

The historical fallacy was to assume that the demand for wheat and other cereals, for "cheap bread," which played such a large part in the French Revolution and in Europe generally since the industrial revolution and no doubt influenced the Marxist view, could remain a continuous criterion for judging agricultural productivity and well-being. Corn is undoubtedly grown best on a large scale, but the demand for it is inelastic, and reliance on it in the past has often proved disastrous to European growers faced with the competition of overseas supplies. The Eastern growers were only able to keep up with it either by depressing the peasants in a direct way or through economic and administrative favors from the state, like those which the landowners in Hungary could still command in the crisis of the 1930's. But even so, though still a country of large estates, by 1937 Hungary's poultry exports had come to exceed its wheat exports. As the wheat market collapsed, the Eastern countries in fact kept afloat on the buoyancy of their peasant economies. The whole episode threw a peculiar light upon the weakness and the strength of their economic system. Subsistence farming could adapt itself to a precarious situation: The fall in prices led many peasants to eat what they produced, rather than take some of it to market, and also to use their spare time in improving buildings and fences, as there was less of the additional work from which they ordinarily raised some ready money; some of the younger folk for the first time could even take off a month or so to attend the peasant schools organized in that period by the peasants themselves. For traders, bankers, and others, however, the loss of exports and the shortage of money meant heavy trouble, nor could the state collect taxes from people who had no cash. But the peasants were

---

* A theory of the location of agricultural production units, developed by the German agriculturalist J. H. von Thuenen in the first half of the nineteenth century.—Ed.

not affected in that way. It was indeed a paradoxical state of affairs, unfathomable by modern economic theory, when, as one might put it, state and trade were bankrupt, but the mass of the people were better off.

The economic fallacy was to assume dogmatically that the larger the scale, the greater the efficiency. Since the Great Depression, doubts about this have grown even in the field of industry. In agriculture, it has always been uncertain, and as regards Eastern Europe, definitely false. The large owners in those parts got better results not because of economic-technical but political and social conditions. Their farming was profitable on a large scale and with extensive methods only as long as it could command semi-servile conditions of labor; and even in cereal crops the well-established peasants in the Banat and in Transylvania consistently got higher yields than any of the large estates. In Poland, the change from extensive corn-growing to mixed farming showed great capacity for expansion in that direction, and in Czechoslovakia, the division of the large estates resulted in an improvement in the number and quality of livestock, an increase in milk production, and even a rise in corn yields, because more livestock meant more manure.

The social fallacy, finally, was to overlook that the quantities thus made available for export were never a true surplus. Economists and socialists, concerned with a surplus for the urban markets, took little heed of how the change to large-scale or capitalist farming affected the village poor; almost always it left those who did the work with an inadequate share of the produce. The Rumanian leaders Maniu and Mihalache * asserted that there was a marked difference in the well-being of the peasants between the regions of large- and small-scale agriculture. In the Eastern countries, the decrease in supplies to the towns meant better supplies for the mass of the people and was therefore in itself a social advance, even if commercial production and exports lagged.

In recent years, and especially since the war, new social considerations have given even the economic factor an altogether different turn. The emphasis now is not merely on quantity, on having enough food, but on having the right kind of food. The closer and more intelligent interest in social health has revealed a serious and widespread shortage in "protective foods" and therefore a rising demand for them. Even in the United States, as the late President Roosevelt disclosed, one-third of the nation did not get enough of these protective foods; in the agricultural countries of Eastern Europe, as stated in the study on *The Economic Development of Southeastern Europe*, the deficiency was appalling, many villages having no milk at all. Awareness of this need has made the argument as to the best scale for agricultural production appear, therefore, in a new light. For reasons both of the people's social health and of external trade, it would seem that the old Eastern system was in any case doomed and that, even if unwittingly, the reforms had in fact given a chance to build afresh on the right lines. Whenever it is a question of intensive farming,

* Iuliu Maniu and Ion Mihalache were the leaders of the Rumanian National Peasant Party in the 1920's and 1930's.—ED.

of personal care of animals, and so on, large-scale undertakings dependent on paid labor must always find it difficult to compete with peasant production in a free market. In spite of the rise of many capitalist undertakings, particularly overseas, specializing in one product or another on factory lines, the support and demand for family farming has continued unabated even in the West.

Besides, perhaps the most important aspect of the matter had almost been lost sight of in the debate about production quantities, namely, the vital need of maintaining the productivity of the soil. That is a need which concerns every country, but not until the shock caused by some disaster, like that in the "dust bowl" of the Western United States, had it received the attention it merits. Good farming means not only what is got out of the soil but also what is put back into it, to keep it "in good heart and condition." Everywhere, and at all times, experience seems to have shown the same close relation between large-scale farming, especially under tenancy, and the impoverishment of the soil. Even in the United States, the policy is now to break up the old cotton lands of the South into small units for mixed subsistence farming as the best way of redeeming the soil (as well as the health and self-respect of the 8 million white and Negro sharecroppers) exhausted by the endless raising of profitable commercial crops. The planter and large tenant often treated the land as an investment, to be used as long as it paid and then sold as scrap: "Land is with him a perishable or movable property." [2] Marx, characteristically, had simply laid it down that small-scale cultivation impoverished and exhausted the soil. Yet how could a peasant, who expects to raise generations on the same bit of ground, treat his land otherwise than as a living thing? The virtue of ancient and recent peasant farming, wrote a reviewer in the scientific journal *Nature*, is that it returns to the soil the elements of life.[3] It may be true that peasant farming does not produce as much as mechanized large-scale farming, but it has never exhausted the soil.

There is a strong element of ideal truth in the old socialist argument that, being God-given and needed by all, the land should be no man's private property. Yet the land as such would be of little worth unless its bearing powers are perpetuated. It is the function of the land, not its raw substance, that society must possess for well-being and survival, and in that sense the claim to individual ownership may be logically rooted in the nature of agricultural production itself. With the factory worker, even the artisan, the quality of his product depends on the quality of the material and on his own skill. Whatever tools or machinery he uses are a passive factor, taken over as they stand from the previous user and passed on to the next, but little affected by their temporary use, or easily replaced. All the variable factors of production, materials, and skill are wholly absorbed in each unit, in each object produced, while machines

[2] From an article by the editor of *Southern Cultivator* (Georgia) in the late 1850's; quoted in Carl Sandburg, *Abraham Lincoln: The Prairie Years* (New York, 1926), Vol. II, p. 206.

[3] *Nature*, December 14, 1946.

and tools are transient. With farmer or peasant, the matter is very different. His chief tool is the soil itself, or rather it is partly tool, partly raw
material, a unique combination in the whole scheme of production. It is
unique in that it is both a variable factor, affected by each period of use,
and at the same time a constant factor, which cannot be replaced. What
the farmer can get out of it depends greatly on the state in which the
soil was passed on to him by the previous user, and his own way of
treating it will affect the results obtained by the next user. Neglect of the
soil by one may make it of little use for many. Quite apart from immediate benefits, therefore, the very nature and spirit of "cultivation" seem to
require that the man who tills the land should have constant use of the
same piece of the same instrument.

All one can ask, as the Weimar Constitution [in Germany] asked, is
that he who claims the right to such constant use should also be responsible for the constant care of the soil's living qualities. To the peasant, such
care is a matter of his own survival. Extensive commercial farming reduced even the young soil of America to poverty in the cotton belt and to
dust in part of the Western wheat belt. Nor did that loss to the soil, and
to society, apparently bring lasting advantage to those who by their
method of farming had been responsible for it. In the United States, even
on the land in the Great Depression of the 1930's, one-tenth of the farming families were on public relief. Perhaps the key to the peasant's deep
attachment to his piece of land, and to the true social meaning of his way
of farming for him, lies in these two facts. To own the land and to be
free to farm it in the traditional peasant way is to him nothing less than
the equivalent of that "social security" which has become the aspiration
of industrial masses even in the advanced countries of the West. The
lifeline that in the West the state has to throw to the worker whenever
he is in difficult circumstances, through the complex of insurances against
unemployment, against sickness and want, for old age, and so on, the
peasant has always found in his traditional economy. As Miriam Beard
says in her *History of the Business Man*, discussing his part through many
centuries, "men suffered on the land but survived; while in the cities they
flourished—and faded." The peasant's way to security may not provide
him with such great material benefits as those now given in the West by
the state, but it is a security that he can achieve with his own hands and
that leaves him free to stand on his own feet.

Social health, social security, the health of the soil—all these new concerns would seem to have brought fresh practical justification for peasant
farming. The small farmer no doubt labors under various disadvantages,
but experience has shown these to be commercial more than technical. In
general, and leaving corn-growing aside, he can hold his own in the
process of production; it is when he enters the market that he finds it
difficult to stand up to the big men. Proudhon had already shrewdly argued that modern communications and distribution would "discipline
the market" and prove a safeguard rather than a danger for the small
farmer. The absence of such communications has been a heavy factor in

the poverty of the Eastern peasant, while the lesson that their chief weakness lay in distribution was gradually learned by the European peasants as much as by the American farmers. In the interwar years, cooperative marketing was fast becoming an integral part of the small-scale farming in the West. Some years ago, under socialist influence, North Dakota tried a system of state marketing of grain, but it proved a failure; the farmers afterward found better help in a scheme of cooperative elevators, which received the blessings of the socialists, too.

Elsewhere, also, the earlier socialist hostility to cooperative arrangements was giving way to acceptance of a movement that was making headway in spite of them. The Italian socialist Gatti, an agrarian expert, had pointed out its special place in agriculture: "Whereas the new technical instrument (that is, concentrated production) has created in industry only one economic current, namely capitalism, in agriculture it has created the capitalist current for the large undertaking and the cooperative current for the small." The Belgian Vandervelde had equal sympathy for it and insisted that even if the agricultural cooperatives had sprung from an antisocialist spirit, they "march unwittingly toward the same goal as the socialist movement itself." Albert Sorel saw in them, indeed, the best type of mutual organization: "It is on the land, much more than in the towns, that socialists must go to see examples that can illuminate the notion of association." [4]

All the peasant parties believed that the shortcomings of small-scale production could be mended by cooperative arrangements. It is not too much to say, indeed, that they had in mind a cooperative society, equally distinct from the liberal capitalist society as from the collective society of socialism. In earlier years, cooperative arrangements in Eastern Europe were but poorly and unevenly established. In some countries, like Rumania, Yugoslavia, and elsewhere, such cooperatives as existed, like everything else capable of giving the peasants a more independent position, never escaped the control of the authorities. In general, rural cooperatives were set up mainly for selling purposes and as such could benefit only the relatively small group of peasants who had a sufficient surplus to sell in the main markets. This was true also of the credit cooperatives, which always depended for their funds on help from the state; and anything that was under the control of the authorities was apt to be looked upon with suspicion by the mass of the peasants.

These beginnings, however, fell far short of the part given to the cooperative idea in the programs of the peasant movement. Whether conceived as "village cooperation," as by the Croat party, or "integral cooperation," as by the group of Dr. Jovanovic,* it was meant to serve every need and every aspect of rural life. Technical, financial, and commercial, and also insurance arrangements were intended to secure to the peasant farmers the benefits of large-scale farming; social and cultural arrange-

[4] From the Introduction to G. Gatti, *Socialism and Agriculture* (Paris, 1961).

* Dragoljub Jovanovic, a leader of the Serbian peasant movement in the interwar years, organized a left-wing political organization that was independent of the main peasant parties.—Ed.

ments were to bring them the advantages that until then had been a privilege of the towns. Especially were they meant to be, as in Croatia, a binding element, to bring the richer and poorer peasants together in the pursuit of their common economic and social interests.

These aspirations found practical expression during the interwar period in manifold cooperative experiments, though with a few exceptions they were no more than beginnings. Apart from their general neglect of agriculture, the obstruction or interference of those in control often came into play through or against the peasant cooperatives. It was natural, therefore, that the cooperative trend should have greatest strength where the peasants were best organized politically. In such parts, the range and spirit of these activities were impressive, as in the interesting experiment with a chain of village health cooperatives in Serbia. Two other instances well illustrate their social significance: One was the experiment in Czechoslovakia with a direct trading arrangement between peasant dairy cooperatives and urban socialist consumers' cooperatives; the other, the beginning of an international connection between the Bulgarian and Serbian cooperatives. The two organizations had started active relations on the eve of the war through a joint selling arrangement and later through a joint insurance scheme, to save the high cost of insurance for their transports. They were aiming to establish similar links with the Rumanian and other peasant cooperatives in the hope of drawing the Balkan people effectively together by such means.

Many of those concerned with these affairs, especially among the younger and advanced elements, felt strongly that the structure of peasant farming would also have to develop somehow toward some kind of communal cooperation; whether such cooperative cultivation was to be undertaken by the village as a whole or some other grouping was not yet clear, but they expected it to give both the form and the content for a peasant democracy. It was perhaps the only way to deal with the difficult problem of scattered strips without rousing the suspicion or opposition of the peasant owners. Yet even those who believed that cooperative farming was an essential and urgent step, without even the exception of the several left-wing peasant groups, wholly rejected all idea of collective farming on the kolkhoz model, because it would mean central control and the loss of peasant initiative and freedom. Perhaps this is as good an example as any of the reaction against socialist ideas that Soviet methods had caused among the neighboring peasant populations.

Be that as it may, these cooperative activities were managed well and with imagination; in most parts, as in Croatia, special attention was paid to the poorer peasants, like those of the penurious villages in the Karst Mountains of Dalmatia. The cooperatives were meant not merely to have economic uses but to become nuclei of a new civic conception. Some of the leaders considered that "the merging of the functions of universal cooperatives with local self-government might create a special form of administrative body." However experimental, therefore, these attempts were reaching, in their purpose and performance, beyond anything known or contemplated as cooperative activity in the West, and they gave an inkling of what the peasant leaders meant when they spoke of a coopera-tive rural society.

Whatever one may think of the claims of large or small farming, the issue cannot be said to have been tested until general conditions and pol-icy give each kind a chance to prove itself. By itself, the break-up of the large estates in Eastern Europe could not solve either the peasant problem or the general economic problem. The circumstances that surrounded these extensive measures and the untoward central policy that followed them, in Russia as in the other peasant countries, therefore revived in the East the old and burning question that had provoked the populist reaction against Marxism: What is the best organization for our people, an agrar-ian one on peasant foundations or an industrial organization, whether capitalist or socialist? The irony of the Eastern revolution was that the break-up of the large estates into millions of peasant holdings was presided over not by populists but by those who stood for the industrial solution. They had to put into action a sweeping change that went contrary to their own beliefs and plans, and that afterward, they had therefore to try to reverse all the more forcibly by means of their general policy. For, ideology and program apart, the division of the land had at once two serious con-sequences for the towns and their industrial plans. For reasons discussed before, it tended at first to reduce the supply of food to the towns; it also reduced the supply of labor. In the first spell, the chance of getting land provoked a real exodus from the towns. "At present, the village," said a Russian writer, "has absorbed a good half of the industrial proletariat." [5] On both counts, therefore, the land reforms, whatever their inspiration and purpose, raised obstacles in the way of plans for rapid industrial ex-pansion and in the same measure prevented control of economic policy by ordinary means by either the capitalist middle class or the proletarian working class.

That could be only a temporary effect. It did not touch the heart of the economic problem and left, moreover, the issue in the political arena. Those who stood for the industrial scheme of things did not adjust it to the new conditions and work to reshape these gradually through economic action. Whether proletarians or capitalists, they strove instead to get con-trol of power and then revive their set conceptions by political means. The crucial issue of agrarian organization cannot be said to have been faced at all as an economic and technical problem: For years, it was left to fester in Soviet Russia and in other countries left to drift. It was naive to think, said a Rumanian peasant leader, that the reform was finished: "Every-thing is still to be done, as far as the work of agrarian development is con-cerned." [6]

Three ways have been advocated for dealing with the agrarian problem in Eastern Europe.

[5] A. Chrjashtchew, "Die Evolutzion der Klassen innerhalb der Bauernschaft," *Rusische Korrespondenz* (Hamburg), January-March, 1922.
[6] Ion Mihalache, *Noul Regim Agrar* (*The New Agrarian Regime*) (Bucharest, 1925), p. 27.

1. Some technical experts and conservative circles urged the creation of "sound" peasant holdings (of the kulak type) of at least ten to fifteen hectares each, on the Western pattern. That was the method tried by Stolypin in 1906 and by King Carol in Rumania before the war; in the latter case they were to be of ten hectares each, indivisible by sale or inheritance (the Nazi *Erbhofgesetz* did not allow sale at all) and were to be given only to Rumanian subjects farming themselves. Such a general policy, broadly speaking, would have reduced the number of holdings by some two-thirds, which meant that new fields of work in the towns or through emigration would have had to be found for at least one-third of the rural population.

2. The socialist school of economics has not so much advocated as taken for granted the proletarization of the peasants through the inescapable working of economic evolution. The towns would then take control of economic policy and transform agriculture into collectivized and mechanical large units of production, on factory lines. Whatever else it might achieve, outside Russia this was bound to be self-defeating in that it would have made the crucial problem of overpopulation even worse than under the kulak scheme.

3. The peasant view has favored diversified farming in family economies, combined with old and new forms of cooperative integration. Some years ago, it was summed up in this way by Dr. Macek, the present leader of the Croat Peasant Party:

> Forty years ago we wanted to preserve and defend the *zadruga* as a unit of production and consumption. The crisis has taught us that this is no longer possible. But it is possible to turn the village into an economic unit. Every peasant holding produces partly for the needs of the peasant family and partly for the market. The part produced for the needs of the family, which never reaches the market, should remain the business of the peasant family also in the future. As to the other part, production for the market, the trend of evolution leads toward cooperative production as a common concern of the village as a whole. Where there is a lack of land, new possibilities of earning a livelihood must be created within the village, ranging from home industries to village factories. But the peasant's connection with the land must not be severed, he must not be driven from the soil.

This Peasant view does not seem very far, in its general idea, from the Soviet agrarian system. Cooperative farming for the market and individual farming for the peasant family's own need look closely similar to the kolkhoz, with its appendage of "home gardens" for the use of individual members of the collective farm. There is a difference between the two ideas, however, which brings out clearly the deep-seated division between the Communist and the Peasant view of society. In the Peasant conception, the whole arrangement would be a cooperative village affair, organized and managed by every village for itself, not one controlled from an urban center in accordance with a centralized plan and imposed as such upon all.

41

FAMILISM IN BULGARIA: A CHANGING WAY OF LIFE

IRWIN T. SANDERS

[The traditional forms of rural social organization have often been cited as obstacles to the modernization of the village in the twentieth century. They have also been cited by political leaders as one reason for their inability to transform the village into a functional entity for the industrial age. In the selection below, an eminent student of Balkan peasant life examines a Bulgarian village (Dragalevtsy) in transition. His analysis, which focuses on the disintegration of the family unit and traditional familism, suggests that it would have been possible to reconcile the interests of the peasantry and those of the state in a more peaceable manner than actually occurred after World War I.]

The day at last arrived when I could anticipate the peasants' answers to most of the questions that I asked them. When I inquired what they would do if they had five hundred dollars to spend, I could list in advance the items they would name. The older people, especially, thought and acted largely in terms of the Dragalevtsy of the "good old days," when life was lived in a *familistic* way, because the family played the major role in the community. When I understood the characteristics of familism, as a result of observing and reading about peasant life in other parts of the world, the many interesting but isolated facts I had noticed in Dragalevtsy began to make sense and to form a pattern. In a familistic society, whether it is in the Balkans or China, life is largely customary and traditional. Individualism is discouraged because of the crisis that the unusual person creates in the daily routine. People prefer a dead uniformity or a leveling of the best toward the mediocre. The family plays the leading part in this

---

Reprinted, by permission, from Irwin T. Sanders, *Balkan Village* (Lexington, Kentucky: The University of Kentucky Press, 1940), pp. 144–60.

task of molding an individual into the accepted pattern. From childhood to old age, the kinship group brings pressure to bear upon any nonconformist, since the family as a whole loses prestige in the community if a member gets out of hand. The family, too, is the chief training ground for the young, and parents cannot blithely transfer any responsibility of this sort to an outside agency, such as the school or the Church. Village opinion holds the parents accountable.

Furthermore, economic life is centered about the family. Since family members grow or make for themselves most of the things they need, they depend only to a minor degree upon stores, factories, and other commercial agencies. The family is the productive, distributive, and consumptive unit. This is one reason why village families can weather so many wars and so many depressions: They can satisfy most of their immediate wants at home.

Visitors suddenly confronted with the familistic way of life for the first time are often shocked at the low level of living they observe: animals sharing the same dwelling; monotonous diet and low health standards; waste of time and energy with inefficient tools and methods. Before the peasant is condemned as unambitious, indolent, or stupid, there are a few things the outsider must bear in mind. In agricultural villages throughout the world, the land base has been shrinking while the population has been expanding. This has meant decreased economic opportunity. Farms that were once adequate are now divided up strip by strip and handed over to many descendants, with the result that the term "eking out a living" has come to have real meaning for the peasant. The outsider often forgets that the rise in the level of living in the cities through the techniques of mass production and mass distribution has been relatively recent and phenomenally rapid. The villager is not really so far behind the time, if one compares his life with that of many cities a few decades ago or with the blighted areas of these same cities today. But one cannot deny that quite a few peasants seem to take pride in resisting social change; they are slow to experiment with new methods, and they assume that what was good enough for their fathers is good enough for them. This resistance is based, to a great degree, upon the realization that accepting too much from outside will seriously affect the social organization of their community. Urban society is not nearly so close-knit and can allow for contradictions and inconsistencies on a much broader scale than can the village, where life is still intimate and face-to-face. Dragalevtsy people, for example, in 1937 were conscious of the far-reaching changes brought about by the abandonment of sheep-raising in favor of dairying. Some time ago, a number of the peasants actively resisted this economic trend. In the opinion of many, these conservatives were stupid; at the same time, they were bright enough to figure out that changes would result in the economy to which they were accustomed. Because they were accustomed to it, they wanted to preserve it.

In a familistic society, religion has usually become rigidly institutionalized and is closely allied with the family. All family events call for the blessing of the religious intermediary; there are usually household shrines; there is considerable emphasis upon observing the forms of the religion; and usually the prevailing religion has a monopoly in its field. Where there once existed two or three competing religions, the peasants now have a syncretistic set of beliefs that almost all of the people accept.

The population in a familistic society tends to be stable. The folk legends and religious beliefs stress the importance of remaining at home. Permanence becomes a virtue, for travel outside introduces too much novelty. Separation places a strain upon the family relationships, which must be kept at full vigor in the interest of community self-preservation.

Recreation is personalized instead of being commercialized. Peasants, as far as possible, spend their leisure hours in the company of others, to say nothing of the many hours women spend working with each other within a family or neighborhood circle. Just as the villagers have ceremonial ways of doing many things, they also have formal ways, or proverbs, of saying many things. . . . Proverbs reinforce those beliefs that help maintain the familistic society and serve as convenient means of self-expression. At the same time, they are standards of behavior.

Because recreation and economic life are personal, the familistic society has little need for much reading and writing. The priest, the middlemen, the tax-gatherers, and a few others who early associated themselves with the village economy needed to "figure," but the rest of the people had little concern with that.

In most family-dominated societies, life is man-centered. In some areas, this arrangement is related to religious beliefs; in others, it is related to the economic organization of the family, in which somebody has to give orders necessary to the carrying out of the daily activities. A recognized head, conscious of his own importance, acts authoritatively in directing his family group.

The local government is traditionally managed by elders, who represent families rather than political parties or individuals. The village elders make their decisions from the standpoint of what is good for the village as a whole in the light of precedents rather than from a narrow legalism. The religious writings or sacred legends are conveniently cited to justify the actions they take. Such governmental activity exists primarily to meet crisis situations and to keep the established ways of life moving smoothly. The giving of relief, the provision of education, healing of the sick, insurance of cattle and crops are all left to the family rather than to the government.

It is quite possible for several societies to use the familistic approach, in the sense that the family is the dominant institution, and still differ as to the relative importance of many community values. Most of them would probably respect the heritage from the past, but even here there would be variations. As far as Dragalevtsy was concerned, the chief values or virtues were land ownership, hard work, frugality, premarital chastity, observance of some of the more important religious rites, and being a good neighbor. In connection with the last, the villagers said, "God help those with bad neighbors," and, "Without good neighbors life couldn't go on."

The Dragalevtsy people, although their underlying organization and philosophy were primarily familistic, had adjusted themselves to a number of modern ways. Some ways persisted because they fitted in with the established customs, and others because they were kept in vogue by force or by the authority of the mayor.

Commerce, as represented by about ten merchant groups, had become established in the village because it was conducted essentially as a family enterprise. From time to time, a local man sold some of his land and started in business for himself. He always employed members of his family rather than outsiders, because he trusted his own. If he needed extra help and had an unmarried son, the normal thing was to urge matrimony. He carried over into his business the same idea of division of labor that prevailed at home and in the field. The men ordered the goods, settled the accounts, sold the liquor in the taverns. The women acted as cooks or clerks. Some of the wives who helped keep the store could not read, write, add, or subtract and had to give whole measurements or else depend upon the customer to hand them the right amount for fractions. A husband explained, when I discussed the matter with him, "It is better to lose money through error than through dishonesty." Both men and women cooperated in keeping the place clean. Here the man made a concession that he would seldom have made in the home.

These merchant groups, with the exception of two or three of the most prosperous, led a precarious, short-lived existence. During the three years in which I knew the village, three successive proprietors managed a business undertaking in one building alone. Bai Penko's tavern, the largest of all, was founded thirty years ago by his father; another tavern, which was founded fifty years ago, had been owned by the present proprietor for ten years; one grocery was started in 1935, and another was taken over by its present managers in 1936.

The largest grocery store had stock, which I carefully inventoried, approximating two hundred dollars in value. It included many articles that would have been found in an American country store a generation ago.

The degree to which the old familistic way of doing things pervaded the local businesses was shown by the nature of the groups that conducted these businesses. In the case of one grocery store, two men were in partnership. One partner took care of the card playing, which he promoted in a small space at the end of the store, and his wife took care of the grocery section. The second partner, in addition to helping with the card playing and the grocery work, mixed bread for the bakery downstairs and sent his wife up to work in the store when she was not busy in the bakery. The stock of goods in this particular store was very small, and so was the clientele. The proprietor of a second grocery store was usually away from his place of business, leaving his wife in charge. She was quite dissatisfied with the present arrangement, saying, "I have to get up at two or three in the morning to do the housework before coming to the store. I go to bed at night between eleven and eleven-thirty. Life is full of hard work, but life is more sure now, because we have food and money." This couple, incidentally, was one of the few childless couples in the village.

Bai Penko, too, made use of members of his family. He himself was the general manager and worked several hours a day in the tavern; his wife was in charge of the kitchen; the older daughter took care of the six or seven upstairs rooms, which were rented to the veterinarian and summer guests when not occupied by members of the family. The older son, Pano, was in charge of serving drink and food and of all accounts connected with this service. His younger brother was in charge of the small grocery store next door, though he often turned the store over to his mother while he served drinks at rush hours in the tavern. The younger daughter helped with both housework and the grocery store, while the eighteen-year-old granddaughter did the heavy, disagreeable work. Both sons married shortly before I left Dragalevtsy, and their wives spent several hours each day working under the direction of Bai Penko's wife. Because of this large family circle, Bai Penko hired two men only on holidays, one as an extra waiter and the other to roast meat freshly killed for the occasion.

Familistic, or at least personal, reasons determined why families traded with one particular merchant. Reasons such as these were most frequently cited:

"We are close friends."

"We are slightly related."

"He lends me money when I need it."

"We were members of the same political party."

"I had a quarrel with the proprietor of another grocery store, so changed to this one."

Only occasionally did the people say:

"He sells pure and fine goods."

"His prices are cheaper."

Just the same, there did seem to be considerable shopping around on the part of the villagers. They favored those places where they could get credit. But here again, family connections helped decide whether or not a man could get credit from a given merchant. Credit was extended with discrimination. A poor risk, when credit was refused, frequently transferred his trade to a different store. The older proprietors were often called upon to give advice, and thus enjoyed an advantage over the younger businessmen trying to establish themselves. One of these young men said to me: "Because of my age, nobody comes to me for advice. That is why my trade is small."

Commerce also made its way into Dragalevtsy through a few commission merchants who regularly visited the peasants to buy eggs, poultry, and livestock. Occasionally they speculated in land.

In Dragalevtsy, therefore, familism had yielded some ground to commerce. People did make occasional purchases in the village and in Sofia. They talked more and thought more about money. They even valued it more highly than a generation ago, but the basis of their economic life remained self-subsistent, with an emphasis upon goods, not cash.

Cooperatives had also come to Dragalevtsy. In a very real sense, village life itself was a cooperative enterprise, although it did not possess the specific characteristics of an economic cooperative. The large joint family, which has been widely prevalent throughout the world, also had many elements of the cooperative, which have been maintained, at least in the sentiments of the people, even though the family group has become individualized and smaller.

Self-subsistent peasant farmers are accustomed to working together when something needs to be done. Theirs is, after all, a cooperative way of life. They also know that their own hard work and their own planning are responsible for whatever success they achieve. They are suspicious of outsiders who seek to organize them and are fearful that any tie-up with the business interests outside the village means loss rather than gain. They are not accustomed to using money to make more money, although they know well enough what it means to pay interest on borrowed money.

Agricultural coperatives often gain adherents more quickly when there is a feeling of distinction or distrust between city and the country people. This is because cooperatives have been identified in such places with the agrarianism that unites the peasants. The profit motive of capitalism is linked, in the minds of many villagers, with the urban businessman, in spite of the fact that the villager who owns his land is also a capitalist. Perhaps it is this idea that Americans find hardest to grasp in their evaluation of peasant Europe. Land is not something to be bought and unfeelingly sold for money. It is rather a means of livelihood, an extension of oneself and one's family.

As the merchant groups in the villages are few and insecure, the cooperatives do not have the opposition of vested interests they face in a more highly developed economy. I realized from the beginning that cooperatives had made much less headway in Dragalevtsy than in many other Bulgarian communities. The secretary of the General Union of Bulgarian Agricultural Cooperatives explained: "The farmers live near the city and prefer to market their goods themselves rather than through the medium of cooperatives. They find that they get higher prices in the Sofia bazaar than they would receive from cooperatives."

Nevertheless, the three cooperatives represented in Dragalevtsy gave me some insight into the reasons for success and failure of those that did get off to a start. The cooperative that had made most progress in Dragalevtsy was a purely local affair, which arose to meet a definite need. In some respects it was more like a corporation than a cooperative, but it was a "combining together" to get something done.

One of the richer families in the village used to spend twenty-five days threshing its grain with horses. As a result, the family began to think of using a machine to do the work. The idea incubated until Trayko Danev decided to take the initial plunge and persuaded his relatives to plunge with him. Two other men joined them in the purchase of a threshing machine in 1930. Their purpose was to thresh their own wheat and, if possible, thresh the wheat of others for a fair return. The first years of the ring's existence, when the price of wheat was high, were the best years. Between 1935 and 1937, the prices were so low that the group just managed to cover its expenses. However, because of their 400,000-leva ($4,-878 at the 1937 exchange rate) investment, the men did not think of giving up the ring.

The structure of this group was simple. Annually, a president, a treasurer, and a manager were elected to control the operations of the ring. The manager, who had technical training, received a salary. Two workers and a machinist were employed from outside and were paid a percentage of the wheat threshed. In 1935, they threshed the wheat of fifty-five farms, including those of the original ten partners. A written agreement existed among all members, who paid in wheat, which was sold for a sum to be divided among the members.

The familistic background of this group was interesting. The originators were all members or cousins of the Danev family, except two rich landowners living in the center of the village, who were close friends of the Danevs. After four of the original partners died, their sons or sons-in-law succeeded to the control of their shares. The five Danevs outnumbered the others, forming a unit around which clustered three other members. There was some friction whenever meetings were held, but the minority was easily suppressed by the majority.

Most of the group considered membership an honor, symbolizing wealth and importance. Generally the village approved its existence, as shown by the increasing number of families who sought its services at threshing time.

Twenty-one Dragalevtsy men also belonged to the Animal Husbandry-Dairy Cooperative, with headquarters in Sofia. This group had a twofold aim: (1) to enable members to get animal feed on credit and more cheaply; (2) to develop a milk-distributing center. Though Dragalevtsy members did not have regular meetings in the village, most of them attended the annual meeting held in Sofia, at which the reports of the officers of the cooperative were read. Before this annual meeting, the Dragalevtsy men got together in the village and agreed on common action at the Sofia meeting. Dragalevtsy had one representative on the Executive Committee and one on the Control Committee. These men kept the villagers informed as to the condition of the cooperative. Two or three Dragalevtsy people had resigned recently, saying that "there were hidden matters." Most of the men who still belonged said that their membership entitled them to cheaper feed for their animals. I asked ten of the members why they belonged to the cooperative:

"I get cheaper feed through the cooperative."

"I joined in order to work collectively; to have a central depot for milk."

"The cooperative gives credit for food at a lower price."

The agricultural crisis through which Bulgaria had been passing reflected itself in the life of this cooperative. With the hard times, peasants said they did not have enough ready cash for their dues and so dropped out. However, one could not consider this a true village organization, because its physical basis was Sofia, and there was no formal organization operating in Dragalevtsy as a local.

In 1934, the Association for the Insurance of Horses and Cows was organized in the village with the help of the veterinary doctor stationed there at that time. He was acting under the guidance of the Bulgarian National Cooperative Bank. The idea back of the association was to make it possible for peasants to obtain additional credit, since no credit could be extended by the bank on uninsured animals. Insured animals were considered better collateral than land and were allowed a greater percentage of money in proportion to value. When the organization was first founded, the fifteen or sixteen charter members entered because they were in favor of insurance. The seventeen members who joined later did so because they needed to insure their animals to get a loan, regardless of their attitude toward insurance.

In the normal life of this organization almost no difficulties were encountered. The members used the schoolhouse for the annual meeting, which was open to all outsiders. There was an executive council, a control committee, and a committee for the evaluation of animals. A president was elected every year and a treasurer every three years. Some of the committee members were changed each year. If a farmer wished to join the association, the proper committee appraised his animals, and insurance was assessed at the rate of 4 per cent of the total value of the animals.

The conservatism of the peasants prevented any rapid growth of such an organization. As one peasant, not a member, explained: "I haven't joined because I feel that here we have good air, good food, and good water for our animals, and therefore they aren't as subject to diseases as are the animals nearer Sofia. God is kind."

A few years ago a private insurance association was organized, which ended unfortunately for the investors. This failure was cited by some people as an additional reason why they should not join the present association, though it was backed by the Cooperative Bank.

In order to get a better idea of the relationships among the members and between the members and the officers of the Insurance Association, I interviewed fifteen of the thirty people registered and found that:

1. Friendship played little part in determining who should become members.
2. The reasons for joining were varied:
    a. "I have six cows. Need help in case a cow dies."
    b. "I wanted to get money from the bank."
    c. "The veterinary doctor enrolled me when he organized the association."
3. All members were satisfied with the officers who represented them.
4. The relations with the Cooperative Bank in Sofia had been cordial. Once a year the bank sent out a commission to see that everything in the village was in order; a commission also came out in case of the death of an animal.

The Insurance Association illustrated the way many village organizations arose in Bulgarian villages. The idea of the organization originated in Sofia and was put into effect by a state employee, and members were recruited from those who thought that their interests would be served by belonging. A glance at the list of members, ranging in age from twenty-four to sixty, showed that they were among the most enterprising in the village. The organization would doubtless have been only half as large had it not been for the ruling of the bank, which required insurance on any animals put up as collateral. Since the association did not attempt to teach the peasants how to feed or stable the animals, it was missing a real opportunity for further service.

The traditional economy of Dragalevtsy had therefore been subjected not only to the incursion of commerce, with its emphasis upon money, but also to the formation of cooperatives to meet some specific needs of a group of interested persons. In addition, there was a concerted effort throughout Bulgaria by the national government to raise the peasants' plane of living. Some of this activity found expression in Dragalevtsy, largely through the initiative of the county agent, or *agronom*, who was concerned with the improvement of agriculture and livestock. Since he had to care for almost a score of other villages, his visits to Dragalevtsy were few and far between, so the peasants were quite correct in saying that little was being done for the improvement of agriculture in the village. While the county *agronom* gave lectures at intervals during the year and consulted with some farmers regarding their work, he could not initiate and carry through a thorough program without the help of a local *agronom*.

As far as livestock was concerned, there were two boars and one village bull for breeding purposes. The law required that each *obshtina* [commune] take charge of its own breeding animals. There was supposed to be a local breeding association, but the mayor was the only member. A fund was being collected for a village barn. Meanwhile, the animals were boarded out to various peasants, who received a fixed sum. Improvement of livestock was more easily managed through the control of male animals, which were inspected each spring. Those of bad quality were castrated (the veterinary's fees for this work being the following: pig, 10 leva; donkey, 20 leva; horse, 40 leva). If the animal died, the state paid for the loss. I happened to visit the village at the time the veterinary doctor was making his inspection of horses. Before he could begin his thorough examination, the representative of the *obshtina* looked over the bills of sale to be sure each man had his own horses. This bill of sale cost 3 per cent of the amount exchanged. If the horses had been foaled at the home of the present owners, the men presented certificates of ownership, which they had previously obtained from the mayor for fifteen leva. If the doctor found that a horse was ill, a second examination was made two weeks later. If the animal was still sick, state officials bought the horse for a small sum and killed it. A fine ranging from two hundred to five hundred leva was charged if the horses were not brought for the examination. While a national program for home demonstration work had been prepared, Dragalevtsy so far had received few benefits.

Recreation, like economic life, had been subjected to efforts at organization. The people of Dragalevtsy customarily associated liquor with holidays and leisure time. In the earlier days there was little organized opposition to the use of alcohol, but by 1922 considerable public opinion had been aroused against the *kruchmi* [taverns]. On January 1, 1922, all the taverns of the village were closed by order of the village council, which thought that the drink shops were a social evil. The village was very much stirred up, most of the men siding with the tavern keepers and the women with the village council. The tavern keepers immediately petitioned the higher court in Sofia, which reversed the decision of the village council on the grounds that the order had been issued illegally, without having a vote of all the people. On March 12, the taverns opened again. A large sum of money was due the tavern keepers in the way of damages, but they did not try to collect for fear a referendum would be carried out and the taverns abolished indefinitely. Between January 1 and March 12, the men of Dragalevtsy had gone to Sofia and to other villages so frequently to drink that they had lost much time from work, to the distress of their families. Since Dragalevtsy became a resort place, it has had summer guests who demanded alcoholic beverages; this clientele aids the tavern keepers, although many peasants are still in favor of closing their places of business.

In 1935, largely at the suggestion of one of the schoolteachers, a temperance society was organized among the young men. The score of members took their organization seriously, though many villagers ridiculed it. This organization gave a *vecherinka* [evening reception], at which a "drunk" comedy was presented in order to discourage drinking. The temperance pledge included not only drinking but also smoking and was so difficult to keep that a year later some of the members had fallen from grace. The village registrar, who was active in the village council in 1922, when the taverns were closed, was not permitted in the temperance association because he smoked. His admission would have greatly strengthened the work of the organization as far as alcoholic temperance was concerned.

The monthly dues were five leva, which were to be spent for buying temperance literature and sometimes in helping the poor. One member was sent to the city of Stara Zagora for a conference of all temperance associations in Bulgaria. The priest could not be a member "because he has to drink in his work," that is, communion. The organization was almost extinct, because the initial enthusiasm had waned and some original members had dropped out. In order to justify their own actions, those who quit talked against the remaining members and accused them of smoking and drinking on the side. The society's value as an aid to temperance would have been hard to estimate. While it must have had some effect on the minds of the young people connected with it, it had little reforming influence upon the older people. The government was trying to control the sale of liquor by limiting hours of sale and by excluding minors from taverns. For example, the taverns were closed during the time of Sunday morning service.

Here, then, we have three efforts on the part of villagers and authorities to promote abstinence or temperance. The first, in 1922, used the local governmental machinery but lacked the support of the men, who were the only ones with the right to vote. The second was the voluntary association of strong-willed youths, who soon found that formal organizations had short lives in Dragalevtsy. The other method consisted of the mayor's arbitrary edicts, which he had power to make people obey. From time to time he overlooked infringements of his rules, being more interested in avoiding excessive drunkenness on the part of well-known sots than in decreasing the tavern keepers' revenues.

The chief objections raised to the use of liquor were economic rather than moral. Although recreation was not commercialized in our sense of the term, the tavern keepers did make an adequate income from catering to patrons with free time on their hands.

The only formally organized recreational group in the village was the *Yunak* [Youth] organization. It began its career in the village in 1932. The local group was one of hundreds scattered throughout the whole of Bulgaria for the purpose of organizing the youth for sport and physical education. The activity of this organization was intense in the beginning. Since then, however, interest died down to the point that the young men gathered only two or three times a year for exercise in the schoolyard, where there were rings and a horizontal bar, and once a year for election of officers. Many of the members felt that it was an honor to belong because it signified to the rest of the villagers that "you want to be healthy." The older people, however, thought that such an organization was unnecessary, since, in their opinion, "if the young people did enough work in the fields and around the stables they would not need any organization for exercise." As is the case with many clubs of this sort, there were four or five people who really carried the load in an effort to keep the group alive. Because this organization was so utterly out of line with the familistic point of view, its members got little encouragement from the older people and had little lasting enthusiasm for its program.

The Reading Room Association (*Chitalishte*) was organized locally on February 10, 1921, upon the initiative of men who had been outside the village and had returned with the desire to raise the cultural level. From its founding, however, it concerned itself more with financial than with cultural problems. In the words of the constitution, the purposes of the organization were: (a) to influence the people of the village, especially the young, to self-improvement; (b) to cause to grow among the people a feeling for public unity in life and for intelligent usage of the village domain; (c) to cultivate love toward the fatherland and toward the good and morally edifying elements of the national literature.

The *Chitalishte* planned to achieve its purpose by opening a public reading room free for all inhabitants and visitors and supplying the room with suitable books. The *Chitalishte* group also planned to organize evening lectures and other public performances and entertainments "in order to create a patriotic feeling and appreciation of the nation's past."

The first act of the newly organized society was to buy a large sign inscribed with the name of the organization. After that the officers spent money for chairs, lamps, benches, bookcases, stovepipes, and tables, while individuals donated inkstands, water jugs, a box for gathering money, and a picture of the Madonna. Unfortunately, this left practically no money for any form of reading matter. The expense of having a share in the construction of the *obshtina* building further drained the financial resources of the organization. It was also a factor in keeping away prospective members who preferred to wait until the building was paid for before they joined. In 1937, twenty-two people, most of them charter members, were looked upon as active supporters of the work of the *Chitalishte*.

Most of the members were critical of the present officers and recognized that the organization's activities were at a standstill. When members were asked to tell how they would improve matters if elected to a position of importance, they answered: "We should choose a new executive committee, put the library in order, lend out the books, have more evening entertainments. To do this we should get in touch with people in Sofia."

Part of the trouble arose from disagreements among the officers. In the words of one member, "An organization cannot get ahead with that sort of business." But even more of the trouble went back to the fact that the organizers had not convinced the villagers of the importance of the group. Meanwhile, most peasants looked upon it as an importation of interest only to the intelligentsia and their hangers-on.

The experiences of the *Chitalishte* and other organizations in Dragalevtsy revealed that the peasants were not organization-minded. Even if we included the governmental groups to be discussed in the next chapter, we would find that fewer than ten women in the village belonged to any formal group, and only 107 of the 510 men over twenty years of age had an organizational membership. Where people's homes were so conveniently located, one would expect greater participation on the part of the men, at least. But almost four-fifths of them avoided any organizational affiliation, largely because they were not accustomed to using an organization to do what they thought needed to be done. One of the most frequent reasons for failure to join was this: "Why should I pay the fees charged when I would get nothing in return?"

In this world of competing "isms," Dragalevtsy represented in 1937 a modification of familism, the oldest and most widespread way of life we know, perpetuated by agricultural villages all over the world. But familism was slowly losing out. In some quarters of the world, the commercialism of a capitalistic system was supplanting the older values with money values; in other quarters, the collectivism of a Communist society was shaking the economic foundations of the large family group.

As far as Dragalevtsy was concerned, commercialism was in its infancy. Back in 1937 Communism might have seemed to the outsider to have a hold on this village, as well as on others in Bulgaria, because of the old affection the Bulgarian peasants had felt for the Russians since the days when the Tsar Alexander II of Russia helped free Bulgaria from Turkish control. Contemporary Russia also was making its appeal through Bulgarian Communists, who had taken the agrarian, or "rights-for-peasants," aspect of the modern Russian system and expounded it to the peasants as Communism. Although it was doubtful whether the Dragalevtsy peasant had any clear idea of collectivism, it was certain that he would have been completely bewildered by the idea of giving up his cherished holdings to the state.

Dragalevtsy, therefore, was something of an anachronism, for the familistic system still had a firm grip on many of the adults. Their ideas had been set a generation ago by parents who subscribed unquestioningly to the familistic way of life. The young people, on the other hand, were receptive to other values and other standards and were ready to look more and more to the "people of the world" for guidance and leadership.

42

AN OPEN LETTER TO THE WORKERS AND PEASANTS OF BULGARIA

GEORGI DIMITROV

[The domestic and foreign policies of the East European governments were criticized by those political forces that sought to remove the existing regimes through revolution. The most ardent exponents of revolutionary change were the Communists, who, however, had no meaningful solutions to the political and socio-economic problems of the masses on whose behalf they were ostensibly acting. This was particularly true in the agrarian states of Southeastern Europe, where the peasantry was in general hostile to the Communists and the Communists distinctly hostile to the peasantry.

Bulgaria was the only agrarian country of Eastern Europe where workable solutions to agrarian problems were provided by the regime in power, and only during the brief rule of Aleksandr Stamboliski. Stamboliski's assassination in June, 1923, by right-wing nationalists was roundly condemned by the Bulgarian Communists, who had, however, been violently

Reprinted from Georgi Dimitrov, *Selected Works (1910–1949)* (Sofia [n.p.], 1960), pp. 39–46.

opposed to Stamboliski during his lifetime. The following "open letter" by the leader of the Bulgarian Communist Party, Georgi Dimitrov, sets forth the basic Communist program for Bulgaria. It is representative of the Communist approach to the problems of the other East European states.]

Dear comrades, after the great revolutionary struggle* which failed, for the time being, to bring liberty to the people's masses, we were constrained, like many other fighters, to leave your midst in order to continue the struggle in the great cause of our people. Although temporarily separated from you by distance, we feel that, in view of the role that fell upon us to play in this struggle, we ought to address you with the present open letter.

And the first word we send to you is:

Heads up! The bloody revenge taken by the White Guard mob in its fear to be deprived of power will not succeed smothering the fighting spirit of toiling Bulgaria. Defeat will teach us how to win. In spite of all, Bulgaria will yet have a government of workers and peasants.

The very parties of the capitalists and landlords, ever clamoring for "law and order," staged *an armed coup d'état* on June 9 † and thus *initiated a civil war*. The events of September represent only an *important episode* in this civil war and can have no other outcome than *the final victory of the toiling masses* over their bloody oppressors, exploiters, and plunderers.

The toiling peasants and workers were united in two large political organizations in Bulgaria for the defense of their vital interests: the Bulgarian Agrarian Union and the Bulgarian Communist Party.

The White Guard government made use of its relatively easy victory of June 9 to deal a heavy blow to the Agrarian Union. Its notables, through towns and villages, were all arrested, a large number of them were treacherously and cruelly murdered, thousands of workers and peasants, treated as insurgents, were subjected to cruel beating, hurled into prisons, and delivered to the courts of class revenge. The very Agrarian Union, the most numerous political party in Bulgaria, was dissolved, its journals were prohibited, and it was legally barred to engage in any political activities.

Considering the menace of the Agrarian Union as no longer extant, the government of generals and bankers turned its attention to the other mass organization of the working people—the Bulgarian Communist Party. Immediately after June 9, it arrested a large number of Communists for their active opposition to the *coup d'état* and subjected them to even greater torments than those endured by the Agrarians. The government used its officer leagues and conspirative bands to hold these Communists in a continuous state of terror. It is a well known fact that, on a certain evening in Turnovo, all Communists were seized by the police and carried

* The abortive Communist insurrection of September 26–28, 1923.—Ed.

† The conspiracy against Stamboliski, directed by officers, Macedonians, and others opposed to his regime.—Ed.

off to the military barracks, to be beaten to death by disguised officers. Another equally well known fact is the assault of the fascist band in Berkovitsa and the acts of terror it perpetrated upon the Communist population of the town and county during a whole week and under the patronage of the government. A large number of similar assaults are known to have taken place in other towns and villages. The entire toiling population, unwilling to acknowledge the new self-established government, lived in a continuous state of terror, intimidation, and coercion. No village could be sure of keeping its peace, no worker or peasant was certain of his life.

At the same time, the agents of the avid and plunderous bourgeoisie, who had misused the state power to suit their rapacious purposes, also exerted themselves to the full. The large landowners engaged in a campaign to regain the lands that had been previously taken away from them. The large real estate owners raised a hue, reclaiming the liberty to skin the poor lodgers to the bone. The big profiteers and exporters grabbed the available bank deposits—better to rob the workers and the poor peasants. The exploitation of hired labor also became harder than ever. In short, the urban capitalists and the large peasant-landowners became the undisputed masters of the country. All this tended to intensify the opposition of the working people against the new regime. On the other hand, the broad masses of the people were especially discontented with the foreign policy of the government, formed by the same old nationalist parties and warlike elements that had thrust the people into two military catastrophes. The incessant conflicts with Soviet Russia and the neighboring states held the people in a state of constant fear lest *Bulgaria be drawn at any moment into a new and even more disastrous war.*

Under these conditions, the bourgeoisie, rallied around the new regime, had to "legalize" its status through a general election. However, while it could entertain no hopes of winning over the confidence of the people, the Communist Party stood firmly on guard, bravely defending the rights and interests of entire toiling Bulgaria. The menace to the Communist Party was now even greater, since the latter, having proclaimed a common front of working people from town and village alike, extended a brotherly hand to the Agrarians and helped them to restore their shattered organizations, thus giving concrete expression to the alliance between the urban proletariat and the toiling peasants. Indeed, the common interests and the general distress of the urban and rural working masses actually cemented the alliance between the Agrarian Union and the Communist Party over the country as a whole. The government of bankers, generals, and professors then decided to provoke the Communist Party and to settle accounts with it, as it had already done with the Agrarian Union. To this end the government concocted the false accusation that the Communist Party was about to stage a *coup d'état* on September 16, and, in order to foil this spurious *coup d'état, mass arrests* of Communists were made on September 12.

We, who hold a responsible and leading position in the Bulgarian Communist Party, declare, at the present historical moment, that the Communist Party had not fixed any general or partial armed action for September 16 or for any other later date. On the contrary, the Communist Party was preparing diligently for the election, because it was generally known that in case of free elections the working majority in the country, headed by the Agrarian Union and the Communist Party, would anyway defeat the government of usurpers and establish a government of workers and peasants. The government, which laid hands on all party archives, could not find any proofs of such a decision and will not find them, unless it fabricates them, because they do not exist. But it needed a pretext to square accounts with the Communist Party, and it found it in a concoction, without thinking of the terrible consequences this provocation might have for the whole people.

This aggression against the Communist Party, the arrest of thousands of its members in town and countryside, the closing of the workers' clubs, trade unions, and cooperative societies, the confiscation of their archives, the stoppage of the whole Communist and workers' press, the banning of all Communist agitation and of all movements of Communists and workers in the countryside exhausted all patience. It was clear that the government would not permit any legal struggle. Not only the Communists, but the vast popular masses, too, felt affected and threatened. Many Communists in the countryside, in peril of being arrested and tortured, fled to the mountains, followed by a mass of sympathizers. The White Guard government unceremoniously proclaimed them bandits and sent troops to persecute and exterminate them.

The Communist Party retaliated by declaring a twenty-four hour mass strike of protest in the towns and by organizing mass meetings of protest throughout the country. The government, however, mobilized all its forces to suffocate this protest. Its brutal actions provoked bloody incidents in Sofia and some other localities. The widespread and unprecedented terror that reigned in Bulgaria led to the further intensification of the general discontent and to the repeated occurrence of bloody collisions, until the latter gradually assumed the character of a people's uprising against the raging government, which had declared war upon the entire working population . . .

At this critical moment, when the government suffocated all possibility for legal struggle and the masses rose spontaneously in many places, the Communist Party faced a test: to leave the masses to rise alone and be beaten separately, or to go to their side and try to generalize the movement, to unite it and to give it political and organizational leadership? The Communist Party, fully conscious of the hardships connected with the struggle and the difficulties incumbent upon organization, could have no other choice, *as a party of the toiling masses*, than to embrace the cause of the people and, notwithstanding the extremely unfavorable conditions, to give the signal for common action with the Agrarian Union all over the country on September 23.

What was the watchword of the uprising? Everybody knows that it stood for overthrowing the present self-established, coercive government of usurpers and the substitution in its place of a government of workers and peasants.

The object of the struggle was not to set up a dictatorship or to establish a Soviet regime in Bulgaria, as the present government maintains with wile, but to abolish the raging military dictatorship and to form a broad democratic government from the midst of the great majority of the Bulgarian people, the toiling masses. And nowhere during the course of the struggle did the insurgents establish a Soviet regime in the districts where they had taken possession of the local power, as the government consistently misleads, only general revolutionary committees of the worker-peasant government having been set up.

The watchword issued by the Communist Party was taken up by the masses that followed in its wake, as well as by the peasants, adhering to the Agrarian Union, and by the entire toiling population. The working masses rose as a single individual to secure their political liberties, to safeguard their vital interests and to establish a government of their own.

The revolutionary struggle of September represented, in the full sense of the term, a general movement of the people, with all the characteristic features of such a movement. The people, striving for the realization of a lofty ideal, *never resorted to pillage, vandalism, or acts of personal revenge.* The banks were most carefully guarded, property was duly protected, the few enemies of the people here and there were rendered harmless, being held in arrest—but they were nowhere maltreated or killed, and not a single hair fell from anybody's head. It is a calumny that extraordinary committees had been put up and that death sentences had been pronounced. The prisoners were kept safe, the wounded of both parties were most carefully looked after, even the lives of the captured members of the Wrangel bands, hurled by the government against the insurgent people, were spared with magnanimity.

After an epic struggle, which lasted nearly a fortnight, the people's uprising was crushed by the government, which was amply provided with artillery and machine guns and had managed to mobilize numerous bands of reserve or noncommissioned officers and thousands of Wrangelite counter-revolutionaries, while the armament at the disposal of the insurgent people was lamentably insufficient.

Having mastered the situation, the frightened-to-death bourgeoisie gave vent to its terrible wrath and enmity against the working people who had ventured to shake the foundations of its domination.

In our own presence, the infuriated gangs of the bourgeoisie commenced an orgy of wholesale extermination of the insurgents. They did not pity even the wounded or the peaceful population, the women and the children. They even did not spare the villages and the property of the working people in the revolted districts.

However, it is not our intention to dwell on the bloody revenge of the now-triumphant mob of White Guards—you, who groan under it, are more familiar with its outrages. This revenge will be cruel, barbarous, fiendish and will surpass in horror the atrocities committed by the White Guards in all other countries. It will thereby dig still deeper the bloody furrow between the class of oppressors and exploiters, on the one hand, and the working people, on the other.

And never, never again will there be peace between them.

Only the abolition of the bloody monarchist government of bankers and generals and the establishment of a government of workers and peasants will give atonement and bring appeasement to the people's masses and the country.

Dear comrades, we all fought together in the great cause of the people. We are now defeated, but the struggle still goes on, and the final victory is nearer than the enemy believes. The Bulgarian working people will never come to terms with the White Guard regime of an insignificant, rapacious, and coercive minority—whatever high-sounding phrases the latter may adorn itself with and whatever "democratic" reforms it may pretend to introduce. We will benefit from the lesson of our defeat, and tomorrow we shall be stronger than yesterday, while our enemies will always continue to lose ground.

Full of unwavering faith in our cause, which is a sacred cause of the people, we, all the working people, will heroically stand the pains and sufferings of defeat and will devote ourselves again, with redoubled energy and greater enthusiasm, to the service of the people's cause, never resting until victory is achieved.

We will again gather together and dress our thinned and shattered rows. We will quickly heal the wounds inflicted by the enemy.

With common efforts and sacrifices, we will help the widows and orphans as well as the families, now fallen in adversity, of the comrades who were constrained to seek refuge abroad.

We will not waste our forces in isolated acts of terrorism, being convinced that victory can be attained only through the organized struggle of the working people and that the overthrow of the White Guard government and the final victory of the worker-peasant government will constitute the most cruel revenge on the jailers of the people.

We will especially cherish and strengthen *the alliance of all working people in towns and villages*—an alliance sealed during the events of September by the commonly shed blood of many thousand combatants who gave their lives for the cause of the people.

Let us not fall in dejection, despair and faint-heartedness.

Heads up, brave combatants!

Long live the workers-peasants government!

Long live toiling Bulgaria!

43

A FEW REMARKS ON DEMOCRACY

CORNELIU ZELEA CODREANU

[The less violent and less visionary solutions proposed by the fascists were more palatable to the East European masses than were the Communist solutions. Among the several brands of fascism that flourished in Eastern Europe between the wars, the most representative of the historical tradition was the Rumanian populist variety expounded by the Iron Guard, which blamed the oppression of the peasant on the Jews and the "Jew-like" ruling establishment. Fascist populism rejected the democratic process and advocated reliance on the *Volk* for the attainment of the fascist revolution in Rumania. The following excerpt from the writings of Corneliu Zelea Codreanu, the leader of the Iron Guard, is characteristic of the views of the Rumanian fascists, who attracted a considerable following in the countryside and among industrial workers and intellectuals in the 1930's.]

I should like to make a few remarks, derived from daily experience, in a manner that can be understood by any young legionary or worker.

We wear the clothes and embrace the forms of democracy. Are they worth anything? We don't know yet. But we do know one thing. We know it for sure. That some of the largest and most civilized nations of Europe have discarded those clothes and have acquired new ones. Did they get rid of them forever? Other nations are doing their best to dispose of them and to get new ones also. Why? Have all nations gone mad? Are the Rumanian politicians the only wise men in the world? Somehow I doubt it.

Those who have changed them and those who want to change them must each have their own reasons.

Translated by Stephen Fischer-Galati from Corneliu Zelea Codreanu, *Pentru Legionari* (Bucharest: Totul Pentru Tara, 1937), pp. 385–87, 396–98.

But why should we concern ourselves with other nations' reasons? Let us rather concern ourselves with the reasons that would make us Rumanians ready to change the clothes of democracy.

If we have no reasons to do so, if the reasons are no good, then we shall keep the clothes, even should all of Europe get rid of them.

However, they are no good for us either, because:

1. *Democracy destroys the unity* of the Rumanian nation, dividing it among political parties, making Rumanians hate one another, and thus exposing a divided people to the united congregation of Jewish power at a difficult time in the nation's history.

This argument alone is so persuasive as to warrant the discarding of democracy in favor of anything that would ensure our unity—or life itself. For disunity means death.

2. *Democracy makes Rumanian citizens out of millions of Jews* by making them the Rumanians' equals. By giving them the same legal rights. Equality? What for? We have been here for thousands of years. Plow and weapon in hand. With our labors and blood. Why equality with those who have been here for only one hundred, ten, or even five years? Let's look at the past: We created this state. Let's look at the future: We Rumanians are fully responsible for Greater Rumania. They have nothing to do with it. What could be the responsibility of Jews, in the history books, for the disappearance of the Rumanian state?

Thus: no equality in labor, sacrifice, and struggle for the creation of the state and no equal responsibility for its future. Equality? According to an old maxim: Equality is to treat unequally the unequal. What are the reasons for the Jews' demanding equal treatment, equal political rights with the Rumanians?

3. *Democracy is incapable of perseverance.* Since it is shared by political parties that rule for one, two, or three years, it is unable to conceive and carry out plans of longer duration. One party annuls the plans and efforts of the other. What is conceived and built by one party today is destroyed by another tomorrow.

In a country in which much has to be built, in which building is indeed the primary historical requirement, this disadvantage of democracy constitutes a true danger. It is a situation similar to that which prevails in an establishment where masters are changed every year, each new master bringing in his own plans, ruining what was done by some, and starting new things, which will in turn be destroyed by tomorrow's masters.

4. *Democracy prevents the politician's fulfillment of his obligations to the nation.* Even the most well-meaning politician becomes, in a democracy, the slave of his supporters, because either he satisfies their personal interests or they destroy his organization. The politician lives under the tyranny and permanent threat of the electoral bosses.

He is placed in a position in which he must choose between the termination of his lifetime work and the satisfaction of the demands of party members. And the politician, given such a choice, opts for the latter. He does so not out of his own pocket, but out of that of the country. He creates jobs, sets up missions, commissions, sinecures—all rostered in the nation's budget—which put increasingly heavy pressures on a tired people.

5. *Democracy cannot wield authority*, because it cannot enforce its decisions. A party cannot move against itself, against its members who engage in scandalous malfeasance, who rob and steal, because it is afraid of losing its members. Nor can it move against its adversaries, because in so doing it would risk exposure of its own wrongdoings and shady business.

6. *Democracy serves big business*. Because of the expensive, competitive character of the multiparty system, democracy requires ample funds. It therefore naturally becomes the servant of the big international Jewish financiers, who enslave her by paying her.

In this manner, a nation's fate is placed in the hands of a clique of bankers.

THE NATION

When we speak of the Rumanian nation, we refer not only to the Rumanians currently living on the same territory, with the same past and same future, the same habits, the same language, the same interests. When we speak of the Rumanian nation we refer to all Rumanians, dead or alive, who have lived on this land of ours from the beginnings of history and will live on it also in the future.

The nation includes:

1. All Rumanians currently alive.
2. The souls and tombs of the dead and of our ancestors.
3. All who will be born Rumanian.

A people becomes aware of its existence when it becomes aware of its entirety, not only of its component parts and their individual interests.

The nation possesses:

1. A *physical, biological patrimony:* the flesh and the blood.
2. A *material patrimony:* the country's soil and its wealth.
3. A *spiritual patrimony*, which includes:

A. *Its concept of God, people, and life.* This concept constitutes a possession, a spiritual patrimony. The limits of this domain are set by the limits of the brilliance of the concept. There is a country housing the national spirit, the expectations of that spirit, a spirit resulting from revelation and the nation's own efforts.

B. *Its honor*, which shines in proportion to the acceptance by the nation, during its historical existence, of the norms derived from its concept of God, people, and life.

C. *Its culture:* the fruit of its life, the product of its own efforts in thought and art. This culture is not international. It is the expression of the national genius, of the blood. The culture is international in its brilliance but national in origin. Someone made a fine comparison: bread and wheat may be internationally consumed, but they always bear the imprint of the soil from which they came.

Each of these three patrimonies has its own importance. All three must be defended by the nation. But the most important of all is the spiritual patrimony, because it alone bears the seal of eternity, it alone transcends all times.

The ancient Greeks are with us today not because of their physiques, no matter how athletic—those are only ashes now—nor because of their material wealth, if they had such, but because of their culture.

A nation lives forever through its concepts, honor, and culture. It is for these reasons that the rulers of nations must judge and act not only on the basis of physical and material interests of the nation but on the basis of the nation's historical honor, of the nation's eternal interests. Thus: not bread at all costs, but honor at all costs.

THE NATION'S ULTIMATE GOAL

Is it life?

If it be life, then the means whereby nations seek to ensure it become irrelevant. All are valid, even the worst.

The question may thus be asked: What are the norms for international behavior? The nations' animal instincts? The tiger in them? Do the laws of the fishes in the sea or of the beasts in the forest apply?

The ultimate goal is not life. It is *resurrection*. The resurrection of nations in the name of Jesus Christ the Savior. Creation and culture are only means—not the purpose—of resurrection. Culture is the fruit of talent, which God implanted in our nation and for which we are responsible. A time will come when all the world's nations will arise from the dead, with all their dead, with all their kings and emperors. Every nation has its place before God's throne. That *final moment*, "resurrection from the dead," is the highest and most sublime goal for which a nation can strive.

The nation is thus an entity that lives even beyond this earth. Nations are realities also in the other world, not only on this one.

To us Rumanians, to our nation, as to every nation in the world, God assigned a specific mission; God has given us a historical destiny.

The first law that every nation must abide by is that of attaining that destiny, of fulfilling the mission entrusted to it.

Our nation has not abandoned that goal, no matter how long and difficult has been its own Golgotha.

And now we are faced with mountain-high obstacles.

Are we going to be the weak and cowardly generation that will relinquish, under threats, the Rumanian destiny and renounce our national mission?

BIBLIOGRAPHY

I. Eastern Europe (General)

BASCH, ANTONIN. *The Danube Basin and the German Economic Sphere.* New York: Columbia University Press, 1943. A study of East European trade relations in the 1930's.

BERNARD, PAUL P. *Joseph II.* New York: Twayne Publishers, 1968.

BRAILSFORD, HENRY N. *Macedonia: Its Races and Their Future.* London: Methuen & Co., 1906. A description of Macedonia under Ottoman rule at the turn of the century.

BRAUNTHAL, JULIUS. *History of the International.* Vol. I: 1864–1914. New York: Praeger Publishers, 1967. An essential work for an understanding of the labor movement up to the time of World War I.

COLES, PAUL. *The Ottoman Impact on Europe.* New York: Harcourt, Brace & World, 1968. A study of Ottoman relations with Europe between 1520 and 1699.

DVORNIK, FRANCIS. *The Slavs: Their Early History and Civilization.* Boston: American Academy of Arts and Sciences, 1956.

———. *The Slavs in European History and Civilization.* New Brunswick, N.J.: Rutgers University Press, 1962. A general and cultural history of the Slavic peoples between the thirteenth and eighteenth centuries.

FISCHER-GALATI, STEPHEN A. *Ottoman Imperialism and German Protestantism, 1521–1555.* Cambridge, Mass.: Harvard University Press, 1959. A study of the Turkish impact on the German Reformation.

GIBB, H. A. R., and H. BOWEN. *Islamic Society and the West.* 2 vols. London: Oxford University Press, 1950, 1957. The basic work on Ottoman society and institutions.

HALECKI, OSKAR. *Borderlands of Western Civilization: A History of East Central Europe.* New York: Ronald Press, 1952.

HELMREICH, ERNST C. *The Diplomacy of the Balkan Wars, 1912–1913.* Cambridge, Mass.: Harvard University Press, 1938.

JACKSON, GEORGE D., JR. *Comintern and Peasant in East Europe, 1919–1930.* New York: Columbia University Press, 1966.

JASZI, OSCAR. *The Dissolution of the Habsburg Monarchy*. Chicago: The University of Chicago Press, 1929. The classic work on the subject.

JELAVICH, CHARLES, and BARBARA JELAVICH. *The Balkans*. Englewood Cliffs, N.J.: Prentice-Hall, 1965. A brief introduction to Balkan history.

———— (eds.). *The Balkans in Transition*. Berkeley and Los Angeles: University of California Press, 1963. Essays on the development of Balkan life and politics since the eighteenth century.

KANN, ROBERT A. *The Multinational Empire: Nationalism and National Reform in the Habsburg Monarchy, 1848–1918*. 2 vols. New York: Columbia University Press, 1950.

KOHN, HANS. *Pan-Slavism: Its History and Ideology*. Notre Dame, Ind.: University of Notre Dame Press, 1953.

KOLARZ, WALTER. *Myths and Realities in Eastern Europe*. London: Lindsay Drummond, 1946. A perceptive if somewhat controversial treatise on ethnic relations in Eastern Europe, primarily in the period 1918–38.

MACARTNEY, C. A., and ALAN W. PALMER. *Independent Eastern Europe: A History*. New York: St. Martin's Press, 1962. A study of East European politics in the interwar period.

McNEILL, WILLIAM H. *Europe's Steppe Frontier, 1500–1800*. Chicago: University of Chicago Press, 1964. A study of the legacy of the steppe in the countries of Danubian and Pontic Europe.

MEYENDORFF, JEAN. *The Orthodox Church: Its Past and Its Role in the World Today*. New York: Pantheon Books, 1962. The best short history of the Orthodox Church.

MILLER, WILLIAM. *The Ottoman Empire and Its Successors, 1801–1927*. Cambridge, England: The University Press, 1936. Although somewhat dated, this is still one of the most useful books in the field.

MITRANY, DAVID. *Marx Against the Peasant: A Study in Social Dogmatism*. Chapel Hill: University of North Carolina Press, 1951. A study of the peasant reaction to collectivization in Eastern Europe.

POUNDS, NORMAN J. G. *Eastern Europe*. Chicago: Aldine Publishing Co., 1969. A socio-economic and political geography of Eastern Europe.

SETON-WATSON, HUGH. *Eastern Europe Between the Wars, 1918–1941*. 3d ed. Hamden, Conn.: Archon Books, 1962. The best work on the subject.

SPINKA, MATTHEW. *A History of Christianity in the Balkans: A Study of the Spread of Byzantine Culture Among the Slavs*. Chicago: The American Society of Church History, 1933.

STAVRIANOS, LEFTEN S. *The Balkans Since 1453*. New York: Rinehart, 1958. The standard work in English on modern Balkan history.

STOIANOVICH, TRAIAN. *A Study in Balkan Civilization*. New York: Alfred A. Knopf, 1967. A provocative study of Balkan intellectual and cultural life.

SUGAR, PETER F., and IVO J. LEDERER (eds.). *Nationalism in Eastern Europe*. Seattle: University of Washington Press, 1969.

TAYLOR, A. J. P. *The Habsburg Monarchy, 1809–1918*. 2d ed. London: Hamish Hamilton, 1948. A stimulating if somewhat unreliable study.

WANDRUSZKA, ADAM. *The House of Habsburg: Six Hundred Years of a European Dynasty*. New York: Doubleday & Co., 1964.

WARRINER, DOREEN. *Economics of Peasant Farming*. 2d ed. New York: Barnes & Noble, 1965.

ZEMAN, Z. A. B. *The Break-up of the Habsburg Empire, 1914–1918: A Study in National and Social Revolution*. London: Oxford University Press, 1961.

II. Albania

NOLI, FAN S. *George Castrioti Scanderbeg, 1405–1468*. New York: International Universities Press, 1947. A biography of the leader of Albanian resistance against the Turks.

SKENDI, STAVRO. *The Albanian National Awakening, 1878–1912*. Princeton, N.J.: Princeton University Press, 1967.

———(ed.). *Albania*. New York: Praeger Publishers, 1956. A general survey of Albanian history, politics, economics, society, and culture.

SWIRE, JOSEPH. *Albania, the Rise of a Kingdom*. London: Williams & Norgate, 1929. A political history of Albania from 1878 to 1928.

III. Bulgaria

BLACK, CYRIL E. *The Establishment of Constitutional Government in Bulgaria*. Princeton, N.J.: Princeton University Press, 1943. A study of Bulgarian internal developments from 1878 to 1885.

CORTI, EGON C. *Alexander von Battenberg*. London: Cassell & Co., 1954. A biography of the first ruler of modern Bulgaria.

DELLIN, L. A. D. (ed.). *Bulgaria*. New York: Praeger Publishers, 1957. A general survey of Bulgarian history, politics, economics, society, and culture.

MACDERMOTT, MERCIA. *A History of Bulgaria, 1393–1885*. London: George Allen & Unwin, 1962. The best history of Bulgaria in English, although not without flaws.

MISHEV, DIMITUR. *The Bulgarians in the Past: Pages from the Bulgarian Cultural History*. Lausanne: Librairie Centrale des Nationalités, 1919.

PASVOLSKY, LEO. *Bulgaria's Economic Position, with Special Reference to the Reparation Problem and the Work of the League of Nations*. Washington, D.C.: The Brookings Institution, 1930. A study of the post–World War I Bulgarian economy.

ROTHSCHILD, JOSEPH. *The Communist Party of Bulgaria: Origins and Development, 1883–1936*. New York: Columbia University Press, 1959.

RUNCIMAN, STEVEN. *A History of the First Bulgarian Empire*. London: G. Bell & Sons, 1930.

SANDERS, IRWIN T. *Balkan Village*. Lexington: University of Kentucky Press, 1949.

SCHUTZE, GLADYS H. *Where East Is West: Life in Bulgaria*. Boston: Houghton Mifflin, 1933. Personal observations on pre–World War II Bulgarian society.

SWIRE, JOSEPH. *Bulgarian Conspiracy*. London: Robert Hale, 1939. A study of the Internal Macedonian Revolutionary Organization in the interwar years.

TODOROV, KOSTA. *Balkan Firebrand: The Autobiography of a Rebel, Soldier, and Statesman*. Chicago: Ziff-Davis, 1943. Absorbing memoirs and description of Bulgarian political life between the two world wars, by a leader of the Bulgarian Agrarian Union.

IV. Czechoslovakia

BENEŠ, EDUARD. *Democracy Today and Tomorrow*. New York: Macmillan Company, 1939.

BROCK, PETER. *The Political and Social Doctrines of the Unity of Czech Brethren in the Fifteenth and Early Sixteenth Centuries.* The Hague: Mouton & Co., 1957.

BUSEK, VRATISLAV, and NICOLAS SPULBER (eds.). *Czechoslovakia.* New York: Praeger Publishers, 1957. A general survey of Czechoslovak history, politics, economics, society, and culture.

CHMELAR, JOSEF. *Political Parties in Czechoslovakia.* Prague: Orbis, 1926.

HEYMANN, FREDERICK G. *George of Bohemia: King of Heretics.* Princeton, N.J.: Princeton University Press, 1965.

————. *John Žižka and the Hussite Revolution.* Princeton, N.J.: Princton University Press, 1955.

KAMINSKY, HOWARD. *A History of the Hussite Revolution.* Berkeley: University of California Press, 1967.

KERNER, ROBERT J. *Bohemia in the Eighteenth Century,* New York: Macmillan Company, 1932. A political, social, and economic history, with special reference to the reign of Leopold II.

KIMBALL, STANLEY J. *Czech Nationalism: A Study of the National Theater Movement, 1845–1883.* Urbana: University of Illinois Press, 1964. A case study of Czech nationalism.

LETTRICH, JOZEF. *A History of Modern Slovakia.* New York: Praeger Publishers, 1955. A survey that emphasizes the period 1918–48.

ODLOZILIK, OTAKAR. *The Hussite King: Bohemia in European Affairs, 1440–1471.* New Brunswick, N.J.: Rutgers University Press, 1965. A study of the rule of George of Podebrady and of the international implications of the Hussite movement.

PECH, STANLEY Z. *The Czech Revolution of 1848.* Chapel Hill: University of North Carolina Press, 1969.

RECHCIGL, MIROSLAV, JR. (ed.). *The Czechoslovak Contribution to World Culture.* The Hague: Mouton & Co., 1964. A collection of fifty-seven papers on all aspects of Czech culture.

SETON-WATSON, ROBERT WILLIAM. *A History of the Czechs and Slovaks.* London: Hutchinson, 1943. The best survey of Czechoslovak history in English.

———— (ed.). *Slovakia Then and Now: A Political Survey.* London: George Allen & Unwin, 1931. A symposium on developments in Slovakia before and after 1918.

SPINKA, MATTHEW. *John Amos Comenius, That Incomparable Moravian.* Chicago: University of Chicago Press, 1943. A survey of the life and work of the bishop of the Unity of Czech Brethren.

TABORSKY, EDWARD. *Czechoslovak Democracy at Work.* London: George Allen & Unwin, 1945. The most thorough study of Czechoslovakia's pre-World War II political system available in English.

VONDRACEK, FELIX J. *The Foreign Policy of Czechoslovakia, 1918–1935.* New York: Columbia University Press, 1937.

WANKLYN, HARRIET G. *Czechoslovakia.* New York: Praeger Publishers, 1954. A historical geography.

WARREN, WILLIAM PRESTON. *Masaryk's Democracy: A Philosophy of Scientific and Moral Culture.* Chapel Hill: University of North Carolina Press, 1941. An analysis of Masaryk's philosophy and practice of democracy.

WHEELER-BENNETT, JOHN W. *Munich: Prologue to Tragedy.* New York:

Duell, Sloan & Pearce, 1963. The classic study of the Munich agreement and its background.

WISKEMANN, ELIZABETH. *Czechs and Germans: A Study of the Struggle in the Historic Provinces of Bohemia and Moravia.* 2d ed. London: Macmillan & Co.; New York: St. Martin's Press, 1967.

V. Greece

CHACONAS, STEPHEN G. *Adamantios Korais: A Study in Greek Nationalism.* New York: Columbia University Press, 1942.

DAKIN, DOUGLAS. *The Greek Struggle in Macedonia, 1897–1913.* Thessaloniki: Institute for Balkan Studies, 1966.

FINLAY, GEORGE. *A History of Greece from Its Conquest by the Romans to the Present Time, B.C. 146 to A.D. 1864.* Revised and enlarged edition. 7 vols. Oxford: Clarendon Press, 1877.

HEURTLEY, W. A., ET AL. *A Short History of Greece from Early Times to 1964.* New York: Cambridge University Press, 1965. The best short history of Greece in English.

KEPHALA, EUPHROSYNE. *The Church of the Greek People Past and Present.* London: Williams & Northgate, 1930.

KOUSOULAS, DIMITRIOS GEORGE. *Revolution and Defeat: The Story of the Greek Communist Party.* London: Oxford University Press, 1965. A study of the Communist movement in Greece from 1920 through 1950.

MILLER, WILLIAM. *Greece.* London: Ernest Benn, 1928. A history of medieval and modern Greece.

PAPADOPOULLOS, THEODORE H. *Studies and Documents Relating to the History of the Greek Church and People under Turkish Domination.* Brussels: Bibliotheca Graeca, 1952.

PETROPULOS, ANTHONY. *Politics and Statecraft in the Kingdom of Greece.* Princeton, N.J.: Princeton University Press, 1968.

SANDERS, IRWIN T. *Rainbow in the Rock: The People of Rural Greece.* Cambridge, Mass.: Harvard University Press, 1962.

WOODHOUSE, CHRISTOPHER M. *The Greek War of Independence: Its Historical Setting.* London: Hutchinson University Library, 1952.

VI. Hungary

BARANY, GEORGE. *Stephen Szechenyi and the Awakening of Hungarian Nationalism, 1791–1841.* Princeton, N.J.: Princeton University Press, 1969.

DEAK, FRANCIS. *Hungary at the Paris Peace Conference: The Diplomatic History of the Treaty of Trianon.* New York: Columbia University Press, 1942.

FEL, EDIT, and TAMAS HOFER. *Proper Peasants: Traditional Life in a Hungarian Village.* Chicago: Aldine Publishing Co., 1969.

HORTHY, MIKLOS. *Memoirs.* New York: Robert Speller, 1957. Autobiography of the Regent of Hungary, 1920–44.

KIRALY, BELA K. *Hungary in the Late Eighteenth Century: The Decline of Enlightened Despotism.* New York: Columbia University Press, 1969.

KORNIS, GYULA. *Education in Hungary.* New York: Teachers College, 1932. A survey of the Hungarian educational system between the two world wars.

KOSARY, DOMOKOS G. *A History of Hungary.* Cleveland: Benjamin Franklin Bibliophile Society, 1941. The best history of Hungary in English.

MACARTNEY, C. A. *October Fifteenth: A History of Modern Hungary, 1929–1945.* 2 vols. Edinburgh: University Press, 1956–57.

MARCZALI, HENRY. *Hungary in the Eighteenth Century.* Cambridge, England: The University Press, 1910. A detailed survey of economic, social, nationality, religious, and political problems.

TELEKI, PAL. *The Evolution of Hungary and Its Place in European History.* New York: Macmillan Company, 1923. Particularly valuable for its treatment of Hungarian nationality problems.

TÖKES, RUDOLF L. *Bela Kun and the Hungarian Soviet Republic: The Origins and Role of the Communist Party of Hungary in the Revolutions of 1918–1919.* New York: Praeger Publishers, 1967.

VII. Poland

DYBOSKI, ROMAN. *Poland in World Civilization.* New York: J. M. Barrett, 1950. A major survey of Polish history and civilization by a leading Polish scholar.

DZIEWANOWSKI, M. K. *The Communist Party of Poland: An Outline of History.* Cambridge, Mass.: Harvard University Press, 1959.

———. *European Federalist: Joseph Pilsudski.* Stanford, Calif.: The Hoover Institution, 1969.

FOX, PAUL. *The Reformation in Poland: Some Social and Economic Aspects.* Baltimore, Md.: The Johns Hopkins Press, 1924.

GIEYSZTOR, ALEKSANDER, ET AL. *History of Poland.* Warsaw: Polish Scientific Publishers, 1968. A Marxist history of Poland.

HALECKI, OSKAR. *From Florence to Brest (1439–1596).* Rome: Sacrum Poloniae Millenium, 1958. A study of the religious unions affecting the Polish-Lithuanian Commonwealth.

——— (ed.). *Poland.* New York: Praeger Publishers, 1957. A general survey of Polish history, politics, economics, society, and culture.

KAPLAN, HERBERT H. *The First Partition of Poland.* New York: Columbia University Press, 1962.

KOMARNICKI, TITUS. *Rebirth of the Polish Republic: A Study in the Diplomatic History of Europe, 1914–1920.* Melbourne: William Heinemann, 1957.

KUKIEL, MARIAN. *Czartoryski and European Unity, 1770–1861.* Princeton, N.J.: Princeton University Press, 1955.

LESLIE, ROBERT F. *Polish Politics and the Revolution of November, 1830.* London: Athlone Press, 1956.

———. *Reform and Insurrection in Russian Poland, 1856–1865.* London: Athlone Press, 1963.

LORD, ROBERT H. *The Second Partition of Poland: A Study in Diplomatic History.* Cambridge, Mass.: Harvard University Press, 1915.

PILSUDSKI, JOSEPH. *Joseph Pilsudski: The Memories of a Polish Revolutionary and Soldier.* London: Faber & Faber, 1931.

REDDAWAY, WILLIAM F., ET AL. (eds.). *The Cambridge History of Poland.* 2 vols. Cambridge, England: The University Press, 1941–50.

ROSE, WILLIAM J. *The Rise of Polish Democracy.* London: G. Bell & Sons,

1944. An analysis of nineteenth- and twentieth-century political and social trends and institutions.

ROTHSCHILD, JOSEPH. *Pilsudski's Coup d'État.* New York: Columbia University Press, 1966.

ROZEK, EDWARD J. *Allied Wartime Diplomacy: A Pattern in Poland.* New York: John Wiley & Sons, 1958.

THOMAS, WILLIAM I., and FLORIAN ZNANIECKI. *The Polish Peasant in Europe and America.* 2d rev. ed. 2 vols. New York: Dover Publications, 1958.

WANDYCZ, PIOTR STEFAN. *Soviet-Polish Relations, 1917–1921.* Cambridge, Mass.: Harvard University Press, 1969.

ZWEIG, FERDYNAND. *Poland Between Two Wars: A Critical Study of Social and Economic Changes.* London: Martin Secker & Warburg, 1944.

VIII. Rumania

FISCHER-GALATI, STEPHEN. *Twentieth Century Rumania.* New York: Columbia University Press, 1970.

——— (ed.). *Romania.* New York: Praeger Publishers, 1957. A general survey of Rumanian history, politics, economics, society, and culture.

HALL, DONALD J. *Rumanian Furrow.* London: Methuen & Co., 1933.

HITCHINS, KEITH. *The Rumanian National Movement in Transylvania, 1780–1849.* Cambridge, Mass.: Harvard University Press, 1969.

MADGEARU, VIRGIL N. *Rumania's New Economic Policy.* London: P. S. King & Son, 1930.

MITRANY, DAVID. *The Land and the Peasant in Rumania: The War and Agrarian Reform (1917–1921).* London: Oxford University Press, 1930.

RIKER, THAD W. *The Making of Roumania: A Study of an International Problem, 1856–1866.* London: Oxford University Press, 1931.

ROBERTS, HENRY L. *Rumania: Political Problems of an Agrarian State.* New Haven, Conn.: Yale University Press, 1951. An account of Rumanian political and socio-economic development in the twentieth century.

SETON-WATSON, ROBERT WILLIAM. *A History of the Roumanians: From Roman Times to the Completion of Unity.* Cambridge, England: The University Press, 1934. The basic history of the Rumanians in English.

SPECTOR, DAVID SHERMAN. *Rumania at the Paris Peace Conference: A Study of the Diplomacy of Ioan I. C. Bratianu.* New York: Bookman Associates, 1962.

WILBUR, EARL M. *History of Unitarianism in Transylvania, England, and America.* Cambridge, Mass.: Harvard University Press, 1952.

IX. Yugoslavia

AVAKUMOVIC, IVAN. *History of the Communist Party of Yugoslavia.* Vol. I. Aberdeen: Aberdeen University Press, 1964.

BYRNES, ROBERT F. (ed.). *Yugoslavia.* New York: Praeger Publishers, 1957. A general survey of Yugoslav politics, economics, society, and culture.

CLISSOLD, STEPHEN (ed.). *A Short History of Yugoslavia: From Early Times to 1966.* Cambridge, England: The University Press, 1966.

HALPERN, JOEL M. *A Serbian Village.* New York: Harper & Row, 1967. An anthropological study of a village in Sumadija.

HOCEVAR, TOUSSAINT. *The Structure of the Slovenian Economy, 1848–1963.* New York: Studia Slovenica, 1965.

HOPTNER, JACOB B. *Yugoslavia in Crisis, 1934–1941.* New York: Columbia University Press, 1962.

LEDERER, IVO J. *Yugoslavia at the Paris Peace Conference: A Study in Frontier Making.* New Haven, Conn.: Yale University Press, 1963.

LODGE, OLIVE. *Peasant Life in Yugoslavia.* London: Seeley, Service & Co., 1942. A study of Yugoslav peasant life in the interwar period.

McCLELLAN, WOODFORD D. *Svetozar Markovic and the Origins of Balkan Socialism.* Princeton, N.J.: Princeton University Press, 1964.

SUGAR, PETER F. *Industrialization of Bosnia-Hercegovina, 1878–1918.* Seattle: University of Washington Press, 1963.

TOMASEVICH, JOZO. *Peasants, Politics and Economic Change in Yugoslavia.* Stanford, Calif.: Stanford University Press, 1955. The best socio-economic and political history of Yugoslavia in English.

VUCINICH, WAYNE S. *Serbia Between East and West: The Events of 1903–1908.* Stanford, Calif.: Stanford University Press, 1954.

WEST, REBECCA. *Black Lamb and Grey Falcon: A Journey Through Yugoslavia.* 2 vols. New York: Viking Press, 1941. A perceptive account of a journey to Yugoslavia just before World War II.

INDEX